HENRY OF GHENT'S SUMMA, ARTICLES 53-55

On the Divine Persons

HENRY OF GHENT'S SUMMA, ARTICLES 53-55

On the Divine Persons

TRANSLATED WITH AN INTRODUCTION

BY

ROLAND J. TESKE, SJ

MEDIÆVAL PHILOSOPHICAL TEXTS IN TRANSLATION
NO. 52
ROLAND J. TESKE, SJ, EDITOR

© 2015
Marquette University Press

LIBRARY OF CONGRESS CATALOGING-IN-PUBLICATION DATA

Henry, of Ghent, 1217-1293.
[Summa quaestionum ordinariarum. Art. 53-55. English]
Henry of Ghent's Summa. Articles 53-55, on the divine persons / translated with an introduction by Roland J. Teske, SJ. — first [edition].
    pages cm. — (Mediæval philosophical texts in translation ; no. 52)
Includes bibliographical references and index.
ISBN 978-0-87462-263-8 (pbk. : alk. paper) — ISBN 0-87462-263-8 (pbk. : alk. paper)
1. Trinity. 2. Medieval philosophy. I. Teske, Roland J., 1934– translator.
II. Title. III. Title: On the divine persons.
BT111.3.H4613 2015
231'.044—dc23

2014044715

The cover art is a photo, by an unknown photographer, of a bust of Henry of Ghent made during the Renaissance. At the DeWulf-Mansion Center in Leuven, Belgium, is a large image, possibly of the original photo. The location of the bust itself is today unknown.

Association of American University Presses

MARQUETTE UNIVERSITY PRESS
MILWAUKEE

The Association of Jesuit University Presses

To my brothers,

John, Robert, Charles, and Paul

EDITOR'S FOREWORD

With the present volume of Mediaeval Philosophical Texts in Translation I have finished my work as editor of the series that I undertook almost a quarter century ago with volume twenty-nine. I have tried to add a volume each year to the series while maintaining the quality of the work of my predecessors, and I have come close to my goal of seeing a volume a year brought to completion firstly with the generous help of Professor Lee Rice and then with that of Professor Andrew Tallon, the director of the Marquette University Press, in getting the volumes into print. I want to express my sincere gratitude to them for without their help and hard work the series would have most probably not have survived. The series began in 1942 under the editorship of the Reverend Gerard Smith, S.J., who saw the first nine volumes through the press. Professor James H. Robb became editor in 1960 and added another eighteen volumes to the series. Richard C. Taylor edited volume twenty-eight, which was the work of the Reverend Francis C. Wade and of myself after Father Wade's death. In 1990 I became editor of the series and saw the next twenty-three volumes through the press. Those years were marked by the rapid rise of the computer with its replacement of the typewriter and typesetting as well as the growth of the Marquette University Press into the respected university press that it is today. With the publication of the present volume, a new editor will take over as editor of the series. In an era when the Latin language is less and less well known, the importance of good translations of important philosophical works can only increase. I wish the new editor success in maintaining and improving the quality of the translations that, as he will soon learn, are not easy to come by. I wish the new editor and the series every blessing and success.

Roland J. Teske, S.J., Editor

INTRODUCTION

The three articles from Henry of Ghent's *Summa of Ordinary Questions* (hereafter *SQO*) translated in this volume are the first that deal with the Trinity. They follow upon Henry's treatment of the divine attributes in articles forty-one to fifty-two. Each of these articles has many questions, and each of them presents many challenges to a reader and to a translator. One of the challenges is the technical terminology of the discussion of the divine emanations and of the divine persons in the Trinity. Another is the difficulty of rendering Latin terms in reasonably intelligible English. And a third is of course the difficulty of speaking of the mystery of the Trinity.

In the sixties of the last century when I firstly studied the traditional trinitarian theology we had a saying that in the Trinity there are five notions, four relations, three persons, two processions, one God, and no proof. I recently discovered that a friend who is now a professor of theology, but went through the same seminary training only a few years after me had no idea of what a notion in this context meant. Regardless of the contemporary value of such items of scholastic theology, one has to know something about them if one is to understand Henry's trinitarian theology, and the questions translated in the volume will certainly help to do that. For article fifty-three asks ten questions about the sense in which a person exists in God, and article fifty-four asks ten questions about the emanations or processions of one divine person from another, while article fifty-five asks six questions about the properties or notions of the divine persons.

Henry was obviously a voracious reader of the Fathers of the Church and the medieval masters of theology in the centuries before him. He cites extensively from Ambrose of Milan, Augustine of Hippo, Boethius, Hilary of Poitiers, Anselm of Canterbury, Peter Lombard, Richard of Saint Victor, and Thomas Aquinas among Western Latin fathers and theologians and from Pseudo-Dionysius and John of Damascus among the Eastern or Greek fathers. But besides such well-known thinkers he cites other masters who are less well-known, such as Praepositinus, Simon of Tournai, Gerard La Pucelle, and Giles of Rome. Henry also quotes such philosophers as Aristotle, Porphyry, and Averroes, who of course have little to say on the Trinity.

What follows will be a brief introduction to the questions that Henry discusses in each of the three articles. In article fifty-three Henry first of all situates the following questions within his *SQO* and explains that he will firstly deal with the persons in general in articles fifty-three and fifty-four and then with the properties or notions of the persons in article fifty-five. Article fifty-three discusses "the manner of the being of persons in God"[1] and article fifty-four is concerned with "the manner of one person's emanating from another."[2]

Article fifty-three has ten questions, the first of which is whether one needs to hold that there is a person in God. In his resolution of the question Henry appeals to what he previously established, namely, that we "must attribute to God whatever is without qualification more worthy or better to be than not to be."[3] Appealing to the authority of Richard of Saint Victor, Henry argues that "person" signifies something incommunicable in a rational or intellectual nature and is something of dignity and nobility. Hence, we must hold that there is a person in God.

As explanation of the issue Henry adds a glossary of seven terms, namely, "individual," "this something," "natural reality," "subsistence," "substance," "supposite," and "person." He explains their meanings and the extent to which they are applicable or not to God. He also notes the difference between the Greek usage of "substance" and that of the Latins. While "substance," "supposite," "subsistence," and the like have an improper meaning in God since God does not stand under anything as those terms imply, "person" is admitted in God without any improper meaning in accord with Richard of Saint Victor's definition of a person as "an incommunicable existence of an intellectual nature,"[4] which corrects Boethius's definition of person as "an individual substance of a rational nature."[5]

In the second question Henry asks whether "person" has being in God in a proper or a transferred sense. In his resolution of the question Henry says that in order to see which things are said of God in their proper sense and which are said through a likeness or transference, we need to look at what a name signifies, not at its use. Those that signify something that is without qualification of dignity are said of God in their proper sense, while others are said of him in a transferred sense. The name "person" signifies in creatures with regard to intellectual substances the same thing as "individual," which Boethius used in his definition. But when used of God, "person" signifies the same thing in a more eminent way. For in God "'person' signifies a concept of the mind by which someone is understood to be incommunicable through his property and to be someone in himself through that property" and "is distinguished from another so that he is not the other,"[6] as Richard's definition says. Since "person" signifies something of nobility and something of the highest nobility in God,

1   *SQO* 52, intro., par. 2.

2   Ibid.

3   *SQO* 53, 1, par. 4.

4   *SQO* 53, 1, par. 15.

5   *SQO* 53, 1, par. 1

6   *SQO* 53, 1, par. 5.

it is said of him in the proper sense, not through a likeness or transference. Henry, however, distinguishes two sorts of transference. One is from the side of the reality in accord with which the reality signified does not belong to God in terms of the same thing signified or in a more eminent manner, such as "imprint" and "mirror," which do not properly have being in God. The other is from the side of the name alone, in accord with which the name is firstly imposed on creatures and is only used with regard to them and is not used in God in a more eminent manner of the reality and is not imposed to signify it. This is the case in names taken from creatures in their proper sense, and such a name is transferred to God as if by a new imposition of the name, and in this way "person" is transferred to God in its proper sense although not in accord with its common and proper acceptance as "person" was firstly used in creatures, where Henry follows the explanation of Richard of Saint Victor, who states that in its common acceptance one does not understand that there are many persons in a single substance.

In the third question Henry asks whether "person" has being univocally and with the same meaning in God and in creatures. After arguments both for and against this, Henry says that we must firstly understand what it is that makes someone a person and then see whether it has being in God and creatures univocally and according to the same meaning. A person is something singular existing in itself in an intellectual nature; hence, a person is not an accident nor a human soul nor the humanity of Christ. Henry explains that "the distinction of the divine persons and of their singularity" is brought about through negation, just as it is in creatures.[7] In this way "person" has being univocally in God and in creatures. Nonetheless, because in creatures such negation is tied to a determinate essence and nature, but in God is tied to the relations, "'person' has being in God and in creatures very equivocally. ..."[8]

Question four asks whether "person" has being in God according to substance or according to relation. In his resolution of the question Henry says that "two ways of being and of predicating are distinguished in God so that whatever is predicated of God and attributed to God is reduced to one of those two," namely, substance and relation.[9] Some names signify the essence or substance alone such as "deity," and others signify a relation such as "paternity." But still others signify both, for example, "Father," although "Father" takes its formal imposition from a relation, while it also signifies the common substance, as "person" also does. Hence, Henry says that "in God 'person' is said according to relation and has being in God according to relation, but not according

---

7   *SQO* 53, 3, par. 9.

8   *SQO* 53, 3, par. 9.

9   *SQO* 53, 4, par. 4

to substance."[10] But for the resolution of the arguments Henry explains that "something is and is said according to relation ... either in itself or in what it is contained under it."[11] Names such as "Father," "Son," and "Holy Spirit" signify a determinate relation, while names such as "person" or "Trinity" are said in the second way and signify indeterminately or signify an indeterminate relation, since they are not said relatively according to their names, but in terms of their contents that imply indeterminate relations.

In question five Henry asks whether "person" signifies in God a reality or only an intention. In his resolution of the question Henry says that we have "firstly to consider what those things are that have to be signified by names and secondly ... to investigate from the use of this name 'person' which of them is signified by it."[12] Names of singular realities, for example, "Peter" and "Paul," signify only realities and in no way signify intentions. Universal names of singular realities, for example, "man" or "horse," represent a nature existing in singular being, but are intentions because they are abstracted by the intellect. Such names are in a sense names of realities and in a sense names of first intentions. Other intentions are produced by the intellect concerning universals and particulars and are pure intentions; hence, names imposed on them are names of second intentions. Henry further distinguishes second intentions into logical intentions, such as "genus," "species," and "difference" and "individual" and "particular," and into grammatical intentions, such as "noun," "verb," etc. First intentions pertain to the real sciences, while second intentions pertain to logical, or grammatical, or linguistic sciences.

At this point Henry turns to the second question, namely, which of these the name "person" is used to signify. At great length he cites and explains the expositions of various masters; he finally concludes that the position "of Richard either has solid truth or less of a defect than some of the others."[13] He further concludes that while in God "these names 'Father,' 'Son,' and 'Holy Spirit' are imposed to signify supposites determined by determinate individual properties," the name "'person' signifies an indeterminate supposite"[14] that includes the substance along with an indeterminate relation. Hence, according to Richard's opinion, "'person' is not the name of an intention, but of a reality to which there belongs the intention of 'singular,' 'incommunicable,' 'subsistence,' and the like."[15]

But Henry then turns to investigate whether this is true from the use of "person" with regard to creatures, since our use of it in God is taken from its use in

10   *SQO* 53, 4, par. 6.

11   *SQO* 54, 4, par. 6.

12   *SQO* 53, 5, par. 11.

13   *SQO* 53, 5, par. 29.

14   *SQO* 53, 5, par. 30–31.

15   *SQO* 53, 5, 32.

creatures. He claims that "person" does not signify intellectual or rational substances, but only signifies their individuation that it implies indeterminately. In the same way "snub" does not signify a nose, but the curvedness of the nose. Hence, as in creatures "individual" is not the name of a reality, but of a second intention, so in rational creatures the name "person" is not the name of a reality, but the name of an intention that expresses the individuality of such creatures.

Hence, although Henry finds himself in disagreement with the authorities that hold that "person" signifies a substance, a property, or both at once, he argues that from its first imposition "person" is "the name of an intention and signifies only the character of an incommunicable supposite ... with regard to an intellectual nature. ..."[16]

Question six asks whether there is an absolute or non-relative supposite in God. Henry refers his readers to his fifth *Quodlibet* where he has dealt with the question, but goes on to explain that this question only asks whether, if one brackets the properties constitutive of the persons, there remains an absolute supposite common to the three. Thus "God" would signify a person distinct from all other natures by his essential properties, as the Jews and some gentiles understood the one God to be. Henry claims that philosophers and presumably the Jews who understood the deity without the trinity of persons had a false and fictitious understanding of God. Similarly, Abbot Joachim could not understand the nature of the deity without understanding it as a supposite, and in order to avoid a quaternity of persons, he understood the three persons as a collectivity, just as we speak of many persons as one people. Thus he fell into Arianism by separating the persons, whereas Sabellius confused the persons by denying their plurality. But the Catholic faith holds one divine essence common to the three persons.

In question seven Henry asks whether "person" signifies something common in God. In his resolution of the question he explains that there are three sorts of commonness: a real commonness, a purely rational commonness, and an intermediate commonness that is partly real and partly rational. The essence and the essential attributes in God are really common to the three persons. Thus we say that the Father is God, the Son is God, and the Holy Spirit is God. The third sort of commonness is that of relation to the three personal relations. Thus we say that paternity is a relation, filiation is a relation, and spiration is a relation since the commonness involved is not that of a true universal, although it approaches it. The second sort of commonness is that in "person." But various theologians explain this commonness of "person" in different ways. After reviewing their various opinions, Henry sides with the view of Richard of Saint Victor who held that "person" does not express something common by its signification, but only by its indeterminateness. For it signifies only something

16 *SQO* 53, 5, 39.

that is distinct from all the others. Hence, Henry explains Augustine's claim that Catholics reply to the question that the heretics asked: "Three what?" by saying: "Three persons," in order that they might have something to say and not remain completely silent.

The eighth question asks whether many persons are to be held to be in God. In his resolution of the question Henry says that we must not hold a person to be in God in terms of something absolute or non-relative, but only in terms of a relation and not just any relation, but only in terms of a relation of origin or in terms of relative properties. Hence, the Catholic faith holds three relative persons in one substance. Henry recalls how Arius divided the substances in God and held as many substances as there are persons, while Sabellius held only one absolute person, which was the Father as generating, the Son as generated, and the Holy Spirit as spirated.

Henry mentions Augustine's and Peter Lombard's proofs from the authority of scripture, but then turns to Richard of Saint Victor's arguments based on God's perfect goodness or love, his supreme happiness and joyousness, and his supreme benevolence. He also adds arguments from Hilary and Richard based on the manner of origin and of one person's emanating from another.

In question nine Henry asks whether three persons are to be held to be in God, no more and no fewer, and he firstly explains how there cannot be only two and then how there cannot be more than three. He argues that there are only two ways of emanating in God, that is, through nature and through will. Through the first of these there proceeds the first emanation from that person who is not from another, and through the second there proceeds the emanation from that person who is not from another and from the person who is from him. Hence, there are only two emanations and only three persons, the one who is not from another, the one who is from him, and the one who is the other two persons. Augustine and other of the fathers have proposed arguments from the traces of God in creatures and from the image of God in the rational creature, all of which lead only to probability according to Henry. Hence, he takes arguments from Richard of Saint Victor that are based on the divine goodness and divine happiness that are supposedly demonstrative.

Question ten asks whether one person has being in another mutually and in the same way, that is, the question asks about what theologians often call the circumincession of the divine persons. After fifteen arguments against it, Henry states that in accord with sacred scripture one must hold that the individual persons are in one another and that the only doubt is about whether one person is in another in terms of substance, in terms of relation, or in terms of both. After citing various positions held by the Fathers, Henry turns to the eight ways of one thing's being in another listed in Aristotle's *Physics* and not surprisingly finds that one divine person is in another in none of those ways, all of which pertain to bodily things. In his rather obscure solution to this obscure question Henry appeals to the explanations of Hilary and Augustine and argues that although one person is in another in terms of both substance and relation, paternity is not in the Son in the same way it is in the Father, nor is filiation in the Father in the same way as it is in the Son. In his reply to the twelfth argument against circumincession Henry presents an amazing example to illustrate the possibility of one person's being wholly in another and wholly in himself and asks us to imagine the risen Christ holding in his bodily hand a consecrated host in which he is wholly present so that Christ holds the whole of himself in his hand holding the host that holds the whole of himself.

Article fifty-four has ten questions. The first asks whether it is necessary to hold that there is a person in God who does not emanate from another. In his resolution of the question Henry again appeals to Richard of Saint Victor who argued that, just as it is necessary that in the universe there be a substance, namely, God, that is from itself and not from another, so it is necessary that in God there be a person that is from himself and not from another. For otherwise we would end up with an endless series of persons from another or with a circular series of emanations, both of which are impossible. After adding another argument from Richard, Henry concludes that there must be a person who is not from another, that is, a person that is unbegotten and innascible.

In the second question Henry asks whether there is only one person in God that does not emanate from another. Henry again appeals to Richard who argues that not being from another is in God an incommunicable property and cannot therefore belong to many. Just as there cannot be more than one God in the universe, as Henry has argued in a previous article,[17] so there cannot be in God many persons that are not from another, that is, many who are innascible. For as Hilary of Poitiers said, to confess many who are innascible is to confess many gods.[18]

The third question asks whether another person emanates from the person that does not emanate from another. In his resolution of the question Henry says that the question only asks whether there is some emanation within God by which one person proceeds from another, as the Catholic faith holds. He argues that a person is constituted in its personality only by a respect or relation by which it is distinguished from another and that the otherness of the persons can only be understood from the character or manner of their origin from one another, which in turn can only be understood through the emanation of one from another. And Henry argues on the basis of the divine perfection and from the character of the divine nature that such an internal emanation can terminate only in a subsisting divine person. As the arguments pro and con were many, so the replies to them are many, long, and convoluted.

---

17 See *SQO* 25, 2,

18 See *SQO* 54, 2, par. 6.

In the fourth question Henry asks whether more than one person emanates in God, and in his resolution of the question, once again following Richard, he argues that being a person from another is not an incommunicable property. For otherwise there would be only two persons in God, one that does not have being from another and the other that has being from another. Henry explains that there are three sorts of plurification existing in an order among themselves and to the first unity. For the manyness of creatures presupposes by an order of duration the manyness of the divine persons, and the manyness of the divine persons presupposes by an order of reason the manyness of the divine attributes, which include intellect and will, the two principles of operation in an intellectual nature. And the person that is not from another contains them in himself in full and unexhausted fecundity for producing two persons in himself, one that emanates through intellect and the other that emanates through will.

Henry further explains that in God intellect and will have their perfection is two ways of acting, one through their essential actions and the other through their personal or notional actions. For the divine intellect does not have its full perfection until there is conceived the Word that proceeds from it through the notional act of speaking, and the will does not have its full perfection until love, that is, the Holy Spirit, proceeds from its notional act. Hence, there are two emanations or processions in God.

Question five asks whether the persons emanating in God emanate equally firstly, principally, and immediately. The resolution of the question is tripartite. Henry firstly asks whether one must in God reduce all plurality and number to a single one in an orderly way. He appeals to the authority of Dionysius to show that every plurality has to be reduced to a first in an orderly way so that two are not reduced to one through equality and uniformity. Hence, in God a plurality of persons has to be reduced to the unity of the deity without a complete uniformity. For otherwise the one person from whom the two originated would have the characters for originating the two equally uniformly, and then neither character nor both would be constitutive of that person. Hence, the characters of the emanations are two, one in the manner of nature and the other in the manner of will, and it is impossible that the other two persons proceed equally firstly and uniformly from the person that is not from another.

Henry emphasizes that his use of "firstly" and "secondly" must not be understood in terms of time, but in terms of a natural order. He appeals to Richard for their non-temporal use and cites Peter Lombard who pointed out the Arian understanding of the temporal priority of one person to another in the Trinity. Although the saints seem to have clearly denied any sort of priority among the divine persons, Henry says, "I do not see that both 'first' and 'second' cannot be accepted in God in accord with the way in which order has being in him, nor do I nonetheless defend that it ought to be done in that way."[19]

The second part of the question asks whether the emanations that proceed from the Father proceed equally principally. Henry argues that the emanation and the person that proceeds in the manner of nature proceeds more principally, again appealing to arguments from Richard, where Henry insists that the Father is more a principle "by the order of natural origin, not of some duration, so that this principality does not express some level of dignity. ..."[20]

The third part of the question asks whether both emanations proceed equally immediately. Henry explains that the second person proceeds immediately from the first person and that the third person proceeds immediately from the first and mediately from the second so that both persons that are from another proceed equally immediately from the person that is not from another. For as nature, the Father is fecund for immediately producing the Son, and as will, he is fecund for immediately producing the Holy Spirit, but the procession "that is absolutely immediate is more principal than the one that is at the same time mediated and immediate."[21]

Question six asks whether one of the two persons that emanate, that is, the Son and the Holy Spirit, does not emanate from the other. Henry points out that no one has held that the Son proceeds from the Holy Spirit. Hence, the question concerns only "the procession or emanation of the Holy Spirit from the Son"[22]—a question on account of which some, Henry reports, have held that the whole Greek church is in heresy, a view that Henry finds harsh because of John Damascene and other teachers of the Greeks. Henry presents three views that attempt to excuse the teaching of the Greeks and admits that before the Church determined the procession of the Holy Spirit from the Son, it was permissible to hold a contrary position, which is surely true, but argues that "and from the Son" was added by the authority of Council of Ephesus according to the *Decretals*, although that does not seem to be true in accord with more recent studies.[23]

Henry turns to arguments that explain this doctrine, firstly to Richard's argument that perfect kinship between the persons requires "that each be immediately joined to each so that from the first there are two and from the two there is the third and the one in between is from the one and the other is from it."[24]

---

19   *SQO* 54, 5, par. 12

20   *SQO* 54, 5, par. 14.

21   *SQO* 54, 5, par. 16

22   *SQO* 54, 6, par. 17

23   Henry's knowledge of the controversy seems mistaken on what the Council of Ephesus said.

24   *SQO* 54, 6, par. 21.

This argument, as Henry points out, does not prove that the Holy Spirit proceeds from the Son rather than the other way around. Others argue that, unless the Holy Spirit proceeds from the Son, there would be no distinction between them, but Henry notes that this argument runs into the same problem as the first. For "the Son would still differ from the Holy Spirit by nascibility, even if the Holy Spirit did not proceed from him."[25] Henry rather argues that we need to seek the distinction of the processions in accord with an order of nature between them and reminds his readers that, as he has shown in the resolution of the preceding question, "it is impossible that many proceed from the same principle through complete equality without any order,"[26] as is the case only in things that differ in terms of matter and only numerically, for example, when one craftsman produces two knives.

Henry explains that being is "the first and more proper of all those things that belong to God because ... it presupposes nothing before itself in God, but all the others are included in the concept of it."[27] Thus from being there proceeds by an order of our understanding living, understanding, and willing, and though living is a sort of being and understanding a sort of living, willing is not a sort of understanding. For the action of willing requires understanding, but not the other way around. Hence, as there is an order of nature between the essential acts of understanding and willing, so there is between the notional acts of understanding and willing. Hence, as the perfection of the will in its essential act requires the perfection of the intellect in its essential act, so the perfection of the notional act of the will, which is the procession of the love that is the Holy Spirit, requires the perfection of the intellect in its notional act, which is the production of the Word. Hence, Henry concludes that "by the order of nature the procession of the Holy Spirit quasi presupposes the production of the Son."[28] Henry confirms this conclusion from texts from John Damascene and Richard of Saint Victor and then turns to the objection of Pseudo-Dionysius to adding anything to the Creed beyond what is found in scripture where he argues for the legitimacy of adding what is inferred from immediate sense of scripture by true reasoning.

In the seventh question Henry asks whether the Holy Spirt proceeds from the Father and the Son equally firstly, principally, and immediately, through himself, and in the same way. The resolution of the question consists in replies to the arguments. With regard to "firstly," he distinguishes so that the Holy Spirit proceeds equally firstly in one way and does not in another. If one looks to the power common to the Father and the Son, the Holy Spirit proceeds

---

25   *SQO* 54, 6, par. 28.

26   *SQO* 54, 6, par. 32.

27   *SQO* 54, 6, par. 33.

28   *SQO* 54, 6, par. 34.

from them equally firstly, but if one looks to the agents, the Holy Spirit does not proceed from them equally firstly. With regard to "principally," he appeals to the same distinction, but also lists and explains four ways of one thing's being a principle of another. Similarly with regard to "properly," he distinguishes three senses of the term and says that the Father spirates the Holy Spirit properly because the Father has the power to spirate from himself and not from another. With regard to "equally immediately," Henry says that, if it refers to the power in the agents, the Holy Spirit proceeds from the Father and the Son equally immediately, but not so if it refers to them as the agents since the Son has it from the Father that he spirates. With regard to "through himself," Henry says that the preposition "through" indicates "some causality over the act it determines"[29] and gives examples of various sorts of causality and ways in which something belongs to something through itself. Although the Son has no causality over any action that proceeds from the Father, he does whatever he does through the Father, as Henry explains, because the Son has his power of acting from the Father.

Henry's eighth question asks whether another person emanates from any of the three persons in God. He explains that the question asks why there are three persons in God and only three. He argues that from the three persons another cannot emanate except by way of nature and of will, either by one of them or by both of them, and "since in God there are only the two ways of emanations through which there emanate only two persons, and besides them there is ... only one person that is not from another, it is for this reason irrefutably concluded that there are only three persons in God. ..."[30]

Question nine asks whether in God the notional acts are acts of understanding and willing. In his resolution of the question Henry firstly explains the difference between the notional acts of generating and spirating and the essential acts of understanding and willing through the way in which these acts are formed in the human intellect and will. He begins with the acts of the intellect since they are clearer to us than those of the will and, following Augustine, takes his start from the way that a sensible body produces a form or species in sight, which is transferred to memory, from which the species in memory, like a parent, produces the species in the imagination. Similarly, according to Augustine, in knowing itself, mind begets an intellectual knowledge of itself in thinking of itself, which is the word that it speaks interiorly. Augustine says that in this production of the word in our knowledge we have an enigma or obscure image of the Word born from the Father. Henry's interpretation of Augustine is influenced by a good deal of Aristotelian epistemology and may leave the reader more puzzled than helped.

---

29   *SQO* 54, 7, par. 16.

30   *SQO* 54, 8, par. 12.

Thus Henry says that God the Father knows his essence by his act of simple awareness and that from that awareness there is naturally formed an explanatory awareness of his quiddity, which is called his Word, as Richard says. Yet our thinking involves change and time, whereas the utterance of the Word in God is without change or time, and while in us there is a difference between the two acts of understanding, in God they differ only by reason.

Henry says that the emanation of the notional act of speaking the Word is not an act of understanding, but is between the Father's two essential acts of understanding, which are only rationally distinct, although in us the two acts of understanding are really distinct, one imperfect and the other perfect. **

Question ten asks whether the emanations of the notional acts of generating and spirating presuppose the essential acts of understanding and willing. Henry explains that the Father has in himself all the essential attributes from himself since he is "the fontal deity," as Dionysius says, and the "principle of the whole divinity," as Augustine says.[31] Hence, he is completely fecund for the first acts productive of something, of which sort are the notional acts productive of the persons. Thus there is a certain order of the essential acts and also of the notional acts, and the notional act of understanding is in a sense founded upon the essential act and presupposes it by an order of reason. Similarly, the act of spirating by the Father and the Son presupposes the essential act of willing.

Article fifty-five on the notions or properties of the divine persons contains six questions, the first of which is whether it is necessary to hold properties of the persons, that is, characteristics that are proper to a divine person. Henry's answer begins by determining what is meant by the name or term "property" and then determining whether there is something of the sort in God. After quoting Ambrose who distinguishes words that express a nature and others that express a mode or quality of a nature, where quality is understood in a broad sense, Henry says that in God there are qualities that belong to the divine substance as such goodness and truth, which are called attributes, and others that belong to a supposite or a person, which are called properties. Although the resolution of the question is brief, Henry's replies to the objections are lengthy, especially to Praepositinus's argument based on various masters' opinions that sides with a certain master who held that there are no properties of the persons in God.

In the second question Henry asks whether there are many properties in God, and he answers that we must hold that there are many properties because the properties denominate or name the many persons. The replies to the objections are almost as brief.

The third question asks whether there are more than two properties in God, and the objections argue that there are only two, only three, only four, more

---

31   *SQO* 54, 10, par. 4.

than five, and even an infinite number of properties. In his reply Henry distinguishes four ways of speaking of "property." In the broadest sense all the essential and personal attributes of God are called properties. But in a broad sense there are only five properties, namely, innascibility and paternity in the Father, filiation in the Son, passive spiration in the Holy Spirit, and common active spiration in the Father and the Son. However, in the strict sense there are only four properties because active spiration is not proper to one person, but common to two. And in a very strict sense there are only three properties, namely, "paternity, filiation, and passive spiration because they alone constitute and distinguish persons from one another."[32]

In the fourth question Henry asked whether all the properties are notional or are notions. In his resolution of the question Henry explains that "notion" is understood in many ways, but concludes that "only those properties that are constitutive of the persons or are in the persons by a character by which they belong to a person, not by a character by which they belong to the essence, are said to be notions."[33] And in that way Henry says that there are only five: two in the Father, namely, paternity or active generation and innascibility, one in the Son, namely, filiation or nascibility, common active spiration in the Father and the Son, and passive spiration in the Holy Spirit, each of which is founded upon a relation of origin. In his replies to the arguments Henry distinguishes concerning notions as he did concerning properties and shows that one can hold various numbers of notions in God in accord with the strictness or looseness of one's understanding of "notion."

The fifth question asks whether the notions or properties in God are relations. In his resolution of the question Henry states that "the properties in God are nothing other than certain qualities of the substance."[34] For paternity and the other properties are really the substance or essence. However, as properties, their character is other than that of the substance, and a property cannot be some absolute reality besides the substance. For that would put composition in God. Paternity, for example, signifies the pure respect by which the Father is the Father, and it is that way with the others. Thus "Father" denotes a relation and a hypostasis, but "paternity" signifies only a relation. The replies to the objection are lengthier and cast light on Henry's view of relations, which he treats more extensively in the next question.

The sixth question asks whether the properties in God are real relations. In the resolution of the question Henry reminds his reader that "the properties that are attributes are not real respects or relations,"[35] although, as he has ex-

---

32 SQO 55, 3, par. 8.

33 *SQO* 55, 4, par. 9.

34 *SQO* 55, 5, par. 7

35 *SQO* 55, 6, par. 6,

plained earlier, they are respects or relations. A relation, Henry explains, consists in a certain order of things related to one another in such a way that the order is (a) from the nature of reality from both sides or (b) is from our way of understanding on both sides, or (c) is on one side from the nature of reality and on the other side from our way of understanding. A relation consisting in an order in the first way is real, and one consisting in an order of the second sort is a relation of reason, while a relation of the third sort is from one side a real relation and from the other a relation of reason. As an example of that third sort of relation Henry appeals to the traditional example of a column's being to the right of a man, and the man's being to the left of the column. In that case the relation is real in the man who has a right hand, but the man's being to the left of the column is a relation of reason in the column because the column has neither a right nor a left side. An example of the second sort of relation involves taking one and the same thing as two in a relation of identity or in a relation of equality. In the latter way the Father is equal to the Son because the greatness of the Father and the Son is the divine essence that is one in the two of them. An example of the first sort of relation is found in things ordered in accord with a relation based upon quantity, quality, or acting or being acted upon, at least when the foundation of the relation is real on both sides. Thus one tree is really bigger than another, and the latter is really smaller than the former.

Henry then comes to "what troubles us most in God where we necessarily have to hold according to the faith ... that there is a real relation between the divine persons lest we hold that the persons are distinguished by reason alone."[36] For how can the relation between the divine persons in terms of their active and passive characters be more real than the relations according to the character of quantity and quality since both sorts are founded upon the divine essence. After citing Boethius, Averroes, and Gilbert of Poitiers on the reality of relations, Henry explains that a relation of itself is only a circumstance or mode of a reality and that a relation gets its reality from that upon which it is founded. The relations of the notions in God therefore take their reality from the divine essence upon which they are founded. The deity then is itself the first principle of all things, and upon it there is founded a respect or order to those things that are from it, and the respect to what is firstly derived from the principle along with the deity constitutes the first person who by reason of his firstness is innascible, and from him every other person and reality has being. For the deity in the first person is an act of understanding fecund for producing the second person or the Word, and the deity existing in both persons is fecund for producing the third person in the manner of will. Hence, because the notional relations are founded on the divine essence, they are real.

---

36   *SQO* 55, 6, par. 11.

At this point Henry raises a doubt as to whether the relations can be called realities along with their being real if they get their reality from the essence, which is only one. He also asks whether the reality of a relation remains in God when the category of relation is transferred to God or passes into the divine substance. Henry states that in God "the reality of a relation from the order to an object is only the mode itself,"[37] and that way there are diverse modes of being toward something else and diverse realities

Henry's first three articles on the divine persons certainly present a challenge to the translator and to the student. The complexity of Henry's treatment of the questions on the divine persons makes me recall the claim that Saint Thomas's *Summa of Theology* was intended for beginners in theology and not for the advanced students—a claim that I had always taken as jocose rather than as serious. But Henry's treatment of the divine persons is certainly not intended for novice theologians, but for the advanced graduate students of his age.

There are relatively few studies of Henry's trinitarian theology. What I was able to find I listed in the bibliography.

The translation indicates the page numbering of the critical edition by inserting the proper page number in the text in brackets. I have preserved the provisional numbering of the paragraphs that the editors dispensed with in the final format of the text since it seemed easier to refer to the paragraphs than to the pages of the critical text. The translator wishes to express his gratitude for the permission to publish the translation to Leuven University Press and to Professors Gordon Wilson and Girard J. Etzkorn.

---

37   *SQO* 55. 6, par. 21.

ARTICLE FIFTY-THREE

On the Manner of the Being of Persons in God

1. Since thus far we have dealt with these characteristics that in God pertain to the common substance, there remains for us hereafter to deal with those that pertain to the distinction of the persons. And we must do this firstly concerning those characteristics that belong to those that are proper and secondly with those that belong to those that are appropriated. And with regard to those that are proper we must firstly deal with those that pertain to the individual persons in terms of themselves and secondly with those that belong to them in relation to one another. And with regard to those that belong to the individual persons in terms of themselves, we must deal with them firstly in general, but secondly in particular. And in general we must firstly deal with the persons, secondly with the properties of the persons that are commonly called notions.

2. With regard to the divine persons in general two things need to be asked: the first concerning the manner of the being of the persons in God; the second concerning the manner of one person's emanating from another.

3. But with regard to the first ten questions are asked, of which the first is whether it is necessary to hold that there is a person in God. But the second is whether "person" has being in God in a proper or in a transferred sense. The third is whether "person" has being in God and in creatures univocally and with the same meaning or equivocally and in accord with different meanings. The fourth is whether "person" is or has being in God according to substance or according to relation. The fifth is whether "person" in God signifies a reality, that is, of the substance or of a relation or only an intention. The sixth is whether an entirely absolute person or an absolute supposite has being in God. The seventh is whether "person" in God signifies something common. The eighth is whether there are many persons in God. The ninth is whether there are three persons in God and not more nor [4] fewer. The tenth is whether one of them has being in another mutually and in the same way.

QUESTION ONE

Whether It Is Necessary to Hold That There Is a Person in God

1. With regard to the first question it is argued that one need not hold that there is a person in God in the first place, as follows: Boethius says in the book, *On the Two Natures and One Person of Christ*, that "*a person is an individual substance of a rational nature.*"[1] But in God there is not a rational nature, but rather an intellectual one, and there is not an individual substance because there is an individual only where there is a universal that can be individuated, and that is not the case in God, as was established above.[2] Therefore, and so on.

2. <It is argued> in the second place, as follows: Augustine says in book five of *On the Trinity*: "'*Three persons' was said not in order that one might say that, but in order that one might not be completely silent.*"[3] But if there were a person in [5] God, "*three persons*" would not be said only "*in order that one might not be completely silent,*" but in order that one might say and express something that exists in God, as is the case. Therefore, and so on.

3. To the contrary Richard says in book five of *On the Trinity*, chapter nine: "*If the divine existence is found to have something one and incommunicable, it is from that alone understood and proven to be a person.*"[4] But there is found "*something incommunicable in the divine existence.*"[5] For either there is nothing communicable in God, or if there is something communicated in him, the property of the one communicating, insofar as he is communicating, cannot be communicated to the one to whom it is communicated, just as by the property of the Father, by which he communicates his essence to the Son, the property of generation cannot be communicated to anyone by him, as will be explained below.[6] Therefore, and so on.

---

1   Boethius, *Against Eutyches and Nestorius* 3; PL 64: 1344C–D; ed. C. Moreschini, p. 214.

2   See *SQO* art. 52, qu. 2; ed. M. Führer, pp. 250–253.

3   Augustine of Hippo, *On the Trinity* 5, 9; PL 42: 918; ed. W. Mountain–F. Glorie; p. 217.

4   Richard of Saint Victor, *On the Trinity* 5, 1; PL 196: 949A–B; ed. J. Ribaillier, p. 195.

5   Ibid.; PL 196: 949A; ed. J. Ribaillier, p. 195.

6   See below, q. 10, par. 37.

<The Resolution of the Question>

4. To this it must be said that, as in accord with what was previously determined on the essential attributes,[7] one must attribute to God whatever is without qualification more worthy and better to be than not to be, so one must
similarly attribute that to him in the personal attributes or properties of the
persons. For as Ambrose says in the book, *On the Trinity*: "*You should understand that there belongs to God whatever can be thought to be more pious, whatever
can be thought to be more splendid with respect to beauty, whatever can be thought
to be more sublime with respect to power.*"[8] And this is the case both in essential
and personal attributes [6] without any difference. But now it is the case that
"person" names something that is without qualification of dignity in creatures
and in the creator.[9] For from what it signifies it names the character of something incommunicable, as is seen from the previously mentioned authority of
Richard,[10] and this comes from the perfection of one who has in himself what
cannot be communicated to another, in accord with which one is said to be a
person, as will be seen below.[11] It also names that with regard to a rational or
intellectual nature, each of which is something of dignity and nobility. For this
reason one must hold absolutely and without qualification that there is a person in God, and one must hold this more truly and more perfectly to the extent
that the character of something incommunicable and intellectual has being in
God more truly and more perfectly, in accord with what will be seen from what
is to be determined.

5. For some explanation of these matters, it must nonetheless be known that
these eight terms, namely, "individual," "this something," "natural reality," "subsistence," "substance," "supposite," and "person," represent and signify almost the
same thing with regard to the nature and essence of a natural reality, when
nature is taken in a very broad sense. And on this Boethius says in *On the Two
Natures*: "*If one wants to say 'nature' of all natural things, such a definition will be
given that can include all the things that exist. [7] Such a nature therefore belongs
to those things that, since they exist, can somehow be grasped by the intellect.*"[12]
This definition therefore defines substances and accidents, but the first two
terms, namely, "individual" and "this something" are found only in the essence
of a creature and both in substances and in accidents, and not in the uncreated

---

7   See *SQO* art. 32, qu. 2; ed. R. Macken, pp. 36 and 50.

8   Ambrose of Milan, *On the Faith* 1, 16; PL 16: 576A; ed. O. Faller, p. 46.

9   See Thomas Aquinas, *Summa of Theology* 1, 29, 3 ad 2um; ed. Leonine 4, p. 332a.

10   See Richard of Saint Victor, *On the Trinity* 5, 1; PL 196: 949A–B; ed. J.
Ribaillier, p. 195.

11   See below q. 5, par. 33, 34, and 26.

12   Boethius, *Against Eutyches and Nestorius* 1; PL 64: 1341B; ed. C. Moreschini, p.
209.

essence or in God. For "individual" is distinguished over against "non-individual" as its contrary. But only something really universal is non-individual. Nor is there the character or the intention of something non-individual save with regard to a universal in terms of reality. Hence, there is an individual only if something really particular or singular is individuated under a universal. And there is the meaning or intention of an individual only with regard to something particular or singular in terms of a reality individuated under that which is really universal.

6. Hence, because in God it is not possible in accord with what has been determined above to find the character of a real universal or particular,[13] it will similarly not be possible to find the character of an individual except by extending the term "individual" to the character of something singular. In accord with this it is said in the beginning of the *Decretals:* "This holy Trinity individual according to the common essence," just as when it immediately continues: "*And discrete in accord with the personal properties,*"[14] the term "discreteness" is there extended to "distinction." For discreteness in the proper sense is not found in God, but distinction is. But it is possible to find the character of an individual in every creature, both from the side of the nature or essence and from the side of the supposite, which is a natural reality. But because a nature subsists in a supposite, whether the nature is substantial or accidental, [8] a nature or essence, such as humanity or whiteness, is not said to be individual unless it belongs to an individual supposite. For as was determined above,[15] humanity is not this humanity unless it is the humanity of this person, and it is similar with whiteness, so that in accord with this a natural reality is properly said to be an individual, but a nature is said to be the essence of a thing whether in itself or as individuated in a supposite.

7. But "this something" names the same thing as "individual" in terms of reality, but differs only by reason. For both signify the character of a part understood under something explicitly divided by negation. But "individual" expresses that negation in relation to what is divided by denying divisibility with regard to the part, from which this term "individual" is imposed. But "this something" expresses the same negation in relation to what is divided and adds along with this the character of a negation in relation to a part divided with it. For when "this" is said, a thing or nature is understood to be something undivided or individual in itself on account of the designation of a thing that can be seen by the eyes. But when "something" is added, it is expressed that it is made something other from which it is divided both in an individual nature and essence and in a supposite. And in God this in no way belongs to one supposite in relation to

---

13   See *SQO* art. 43, qu. 2; ed. L. Hödl, pp. 52–53.

14   Gregory IX, *Decretals* 1, 1, 1, 1; ed. A. Friedberg, 2, p. 5.

15   See *SQO* art. 28, qu. 5; ed. Badius 1, fol. 169vB.

another insofar as "other" expresses a difference in nature and essence. For if one supposite in God is other than another in supposite, <it is> still not other in essence and nature, as will be seen below.[16] Hence, since "other" in the neuter names by itself an essential difference, for this reason when it is used absolutely, as when one says "this something," it is in no way admitted in God so that one of the divine supposites is said to be absolutely something other [9] than another one, but <it is said> only with the determination of "supposite" so that one of them is said to be another supposite than the other. Hence, if we want to speak properly in God as in creatures, we must distinguish in this term "other" the sense of the masculine gender and of the neuter. Thus, as we properly say in creatures that an individual supposite is a "this something," "this," that is, an individual or something individuated in itself, but something other than another supposite, that is, something in a common essence, but in an individual essence something other than the essence of what is divided with it. Thus in God a supposite is properly said to be "this someone," "this," that is, a singular existent in a supposite, but someone other than another and distinct from him.

8. The other six terms, however, are found both in the uncreated reality and in a created reality. But "singular" is found in common in accidents and in substances, while the other five are found only in substances. The character of something singular, however, is that is one solitary something. But it must be understood that, in including "solitary," "singular" can be understood absolutely or with a determination. In the first way it is not admitted in God in accord with what the Master teaches in distinction twenty-three of the first book of the *Sentences* in the chapter: "Now sufficiently," because—as he says in the same place—"*singularity or solitariness shows that a plurality of persons is excluded*."[17] Hence, according to this way it asserts something false in human beings, if one says that Socrates[18] is singular, because it would exclude the fellowship of others in human nature, but it does so in one way in God and in another in [10] human beings. For in God there cannot be solitariness either in act or in potency; in human beings there can be solitariness in act. For humanity could exist in only a single supposite. But in the second way it can very well be admitted in both with regard to the essence and with regard to the supposite. For the deity is a certain singularity and a singular essence. Hence, Gregory says in *On Ezekiel*, in homily two, part five: "*By one and the same power of his singular nature he who is indivisible always arranges* in that way *dissimilar things*."[19] And the Father

16 See below, q. 5, par. 39 and 40.

17 Peter Lombard, *Sentences* 1, d. 23, c. 5; PL 192: 586; ed. I. Brady, 1, p. 186.

18 Though the editors of the critical edition preserve "Sortes," which is found in all the manuscripts, I have taken it as an abbreviation for "Socrates," especially since it is linked at times with "Plato."

19 Gregory the Great, *Homilies on Ezekiel* 2, 5; PL 76: 991A; ed. M. Adriaen, p. 283.

is a certain singular person. And this singularity does not exclude the fellow-ship of many persons, just as when it is said that Peter is a singular person, the fellowship of other human beings is not excluded, but it only excludes the plu-rality or multiplication of that in which such singularity is said to exist, wheth-er it is an essence or a supposite. But it belongs to the essence and the supposite differently in God and in creatures, because in God it belongs to the essence of itself, not because it has being in a person. For the deity is a certain singularity or a certain singular essence of itself, as was established above.[20] But humanity is not that way, because it is not a "this" of itself, but only because it belongs to this person, as was similarly established above.[21] Similarly, singularity has being in a different way in God and in creatures, as will be explained below.[22]

9. But "natural reality" differs from the character of something singular be-cause, as was said,[23] "singular" belongs both to an essence and to a supposite. But "natural reality" belongs only to a supposite. Hence, the character of a sup-posite is not found in [11] accidents, but only in substances, but a natural thing belongs only to a supposite. Hence, the character of supposite is not found in accidents, but only in substances. For an essence is itself a nature, whether it is that of a substance or of an accident. But only the supposite of a substance is a natural reality, because an essence, whether substantial or accidental, has the ratification of its existence only in the supposite of a substance.

10. Hence, in creatures "subsistence" according to the common usage of the Greeks and the ancient usage of the Latins belongs in common to something universal, that is, to a genus and to a species, and to individuals, but "substance" belongs only to individuals. For "to subsist" or "subsistence" is said as if to stand by holding oneself up, and it belongs to everything that is in the category of substance insofar as it is substance.

11. But "substance" or "to stand under" is said as if to stand under something else, that is, under accidents or under universals, which properly belongs only to an individual substance. On this account in the *Categories*, first substance is *"most of all and principally* said to be *that which is neither* in another *nor said of* another,"[24] but other things are in it and said of it. Hence, Boethius also says in *On the Two Natures*: "Substances *subsist only in particular individuals.* [12] *For the understanding of universals is taken from particulars. Hence, since essences exist in universals, they receive substance in particulars.*"[25] But it stands under because

---

20   See *SQO* art. 52, qu. 2; ed. M. Führer, pp. 250–253.

21   See *SQO* art. 28, qu. 5; ed. Badius 1, fol. 168vB.

22   See below q. 3, par. 8.

23   See above, par. 5.

24   Aristotle, *Categories* 5.2a11–13; Boethius, trans. ed. L. Minio-Paluello, p. 7.

25   Boethius, *Against Eutyches and Nestorius* 3; PL 64: 1344B; ed. C. Moreschini, p. 216.

it offers a subject to accidents so that they can be. For it is under them when it stands under. "*Therefore, genera and species only subsist. For accidents do not belong to genera or species. But individuals not only subsist, but also stand under.*"[26] "*For this reason, however,*" as he says in the same place, "*the Greeks also call individual substances hypostases, because they stand under other things and are subject to certain things as to accidents. For this reason we too call substances what they call hypostases as if they were placed under.*"[27]

12. But "supposite" among us is entirely the same as "subsistence," and it belongs both to what is universal and to what is singular in the category of substance. For they stand for either what is signified or what is named. But there is a difference only insofar as in something singular the same thing is signified and named, but not in universals

13. And one must know that there is now a different usage of the name "substance" among us and among the Greeks because we do not now use "substance" as the Greeks do. In accord with this Augustine says in book seven of *On the Trinity*: "*The Greeks understand 'substance' in another way than the Latins,*" because "*in our language, that is, Latin, 'essence' is usually not understood otherwise than 'substance.'*"[28] But "person" signifies the same thing in reality as hypostasis or substance does among the Greeks, while [13] the only difference between us and them is with regard to the generality of the usage and the proper meaning of the name—with regard to the generality of usage since, although we use the name "hypostasis" or "substance" without any difference both in intellectual and non-intellectual and in non-living beings, they use "substance" only in rational beings, as Boethius says. "*Hence, a Greek does not say 'hypostasis' concerning non-rational animals, and the reason is that it is applied to better things, as something that is more excellent.*"[29] And similarly there is the same observance among the Greeks concerning the name "*prosopon,*" because as Boethius says: "*When they say 'prosopa,' we can also call the same substances persons,*"[30] Hence, we also use "person" only in intellectual or rational beings. For although it signifies the same intention in creatures as this name "individual," as will be seen below,[31] it nonetheless signifies it with regard to a determinate matter, namely, a rational one, as Boethius says in *On the Two Natures*, chapter three, in the beginning. For just as "curved" and "snub" signify the same thing, but "curved" signifies it

---

26   Ibid.

27   Ibid.; ed. C. Moreschini, p. 218.

28   Augustine of Hippo, *On the Trinity* 7, 4; PL 42: 939; ed. W. Mountain and F. Glorie, p 255.

29   Boethius, *Against Eutyches and Nestorius* 3; PL 64: 1344B; ed. C. Moreschini, p. 216.

30   Ibid.; ed. C. Moreschini, p. 217.

31   See below q. 2, par. 4.

indifferently with respect to any matter, but "snub" signifies the same thing as determined in relation to a nose and as proper to it, so "individual" signifies something indeterminate in relation to a rational and non-rational nature, but "person" signifies something determinate and proper to a rational nature. And in accord with this, "person" implies by its name [14] a character of dignity that the former does not imply with respect of the proper meaning of the term.

14. Hence, since "substance," "supposite," "subsistence," and suchlike, are said with an improper meaning in God insofar as it depends on the character of the term, because what subsists in God does not stand under something, neither under a higher universal nor under accidents, as is the case in creatures, and the imposition of the name was taken from this. But "person" rather subsists in the essence, as will be seen below.[32] "Person," however, is admitted in God without any improper meaning of the term, as Richard says in the place above: "*The fact that persons are called subsistences by some and substances by others is seen to be with regard to the same thing. For it is certain that they are said to be 'substances' or 'subsistences' with respect to those things that are usually said to be in them, although they can less properly be said to be substances or subsistences.*"[33] And he adds after a bit: "*Among the Latins I think that no term can be found that can be better suited to the divine plurality than the name 'person.'*"[34] And he proves this from the common usage of all Christians and the authority of sacred scripture, when he adds: "*And certainly nothing ought to be more authoritative for the believing soul than what is heard from the lips of all and that the Catholic authority confirms.*"[35]

<Replies to the Arguments>

15. To the first argument to the contrary that "'rational' and 'individual,' which do not belong to God, are according to Boethius placed in the definition of person."[36] [15] it must be said that Boethius takes "rational" in a broad sense so that it includes the purely intellectual, and he does the same with "individual" so that it also includes incommunicable, and in that manner of extension both belong to God. Hence, in such an extension both belong to God in an improper sense and, as was said, the name "substance" also does, which Boethius also puts in that definition. For this reason, in book four of *On the Trinity*, chapter twenty-one, Richard corrects the definition of Boethius and makes it quasi proper to the divine persons. For where Boethius says that "*a person is an individual substance*

---

32   See below q. 2, par. 5.

33   Richard of Saint Victor, *On the Trinity* 4, 20; PL 196: 943C; ed. J. Ribaillier, p. 184.

34   Ibid.; PL 196: 944C; ed. J. Ribaillier, p. 186.

35   Ibid.

36   See above par. 1.

of a rational nature,"[37] [16] Richard says that *"it is an incommunicable existence of an intellectual nature."*[38] But how this definition has to be understood and explained, will be seen below.[39]

16. To the second argument that "there are said to be *three persons, not in order that one might say that, but in order that one might not be completely silent,"*[40] it must be said that Augustine does not say this on account of some falsity, but on account of the novelty of the use of the name with regard to God. For that which is expressed by the name "person" was in truth from eternity in God according to its true meaning, or it could have been conceived with regard to him, but the usage did not have it that it should be expressed by this name. And it would not have been expressed by this name if the attacks of heretics had not forced this, as Augustine says in book seven of *On the Trinity.*[41] Hence, Augustine's words, *"Not that one might say that,"* have to be [17] understood in that way; when heretics asked: *"Three who or what?"* the reply was: *"Three persons, not in order that one might say that,"* that is, that one might answer the question of the heretics, when they asked: *"Three what?"* but *in order that one might not be completely silent."*[42] For by this answer he did not satisfy the question in accord with their intention, as will be seen below,[43] but only satisfied the questioners who had nothing further that they might ask, and by that the faithful were set free from their attack without the confusion that they would have incurred by his being silent. Hence, Richard says in book four of *On the Trinity,* chapter five, *"Those who firstly transferred this name 'person' to God did this out of necessity, but the Holy Spirit who presided over their hearts knew with what reason and truth he wanted them to do what they did out of necessity, and we are now seeking with all diligence not the understanding with which human beings firstly imposed it, nor the necessity out of which it was later transferred to God, but the truth by which the Holy Spirit inspired it in those who transferred it and by which it has been universally used in the whole Latin church."*[44]

---

37   Boethius, *Against Eutyches and Nestorius* 3; PL 64: 1343C–D; ed. C. Moreschini, p. 214.

38   Richard of Saint Victor, *On the Trinity* 4, 18; PL 196: 941C; ed. J. Ribaillier, p. 181.

39   See below q. 5.

40   Augustine of Hippo, *On the Trinity* 5, 9; PL 42: 941–942; ed. W. Mountain and F. Glorie, p. 217.

41   See ibid. 7, 4; PL 42: 491–492; ed. W. Mountain and F. Glorie, p. 259.

42   Ibid. 5, 9; PL 42: 918; ed. W. Mountain and F. Glorie, p. 217.

43   See below q. 7, par. 16.

44   Richard of Saint Victor, *On the Trinity* 4, 5; PL 196: 933C–D; ed. J. Ribaillier, p. 167.

Whether "Person" Has Being in God in a Proper or a Transferred Sense

1. With regard to the second question, it is argued that in God "person" is not said in the proper, but in a transferred sense, in the first place as follows: That which properly and principally signifies something unworthy and lowly and is imposed to signify that cannot be properly said of God because, as is clear from what has already been determined,[45] nothing is properly said of him except that which is unqualifiedly more noble and more worthy with respect to anything. "Person" is such, <that is, it signifies something unworthy and lowly>, because according to Boethius in *On the Two Natures*, chapter three: "*The name 'person' is seen to have been taken from elsewhere, namely, from these masks* (personae) *that in comedies and tragedies represented those human beings who were involved.*"[46] And such representation was something lowly because "it was *produced by actors and lowly human beings,*" as he says there,[47] and in a disreputable place. Therefore, and so on.

2. Likewise, it is clear through Boethius who explicitly says in the same place: "*On account of a lack of words to convey the meaning, we have retained a transferred term, calling a person that which they,*[19] *namely, the Greeks, call an hypostasis.*"[48] But a naming expressed in a transferred sense is not a proper naming in God because it is distinguished in an opposite way in accord with what was determined above.[49] Therefore, and so on.

3. To the contrary there is that which Richard said above:[50] "*No name can be found that is better suited to the divine plurality,*"[51] and that would not be the case unless it was possible to use it in God in the proper sense.

<The Resolution of the Question>

4. To this it must be said that, since certain things are said of God through their proper sense or properly, while certain others are said through likeness or transference, in order to see which are which one must look at what is signified by the name, not to the use of the word. For whichever ones imply in what they

---

45   See *SQO* art. 32, qu. 1; ed. R. Macken, pp. 30–32.

46   Boethius, *Against Eutyches and Nestorius* 3; PL 64: 1343D 3; ed. C. Moreschini, pp. 214-215.

47   Ibid.

48   Ibid.; PL 64: 1344A; ed. C. Moreschini, p. 215.

49   See *SQO* art. 32, qu. 1; ed. R. Macken, p. 30–32.

50   See above qu. 1, par. 13.

51   Richard of Saint Victor, *On the Trinity* 4, 20; PL 196: 944C; ed. J. Ribaillier, p. 186.

signify something that is of dignity without qualification are said of God in a proper sense, but all the others are said of him in a transferred sense, in accord with what is clear from what was determined above.[52] But now in the present question it is the case concerning what "person" signifies that this name "individual" signifies concerning anything to which the character of an individual is attributed, whether it is a substance or an accident, a concept of the mind by which a thing is understood to be singular and determinate or designated as indivisible through its essence under some universal to which the character of divisible of itself belongs. And by that signification that essence is understood to be something not distinguished in itself and incommunicable or indivisible through its essence and divided from anything else of its nature. And thus it is something one in itself that is not able to be this and something else, but is this [20] in such a way that <it is> this and not able to be something else. On the other hand, the nature of a genus <is able to have> diverse species and <is> in potency in relation to them, and the nature of a species similarly <is able to have> diverse individuals. So this term "person" signifies the same thing with regard to created intellectual substances, as Boethius's definition of person assigns.

5. But when it is used for God, it signifies the same thing, but in a more eminent way or manner, as things taken from creatures signify in God, however properly they are said of God, as is clear from what has been already determined.[53] For in God "person" signifies a concept of the mind by which someone is understood to be incommunicable through his property and to be someone in himself through that property, unable in accord with that to be this one and another, but is distinguished from another so that he is not that other, in accord with what the definition of person assigned by Richard maintains. And this manner of existing is noble in the highest way, that is, that many who are incommunicable in accord with their properties have one singular shared essence, which will be clearer below.[54] On this account it was already said above that "person" signifies something that is of nobility without qualification and of the highest nobility in God.[55] Hence, since in accord with what was determined above, something of the sort has being in God in the proper sense, it must for this reason be said without qualification that "person" has being in God in the proper sense and not through a likeness or transference.

[21] 6. Nonetheless, on account of the arguments for the first side, it must be understood that transference is of two sorts. One is from the side of the reality, that is, when the reality does not belong to God in terms of the same thing signified

52 See above qu. 1, par. 5–13.

53 See above qu. 1, par. 5 and 13.

54 See below qu. 3, par. 12.

55 See above qu. 1, par. 5 and 13.

and also not in a more eminent manner, but only in terms of a certain likeness, in the way that 'imprint,' "mirror," and suchlike are said to be in God, and ones of this sort do not have being properly in God. But there is another transference from the side of the name alone, namely, when the name is firstly imposed on creatures and only used with regard to them in accord with one character of the reality and is not used in God in accord with a more eminent manner of the reality and is not imposed to represent it, as is the case in individual <names> that are taken from creatures through their proper sense. And in this way some are taken by an assumption or transference as if a new imposition of the name is made, and by such a transference the name "person" is transferred to God and still through its proper sense, although not in accord with its common and proper acceptance, in accord with which the name "person" was firstly used in creatures. For, as Richard says in book four of *On the Trinity*, chapter one: "*If one would want to understand the name 'person' under its common and proper acceptance, he in no way supposes that many persons can subsist in the unity of a substance. For human understanding does not easily grasp how there can be more than one person where there is not more than one substance. From this <there have come> countless errors of unbelievers. From this <it has come about> that some divide the unity of the divine substance. From this <it has come about> that the Arians and Sabellians were divided in contrary sects.*"[56]

7. And through this the reason for both arguments is seen,[57] but especially for the second.

[22]   **<Replies to the Arguments>**

8. But with regard to that which is argued in the first argument, namely, that "'person' was firstly imposed to represent *something lowly* and useless, such as individual human beings whom *the actors* in theatrical plays represent,"[58] it must be said to this that there are diverse opinions about the imposition of the name "person" and about those from whom it was transferred. For as Master Alexander says in his *Summa*, "*According to some, this name 'person' in substances took its origin from a grammatical person, which is nothing other than the property by which someone is the one who speaks or the one to whom someone speaks or the one about whom someone speaks to another. In the first way it is said to be the first person; in the second way the second person, and in the third the third person.*"[59] And this property belongs to each of them as he is one in himself and through himself. For this reason, as he exists in such a relationship, anyone of them is said to be a person. And in accord with the meaning of the word, a

56   Richard of Saint Victor, *On the Trinity* 4, 1; PL 196: 931B and 931A; ed. J. Ribaillier, pp. 163 and 162.

57   See above par. 1 and 2.

58   See above par. 1.

59   Alexander of Hales, *Summa* 2, 2, 2, q. 1; ed. Quaracchi, I, p. 565–566.

person is said to be as if "one through himself (*per se una*)."[60] But the opinion of Boethius in *On the Two Natures* is different. From it the argument was taken, namely, that the name "'person' was taken from those *who represent them in comedies and tragedies* [23] of theatrical plays in a place in which they produced theatrical dramas, such as Hecuba and Chremetes and other such people who are regarded as great and more honorable people."[61] And on this account the actors representing them as worthy and more honorable men were called persons. In the same way, those placed in ecclesiastical dignities are called persons because they ought to be great and more honorable men and at least represent them. And according to the proper meaning of the word in this transference, according to Boethius, "*person was said* in accord with the meaning of the word, 'person' from 'sounding' (personando),"[62] that is, by sounding perfectly and in loud voice. And this is so because those actors had tied before their faces a mask, that is, a face made of wood or copper, which represented the one in whose role they sang, as something well known and admirable at which everyone looked. And that mask hid their faces and eyes, and from "*that hollowness a greater sound was necessarily* produced. Hence, the Greeks called "*prosopa*" those masked in that way, whom the Latins called persons, [24] *because* that mask was put in front of their faces. For in Greek πρόσοπον is said to be from πρός, which is "on," and ὤψ, ὠψός, which is "face," as having something *on the face*."[63] And because such people were recognized and known to all because of that mask, they were called persons, and for this reason the usage became customary, as Boethius says, that "all elegant human beings who were known *for their stature and dignity* were called persons."[64] And afterwards all individual intellectual natures were universally called persons, and this was because of the dignity of that nature above the others. And from there it was finally transferred to God. For if it was taken from lowly human beings and ones placed in lowly offices, as the objection runs, it still was not insofar as they were lowly, but insofar as they represented noble and honored men. Thus the name "person" represents something entirely of dignity and nobility so that it can be worthily transferred to God through its proper sense, not merely through a likeness.

---

60   See Simon of Tournai, *Summa* 1, 3; ed. M. Schmaus, p. 62. Also see below qu. 5, par. 22 and William of Auxerre, *Golden Summa* 1, tr. 6, 1; ed. J. Ribaillier, p. 78–82; and others.

61   See Boethius, *Against Eutyches and Nestorius* 3; PL 64: 1343D–1344A; ed. C. Moreschini, p. 215.

62   Ibid. 3; PL 64: 1343D; ed. C. Moreschini, p. 215.

63   See ibid. Also see Thomas Aquinas, *Commentary on the Sentences* 1, d. 23, 1, 1; ed. P. Mandonnet, p. 557.

64   Boethius, *Against Eutyches and Nestorius* 3; PL 64: 1343D–1344A; ed. C. Moreschini, p. 215. Also see Thomas Aquinas, *Summa of Theology* 1, q. 29, a. 3 corp. and ad 3um; ed. Leonine 4, pp. 331b and 332a.

QUESTION THREE

Whether "Person" Has Being in God and in Creatures
Univocally and with the Same Meaning or
Equivocally and According to Diverse Meanings.

1. With regard to the third question, it is argued that "person" has univocally and according to the same meaning in God and in creatures in the first place as follows: That which has being in several things in accord with the same name and the same definition belongs to them univocally and in the same way. In that way "person" has being in God and in creatures, as is seen from the definition of person according to Richard.[65] Therefore, and so on.

2. <It is argued> in the second place as follows: That whose formal and complete meaning has being in several things has being univocally and in the same way in those same things. But the formal meaning of "person" is that it is someone, that is, someone singular in himself and incommunicable, and other than any other of the sort and distinct from him. And this has being univocally in God and creatures because what is singular and incommunicable in itself implies only negation, and similarly that it is not some other distinct from it <implies only negation>. But negation has being univocally and in the same way in God and in creatures, just as not to be a stone belongs to them univocally and in the same way. Therefore, and so on.

3. To the contrary it is argued in the first place as follows: Nothing that signifies some reality and nature has being univocally and in the same way in those things that do not have [26] some common nature because univocity comes from the unity of something common, as is clear from the definition of univocal things in the *Categories*.[66] But no common nature has being in God and creatures, and the name "person" signifies a subsisting reality and nature, as will be clear below.[67] Therefore, and so on.

4. <It is argued> in the second place as follows: To be a person does not belong univocally to those to which those things pertaining to the meaning of person and its integrity do not belong univocally. But a nature or essence and the character of incommunicability pertain to the meaning of person and its integrity, as is clear from its definition explained above.[68] But neither of these belongs univocally to the meaning of person in God and creatures because the

---

65   Richard of Saint Victor, *On the Trinity* 4, 21; PL 196: 945A; ed. J. Ribaillier, p. 186.

66   Aristotle, *Categories* 1.1a.6–8; trans. Boethius, ed. L. Minio-Paluello, p. 5.

67   See below par. 5 and 11. Also see *SQO* art. 21, qu. 2, ed. Badius 1, fol. 124rF.

68   See above qu. 1, par. 4.

essence pertains to the meaning and integrity of person in God as it is something communicable in the same singularity, but in creatures as it is not communicable in the same singularity, but only in a community of reason. Hence,
in God there is one singular essence of many persons, but in creatures there is
not. There are rather necessarily many essences of many persons. Similarly, in
God the incommunicability of a person also comes from a relative property, but
in creatures from negation alone.[69] Therefore, and so on.

[27]   <The Resolution of the Question>

5. For the understanding of what was asked in this question it is necessary to
see what is understood by the name "person," that is, what makes something to
be a person, and to see whether that has being in God and in creatures univocally and according to the same meaning. For if it does, "person" would also have
being in them univocally and according to the same meaning. But if it does not,
it would not by any means. And being a person, according to Boethius in *On
the Two Natures*,[70] does not belong to something universal, but only to something singular, and according to that character by which it is singular, although
not just any singular, but one existing in itself, not in another. For a person is
not found in accidents, nor is our soul as it is the act of a body a person. Nor is
the deity itself that exists in supposites a person, nor universally is something a
person that does not have its own being in itself and through itself, not united
to something else. Hence, the humanity of Christ is not a person in Christ.
Therefore, it is necessary in this question to look at the meaning of what is singular in itself and existing in terms of itself, which is understood by the name
"person." But the meaning of "person" does not add anything beyond the meaning of such a singular, although by its name, "person" names such a singular only
with regard to a determinate matter, that is, an intellectual matter, as was said.[71]

6. With regard to the meaning of such a singular, as it is commonly understood, without determining for itself this or some other matter, but as it is understood by the name alone, it must be known that two things are understood
by the name "singular": both a certain intention of non-distinction of the reality
in itself along with its distinction from others and [28] the reality itself with
regard to which such an intention is understood. And we must look at both.
Therefore, if one looks firstly at the reality itself, it must be known that in some
sense it has being in one way in creatures and in another way in God and that
in some way <it has being> in a similar way. For in creatures nothing has singular being unless it is an individual under some form that, considered in itself,
is only a form and essence without the character of universal and singular. And

---

69   See above par. 7–8.

70   See Boethius, *Against Eutyches and Nestorius* 2 and 3; PL 64: 1343C–D; ed. C.
     Moreschini, p. 214.

71   See above qu. 1, par. 10.

to that form or essence the character of universal is added from the consideration of the intellect with regard to it, that is, insofar as the intellect considers it as abstracted from singulars and again as applicable to the same through predication. Hence, on the basis of its nature such a specific form is non-individual, that is, able to be divided—I do not mean by that division into the form of genus and difference as integral parts of the essence, about which nothing pertains to the present question—but into subjective parts, to which the whole integrity of the form is in potency so that it is whole in this and whole in that, as humanity is in this humanity, namely, Peter's and in that humanity, namely, Paul's, in which it is individuated by the fact that it became "this" and "that." And according to the Philosopher,[72] this takes place only through matter subject to it, in which it is of itself firstly divisible into parts. Thus humanity is not "this," except because it is in this part and not in that part of matter,[73] just as whiteness is not "this" except in this subject. Hence, he maintained that all immaterial forms are of themselves singular, just as we hold [29] that deity is of itself a certain singularity, which one should not hold. On the contrary, <one should hold> that any specific form of a creature is immaterial and undivided into many subjective parts, even though it is able to subsist in itself without any subject and matter. But that individuation of it is effectively produced in a subjective part, as humanity in this humanity, or rather in this human being, only though an agent that gives it being, and not through matter, although it has matter. And <it is> not <produced> through some accident that inheres in it, but is produced firstly through its designation and determination, which it has from the one causing it.

7. For although according to Ambrose in book one of *On the Trinity:*[74] *"Every creature is contained by certain limits of its essence,"* humanity nonetheless has a more ample spiritual breadth by reason[75] of its essence than this humanity. And for this reason this humanity is determined, limited, and designated with respect to humanity without qualification, in which designation the character of a singular form firstly consists subjectively, just as the individuation of the common form also does. But as a consequence, each of them comes to be by the negation consequent upon that determination and joined to it, not through a single one, but through two, that is, by which it is separated from that which is under it and from that which is on a par with it. For humanity is divided, as was said, into this humanity and that humanity. Even if it were not divided, it

---

72   See Aristotle, *Metaphysics* 1.6.988a10-13; trans. anon., ed. G. Vuillemin-Diem, p. 23.

73   I have omitted *"nisi quia in illa,"* which does not seem to fit.

74   Rather, Ambrose of Milan, *On the Holy Spirit* 1, 7; PL 16: 723A; ed. O. Faller, p. 48.

75   I have conjectured *"ratione essentiae"* instead of *"sive rationis."*

would still be divisible, insofar as it is considered in itself, and in that way it is not separated from that which is under it by any negation. But by reason of the fact that "this humanity" is "this," it is neither [30] divided nor divisible into some things under it of its nature, and for this reason it is negatively related to those things that could be imagined under it. It is also related negatively to those things that are on a par with it and divided over against it under the species. For the singularity of its form is neither communicable to some things under it nor to something on a par with it. For from this an individual of a creature has it that it is a "this something," that is, something one in itself, which is not "this" and something else under it, and similarly <it is> something other than anything else under the form of its species. It also has it from this that it is singular and a supposite, whether it is intellectual or non-intellectual, and it also has it that it is a person when it is in an intellectual nature. For the character of supposite or person in a creature comes from the fact that it is something existing in itself and in terms of itself in a communicable nature, and that is necessarily had in creatures from that twofold negation with regard to the determinate form and nature of the reality.

8. But in God the character of singularity does not come from the side of the reality because in God the form of deity, even as it is considered without qualification and absolutely, is singular, in no way able to be divided in something under it by receiving a determination. Hence, it is not able to be individuated in a supposite. Nonetheless, it is able to be communicated through the relative properties, while remaining in the same singularity of essence, and through those properties the character of a supposite and a person and the singularity of the same are constituted in God, not insofar as those properties are merely relative, but insofar as they are relatively opposed. And from that there follows a twofold negation. The one is by reason of each personal property. For because it is of itself incommunicable, there follows from this [31] a negation that removes the plurality of communicating its property to another in the same nature and that there are not in God many persons with the same respect, for example, many fathers or many sons or many holy spirits. The other is by reason of the distinguishing opposition by which there is had the negation that removes each person from its correlative.

9. And in that way there is realized through negation the character of the distinction of the divine persons and of their singularity, just as that of creatures, and with regard to this, "person" has being in God and in creatures univocally and according to the same meaning, as the second objection to the first side proceeded.[76] Nonetheless, as such, negations accompany in God the relative properties that principally constitute and distinguish the persons in the common essence, although not without the force of the added negations. But in

---

76 See above par. 2.

creatures they accompany the determination of the nature and essence that contracts the essence to the supposite and person, although not without the force of the added negations, as was said above.[77] And in accord with this, although by reason of the negations "person" has being and is constituted in God and in creatures univocally and according to the same character, still by reason of those things to which the mentioned negations are attached in the one case and the other, because in creatures it is the determinate essence and nature, but in God the relation of the properties, "person" has being in God and in creatures very equivocally and with different characters, insofar as the basis of [32] constituting a person is different and equivocal—in a creature the determination of the created essence and in God the relation of the properties.

10. Nonetheless, from the side of the negations there is some difference concerning the negation with respect to that which is under it and with respect to that which is on a par with it. Because from the side of that which is completely denied, there is a single negation under it because, as a single divine person cannot be made many in itself, so a created person also cannot. But from the side of that which is denied on a level with it, it is in some way univocal and in some way equivocal. For that in God one person is denied of another is not by reason of the nature and essence, but by reason of a personal property. But in creatures one person is removed from another by reason of the essence and by reason of the personality. For in God there is one singular common essence for many persons, but it is not that way in creatures.

11. Thus if one looks at the reality itself with regard to which the intention of "singular" is considered in God and in creatures, "person" has being in them in one way univocally and in one way equivocally. But if we look at the intention, the character of the intention is not diversified on account of the diversity of the realities with regard to which it is. For there is not another meaning of species, which is a logical intention, insofar as it is considered with regard to a substance, such as with regard to a man and a horse, and insofar as it is considered with regard to an accident, whether it is absolute, such as with regard to whiteness or blackness, or relative such as with regard to lordship or servitude. It must therefore be said that the intention has being entirely univocally and in accord with the same meaning in God and in creatures, although in God it is considered with regard to something relative, but in creatures with regard to something absolute, except that the intention of person is considered in God [33] in many persons with respect to the singular essence, while it is not that way in creatures. But this does not change the meaning of the intention in any way.

---

77   See above par. 7 and 8 and also *SQO* art. 39, qu. 3; ed. G. Wilson, pp.185–186 and art. 39, qu. 4; ed. G. Wilson, pp. 198–199.

<Replies to the Arguments>

12. To the first argument showing that "it is entirely *univocally and* with the same meaning *in God* and *in creatures* because *the definition of person* is the same in both cases,"[78] it must be said that it is not true because the equivocation in the definition is the same as in the name. For an incommunicable existence is in a created and an uncreated person, but with an equivocal incommunicability. For the incommunicability of existence in a created person results from the determination of the essence, but in an uncreated person from the relation of the properties, as was seen.[79]

13. To the first argument to the contrary showing that person is entirely equivocal in them because "*no reality or nature* is univocally common *to God and to creatures*,"[80] it must be said that this argument proves that it does not belong to them completely univocally. If nonetheless "person" is a name of a reality and of a nature, as the names of essential attributes also are, it does not belong to God and creatures completely univocally, as is clear from what was determined above.[81] It still does not follow from this that <it belongs to them> completely equivocally because analogy lies in between. And in accord with it, both essential and personal attributes belong to God and creatures in common. They firstly belong to God insofar as it depends on the meaning of what is signified by the word, although insofar as it depends on the imposition of the word they belong to them in the opposite way. Because every transference of words that we use with regard to the creator is made from creatures, as will be better explained below [34] when we discuss the manner of speaking about God.[82] But if "person" is the name of an intention, then the argument supposes something false about what "person" signifies, namely, that it signifies a reality and a nature. On the contrary, it rather signifies a certain manner of a concept with regard to a reality, and nothing prevents it from being in God and in creatures in some way univocally and according to the same meaning and in some way equivocally, as has been said.[83] But there will a discussion concerning that in the following question in which we will speak about what is signified by this name "person." For although no reality belongs to God and a creature purely univocally, nothing nonetheless prevents some intention from belonging

---

78 See above par. 1.

79 See above par. 10.

80 See above par. 3.

81 See above par. 10.

82 See below qu. 4, par. 5 and 6.

83 See above par. 9.

to them purely univocally because it does not put something in God, but rather in a concept of the intellect, as will be seen below.[84]

14. To the second argument that "essence is not said univocally concerning of the meaning of 'person' in God and creatures, because *in God* it has the meaning of something *communicable*, but *in creatures* it has that of something incommunicable,"[85] it must be said that, in accord with Richard in book four of *On the Trinity*, chapter eight, as will be expressed more fully below,[86] "*We understand 'person' in accord with the same understanding in the singular and in the plural. But it makes no difference whether the essence is communicable or not and whether there are many <essences> or one and the same singular essence in many persons.*"[87] Hence, since there are two things that belong to the integrity of a person, namely, the essence and a personal property, as will be seen below with regard to the divine persons,[88] the essence is like something material in it and the property like something formal, so that the character of the person consists in the character of the property. And in that way the person is one if the property is incommunicable and one, and the persons are many if there are many of that sort, whether the substance is communicable to many in one singularity or only in many singularities. For as [35] Richard says in book four, chapter ten: "*Just as to be different things substantially does not everywhere destroy the unity of a person, so to be one person and another in the plural does not everywhere divide the unity of a substance. For in human nature the soul is one substance and the body another, although they are only one person. But in the divine nature one is one person and another is another, although there is still only one and the same substance.*"[89] And as he says in chapter twenty-five: "*It is proper to the divine nature to have a plurality of persons in the unity of the substance. But it is on the contrary proper to human nature to have a plurality of substances in the unity of a person. For that a human person is found in the simplicity of a substance does not come from the condition of his nature, but is found to be from the corruption of his condition.*"[90] And this is only from that which is formal in the being of a human being, from which he principally derives his personality, as it is in the separated soul. When it is also added that "incommunicability is not of the same character in creatures and

---

84   See below q. 5.

85   See above par. 4.

86   See below qu. 5, par. 24 and qu. 6, par. 7.

87   Richard of Saint Victor, *On the Trinity* 4, 8; PL 196: 935B–C; ed. J. Ribaillier, p. 170.

88   See below qu. 5.

89   Richard of Saint Victor, *On the Trinity* 4, 10; PL 196: 936C–D; ed. J. Ribaillier, p. 172.

90   Ibid. 4, 25; PL 196: 947A–B; ed. J. Ribaillier, p. 190.

in God,"[91] it must be said that insofar as it comes from the side of something positive that is implied by the name "property" in God, there is not something correlative in the individuation of a creature, and in this respect the character of individuation and of personality is not univocally in creatures and in God. But insofar as it comes from the side of the added negations, there is partly univocation and partly equivocation, as has been explained.[92]

---

91   See above par. 4.

92   See above par. 9.

[36]   **QUESTION FOUR**

Whether "Person" Has Being in God According to Substance or According to Relation.

1. With regard to the fourth question it is argued that "person" is said and has being in God according to substance and not according to relation by the Master who says in distinction twenty-three, chapter one of the first book of the *Sentences*: "*There is one name, namely, 'person,' which is said of the individual persons according to substance.*"[93] And the authority of Augustine in book seven of *On the Trinity* confirms this.[94]

2. <It is argued> in the second place as follows: In the same authority Augustine says: "*The Father is said to be a person with respect to himself, not with respect to the Son or to the Holy Spirit, just as he is said to be God with respect to himself.*"[95] But according to the rule of Augustine in book five of *On the Trinity*, which the Master discusses in distinction twenty-two:[96] "*Whatever that most excellent and divine loftiness is said to be with respect to itself is said substantially.*"[97] But what is said substantially [37] in God is said according to substance and not according to relation. Therefore, and so on.

3. But it is argued that it is not said according to substance, but according to relation from what Boethius says in the end of *On the Trinity*: "*It is necessary that that word which takes its origin from the persons not pertain to the substance.*"[98] But "*that on account of which each thing is such is such to a greater degree,*" as the Philosopher says in the *Topics*.[99] Therefore, and so on.

<The Resolution of the Question>

4. It must be said to this, without as yet getting down to what is signified by "person," that according to the two categories that are in God, namely, sub-

---

93   Peter Lombard, *Sentences* 1, d. 23, c. 1; PL 192: 583; ed. I. Brady, 1, p. 181.

94   See Augustine of Hippo, *On the Trinity* 7, 6; PL 42: 943; ed. W. Mountain and F. Glorie, p. 262.

95   Ibid.

96   Peter Lombard, *Sentences* 1, d. 22, c. 1; PL 192; 582; ed. I. Brady, 1, p. 179.

97   Augustine of Hippo, *On the Trinity* 5, 8; PL 42: 916–917; ed. W. Mountain and F. Glorie, p. 215.

98   Boethius, *Whether the Father and the Son*; PL 64: 1302B; ed. C. Moreschini, p. 184.

99   Rather, Aristotle, *Posterior Analytics* 1.2.72a29–30; trans. Jacobus; ed. L. Minio-Paluello–B. G. Dod, p. 9.

stance and relation, in accord with the way it was determined above,[100] two ways of being and of predicating are distinguished in God so that whatever is predicated of God and attributed to God is reduced to one of those two, that is, that it is said of God or has being in him either according to substance and by reason of the substance or according to relation and by reason of a relation. And this is true because every name formally signifies in God either the substance or a relation, or its formal character of signifying is taken from the substance or a relation, which are really in God, even if it does not signify one of these according to reality, but signifies some intention of reason with regard to that which principally signifies the substance or a relation in God.

[38] 5. It must therefore be understood that, although in God a name can sometimes signify the essence or substance alone, such as this name "deity," but sometimes a relation alone, such as the name "paternity," but at times both at the same time, such as this name "Father," as will be seen below,[101] to be said or to be in God is still only said in accord with that from which the signification of the name is formally taken or imposed to signify. Thus that name that formally takes its origin from the substance in its imposition is said and is in God according to substance, but one <which takes its origin> from a relation <is said and is in God> according to relation, even if the rest is signified quasi materially in the name. Hence, because this name "Father" is formally imposed from a personal relation, although it includes in what it signifies the common essence, as will be seen below,[102] it is said and has being in God according to relation. But now it is the case that, whatever is signified by this name "person," its formal character, to signify which is imposed, is still either a relation or is taken from a relation. For if there were not in God a relation that distinguishes them, there would in no way be held to be in God any of those persons that in fact constitute the ineffable Trinity, as will be seen below.[103] But how it signifies a relation or is taken from a relation is seen from the preceding question,[104] where it was explained how the character of the singularity of the divine persons, in which the personal character consists, was taken firstly and positively from a relation. But this will be seen more in the following question.[105]

6. For this reason it must absolutely be said that in God "person" is said according to relation and has being in God according to relation, but not according to substance. For the sake of the resolution of the arguments, it must nonetheless be understood that something is and is said to be according to

---

100 See above par. 3 and *SQO* art. 32, qu. 5; ed. R. Macken, pp. 81–94.

101 See below par. 6.

102 See below qu. 9, par. 5 and *SQO* art. 75, qu. 1; ed. Badius 2, fol. 289vA.

103 See below qu. 5, par. 28.

104 See above qu. 3.

105 See below qu. 5.

relation [39] in two ways: either in itself or in what is contained under it. In the first way those things are said relatively that signify a relation determinately or a determinate relation, such as "Father," "Son," and "Holy Spirit," because the Father is said to be the father of the Son and the Son the son of the Father, which are said according to relation in terms of their name and in terms of the formal character of the name from which they are imposed, as Augustine says in book five, chapter five of *On the Trinity*: "*These are not said according to substance because each of them is not said with respect to himself, but they are said with respect to one another and to another.*"[106] In the second way those things are said relatively that signify indeterminately or signify an indeterminate relation, such as this name "person" and this name "Trinity," and the like. They are not said relatively in accord with their name because they do not have a correlative that corresponds to them outside of themselves, although in terms of the formal character of the name they signify a relation or have it as something taken from a relation, but they are said relatively in what they contain which are names that imply indeterminate relations.

<Replies to the Arguments>

7. Through these points the reply is clear to the first argument that according to Augustine "*person* is said *according to substance*,[107] it must be said that it is true with regard to the fact that it is not said relatively according to its name, but <it is> not <true> that it is imposed with regard to its formal character from substance because it includes substance in what it signifies only materially, but does not take what it signifies from it. [40] And the text of Augustine's *On the Trinity*, book seven, explains this well where he speaks as follows: "*In that way 'person' is said relatively with respect to itself, as we say three persons, the Father, the Son, and the Holy Spirit, just as some people are said to be three friends or three neighbors because these names have a relative signification. What follows then? It is not all right, is it, to say that the Father is the person of the Son and of the Holy Spirit or that the Son is the person of the Father and of the Holy Spirit or that the Holy Spirit is the person of the Father and of the Son? But when in this Trinity we say the person of the Father, we do not say anything other than the substance of the Father.*"[108] And this is true insofar as it depends on the proper sense of the name in itself because in terms of his name when we say "*the person of the Father, we do not say anything other than the substance of the Father.*"[109] And this is true insofar as it depends on the proper sense of the name in itself because

---

106   Augustine of Hippo, *On the Trinity* 5, 5; PL 42: 914; ed. W. Mountain-F. Glorie, p. 210.

107   See above par. 1.

108   Augustine of Hippo, *On the Trinity* 7, 6; PL 42: 943; ed. W. Mountain and F. Glorie, p. 262.

109   Ibid.

its name is not said relatively, as on the contrary three people are said to be neighbors or close to one another. Nonetheless, from the side of the reality on account of what it formally signifies, it is said according to relation, and for this reason he adds and says that *"the person of the Father is nothing other than the* Father himself."[110]

And the reply to the second argument is clear through the same explanation.[111]

---

110   Ibid.

111   See above par. 2.

QUESTION FIVE

Whether in God "Person" Signifies a Reality, Namely, of the Substance or of a Relation, or Only an Intention

1. With regard to the fifth <question> it is argued that "person" does not signify the divine substance or a relation that falls under what the Father, the Son, and the Holy Spirit signify: That <it does> not <signify> the substance <is argued> in this way: Whatever a name signifies in the singular becomes many in its plural, whether it comes under the signification quasi materially or quasi formally, as is seen when we say "man" and "men." Hence, if there are many men, there are many animals and many rational beings. Therefore, if "person" signifies the essence of the deity, since it has being in the plural in God, there would be many deities in God. The consequent is false. Therefore, and so on.

2. Similarly, <it does> not <signify> the substance alone because then "person" would not be relative, as "substance" also <is> not. Therefore, it signifies both or neither. It does not signify both because nothing univocally signifies those things that belong to diverse categories, as substance and relation do. "Person" would therefore be an equivocal name. The consequent is false. Therefore, and so on.

3. <It is argued> that it does not signify a relation as follows: A name taken in its proper sense from creatures for God signifies that same thing in God that it signifies in creatures, although under a more eminent character, as is clear concerning the names of the [42] attributes in accord with what was determined above.[112] <But>, as was determined above,[113] "person" is taken in its proper sense from creatures for God, and in creatures it in no way signifies a relation, as is seen by running through singular persons among creatures. Therefore, and so on.

4. <It is argued> that it does not signify a relation alone because then it would be the same to say: "The Father is a person" as "The Father is paternity or sonship or spiration" because there are no other personal relations in God. The consequent is false because the Father is not a person from paternity alone, as will be seen below.[114] Therefore, and so on.

5. <It is argued> in the third place against both that it does not signify a reality, but an intention, as follows: "Person" signifies the same thing in rational or

---

112 See *SQO* art. 32, qu. 2; ed. R. Macken, p. 41.

113 See above qu. 3.

114 See *SQO* art. 57, qu. 2; ed. Badius 1, f. 120vH.

intellectual beings as "individual" does in non-rational or non-intellectual be-ings, in accord with Boethius, who says that "*A person is a rational individual,*"[115] but the name "individual" signifies an intention and is the name of an intention. Therefore, and so on.

6. To the contrary it is argued that "person" does not signify only an intention in the first place as follows because, if "person" signified an intention, not a re-ality, since the glorious Trinity consists of persons, it would then consist only of intentions and not of realities. And that is false, as Augustine says in book one of *On Christian Doctrine*: "*The realities to be enjoyed are the Father, the Son, and the Holy Spirit. The same Trinity is* nonetheless *a certain supreme reality.*"[116] Therefore, and so on.

[43] 7. <It is argued> in the second place as follows: That which is signified by the name "person" is to be adored because the Trinity is to be adored. But only the divine reality is to be adored, and that is only essence and relation. Therefore, and so on.

8. But it is argued that it signifies substance because it signifies something subsisting, and in God only the substance subsists. Therefore, and so on.

9. Similarly it is argued that it signifies a relation because its contents signify a relation, and they are the Father, Son, and Holy Spirit. But this would not be so unless it signified a relation. Therefore, and so on.

10. From this it is further concluded that it signifies both at the same time, that is, both the substance and a relation.

<The Resolution of the Question>

11. Because this question is about what is signified by this name "person," that is, what a person is, but what is signified by any name can only be known if one firstly knows in general those things that have to be signified by names and how it is customary to use this name in question. For this reason it is necessary firstly to consider what those things are that have to be signified by names, and it is necessary secondly to investigate from the use of this name "person" which of them is signified by it.

12. With regard to the first of these <questions>, it must therefore be known that certain names signifies a reality alone, and certain names signify an in-tention alone, while certain names signify something that stands in an inter-mediate way, that is, something that is in some way a reality and in some way an intention. [44] The names of singular realities signify a reality alone. For singular beings are only realities and in no way intentions because they have being only from nature and in no way from the consideration of reason, for

---

115 Boethius, *Against Eutyches and Nestorius* 3; ed. C. Moreschini, p. 214; PL 64: 1343C–D.

116 Augustine of Hippo, *On the Christian Doctrine* 1, 5; ed. J. Martin, p. 9; PL 34: 21.

example, this man, this stone. Hence, when names were imposed on them, in accord with which "Peter" or "Paul" is the name of this man, they are called names of realities without qualification. But universals of singular realities are in certain sense realities and in a certain sense intentions. <They are> realities insofar as they represent the nature that has being in singular beings, but they are intentions insofar as they have a character of something abstract in the consideration of the intellect. On this account names imposed on them are in a certain sense names of realities and in a certain sense names of intentions, but of first <intentions>.

13. For certain intentions are first, but certain others second. And in that way any real universal, insofar as it has the character of something abstract, is a predicable intention, because it exists outside of singular things only in the consideration of an intellect. But the others that are considered or produced by the consideration of an intellect both concerning universals and concerning particulars, whether mediately or immediately, are pure intentions. On this account the names imposed on them are called the names of intentions, but of second <intentions> because the intellect conceives them both with regard to the universals of realities and with regard to singulars after conceiving the meaning of something really universal.

14. But these are found in two kinds because some are understood by the intellect as properties principally with regard to realities, but others are understood as properties with regard to the names of realities. Of the first kind there are logical intentions, such as the character of a universal, that is, of "genus," "species," "difference," and the like with regard to the universals of realities, and "individual," "particular," and [45] the like with regard to the singulars of realities. For these names signify only the respects and relationships between those realities compared to one another by the consideration of the intellect. Of the second kind there are the grammatical intentions, such as the concept of noun, verb, adjective, substantive, and the like, which signify only modes of names. And on this account they are called the names of names.

15. Because the consideration of first intentions is a consideration of realities in terms of themselves, it pertains to the real sciences. But because the consideration of second intentions is either a consideration with regard to realities as they are able to be expressed by words, and this is with regard to logical intentions, or <it is a consideration> with regard to the words themselves, and this is with regard to grammatical intentions, it pertains to the linguistic sciences. And yet logic is less linguistic and more real than grammar and is as it were in between the real and grammatical sciences.

16. With regard to the second question, however, it must be known that the use of this name "person" appears different to the different people insofar as they judged differently about its signification in God. But all whom I was able to hear or see deny that it is the name of an intention, but hold that it is the

name of a reality and signifies the substance or essence, although not alone. But some of them say that "person" signifies many things and equivocally,[117] but some others <say that it signifies> many things, but univocally,[118] while others <say that it signifies> only one thing.[119]

17. But none of those who hold that it signifies many things and equivocally holds that it signifies many things equally firstly and in the same way as equivocal terms in the proper sense signify, but they all say that it signifies firstly and from the first [46] imposition of the name only the substance or essence but other things as a consequence and by accident. Some of these say that it signifies other things as a result of an addition.[120] But some <say> that <it does so> as a result of use,[121] while a third group <say> that <it does so> from its consignification.[122]

18. The first ones[123] say that by itself it signifies substance, but <signifies> a certain personal property as a result of an addition, but that at times <it signifies> an hypostasis containing both. And Praepositinus explains this in his *Summa* when he says: "*Certain people reply and say that this name 'person' is understood in three ways. For at times it signifies the essence, that is, when it is put in the predicate position without some addition, for example, 'the Father is a person,' 'the Son is a person.' At times it signifies an hypostasis, that is, a subsistence, as when something is added to it, for example, 'the Father is a person, and the Son is another person, and the person of the Father is other than that of the Son.' And at times <it signifies> a property, as 'the Father is distinguished from the Son in his person, that is, by his personal property.'*"[124] And this is the position of the Master of the Sentences in distinction twenty-five, the chapter: "It must be known," where he says: "*This name 'person' produces a multiple understanding, not merely one. Therefore, separating out the reasons for saying this name 'person,' we distinguish its signification and say that it is properly said substantially and signifies the essence, when it is said: 'God is a person,' 'the Father is a person,'*" and so on.[125] Hence, he concludes in the chapter, "Also in this way": "*From what has been said we conclude that the name 'person' produces a threefold understanding in the Trinity. For there is the*

---

117   See below par. 17–21.

118   See below par. 22–25.

119   See below par. 26–27.

120   See below par. 18–19.

121   See below par. 20.

122   See below par. 21.

123   See above par. 17.

124   Praepositinus, *Summa against the Heretics* 3, 2; ed. J. Garwin, p. 200. Also see Simon of Tournai, *Summa*; ed. M. Schmaus, pp. 61–63

125   Peter Lombard, *Sentences* 1, d. 25, c. 2; PL 192: 580; ed. I. Brady, 1, p. 192.

case where it produces the understanding of the essence, and there is the case where it produces the understanding of an hypostasis, and there is the case where it produces [47] *the understanding of a property.*"[126] And he confirms this by authorities in the following chapter.

19. This opinion supposes that "person" principally and by itself signifies the substance, but an hypostasis or property as the result of an addition. And Praepositinus argues against this, saying: "*If this name 'person' principally signifies the essence, what argument demands that since this is its principal signification, it loses this immediately as the result of* an addition?"[127] Actually, none. It falsely supposes that "*the essence is its principal signification,*" as will now be seen. For by the same argument the same thing could be said of this name "man" and of this name "supposite," because they are used in speaking in the three ways already mentioned.

20. But Praepositinus holds that it is equivocal by the extension of its use, when he speaks in this way: "*This name 'person' does not today signify the essence, although it did once signify it. But when necessity demanded, it was, as Augustine says, transferred from the signification of the essence to the signification of distinction.*"[128] But this cannot stand, since before that need of the Church it was not taken to signify the substance or a distinction in God, but <it was used> only in creatures, in which it is clear that it did not signify the substance, which is the essence of a reality, because then it would not be different to say: "Socrates is a person" and to say: "Peter or Socrates is a man." And there would be the same commonness in "person" for Peter, Paul, and Andrew as there is in "man," which is not true, as will now be seen.

[48]　21. But the third group[129] who say that it is equivocal from its consignification say that from itself and in its first imposition it signifies only the essence in the singular, but in the plural by reason of number consignified, it signifies the distinction of persons. And this cannot stand, because what is consignified by the plural number does not add anything to what is signified by the singular except its duplication or multiplication. Hence, it does not change the signification.

22. But all of those who hold that "person" signifies many things univocally say that it does not signify them equally principally and in the same way. For otherwise it could not be univocal if it signified many things unless it signified them under the character of one thing that is principally signified by the name. But some of them said that "it principally *signifies substance*, but secondarily a

---

126　Ibid. 1, d. 25, c. 3; ed. I. Brady, 1, p. 195; PL 192: 590.

127　Praepositinus, *Summa agains the Heretics* 3, 2; ed. J. Garwin, p. 208.

128　Ibid. 3, 5; ed. J. Garwin, p. 209.

129　See above par. 17.

distinguishing relation,"[130] as Simon of Tournai and his followers. Hence, he says in his *Summa*: "*I say that by reason of its etymology person is said to be something one though itself* (per se unum). *Hence, this name 'person' implies two things: both the signification of the unity of the essence and the consignification of a personal distinction, which the union of the words "one through itself" designates,*"[131] and so on, in accord with which he continues. And in accord with this, Praepositinus explains that position in his *Summa*, when he says: [49] "*There are some who say that this name 'person' principally signifies the essence and consignifies a distinction, because when I say: 'The Father is a person,' it only amounts to: 'The Father is something one and through himself,' that is, distinct, as this term "one" signifies the essence and this pronoun "himself" in the masculine gender consignifies a distinction.*"[132]

23. Master William of Auxerre agrees on this position in his *Summa*, but adds a modification, namely, that along with its signifying the distinction of a relation, it signifies a quasi specific essence in some way, that is, one of an intellectual nature. "*For*," as he says, "*a person is a substance of a rational* or intellectual *nature.*"[133] But if this were the case, then the essence would principally give to the person personal being. For the being of realities principally consists in that which is principally signified by its name. And that is false because in the constitution of a divine person the essence is like a genus and something material, but the distinguishing property is like a difference and something formal. But what is formal is always principally signified in a term and gives being to the reality, according to the determination of the Philosopher in book eight of the *Metaphysics*.[134]

24. But Richard determines in book four of *On the Trinity*, chapter five and the following,[135] that it principally signifies a property, but along with the essence [50] that it includes in its signification. For he says in chapter six: "*Others said that it is said according to substance and signifies the substance. Still, there is a big difference between the signification of the one and the signification of the other.*"[136] Because, as he says in chapter seven, "*The name 'substance' signifies not so*

130   Simon of Tournai, *Summa* 1, 3; ed. M. Schmaus, p. 62. Also see Thomas Aquinas, *Commentary on the Sentences* 1, d. 25, qu. 1; ed. P. Mandonnet, p. 605

131   Simon of Tounai, *Summa* 1, 3; ed. M. Schmaus, p. 62.

132   Praepositinus, *Summa against the Heretics* 3, 4; ed. J. Garwin, p 210; see Simon of Tournai, *Summa* 1, 3, ed. M. Schmaus, p. 62

133   William of Auxerre, *Summa Aurea* 6, 3; ed. J. Ribaillier, p. 88.

134   See Aristotle, *Metaphysics* 8.3.1043b28-30; trans. anon. ed. G. Vuillemin-Diem, p. 162.

135   See Richard of Saint Victor, *On the Trinity* 4, 5–7; PL 196: 933B–935B; ed. J. Ribaillier, pp. 167–170.

136   Ibid. 4, 6: PL 196: 933D–934A; ed. Ribaillier, p. 168. Also see Peter Lombard, *Sentences* 1, d. 23, c. 1; ed. I. Brady, 1, pp. 181 and 182, and Augustine of Hippo, *On the Trinity* 7, 6; PL 42: 943; ed. W. Mountain and F. Glorie, p. 262.

much 'who' as 'what.' But conversely the name 'person' signifies not so much 'what' as 'who.'"[137] And as he consequently determines, "what" pertains to the quality of a substance and asks about it, but "who" pertains to the individual or incommunicable property of a person. Hence, it also asks about substance in creatures, firstly in general, secondarily in particular. For "when something is distant from us so that it cannot be distinctly seen, we ask what it is. And if the answer is that it is something, after the same question has again been asked, we need the answer that it is an animal or a horse or something of the sort. But when we know that it is a human being, we do not ask what it is, but who it is, and the answer is 'Matthias' or 'Bartholomew.' Therefore, by means of 'what' one asks about a common property, but by means of 'who' one asks about a singular property."[138] "For by the name 'person,'" as he says, "one understands only a single someone distinguished from all the others by a singular property."[139] And as he says in chapter six: "When we mention a person, we understand only one solitary and singular substance, as by the name "perons," so that, although by the name 'substance'[140] there is signified the substance of an animal or of a man or of the deity, still as the name "person" [51] is distinguished from other names, it is imposed only from a singular incommunicable property that belongs only to one who exists in singularity. Yet it is imposed from none determinately, as a person is designated by a proper name,"[141] such as "Peter" or "Paul," in creatures or by the name "Father" or "Son" in God, just as if "animal" were imposed to signify a specific property, yet none determinately of either a man or some other <being> and signified no general property common to those specific ones.

25. And in that way it is clear that the statement of certain men[142] is false concerning what is signified by this name "person," namely, that as "Father" signifies the substance with the relation that is paternity from which the name is imposed and "Son" signifies it with the relation that is filiation, so "person" signifies a relation common to paternity, filiation, and spiration along with the substance. And this is not true because it does not signify something of a real relation common to the three relations, but signifies along with the substance an incommunicable relation indifferently and indeterminately with respect to any of them so that the signification of "person" does not differ from what is

---

137   Richard of Saint Victor, *On the Trinity* 4, 7; PL 196: 934C; ed. Ribaillier, p. 169.

138   Ibid. 4, 7; PL 196: 934C–D; ed. Ribaillier, p. 169.

139   Ibid. 4, 7; PL 196: 946C; ed. Ribaillier, p. 189.

140   I have conjectured "*substantiae*" instead of "personae."

141   Richard of Saint Victor, *On the Trinity* 4, 6; PL 196: 934B; ed. J. Ribaillier, p.168–169.

142   See Albert the Great, *Commentary on the Sentences* 1, d. 25, B, a. 2; ed. A. Bourgnet, 25, p. 587B.

signified by "Father," "Son," or "Holy Spirit" except as determinate and indeterminate without the signification of anything common to them.

26. But there is a single opinion and that of one man that "person" signifies only the essence. And Praepositinus reports and explains it in his *Summa*, when he says: "*Master Gerard la Pucelle said that this name 'person' signifies the divine essence in another way than this name 'essence' because this name 'essence' signifies the divine nature for its own sake and stands for it and not for one of the persons.* [52] *And this name "person," on the contrary, signifies the divine nature not for its own sake, but for the sake of what it contains, that is, the Father and the Son and the Holy Spirit, and in that way it signifies it and does not stand for it, but for one of the persons, as can be seen in this similar case. For when one says this species 'man,' this species is signified for its own sake, and it stands for it. But this name 'man' signifies the same species not for its own sake, but for the sake of what it contains,"* and it stands for them. *And it is almost that way concerning this name 'person,' and hence it is that this name 'person' signifies the essence in the plural. For this reason, when it is said, it is the same <to say> that the Father is a person and is a substance, this is the sense: The same thing is signified by these names 'person' and 'essence,' although in different ways. And when I say the person of the Father, I say nothing other than the substance of the Father, that is, I signify nothing other by this name 'person' than by this name 'substance.' And thus whatever is added, it always signifies the substance."*[143]

27. But now Praepositinus argues against him and well: "*According to this one should grant that the Father is not a person by a property, but only by the nature,*"[144] which is contrary to Hilary who says: "*The Father is a person by a property, not by the nature.*"[145] By the same argument he refutes the opinion of those who say that person firstly and principally signifies the substance. For then the Father would be a person by the nature rather than by a property.

28. One must however note that in all the opinions that have been mentioned except those of Simon and Richard, the substance, which is the essence, is held to belong to what "person" signifies. Hence, the authorities that say [53] that a person is the substance or that a person and the essence are the same thing, and such things, are explained in accord with how Master Gerard la Pucelle explains them. And the Master of the *Sentences* conveys this well in distinction twenty-five in the chapter, "Person," where he says: "*Hence, it is clearly inferred that we predicate the divine essence when we say: 'The Father is a person,' 'the Son is a person,' 'the Holy Spirit is a person,' that is, the essence, and the name 'person' signifies absolutely one and the same thing, namely, the divine essence, as the name*

---

143   Praepositinus, *Summa against the Heretics* 3, 3, ed. J. Garwin, p. 209.

144   Ibid.

145   Hilary of Poitiers, *On the Trinity* 2, 6; PL 10: 55B; ed. P. Smulders, p. 43.

'God' *signifies it when one says:* 'The Father is God,' 'the Son is God.'[146] And when something problematic was raised against them from this, such as that, since the essence of the Father is the essence of the Son, if "essence" and "person" signify the same thing, then the person of the Father would be the person of the Son, they reply that it stands for something else with respect to the Son, although it signifies only the essence.[147]

29. But in the position of Simon and Richard, "substance," that is, "hypostasis," is held to belong to what "person" signifies. And because what an hypostasis is includes the common essence with a distinguishing property, both Master Simon[148] and Master Richard[149] for this reason hold that those two belong to what "person" signifies, although in different ways, as was said,[150] and they have more of the truth among the others because in the divine persons [54] the Trinity consists in the unity and the unity in the Trinity. For the unity of the essence belongs to what is signified by the Trinity, although the character of the Trinity formally comes from the three properties, because the name is imposed from them, as will be seen below.[151] For a property is formal with respect to the essence in the signification and constitution of a person, as will similarly be seen below.[152] On this account the position of Richard that holds that "person" principally signifies a property is more reasonable than that of Simon that holds <that it> principally <signifies> the essence. For although each of the others has some truth, they are still lacking in much. But that of Richard either has solid truth or fewer defects than some of the others.

30. And this is clear from the explanation of it that Simon puts in his *Summa* where he is seen to agree with Richard when he says that "*substance is said in two ways: that which subsists* as a supposite and *subject* and *that by which it subsists, that is, a substantial property.*"[153] For a substance that subsists in creatures is twofold, insofar as supposite in them is twofold, that is, a universal one of genus and species, as animal and man, and a singular individual one under the species. And the first of them produces a "what," but the second produces a "who." And that which produces a "who" can be signified under the character of singularity or individuation either determinately or indeterminately. In the

---

146   Peter Lombard, *Sentences* 1, d. 25, c. 1; PL 196: 588; ed. I. Brady,1 , p. 190.

147   See ibid.

148   See Simon of Tournai, *Summa* 1, 3; ed. M. Schmaus, p. 62 and above par. 22.

149   See Richard of Saint Victor, *On the Trinity* 4, 6; PL 196: 934B; ed. J. Ribaillier, p. 168, and above par. 24.

150   See above par. 28.

151   See below par. 37.

152   See below art. 55, qu. 1.

153   Simon of Tournai, *Summa* 1, 3, ed. M. Schmaus, p. 162.

first way it is signified by these names: "Peter" and "Paul"; in the second way <it is signified> by this name "individual" or "person." And although it is a name by which someone is called, it is a name in another way than the names "genus" and "species" are names by which someone is called. For the latter are imposed from one [55] common property. But the name "person" is imposed from no one property, whether universal or singular, but from a singular property though indeterminately in relation to all. Hence, in the deity this name "God" is imposed to signify that nature that is the common essence under the manner and character of a supposite. But these names "Father," "Son," and "Holy Spirit" are imposed to signify supposites determined by determinate individual properties.

31. But "person" signifies an indeterminate supposite and one indeterminate by reason of the fact that it is not under any determinate individual property, so that in accord with this, "person" signifies the substance that is an indeterminate supposite or hypostasis. I do not mean this intention that is implied by the name "supposite" or "hypostasis," but that which is a reality, and this as "Father" or "Son" or "Holy Spirit" signify the substance that is a determinate hypostasis, and that substance–hypostasis includes in what "person" signifies the substance that is the divine essence, as what is signified by "Father," "Son," and "Holy Spirit" also includes it. And it similarly includes the relation, which is an incommunicable property constitutive of the person along with the essence. But that is included indeterminately and indifferently in the name "person," but <is included> determinately in the name "Father," or "Son," or "Holy Spirit."

32. And it is clear in accord with this way of explaining what "person" signifies that it is a name of a reality, and from what it principally signifies it signifies a reality, not that which is the essence nor that which is a relation, but that which is constituted from both, that is, that includes in itself both the essence and a relation. And by this means both come under what is signified by "person." And in this way a person is a certain reality and is in some way another reality than the reality that is the essence or the relation, in accord with which it will be seen further below.[154] Through this [56] it is also clear that, according to the opinion of Richard,[155] "person" is not the name of an intention, but of a reality to which there belongs the intention of "singular," "incommunicable," "subsistence," and the like.

33. And in that way, as we say in creatures that, in accord with the Philosopher in books seven and eight of the *Metaphysics*,[156] a name signifies through itself and principally a composite, secondarily the form, and thirdly the matter,

---

154   See below par. 34.

155   See Richard of Saint Victor, *On the Trinity* 4, 5; ed. J. Ribaillier, pp. 168–169.

156   See Aristotle, *Metaphysics* 8.2.1042b25–26 and 8.3.1043b28–32; trans. anon; ed. G. Vuillemin-Diem, pp. 159 and 162.

so in God this name "person" by itself and principally signifies that which is constituted from the essence and a property, and quasi secondarily a property, and quasi thirdly the essence. But it signifies the determinate property of a person, yet indeterminately in relation to that which is the Father's and to that which is the Son's, and that which is the Holy Spirit's, just as each of these signifies by its name a determinate property and determinately. Hence, if the name "person" is taken generally, it signifies an intellectual substance that is an incommunicable hypostasis, whatever that is and however that incommunicability is produced, whether it is by the nature of the determination of the common essence, [57] as is the case in creatures, or by an incommunicable relative property, as is the case in God, as was established above.[157]

34. Hence, because this name "person" in its totality signifies a substance that is an hypostasis that includes in itself the substance, that is, the essence along with a relation, Boethius defines "person" as taken in common in God and in creatures, when he says that it is *a substance*,[158] better than Richard, when he says that it is *an existence*.[159] For "substance" according to the usage of the Greeks can stand for an hypostasis, which "existence" cannot do in an equally familiar usage, although in saying "incommunicable," Richard specifies it better than Boethius in saying "individual." For "individual," as was said above,[160] is not admitted in God. And similarly in saying "of an intellectual nature," he specifies it better than Boethius in saying "of a rational nature." For "rational" is not taken as properly in God as "intellectual" is.

[58]   35. Therefore, in accord with the way stated, the opinions of all those previously mentioned hold that "person" is the name of a reality and not the name of an intention. But we must investigate whether this is true from the use of this word "person" with regard to creatures because the use of it in God was taken from the use it had in creatures. But now in intellectual creatures we clearly see that this name "person" does not signify with regard to intellectual substances something other than this name "individual" signifies with regard to subsisting non-intellectual substances or with regard to non-intellectual creatures, as Boethius says in *On the Two Natures*: "A person is a rational individual,"[161] and in the same place: "A person is an individual substance of a rational nature."[162]

---

157   See above qu. 3, par. 7.

158   Boethius, *Against Eutyches and Nestorius* 3; PL 64: 1343C–D, ed. C. Moreschini, p. 214.

159   Richard of Saint Victor, *On the Trinity* 5, 1; PL 196: 949A–B; ed. J. Ribaillier, p. 195.

160   See above qu. 1, par. 3 and 6.

161   Boethius, *Against Eutyches and Nestorius* 3; PL 64: 1345A; ed. C. Moreschini, p. 218.

162   Ibid.; PL 64: 1343C–D; ed. C. Moreschini, p. 214. See also above qu. 1, par. 1.

But I say that it signifies that with regard to intellectual or rational substances because "person" does not signify those substances, but only the individuation that it implies determinately, as a certain intention of singularity with regard to such substances, just as "snub" determines the curvedness that it signifies with regard to the nose, but not the nose itself.[163] And those substances are not part of what is signified by "person," as "nose" is not part of what is signified by "snub," but only part of its concept. And Boethius explicitly says this when he asks about "person": "*Why does a Greek not say it of non-rational animals, as we predicate the name "substance" of them?*" And he answers, saying: "*The reason is that it is applied to better things, as something that is more excellent.*[164] If it is applied to them, they do not therefore come under what it signifies, [59] just as singular non-rational substances <do> not <come> under the signification of this name "individual."

36. Hence, since there is no doubt that this name "individual" with regard to non-rational substances is not a name of a reality, but the name of a second intention, which is nothing other than the way the intellect conceives a reality with respect to something superior and to something on a par with it, as determinate and not divided in some thing under it and divided from that which is on a par with it, there is no doubt that this name "person" in rational creatures is not the name of a reality, but the name of an intention that expresses the previously mentioned manner of individuation with regard to those things, so that it does not signify the reality to which individuation is added, but signifies the intention of individuality. Thus it is absolutely the same thing to say: "Peter is an individual" and "Peter is a person." And <person> signifies the same thing as "incommunicable supposite." For "supposite" is the name of a second intention common to a common and singular substance, and "incommunicable" is common to something singular of substance and accident, as was established above.[165] And one mutually narrows down and specifies the other. Hence, what is here called "an incommunicable supposite," Boethius says in the definition of person is "*an individual substance,*"[166] where he takes "substance" in the manner of the Greeks for "subsistence," but "individual" for "incommunicable." And in terms of this Richard corrects him. But what is said in the one case to be "*of an intellectual nature,*"[167] [60] is put in the other as a subject <is put> in the defini-

---

163   See above qu. 1, par. 13.

164   Boethius, *Against Eutyches and Nestorius* 3; PL 64: 1344D; ed. C. Moreschini, pp. 217–218.

165   See above qu. 2, par. 4.

166   Boethius, *Against Eutyches and Nestorius* 3; PL 64: 1342C–D; ed. C. Moreschini, p. 214.

167   See Richard of Saint Victor, *On the Trinity* 4, 18 and 4, 22; PL 196: 941C and 945C; ed. J. Ribaillier, pp. 118 and 187.

tion of an accident, insofar as it is properly a modification of it. For "person," as was said,[168] is appropriated to an intellectual nature, as "snub" is to a nose.

37. And in that way this question that the previously mentioned opinions greatly confuse can be briefly explained in accord with that which Richard say in book four of *On the Trinity* in the beginning: "*Some of the moderns take the name 'person' under a multiple signification and confuse with greater ambiguity the understanding of a profound truth that they ought to have explained.*"[169] What then shall we say to the authorities of the saints that cry out that it signifies a substance or distinct property or both at the same time, as is clear to one who looks at distinction twenty-five of the first book of the *Sentences*?[170]

38. It must therefore be known in order to bring ourselves into agreement with the others and with the statements of the saints that, although wherever any name is put in a proposition, it essentially and principally stands for and represents what it signifies as a sign designated for the representation of which it is imposed. But at times that name stands for that which is signified, while at other times it does not stand for what is signified, but for what it names or as if for that, for example, in a name that signifies a reality. For in whatever proposition "man" is put, it stands for humanity that it signifies, and at times it stands for humanity itself, [61] as when it is said: "Man is a species," but at other times it stands for what it names, as when it is said: "The man is running." For a term is said to stand for that for which it is able to verify the utterance and for which it is related to something else in a proposition. It is similar in a name that signifies an intention. For example, in whatever proposition "species" is put, it stands for the character of a universal which is a certain respect and intention that it signifies. And at times it stands for it, as when it is said: "A species is an intention of reason and a certain universal." But at other times it stands for what is named, as for "man" or for "horse" or suchlike, as when it is said: "A species is *what is predicated of many that differ in number*,"[171] where "species" is defined, not as it is an abstract intention and as it stands for what it signifies. For in that way it is not predicated of things that differ in number. For it is not truly said: "Peter is a species," "Paul is a species," but it is defined as it is in a reality to which it belongs and as it stands for that with a certain indifference in relation to any of them. Of this sort are "man," "horse," and suchlike, which are predicated only of individuals. And much remains to say about what it signifies as it is considered in terms of itself and as it stands for what it signifies and as its stands for what

---

168   See above qu. 1, par. 13.

169   Richard of Saint Victor, *On the Trinity* 4, 1; ed. J. Ribaillier, pp. 163–163; PL 196: 931A–B.

170   See Peter Lombard, *Sentences* 1, d. 25, c. 1; PL 192: 587–591; ed. I. Brady, 1, p. 90.

171   See Porphyry, *Introduction*; trans. Boethius; ed. Minio-Paluello, p. 11.

underlies it or what it names or for what it quasi names, if it cannot be properly be said to be what is named. For if it is considered by itself and as it stands for what it signifies, it then signifies an intention of reason alone from which the name is imposed. But if it is considered insofar as it stands for a reality with regard to which it denotes an intention and if it is asked about what it signifies, if one is speaking in a broad sense about what it signifies as it stands for it in that way, that reality in that way comes under what it signifies if one is speaking in a broad sense about what it signifies.

[62] 39. Therefore, coming down to the question at hand, we say that this name "person" is through itself and from its first imposition the name of an intention and signifies only the character of an incommunicable supposite from its first imposition from which the name was imposed only with regard to an intellectual nature, not as that which it signifies, but as that which belongs to its concept, as in some way a subject belongs to the concept of a proper modification. At times, nonetheless, it can stand for that which it signifies, which is an intention of reason for what it signifies, as when it is said: "Person is a supposite or certain hypostasis," but at times it can stand for what it names or quasi names, as for its quasi subject with regard to which it connotes such an intention, as when it is said: "A person is said to generate or to be generated, to spirate or to be spirated." "The Father is a person," or "A person is the Father." And although as it is considered in terms of itself, as it stands for what it properly signifies, it signifies only an intention of reason, still as it stands for the reality with regard to which it denotes that intention, if one asks about what it signifies in terms of this intention, it then includes in what it signifies only the reality and the character of the intention. And the saints and doctors speak in this way concerning the name "person" when they ask what it signifies. But to speak in that way about what it signifies is to extend its signification greatly, and Boethius does not speak in that way concerning what "person" signifies. Hence, in the definition of "person," that which pertains to the character of an intention is put in the place of a genus as "individual substance," and that which pertains to the character of the reality is put in the place of a difference, as "of a rational essence," just as in the definition of a proper modification that which belongs to its nature is put in the place of a genus, and that which pertains to the subject is put in the place of a difference, in accord with the art of the Philosopher.

[63] 40. Therefore, all the arguments introduced above come to a conclusion in accord with different significations of this name and do not come to a conclusion in accord with different ways. But it is necessary to respond to them on account of different difficulties that they imply.

\<Replies to the Arguments\>

41. To the first argument that "'person' does not signify the essence or substance because then "person" would signify in God the essence in the plural

or substance as having become many,"[172] it must be said that it is true, if the character of singularity which that name expresses were found with regard to it. But if the character of that singularity is not found with regard to it, it is in no way necessary. For example, "man" when said in the singular is able to be become many so that "men" is said in the plural only because "man" in the singular that stands for what it names expresses the character of the singularity of the essence in a supposite of the sort that belongs to the supposite. For just as this man is a singular determinate supposite, so animality and rationality in him are determinate, so that not only the supposite is individual through the determination, but also the whole essence of the species is determinate both from the side of the genus and from the side of the difference. And from this determination, being something singular belongs to a man so that he is one single someone discrete from another singularity and is unable to become many in himself. And it similarly belongs to his essence to be singular, that is, one single something distinct from every other in its singularity and unable to become many so that it cannot become many in itself or be communicable to another supposite. On this account, when it becomes many, everything in a man with regard to which such determination is found, whether it is the supposite or the essence, is understood to become many.

[64]   42. Now however it is otherwise in God with regard to this name "person," because "person" said in the singular is only able to become many so that "persons" is said in the plural because "person" in the singular, as if standing for someone named, expresses the character of the singularity of a supposite, although it does not in that way express the character of singularity in the essence as it is in the supposite. For the deity is not a singular supposite determined by a relative property as this person, for instance, the Father, is. For the deity has it from itself and essentially that it is singular and a certain singularity, not through some determination, because it receives none in itself. For it does not have the character of a universal in accord with what was determined above.[173] But in God a supposite becomes incommunicable through the determination of a property so that, although there cannot be many fathers in God or many sons or many holy spirits, as will be established below,[174] the deity is still not made incommunicable through some determination, although it also has it from itself and from its nature that it cannot become many. For there cannot be many deities. Hence, through its being in one supposite, it does not have it that it cannot be communicated to another. Because therefore "person" in God does not have the character of its singularity, in accord with which it is made many, from the side of the essence, as is the case in creatures, but only from the

172   See above par. 1.

173   See *SQO* art. 43, qu. 2; ed. L. Hödl, p. 51.

174   See below qu. 9, par. 11.

side of the supposite and the relative property determining the supposite, for this reason, although "person" signifies the essence in God, it does not make the essence many[175] when it is plural. On this account Boethius says [65] in the last chapter of *On the Trinity*: "*The manyness of the Trinity is brought about insofar as there is the predication of relation, while the unity is preserved in it insofar as there is no difference of the substance. In that way then the substance contains the unity, and relation makes the manyness of the Trinity.*"[176] Hence, with regard to the relation of the singular and the plural in the name "person," it makes no difference whether the substance is one of many or is diverse, as Richard says in book four of *On the Trinity*, chapter eight: "*In accord with the understanding by which we take 'person' in the singular, we also take it in the plural, except that in the one case we are given to understand many, but in the other only one. Thus, when 'person' is said, we are immediately given to understand someone one who is a rational substance. When 'three persons' are named, some three are undoubtedly understood, each of which is a substance of a rational nature. But whether many or all are one and the same substance makes no difference. But in human nature there are as many substances as there are persons, and daily experience compels one to think similar things about the divine persons.*"[177] And there follows in chapter nine: "*Wherever there are three persons, it is absolutely necessary that this one is one, and that one another, and the third still another. But where there are three substances, it is absolutely necessary that the one is one thing, the other another, and the third another. The diversity of substances causes there to be one thing and another; the diversity of persons causes there to be someone and someone else.*"[178] On this account we said above[179] that in God there is "this someone," but in creatures "this something."

43. To the second argument it must be said that it is true that it does not signify the substance or not the substance alone, but both or neither. And when it is argued that "*it does not signify both because* in that case it would be *an equivocal name,*"[180] it must be said that it is true unless it signified those two as constitutive of the one thing that it principally signifies, that is, a substance that is an incommunicable supposite, in accord with Richard's explanation.

---

175   I have followed "make many, *plurificat*" in one ms. and Badius instead of "signify, *significat*" in the critical edition.

176   Boethius, *On the Trinity* 5; PL 64: 1254D–1255A; ed. C. Moreschini, p. 179–180.

177   Richard of Saint Victor, *On the Trinity* 4, 8; PL 196: 935A; ed. J. Ribaillier, p. 170.

178   Ibid. 4, 9; PL 196: 935D–936A; ed. J. Ribaillier, p. 171.

179   See above qu. 1, par. 7.

180   See above par. 2.

[66]   44. To the third argument that "*it does not signify a relation* because it does not *signify* that in creatures,"[181] it must be said that, if we understand that this name "person" signifies an intention and is principally transferred to God in accord with this, it would in that way be transferred from creatures to God more according to the character of its signification than names of realities are because God and a creature are more truly spoken of univocally in an intention than in some reality. And if one replies in that way, the objection does not have any place because it proceeds about "person" insofar as it is the name of a reality. For the transference of a name from creatures to God is not principally made in signifying a reality because in terms of a reality "person" subsists purely equivocally in God and in creatures since in God it subsists only relatively, but in creatures only non-relatively, as was said above.[182] But a name transferred to God in terms of a reality ought to signify the same reality in God and in creatures, although par excellence and in a supereminent way. Or if we would absolutely want that it be transferred to God from a creature insofar as it signifies a reality, it must be said that the fact that in God a relation signifies a reality of a respect, but not in a creature, pertains to the more eminent way of taking "person" in God than in creatures, and thus it does not with regard to this signify in God what it does in creatures, even in signifying the substance, which is an hypostasis, because in creatures "person" is absolute, but in God relative, as was said above.[183] Hence, this does not prevent "person" from being understood most properly in God.

45. To the fourth argument that "*it does not signify a relation alone*,"[184] it must be granted.

46. To the fifth argument that "*a person is a rational individual*, and '*individual*' is *an intention; therefore, and so on*,"[185] it must be said that by the same argument one can conclude: "But [67] 'rational' is a substance; therefore, 'person' signifies a substance." And it must be said that besides the already mentioned two sorts of signification of person, a third signification of it can still be assigned in God on the basis of this statement of Boethius that the signification of person is threefold. For if one is speaking properly of what it signifies, insofar as its signification is called that to represent which it was through itself imposed, it is in that way the name of an intention and it signifies only an intention, which is a concept of reason with regard to an intellectual reality, as this name "individual" commonly signifies with regard to any creature. And in God it has the substance which is obliquely "this someone" from its concept, as was said,[186] and

---

181   See above par. 2.

182   See above qu. 1, par. 6.

183   See above par. 40.

184   See above par. 4

185   See above par. 5.

186   See above par. 3.

in that way it is the name of an intention alone. But if one is speaking in a wide sense of what it signifies insofar as it is said to signify what it names and what is signified by it, as the saints and masters are commonly accustomed to speak about what it signifies, in that way it signifies the substance with a relation in accord with the way that Richard states. But it signifies quasi immediately that which is "this someone," but indeterminately, and the signification of it there belongs to the substance and an incommunicable relation. And on this account they also belong to the signification of "person," and in that way it is the name of a reality alone, and it is an intention from its concept with regard to such a reality as proper to it. But if one is speaking in the widest sense about what "person" signifies, it is said to signify both of those mentioned at the same time, and it does this directly, just as if "something white" would signify an accident and a subject, and in that way it is the name of a reality and of an intention. And Boethius speaks in that way when he says that "a person is a rational individual."[187]

47. To the sixth argument that "if person signifies an intention, not a reality or a substance, then the Trinity of persons would consist only of intentions,"[188] it must be said that it is true if it in no way signified something else, and it is not the case, as is clear from what has been determined. Hence, the Trinity is <a trinity> of the three in terms of persons in [68] the properties of the persons, but a unity in the essence, as will be seen below.[189] And both the unity of the essence and properties of the three persons are signified by the name "person" along with the character of an intention, as was said.[190]

48. The reply to the seventh argument[191] is clear through the same reply.

49. The last two must be granted in accord with what has already been determined.[192]

---

187 Boethius, *Against Eutyches and Nestorius* 3; PL 64: 1345A; ed. C. Moreschini, p. 218.

188 See above par. 6.

189 See below qu. 6, par. 12.

190 See above par. 12 .

191 See above par. 7.

192 See above par. 8–9.

QUESTION SIX

Whether a Completely Absolute Person or an Absolute Supposite Has Being in God.

1. With regard to the sixth question it is argued that it is necessary to maintain in God one absolute supposite common to the three that are relative in the first place as follows: "Person" includes in its signification a supposite with a distinguishing relative property, according to the common and magisterial definition of person, which says that a person is an hypostasis distinguished by a property. But "hypostasis" implies the character of a supposite. Therefore, it is necessary to maintain in God the character of a supposite besides a distinguishing relative property. But in God apart from the distinguishing relative property there is only what is common and absolute. Therefore, and so on.

[69]   2. <It is argued> in the second place as follows: Augustine says in book seven of *On the Trinity*: "*Every essence that is said to be relatively is also something apart from what is relative.*"[193] And there follows: "*Hence, if the Father were not something with respect to himself, there would absolutely not be anyone who is said to be relatively.*"[194] But the same thing can be said of the Son and of the Holy Spirit. They are therefore something with respect to themselves besides that by which they are said to be relatively to one another. But apart from this there is only the one thing common to the three because, according to Boethius, only "*relation makes the Trinity many.*"[195] But something existing with respect to itself is only a supposite. Therefore, and so on.

3. <It is argued> in the third place as follows: The Father is someone and is the Father, but he is not someone and the Father by the same thing because he is the Father by paternity. But he is not someone by paternity. For then the Son would not be someone because he does not have paternity in himself, nor does "being someone" include "being the Father" because then, in the same way as before, the Son would not be someone. The Father is therefore someone apart from that by which he is the Father and by which he is one with the Son. But to be someone is to be a supposite. But that which is common to the Father along with the Son is only something one and absolute because, according to

---

193   Augustine of Hippo, *On the Trinity* 7, 1; PL 42: 935; ed. W. Mountain and F. Glorie, p. 247.

194   Ibid.

195   Boethius, *On the Trinity* 6; PL 64: 1255A; ed. C. Moreschini, p. 180.

Boethius[196] and Augustine,[197] the Father and the Son are one in all things apart from that which they are said to be relatively. Therefore, and so on.

4. <It is argued> in the fourth place as follows: Augustine says in book seven of *On the Trinity*: "*Everything subsists with respect to itself. For how much better reason does God!*"[198] But only a supposite subsists with respect to itself. There is therefore in God an absolute supposite. But there is only one absolute in God, as was said before. Therefore, and so on.

[70] 5. <It is argued> in the fifth place as follows: The divine essence, as it is an essence, has the character of a person because it is undivided in itself on account of its simplicity and divided and distinct from anything else, that is, from any created essence. But what is such has the character of a person in an intellectual nature, as is seen in human beings and angels. But the divine essence, as it is an essence, is something absolute. Therefore, and so on.

6. <It is argued> in the sixth place as follows: Because to understand is in God among the essential and absolute attributes, it precedes in accord with our way of understanding everything real that is relative. And in that way it precedes every relative person, and yet it presupposes a person who understands, and that can only be something absolute and common to the three relative persons. For if it were a relation, if it would similarly presuppose its correlative, since "relative things" are, according to the Philosopher, "*by nature simultaneous.*"[199] Therefore, and so on.

7. <It is argued> in the seventh place as follows: An act of speaking presupposes a person who speaks, and if the person were relative, he would simultaneously presuppose his correlative, namely, the person he spoke, and in that way he would be before he was spoken. The consequent is false. Therefore, and so on.

8. It is argued. to the contrary that, since that supposite belongs only to an intellectual nature, it would be a person. Therefore, there would be in God a quaternity of persons, which is contrary to the faith.

[71]   <The Resolution of the Question>

9. We disputed this question in our fifth *Quodlibet*,[200] and in briefly gathering together some points from it along with what was determined above,[201] let us say that since, in accord with what was determined above, there is not in God

---

196 See above par. 2.

197 See above par. 2.

198 Augustine of Hippo, *On the Trinity* 7, 4; PL 42: 942; ed. W. Mountain and F. Glorie, p. 260.

199 Aristotle, *Categories* 7.7b15; trans. Boethius, ed. L. Minio-Paluello, p. 21.

200 See *Quodlibet* 5, qu. 8; ed. Badius 1, fol. 164rD.

201 *SQO* art. 43, qu. 2; ed. L. Hödl, p. 51

the character of a universal, for this reason there is also not the character of an absolute universal or common supposite, in the way that we already said above[202] that a supposite exists in universals and singulars, although a supposite does not in the proper sense have being except in singulars, as was determined in the previously mentioned *Quodlibet.* If therefore there is in him the character of an absolute supposite, it will be singular and unique because nothing absolute in God is many, as was said in opposition. What is unique and absolute in God is only the form of the deity. But an absolute supposite in God can only be maintained in the form of the deity if the relative properties are bracketed by the intellect. And this question only asks whether, if the mentioned properties constitutive of the three persons are bracketed, there remains in God one absolute supposite common to the three.

10. But the opinion of some is noted on distinction twenty-six of the first book of the *Sentences*[203] that, if there is removed the plurality of the names, that is, "Father," "Son," and "Holy Spirit," which are imposed from the relative and distinguishing properties, this name "God" signifies a certain person distinguished by essential properties from all other natures, that is, of creatures, as certain Jews and gentiles understand one God eminent in terms of the properties of things that exist.

[72]   11. And this cannot stand because, as was determined in the previously mentioned *Quodlibet,* nothing has the character of a supposite unless it has the character of a determinate being.[204] For a form is not a supposite as it is signified by the name "form," but only what has a form is a supposite. But to have a form does not belong to anything except through a determinate way of having it. For otherwise a form would be only a form, such as humanity or equinity, but not had by something such as a supposite, for example, a man or a horse.[205] But the determination cannot exist in what has the form except through something founded on the form or essence, which is of another character than the form itself is. For by itself from the character by which it is a form, it has no determination. But that character cannot be purely negative because that determines nothing. It is therefore positive either absolute or relative. It is not absolute because, since it cannot be some other reality added to the essence of a form, it is necessary that it be founded on the essence of the form, and in that way it would determine the essence of the form, which happens only in creatures and created forms, but not in the uncreated form because it is unlimited and unable

202   See above qu. 5, par. 30.

203   See Peter Lombard, *Sentences* 1, d. 26, cc. 1–8; PL 192: 591–594; ed. I. Brady, 1, pp. 196–203.

204   See *Quodlibet* 5, qu. 8; ed. Badius 1, f. 164rD–167rC.

205   See *SQO* art. 28, qu. 2; ed. Badius 1, f. 166rA–vG.

to be determined, as was established above.[206] But the character of an absolute supposite cannot be constituted in another way. If therefore there is a supposite in God, it is necessary that it be constituted by a relative character founded on the essence that does not signify some determination of the reality considered in terms of itself, on which account it does not determine the essence. But <it signifies the determination> only of a reality compared to another according to relative opposition. And this pertains to that which is itself related, which is itself constituted as if from the essence and the relation and is itself determined and distinct, as will be said below.[207] Therefore, if the properties and their names are removed by the intellect, [73] there in no way remains in God the character of a supposite, and it is not possible to hold another character of a supposite in God than of a relative one.

12. Hence, the philosophers[208] who had a true understanding of the deity, although not of the Trinity of related persons, understood it in a curtailed fashion as a certain absolute undetermined and unlimited singularity so that their understanding was false and fictitious, and they did not understand the essence of the deity, but that of a figment that they framed for themselves in their imagination, if they understood it under the character of an absolute supposite, just as they would have also understood it falsely if they understood it without understanding that it exists under the relative properties and in a subsisting relative supposite, or rather, to speak more truly, in understanding that it exists without the relative properties and not in a relative supposite. Hence, Hilary says in book three of *On the Trinity*, chapter seven: "*Were they ignorant of the name of God? Moses heard this from the bush; Genesis announced it in the beginning of the created world. The law explained this; the prophets proclaimed it. Human beings found it in the works of this world. Even the nations venerated it falsely. The name of God was therefore not unknown, but God was clearly not known. For no one knows God unless he confesses the Father of the only-begotten Son.*"[209] And in book five, chapter seventeen, he says: "*One must firstly confess the Father and the Son in order that the one God can be understood. Impiety ignorant of the evangelical and apostolic preaching will not apprehend the one true God.*"[210] For just as it belongs to the nature of a creature's essence that it only exists [74] in an absolute supposite determined by participation of a nature, so it belongs to the nature of the deity that it exists only in a supposite determined by a relation.

---

206   See above in this par.

207   See below qu. 7, par. 12.

208   See, for example, Aristotle, *Metaphysics* 12.10.1075v25–27 and 1976a5.

209   Hilary of Poitiers, *On the Trinity* 3, 17; PL 10: 85C–86A; ed. P. Smulders, p. 88.

210   Ibid. 5, 35; PL 10: 153B; ed. P. Smulders, pp. 188-189.

13. Abbot Joachim[211] could not understand the one nature of the deity, while at the same time understanding the personal properties, without understanding the nature under the character of a supposite and a person. Hence, in order to preserve in God the trinity of persons and to deny a quaternity, although he granted *"that the Father and the Son and the Holy Spirit are one essence, one substance, and one nature,"* he did not nonetheless confess that *"such true and proper unity"* as if it were one something really singular in the Father and the Son and the Holy Spirit, but understood it in a collective sense[212] and in a likeness, *"just as many human beings are said to be one people and many believers one Church."*[213] And he fell into the Arian heresy by separating the persons. Hence, "he also called the *Master Peter Lombard, a heretic, because 'he said in his Sentences that a certain highest reality is the Father and the Son and the Holy Spirit.'*[214] Hence, *he claimed that <Master Peter> construed in God not a trinity, but a quaternity, namely, three relative persons and one common essence [75] like a fourth,* namely, an absolute person, *clearly protesting that there is no reality that is the Father and the Son and the Holy Spirit, neither an essence nor a nature."*[215] And he said this because, if he had held that, it seemed to him that he necessarily had to maintain that the essence was by itself a person, which is not true. For the essence is in the persons not distinguished from them, but is not a person. And thus the Church believes that a certain reality and nature is the Father, the Son, and the Holy Spirit so that the three together and each of the three persons by themselves are that nature, so that there is unity in the nature and distinction in the persons. And in accord with this, all these things are maintained in the beginning of the *Decretals,* in the chapter: *"We condemn therefore and reject,"* and so on.[216]

14. And just as it turned out that Joachim separated the persons along with Arius for fear of putting in God a quaternity of persons because he could not understand the unity of the essence or nature without the character of personality, so it turns out in the opposite way for Sabellius that he confused the persons for fear of denying the unity of the substance or nature, which he could only understand in a single personality that he held was in the three, just as we hold the essence in the three without its own personality. For insofar as he held one absolute person in the essence, he necessarily had to hold that the relative personal properties are founded on that person, just as we hold that they are

---

211   See Gregory IX, *Decretals* 1, 1, 1; ed. A. Friedberg, 2, p. 6.

212   I have followed "collective, *collectivam*" with Gregory instead of "conjectural, *conjectivam*" in the mss.

213   Ibid.

214   Peter Lombard, *Sentences* 1, d. 25, c.2; PL 192: 590; ed. I. Brady, 1, p. 194.

215   Gregory IX, *Decretals* 1, tit. 1, c. 1, 1; ed. A. Friedberg, 2, p. 6.

216   See ibid.

founded on the essence, and he had to hold that the one essence, just as we do, is the Father and the Son and the Holy Spirit so that those properties did not distinguish their own persons upon that personality of the essence, but so that that one personality was poured out in them and they at the same time were confused in it. Thus just as according to Arius, the Father is one thing, the Son another, and the Holy Spirit a third, so according to Sabellius he who is the Father, is the Son, and is the Holy Spirit. They really had to hold these things [76] when they held one absolute person in God because it would essentially belong to it to do the divine actions and to be the terminus of the personal actions, so that it would be the Father because it generates and the Son because it is generated and the Holy Spirit because it proceeds. Thus the relations would be adventitious to the person from the act, in no way the reasons for eliciting or terminating the act, and one who generates would be the one who is generated, and the one who spirates would be the one who is spirated, and he would generate and spirate himself. And the Catholics bring this forth against the Sabellians as impossible and absurd.

15. Let us therefore hold a middle path between the two plagues, avoiding Scylla and Charybdis, by saying that in God there is one essence with the singularity of the essence common to the three persons, so that we do not divide the persons like Arius, but so that we do not confuse them like Sabellius by the singularity of a person,.

\<Replies to the Arguments\>

16. As for what is argued in the first place to the contrary that "*a person* is an hypostasis *distinguished by a property*,"[217] it must be said that "person" is not there defined in general, as it is considered in its generality or commonality in the way it is to be found in all rational and intellectual beings, but specifically as it has being in God. And "hypostasis" stands there in that generality as it belongs to every individual subsisting substance in accord in the manner of the Latins, whether it is intellectual or non-intellectual. Hence, it does not include the determinate character of a distinction, whether by the determination of the essence or of the nature, as is the case in creatures, or through relative properties, as is the case in God in accord with the way determined above. But a divine person includes the determinate character of a distinction, namely, by a relative property. And thus in this definition of a divine person when [77] it is said that it is an hypostasis distinguished by a property, "hypostasis distinguished" in that definition is like a genus, and "by a property"—understand a relative one—is like a difference, and in that way "hypostasis" stands there for something common in terms of character and intention, but not for something common in terms of real being, as "essence" does, and the argument supposes

---

217   See above par. 1.

that. For otherwise there would not be understood one absolute person that remains when the properties are removed.

17. To the second argument that "what is said to be *relatively* is *something apart from what is relative*,"[218] it must be said that the understanding of this statement is that everything that is said to be relatively, apart from the character of the respect by which it is said to be relatively and toward something else is something in an absolute reality on which that respect is founded. But from the side of that which is said to be in relation to something, it must be known that it can have a simple supposition for an essence or a personal one for a supposite. But it is taken in the first way in the statement of Augustine, and in that way the Father is something in God, that is, the divine essence, which is something other than a created essence, apart from what is relative, that is, from the character of the respect or relation, which is formally imposed by the name "paternity." In the second way the argument does not proceed in accord with the intention of Augustine.

18. To the third argument that "*the Father is someone* by one thing and *is the Father* by another,"[219] it must be said that it is false, just as he is not a person by one thing and this person of the Father by another, although "person" stands indeterminately for that which the person of the Son, of the Father, and of the Holy Spirit stands determinately. And it signifies in common that intention that each of them signifies determinately, in accord with what is seen from what has been determined above. And as for the argument that [78] "*he is the Father by paternity, but is not someone by paternity because then the Son would not be someone*,"[220] it must be said that he is the Father determinately by paternity, but is someone indeterminately. On this account it does not follow that "*the Son is not someone*" because by his filiation he is someone determinately, and it would not follow that "*the Father is someone by paternity, therefore, the Son is not someone*,"[221] unless "someone" expressed something determinate. Therefore, the further conclusion would not follow.

19. To the fourth argument that "God *subsists with respect to himself*,"[222] it must be said that according to Augustine in book seven of *On the Trinity*, from where the argument was taken, "*we say that substance comes from to subsist*,"[223] and we can take "substance" in accord with what has already been said accord-

218   Augustine of Hippo, *On the Trinity* 7, 1; PL 42: 935; ed. W. Mountain and F. Glorie, p. 247. See above par. 2.

219   See above par. 3.

220   Ibid.

221   Ibid.

222   See above par. 4.

223   Augustine of Hippo, *On the Trinity* 7, 4; PL 42: 942; ed. W. Mountain and F. Glorie, p. 260.

ing to the custom of the Latins for "essence" or according to the custom of the Greeks for "subsistence." Similarly, "to subsist" can be taken in two ways: in one way from what is said to be a substance, which is essence; in another way from what is said to be a substance, which is subsistence. In the first way it is the same thing for God to be as to subsist, and with respect to himself God subsists non-relatively. For now, as the argument concludes, substance is not a substance, but something relative. And in this way Augustine is speaking there about "to subsist." But in the second way it is not the same thing for God to be as to subsist, just as it is not the same thing to be and to be the Father. And in this way he subsists relatively, not with respect to himself, as he is also a person relatively, not with respect to himself.

20. To the fifth argument[224] it must be said that the divine essence, as it is an essence, cannot have the character of a person because a person, as a person, has the character of something incommunicable and of determinate being in its singularity. But the essence, under the character by which it is an essence without qualification, does not in that way have it that [79] it has determinate being and is something incommunicable. Rather, every essence, as it is an essence without qualification, is something communicable to many supposites, although in God according to the character of indeterminate singular being, but in creatures under the character of indeterminate universal being, even though because the essence of the deity is of itself singular, it may seem to have the character of a person more than a created essence because it is universal of itself. For whether the essence is singular or universal makes no difference to its not being a person, provided nonetheless that it is of itself communicable either in a singularity or plurality of substance because only that character that confers incommunicability in an intellectual nature confers personality. Hence, to the form of the argument it must be said that non-division is twofold and division or distinction is similarly so, just as there is a twofold unity and plurality, namely, essential and personal. Although the divine essence, as it is an essence, is therefore undivided in itself and divided from every other because that division is essential, and the non-division is similarly so, it is however not personal because it is not within the character of something incommunicable, as was said. It is for this reason not necessary that the divine essence, insofar as it is an essence, have the character of a person.

21. To the sixth argument that. "*because to understand belongs among the absolute attributes, it precedes everything relative and personal*,"[225] and so on, it must be said that according to our manner of understanding that is prior which of itself forms a simpler and more absolute concept, and in that way something absolute, as absolute, is universally prior to something relative that includes

---

224 See above par. 5.

225 See above par. 6.

that absolute, as a person includes an essence. But if something relative does not include in terms of its concept the concept of something absolute, it is not necessary, as is the case in the present question. Hence, it is necessary to distinguish concerning absolute attributes in God because some signify in the manner of a habit and some <signify> in the manner of acting or of an act. Concerning those that signify in the manner of a habit, it is universally true [80] that they precede every real relation. But it is not true concerning those that signify in the manner of acting, as "to understand" and "to will" do. Rather they presuppose a relative supposite that does not exist from another, to which "to understand" and "to will" belong firstly according to reason. And they do not nonetheless at the same time presuppose their correlative with respect to the act of understanding, nor similarly with respect to the act of speaking, concerning which the last argument proceeded, although they do with regard to our act of understanding.

22. It must therefore be known for the resolution of this assumption in each argument that something relative can be considered as relative without qualification and as it is related to the act of understanding of anything passively or as it is something pertaining to its origin and is related to the act of originating, either actively or passively. In the first way it is true that they are simultaneous by nature, that is, by natural understanding, because one cannot be understood without the other. Rather, one is the reason for understanding the other. But in the second way one can be prior to the other insofar as the act is originated by one and terminated in another. And this is according to the manner in which, according to our reason, prior and posterior come under the order of origin, with regard to which there will be a more ample discussion below.[226] But by means of the act of understanding and speaking "the first person speaking and understanding" simultaneously provides the understanding of its correlative, as will be explained more below.[227]

---

226   See below art. 54, qu. 5, par. 7.
227   See below qu. 10, par. 26.

[81]   QUESTION SEVEN

Whether "Person" Signifies Something Common in God

1. With regard to the seventh question it is argued that "person" does not
signify something common in God in the first place as follows: Commonness
is only some unity that belongs to many. There are not many in God except
the three persons, but a person is not something one that belongs to the three
because they differ in personality. But in that in which some differ, they do not
have unity and agreement. Therefore, and so on.

2. <It is argued> in the second place as follows: Something common and
univocal is a true universal in relation to those to which it is common. But
"person" belongs to the divine persons univocally[228] because it belongs to them
according to the same name and ths same meaning assigned by Boethius[229]
and corrected by Richard,[230] as was said. Therefore, if [82] "person" is common
to the three persons, it is a true universal in God, the contrary of which was
determined above.[231]

3. To the contrary there is what Augustine says in book seven of *On the Trinity*: "*Hence, we say 'three persons' because that which is a person is something common to them.*"[232]

<The Resolution of the Question>

4. It must be said that commonness is threefold: one of reality alone, another
of reason alone, but still another in between, partly of reality and partly of reason. In the first way the three persons have a commonness of the essence alone
and of the essential attributes. And in accord with this commonness it is said
that the Father is God, the Son is God, and the Holy Spirit is God. And this
is most remote from the character of a universal because it is founded on the
unity of a singular reality, but the commonness of a universal is not such.

5. Commonness stated in the third way is the commonness of relation for
the three personal relations, which are paternity, filiation, and spiration. And
relation is one of the categories in God, not merely the character of a category.

---

228   See above qu. 3.

229   See Boethius, *Against Eutyches and Nestorius* 3; PL 64: 1343C–D; ed. C.
      Moreschini, p. 214.

230   See Richard of Saint Victor, *On the Trinity* 4, 18 and 4, 22; PL 196: 941C and
      945C; ed. J. Ribaillier, pp. 181 and 187.

231   See *SQO* art. 43, qu. 2; ed. L. Hödl, p. 51

232   Augustine of Hippo, *On the Trinity* 7, 4; PL 42: 940; ed. W. Mountain and F.
      Glorie, p. 275.

For in accord with this commonness we say that paternity is a relation, filiation is a relation, and spiration is a relation, and as if concretely, we say that the Father is something relative, the Son is something relative, and the Holy Spirit is something relative. And this commonness approaches more closely to a universal than the preceding one because it does not consist in the unity of a singular relation, but as if in <a unity> abstracted from the three real singular relations already mentioned. And [83] there is still not the true character of a universal in it because there are not in them three realities in the foundation of the supposites, but only a single one because they are founded in one singular reality, which is the deity, as will be clear below.[233] And a true universal must have a diverse reality in its supposites, in accord with what was sufficiently established concerning this above.[234] And on this account it was said that this commonness is in part that of reality and in part that of reason, although there is not a true universality in it. But it will be seen later how those three relations are said to be real and how they are said to be three realities not only on account of the reality of the nature and essence, which is their foundation, but on account of the reality of the hypostases that they constitute.[235]

6. But commonness said in the second way is the commonness that is in the name "person." But different people hold this in different ways. For some say that the commonness of "person" is in terms of negation,[236] just as the commonness of "individual" is in relation to Peter and to Paul, that is, because their singular essence does not admit their division into many, as the essence of humanity without qualification does not admit division into the humanity of this one or of that one, in accord with what was touched upon above.[237] But this is not true because "person" in God does not consist in pure negation, even if it signified only an intention, as "individual" signifies. Rather, in creatures it is founded on a positive determination of the common nature, and in God it is founded upon the relations of the divine supposites, as was already said.

[84] 7. For this reason one must reply otherwise and by holding that in one way "person" signifies the substance or essence, but in another way by holding that it signifies an intention. But in holding that "person" signifies the substance or essence, some look to the nature of the relations that are constitutive of the persons in maintaining its commonness,[238] while others look to the persons

---

233   See below art. 55, qu. 6.

234   See *SQO* art. 34, qu. 2; ed. R. Macken, p. 77 and art. 52, qu. 2; ed. M. Führer, p. 250.

235   See below art. 55, qu. 6

236   See William of Auxerre, *Golden Summa* 1, 6, c. 2; ed. J. Ribaillier, p. 83.

237   See above qu. 1, par. 10.

238   See below par. 8.

themselves or singular hypostases constituted.[239] But one cannot look to the common essence because *"it accounts for the unity* and does not *make the Trinity many*,"[240] according to Boethius, and without that multiplicity there is not a commonness of person, as was already said above according to Richard.[241]

[85] 8. In accord with the first way some say that the commonness there lies in the reality of the relations that are constitutive of the persons,[242] upon which there is <founded> the character of relation common, as was said, to paternity, filiation, and spiration, and they say that it is signified by the name "person," just as the specific relations are signified by the names of the Father, the Son, and the Holy Spirit, and in that way "person" is common to the Father, the Son, and the Holy Spirit, as relation without qualification is common to paternity, filiation, and common spiration.

9. But this cannot stand because, as was said above according to Richard,[243] the name "person" signifies something singular, unique [86] in itself, unable to be distinguished in itself, and distinguished from everyone else, and that something of the sort signifies no common reality. Hence, if it were as they say, then when it is said: "The Father is a person," "The Son is a person," and "The Holy Spirit is a person," no other commonness would be expressed than when it is said: "The Father is something relative," "The Son is something relative," and "The Holy Spirit is something relative." And this is false because to be something relative without qualification implies no character of distinction, as this name "person" implies. And truly if "person" properly and by itself by its first and absolute signification were said to signify the substance that is an hypostasis or something relative, then it could not be something common to the three relative hypostases except by signifying a relation common to their relations, or absolutely nothing real that is common is understood by the name "person," and that is undoubtedly true.

10. And for this reason those who hold that "person" signifies the substance or essence hold its commonness without the signification of something common. Master Gerard la Pucelle holds that "'person' *signifies* the essence *not for its own sake, but for the sake* of the supposites, *so* that it stands *for* the persons,

---

239   See Gerard la Pucelle, below par. 10.

240   Boethius, *On the Trinity* 6; PL 64: 1255A; ed. C. Moreschini, p. 180.

241   See Richard of Saint Victor, *On the Trinity* 4, 8; PL 196: 935B; ed. J. Ribaillier, p. 170.

242   See Thomas Aquinas, *Commentary on the Sentences* 1, d. 25, qu. 1, art. 3; ed. P. Mandonnet, pp. 609–610.

243   See above qu. 5, par. 26.

not for the essence,"[244] as was explained above,[245] and by reason of this [87] supposition he says that "it is understood in the plural and yet signifies the substance in the plural as in the singular and thus that its commonness is not in its signification, but in its supposition.[246] And Praepositinus argues against him in this way. "*Although at times this name 'God' stands for a person and at times for the essence, still where it stands for a person insofar as it stands for a person, it does not stand for the essence.*"[247] Therefore, where it stands for any person, it has the same commonness as "person" and can be predicated in the plural of the three, just as "person" also can. And that is not true; therefore, that account is not sufficient.

11. But speaking in accord with his previously stated view, Richard would say that "person" does not express something common to the three by its signification, but only by its indeterminateness. For it signifies only something one that is distinct from all <the others>. And its character, insofar as it is such, can only be common because it does not determine someone of the sort signified by person, either in the singular or in the plural, insofar as it is considered from the side of what is signified. In the singular it signifies someone of the sort, but [88] in the plural several of the sort. And on this Simon of Tournai agrees,[248] and says, as Praepositinus reports, that "*because of its consignification, this name 'person' passes into plurality, so that* it is said: *The Father and the Son and the Holy Spirit are persons, that is, they are something one and through themselves, that is, distinct, so that this pronoun 'themselves'* (se) *is plural in number and in the masculine gender,*"[249] as the Father is a person in the singular, that is, something one through himself, that is, distinct, so that "himself" is in the masculine gender. But by the name "person" it is understood singularly in the singular and plurally in the plural. And this position with regard to this commonness returns to the same thing as the position that says that "person" signifies only the essence and stands for the hypostasis so that, if one holds nothing else concerning what "person" signifies but the essence or a distinguishing relation or a singular hypostasis, there is nothing common in what is common to the three except the word "person."

12. I say that, as this commonness is taken, it cannot be taken from the side of the essence, as was said.[250] And in that way there would be only a com-

---

244   See Praepositinus, *Summa against the Heretics* 3, 3; ed. J. Garwin, p. 209 and above q. 5, par. 30.

245   See above qu. 5, par. 30.

246   Praepositinus, *Summa against the Heretics* 3, 2; ed. J. Garwin, p. 210.

247   Ibid. 3, 2; ed. J. Garwin, p. 210.

248   See Simon of Tournai, *Summa*, ed. M. Schmaus, p. 62.

249   Praepositinus, *Summa against the Heretics* 3, 4; ed. J. Garwin, p. 210.

250   See above par. 6–7.

monness of equivocation, which it does not seem should be granted. Hence, it seems that one must return to the position that says that from what it absolutely signifies, "person" is a name of a second intention in accord with the previously stated manner,[251] although it only stands for a reality that is [89] a singular hypostasis under that indifference that Richard holds, as was said.[252] And that intention is the character under which the intellect conceives a real supposite, which is an hypostasis, signified by the name of a reality, such as the Father and the Son in God, and Peter and Paul in creatures. I mean, it conceives one as distinct through himself from anyone else. And this intention consists in a certain respect and way of such a reality's being in relation and respect to the common essence and to anything else that has a similar distinction, whether in one singular essence, as is the case in God, or in one specific essence, as is the case in human beings, or in many specific essences as is the case in human beings and angels.

13. For in all of them "person" is as if of the same intention, except that it is taken from something absolute in creatures, but from something relative in God. Hence, because the character of such an intention consists in a certain relation, as that of other intentions "genus" and "species" do, and for this reason the commonness of the intention is a commonness of proportion. For Peter is an individual and a person, as Paul is, because he stands in the same way in relation to his species and to that from which he is divided, as Paul does, and in a similar way "man" is said to be a species, as "horse" is, and "quantity" is said to be a genus as "quality" is, and this is so because of a similar relation to what is under them. And in that way in the name "person" nothing common can be taken from the side of what it signifies, in terms of which it is distinguished in what it contains except the character of an intention, which in its commonness has no external reality, but consists only in a concept of the intellect. Nor does it have the character of a real universal, but only of an intentional one, although it is considered [90] with regard to a reality and has the character of an accident that does not exist in a thing, but only in a concept of an intellect. On this account it is not problematic if we hold that it has the character of a true intentional universal, although the character of a real universal is in no way held to be in God. But because that is somehow in a thing, it would put some composition in God, which this position does not do because it is held to be only in the conception of an intellect.

14. But one should note that it is the case that such a universal intention is at times related to something as to a subject with regard to which it is considered, as "person" is to the Father and the Son and to Peter and Paul, and as "species" is

---

251   See above qu. 5, par. 32.

252   See Richard of Saint Victor, *On the Trinity* 4, 6; PL 196: 934B–C; ed. J. Ribaillier, p. 168.

to man and horse, and "genus" is to quantity and quality. And such an intention has as it were the character of a most specific species containing quasi individuals, of which sort are this person "Peter" and this person "Paul," and this species "man" and that species "horse," and this genus "quantity" and that genus "quality." But at times it is the case that it is related to something as to another intention placed under it, of which it is predicated as a genus of a species, as this intention "universal" is of this intention which is "species" and of that which is "genus."

15. Hence, in the present question the character of "person" is like an intention of a most specific species with regard to a subject that contains quasi particular intentions with regard to particular subjects, as this person or that one. But in the name "person" there is not understood something with regard to which it is considered except indeterminately, in accord with what was determined above according to Richard.[253] And through this commonness of intention the commonness by which "man" is predicated of Peter and of Paul is other than that by which "person" is predicated of the same. And "person" does not have [91] another commonness in God. And this name "person" was firstly transferred to God to express this because there could not be another commonness that could be made many regarding the three and be the substantive of this adjective "three," in accord with what Praepositinus says. *"For since scripture says the Father, the Son, and the Holy Spirit are three, it was asked what or who the three are. And it could perhaps have been said 'three things,' but since this word is extremely common, it was necessary to find another less common word that could be joined to this word 'three,' and this name 'person' was transferred, and the answer was 'three persons,' as Augustine says, not so that we might say that, but so that we did not say anything at all, that is, not in order that we might respond fully, but in order that we might not be completely silent."*[254] For as he says in book seven of *On the Trinity:* *"For the sake of speaking about the ineffable in order that we might be able to speak in some way—and we can in no way express it—the Greeks said 'one essence, three substances,' but the Latins said 'one substance, three persons.' For when we are asked what the three are, we try to find some specific or generic name by which we may think of these three, and none comes to mind because the supereminence of the deity surpasses the ability of our ordinary language."*[255] *"Therefore, because the Father, the Son, and the Holy Spirit are three, we ask what the three are and what they have in common. For if they are three persons, 'person' is what is common to them. Otherwise, they can in no way be spoken of in that way."*[256] *"But*

253   See above par. 9 and 11, as well as Richard of Saint Victor, *On the Trinity* 4, 6; PL 196: 934B–C; ed. J. Ribaillier, pp. 168–169.

254   Praepositinus, *Summa against the Heretics* 3, 5; ed. J. Garwin, p. 211.

255   Augustine of Hippo, *On the Trinity* 7, 4; PL 42: 939; ed. W. Mountain and F. Glorie, p. 255.

256   Ibid.; PL 42: 940; ed. W. Mountain and F. Glorie, p. 256.

we say 'three persons,' because we want one word to serve for this signification by which the Trinity is understood,"[257] that is, which signifies something common to the three under which those three are understood in common.

[92] 16. And there is only the stated commonness of reason that Augustine investigates there by removing from the nature of person all real commonness, as is stated especially in chapter six.[258] And the answer by which one answers: "three persons" does not satisfy the question, but only the questioner. For when they asked what the three are, their intention was that some common reality be given them in reply that is signified by that one name that might be predicated of them in the plural, as the subject of that adjective "three," just as when it is said: "There are three who are running," and it is asked what the three are, and it is answered: "three men," and <when it is> further <asked> which men, it is answered: "Peter, Servatius, and John." But such a name could not be found in God. Hence, because nothing could be common to them but the intention of person, <such a name> does not satisfy either the question or the intention of the questioner, but only the stubbornness of the heretics since they had nothing further to ask, just as if one asked what the three Peter, John, and Paul are, and the reply was given: "three persons." Hence, if with this commonness of intention one understands that the reply is the commonness of indifference in accord with the position of Richard, it then most completely satisfies the question and the questioner insofar as it is possible.

17. And still neither this response in saying "three things," nor that response in saying "three persons," whether "person" is understood to stand for an intention or for the individual supposites under indifference, completely satisfied the question and similarly the questioner. For the question and the intention of the questioner were asking about the substantive for the substance of that adjective "three," intending [93] that the substance be given in the plural in answer and that the plurality be determined with regard to it by that adjective "three." Thus with respect to this nothing other was asked by "what" than by "who," but only with regard to the fact that "what" asked about the substance made many absolutely and under the character of an essence, but "who" asked about a substance made many in supposites. Hence, since such a substance or essence cannot be found in God, the question supposes something false in God, and for this reason the question was not to be answered[259] since it was impossible. Nor likewise was the intention of the questioner to be satisfied because it similarly supposed something false in God, but only the stubbornness <of the questioner> was to be satisfied to the extent it was possible. Hence, Richard says in book four of *On the Trinity*, chapter five: "*Those who firstly transferred*

---

257   Ibid. 7, 6; PL 42: 943; ed. W. Mountain and F. Glorie, p. 262.

258   See ibid; PL 42: 943–946; ed. W. Mountain and F. Glorie, pp. 262–267.

259   I have removed: "or satisfied, *nec satisfaciendum*," which seems out of place.

the name 'person' to God did this out of necessity in order to have what they might reply to those asking what three those three in the Trinity were since they could not say 'three gods.'"[260]

18. And it must nonetheless be noted that it is not necessary to hold that this question supposed something false of itself, but only insofar as it was from the intention of the questioner. For insofar as it is considered of itself, neither question has to suppose something false because each question, insofar as it is considered from the side of "three," does not have to suppose anything but three supposites, and it is not necessary to understand that "what" asks about anything other than their essence and quiddity without qualification. And it does not suppose that it is triple rather than it is simple and single. Hence, in replying whether the essence is explained as triple or as simple and singular, the response satisfies the question. Hence, by "what" the question does not intend anything but what those three are in substance, and it is sufficiently answered in saying "God." It is not necessary however that "who" is understood to ask about anything other than the properties of the supposites in which it is not necessary to understand the substance to be triple rather than single. Hence, in responding it is not necessary [94] to express the essence, but it satisfies the question if one answers a trinity of persons. Hence, by "who" the question does not intend anything but those three that are in the supposites, and it responds quite sufficiently by expressing this under the proper names and by saying "the Father, the Son, and the Holy Spirit," either under one name common to the three that contains the concept of the three, whether it signifies them by its principal signification, although under indetermination, as Richard holds,[261] or it does not, but only signifies a common intention and by standing for them, in saying "three persons" or "things."

19. And it makes no difference to respond in this way or in that because by the name "person" one has an understanding of the three under a certain indetermination and indifference without the signification of something real common to them, as is had by this name "thing" that is predicated in the plural of the three. But "person" adds the character of a common intention, and for this reason one responds better by saying "three persons" than by saying "three things." For the question is about singular supposites and according to the intention of the questioner as they are under something common, not that which is the essence, nor that which is a relation, nor that which is an intention, and especially because of itself it does not have its supposition determined to singular supposites. Hence, in order to completely satisfy the question and the stubbornness of the questioner, as far as it was possible, especially when the

---

260   Richard of Saint Victor, *On the Trinity* 4, 5; ed. J. Ribaillier, p. 167; PL 196: 933C.

261   See ibid. 4, 6; PL 196: 934B–C; ed. J. Ribaillier, p. 169, as well as above par. 9 and 11.

question is asked by "what," one responds by the name "person" because it has a determinate supposition for singular supposites, and along with this it signifies a common intention, although neither the intention of the questioner nor the thrust of the question was about that, and such is this name "person." On this account Augustine says in book six of *On the Trinity*: "*We want at least one word to serve this signification by which the Trinity is understood,* [95] *so that we are not entirely silent when someone asks: 'Three what?' when we say that there are three.*"[262] But that is the signification of the common intention in the name "person," not by which the Trinity is signified, but by which it is understood, as was said.

⟨Replies to the Arguments⟩

20. To that which is argued in the first place that "'*person*' *does not signify something common in God, because in the name 'person' there is not signified something one common to the three,*"[263] it must be said that it is true. Nonetheless, this does not exclude that "person" is something common with regard to the three, that is, by supposition, as the opinion of Master Gerard la Pucelle says,[264] nor does it exclude a certain indifference, as Richard[265] and similarly Simon say,[266] as is evident from what has been said.

21. To the second argument that "*something common and univocal is universal*"[267] it must be said that it is true of something univocal by the unity of a reality, but not of something univocal by the unity of proportion, such as is in the name of an intention, as was said, just as a governor in a city and a governor on a ship are not said univocally. And Augustine is speaking of such a commonness, when he says that "*person is something common.*"[268]

---

262   Augustine of Hippo, *On the Trinity* 7, 6; PL 42: 943; ed. W. Mountain and F. Glorie, p. 262.

263   See above par. 1.

264   See Praepositinus, *Summa against the Heretics* 3, 5; ed. J. Garwin, p. 209, and above par. 10.

265   See Richard of Saint Victor, *On the Trinity* 4, 6; PL 196: 934B–C; ed. J. Ribaillier, p. 168 and above par. 9, 11, and 12.

266   See Simon of Tournai, *Summa*; ed. M. Schmaus, p. 62 and above par. 2.

267   See above par. 2.

268   See Augustine of Hippo, *On the Trinity* 7, 4; PL 42: 940; ed. W. Mountain and F. Glorie, p. 257 and above par. 3.

[96]   **QUESTION EIGHT**

Whether There Are Many Persons in God

1. With regard to the eighth question it is argued that many persons are not to be held to be in God in the first place as follows: Of those of which a specific name, whether it is a specific name of a reality or of an intention, can be said in the plural of them, a generic name can also be said, "*as when Abraham, Isaac, and Jacob* are said to be *three men and three* living beings, or when they are said to be *three individuals* of man or of horse and *three men or three living beings*,"[269] according to Augustine in book seven of *On the Trinity*: "God" and "person" are in God like something generic and specific. For "God" is something common to person, whether "God" is the name of a reality or of an intention. If then the Father and the Son and the Holy Spirit are many persons, they are also many gods. The consequent is false; therefore, and so on.

2. <It is argued> in the second place as follows: Boethius says in book two of *On the Trinity*, chapter four: In God "*there is no plurality because of diversity.*"[270] But there is a plurality of persons only because of some diversity of them because where there is complete identity. there is perfect unity, and thus no plurality at all. Therefore, and so on.

3. Likewise <Boethius says> in the same place: "*Where there is no difference, there is absolutely no plurality. Hence, there is no number, but only unity.*"[271] These are found in God in the greatest degree. Therefore, in [97] God there is absolutely no number, but there is not a plurality of persons without any number. Therefore, and so on.

4. Likewise, whatever in something are of one and the same character, if one is not multiplied, the other cannot be multiplied. Person and being in the Father, the Son, and the Holy Spirit are of one and the same character, as Augustine says in book seven of *On the Trinity*, chapter six that "*for him it is the same to be as to be a person.*"[272] Hence, because being is not made many in the Father, the Son, and the Holy Spirit, person is also not. Therefore, and so on.

---

269   Augustine of Hippo, *On the Trinity* 7, 6; PL 42: 944; ed. W. Mountain and F. Glorie, pp. 262–263.

270   Boethius, *On the Trinity* 2; PL 64: 1251A; ed. C. Moreschini, p. 171.

271   Ibid. 3; PL 64: 1251A–B; ed. C. Moreschini, p. 171.

272   Augustine of Hippo, *On the Trinity* 7, 6; ed. W. Mountain and F. Glorie, p. 262; PL 42: 943.

5. Likewise, simplicity follows upon unity, as was established above.[273] Therefore, where there is greater unity, there is greater simplicity. But there is greater unity where there is the unity of person along with the unity of essence than where there is a plurality of person. Therefore, there is also greater simplicity. But in God there is found the highest simplicity. Therefore, and so on.

6. To the contrary it is argued that in that in which it is necessary to hold otherness of persons, <it is> also <necessary to hold> a plurality of persons because there is no otherness except from plurality. In God it is necessary to hold the otherness of persons in accord with what is said in the Symbol of Athanasius: "*The person of the Father is one; that of the Son another, and that of the Holy Spirit another.*"[274] Therefore, and so on.

<The Resolution of the Question>

7. To this it must be said that, in accord with what has already been determined,[275] it is not possible to hold in God that person is to be admitted in accord with some absolute character, but only in accord with a relation or a relative property, and this not in accord with just any relation, but only through that by which a person is ordered to an act of emanation, as from which that which proceeds emanates, or as that which [98] proceeds through emanation, which is only a relation that pertains to origin. And this is also not to be admitted in God in relation to something external, as to a creature, because the relation of God to a creature is only in terms of being said and quasi accidental. But the character of personality is essential to that to which it belongs. But a relative property never exists in the singular or as unique and solitary. There ought therefore to be many relative properties in God in accord with which the character of person is understood in them, and for this reason many persons must be held to be in God, and in that way it is necessary to hold in God a plurality of persons along with the unity of substance, with which we dealt above.[276] And Augustine[277] and Hilary[278] show this quite well by the authority of sacred scripture, as the Master treats this in book one of the *Sentences*, distinction two, the chapter: "Also the Plurality of Persons."[279] But Arius[280]

273　See *SQO* art. 28, qu. 1; Badius 1, fol. 165rN and art 51, qu.3, ??5; ed. M. Führer, pp. 236–239.

274　Pseudo-Athanasian Creed, Denzinger–Schönmetzer, #75.

275　See above qu. 4.

276　See *SQO* art. 25, qu. 1–3; Badius 1, fol. 147ra–157rZ.

277　See Fulgentius of Ruspe, *On the Faith for Peter* 5; ed. J. Fraipont, p. 715.

278　See Hilary of Poitiers, *On the Trinity* 4, 18; ed. P. Smulders, 21; PL 10: 111A–B.

279　See Peter Lombard, *Sentences* 1, 2, 4; ed. I. Brady, 1, pp. 64–65; PL 192: 973D.

280　I had added "Arius" with Badius and one ms.

opposed the unity of substance and divided the substances, holding as many substances in God as persons. Sabellius opposed the distinction of persons, holding one absolute supposite and that it is the Father when it generates, and the Son when it is generated, and the Holy Spirit when it proceeds, in accord with what was touched on above.[281] And the already stated reason for holding many persons in God proceeds from the formal proper character constitutive of a person.

8. But in book three of the book, *On the Trinity*, Richard takes for the same point other arguments from the common characters that follow as it were upon the being of a person [99] already constituted. And he takes the first of these in chapter two from the character of perfect goodness or of love or charity that it is necessary to hold in God. And it is as follows. *"In God there is the fulness and perfection of complete goodness to which the true and highest charity cannot be lacking. But no one is properly said to have charity for the private love of himself. For it is necessary that love tend toward another in order that it may be charity."*[282] It is necessary therefore that there be in God one person and another and in that way many persons in order that perfect charity can exist in him. For it cannot be said that he has that charity for a creature because a creature is not loveable in the highest degree, in accord with what he deals with there.

9. But he takes a second argument from the character of the highest happiness and joy that it is similarly necessary to hold in God in this way: *"Thus there cannot be lacking in the fullness of the highest happiness that than which nothing is more joyous. Love cannot be joyous unless it is mutual,"*[283] because, as he says in chapter sixteen, *"The delights of intimate charity are drawn from the heart of another."*[284] *"But in mutual love it is necessary that there be one who gives love and one who returns love. But where there is shown to be one and another, a true plurality is found."*[285] Therefore, and so on.

10. In chapter four he takes a third argument from the character of the highest benevolence in this way. *"If there were only a single person, he would not have one with whom to share his [100] abundance, and this <would be> either because he could not have one with whom to share it when he wanted or because he did not want to when he could. But the almighty can undoubtedly not be excused on the grounds of impossibility. And he also can not on the grounds of a lack of benevolence because this would be a lack in him,"*[286] as he clearly shows, and so

281   See above qu. 6.

282   Richard of Saint Victor, *On the Trinity* 3, 2; PL 196: 916C–D; ed. J. Ribaillier, p. 136.

283   Ibid. 3, 3; PL 196: 917C; ed. J. Ribaillier, p. 138.

284   Ibid. 3, 16; PL 196: 295D; ed. J. Ribaillier, p. 151.

285   Ibid. 3, 3; PL 196: 917D; ed. J. Ribaillier, p. 138.

286   Ibid. 3, 3; PL 196: 918A; ed. J. Ribaillier, pp. 136–139.

on. And in this truth there is an worry of doubt only because, as he says there in chapter nine: "One wonders *how there* can be *more than one person where there is not more than one substance.*"[287] But he argues against this worry from the contrary: We see that in a human being where there is "*more than one substance, there is* still *not more than one person.*"[288] Yet the substances are as diverse as the body and the soul, as he argues in chapter ten. Hence, he also says in book four, chapter ten: "*Just as being one thing and another substantially does not take away the unity of a person in every case, so being one person and another does not in every case divide the unity of substance. For in a human person,*"[289] and so on.

11. But a plurality of persons in God is shown from another argument, that is, from the character of one person's origin and mode of emanating from another. For the character of origin and emanation has necessarily to be maintained in God, as will be seen below,[290] but the character of origin or emanation is only of one person from another, and thus only of many. For Hilary says in book one of *On the Trinity*, chapter nine: "*Birth does not permit God born from God to be the same one nor something else,*"[291] that is, neither the same in person nor other in substance. For this reason it is necessary to hold that there are many persons in God. And in accord with this Richard says in book four of *On the Trinity*, chapter thirteen: "*Existence can vary in three ways:* [101] *either according to a quality of a thing alone, or according to origin of a thing alone, or according to the concurrence of both. Existence varies according to quality of a thing alone when many persons have one and the same origin in every respect each with its own substance. For substances cannot be many without different quality.*"[292] "*They differ according to origin alone if one has an origin and the other lacks it, or if the origin of one of those that has an origin differs from the origin of the other. Existence varies both according to quality and according to origin where individual persons have a single substance and their proper origin is diverse.*"[293] And then there follows in chapter fourteen: "*In human nature the existence of persons varies both according to quality and according to origin. But in angelic nature there is no propagation, but only simple creation. Therefore, it is necessary that they differ in quality.*"[294] And there follows in chapter fifteen: "*But in God they can in no way differ from one*

---

287 Ibid. 3, 9; PL 196: 921A–B; ed. J. Ribaillier, p. 144.

288 Ibid.

289 Ibid. 4, 10; PL 196: 936B; ed. J. Ribaillier, p. 172.

290 See below art. 54, qu. 3, par. 14.

291 Hilary of Poitiers, *On the Trinity* 1, 17; PL 10: 37C; ed. P. Smulders, p. 18.

292 Richard of Saint Victor, *On the Trinity* 4, 13; PL 196: 938A–B; ed. J. Ribaillier, p. 175.

293 Ibid.; PL 196: 938C; ed. J. Ribaillier, p. 175–176.

294 Ibid.; PL 196: 938D–939A; ed. J. Ribaillier, p. 176.

another by some difference of quality. It remains therefore *that they* are said to have *some difference according to the manner of origin. For where there is no difference, there can be no plurality."*[295]

<Replies to the Arguments>

12. To the first argument to the contrary that "in the deity God and person are related as generic and specific; therefore, and so on,"[296] it must be said that common being and generic or specific being differ because everything generic or specific is common, but not the converse. For only what is common in terms of a diversity of nature that is present in subjects is generic or specific, as [102] "animal" is in man and horse, and "man" is in Isaac and Jacob. But there is something common in the identity of nature, although it is in diverse supposites, as deity is in the divine persons, and the character of person without qualification is in the individual persons. But deity is common in one way, person in another, because deity is common to many in accord with one and the same character of deity, but person is common only in accord with different characters of personality. Something common in the first of these ways in no way has the character of something universal, whether generic or specific. But something common in the second way and similarly in the first and principal way has the character of universal and generic or specific, in accord with what was determined above in the question on the commonness of person.[297] And it is true in such things that of those things of which something specific can be said in the plural, something generic can also be. But in the deity "God" is not unqualifiedly something common in that way, either generic or specific, in relation to a person, because it is of the same commonness with regard to the subjects, God and person without qualification, although in different ways, as has already been said.[298] And according to those different manners of commonness, "person" is predicated in the plural of the Father, the Son, and the Holy Spirit, but "God" or "deity" or "divine essence" is not. Through this the lengthy treatment of this matter in book seven of Augustine's *On the Trinity*, especially chapters four and six, is clear.[299]

13. To the second argument it must be said that diversity is taken in a proper sense or a broad sense. For in the proper sense it denotes otherness in substance or essence. But in a broad sense it denotes only otherness and distinction in accord with the respects of relations. In the first way there is no plurality in God because of diversity. There is nonetheless [103] in the second way. On account of this Augustine says in book seven of *On the Trinity* that in saying

295   Ibid.; PL 196939B–C; ed. J. Ribaillier, p. 177.

296   See above par. 1.

297   See above qu. 7.

298   See above par. 7–8.

299   See Augustine of Hippo, *On the Trinity* 7, 4 and 6; PL 42: 939–942 and 943–946; ed. W. Mountain and F. Glorie, pp 255–260 and 261–267.

"three persons" the Church "*did not want a diversity to be understood by these names, but did not want singularity to be understood.*"[300]

14. Through the same thing the reply to the third argument[301] is clear because where there is no diversity at all, neither in the first nor the second way, there is no plurality or number in any way. But where there is diversity of some sorts, there is a plurality according to it. And thus in God there is plurality and some sort of number in accord with the way there is diversity in him, as is seen more fully from what was determined above[302] concerning the manner of holding number in God.

15. To the fourth argument that "in God *person and essence are of the same character,*"[303] it must be said that it is true according to the manner of predicating and speaking in themselves, because in themselves both are said with respect to themselves and according to substance. Nonetheless, according to the manner of predicating and speaking in their proper subjects they are of another character because being in God is said entirely with respect to itself, but person in its subjects is said in relation to another, as is seen more from what has already been determined.[304]

16. To the last argument[305] it must be said in accord with what was explained above in the first question on the simplicity of God[306] that unity is twofold. A certain unity is called a monad according to the Greeks, and that unity is incompatible with a multitude of discrete things in diverse ones. But a certain unity is called a henad, and it is incompatible with a multitude of things united in the same thing. Simplicity follows upon unity in the second way, and where there is greater unity, there is greater simplicity, and [104] it belongs to each person in himself, just as <it does> to the essence. For a person is just as simple as the essence, as was established above[307] and will be more fully established below.[308] But simplicity does not follow upon unity in the first way, but singularity does. For in that way it is not necessary that something one be simple, as is clear in the world. And it does not follow that there is greater simplicity where there is greater unity. For in this way the unity of the world is greater than that of an angel, and it still would not follow that there cannot be many angels,

---

300   Ibid. 7, 4; PL 42: 942; ed. W. Mountain and F. Glorie, p. 259.

301   See above par. 3.

302   See *SQO* art. 29, qu. 7; ed. Badius 1, fol. 177vR–177rG.

303   See above par. 4.

304   See above qu. 4, par. 7.

305   See above par. 5.

306   See *SQO* art. 25, qu. 1; Badius 1, fol. 147rB–148rE.

307   See *SQO* art. 51, qu. 3; ed. M. Führer, pp. 234–241.

308   See below art. 54, qu. 8.

although there cannot be many worlds. And this second unity belongs to the divine essence insofar as there cannot be many divine essences, and it similarly belongs to a person according to any character of person, insofar as there cannot be many fathers in God, nor many sons, just as there cannot be many gods, as will be seen below.[309] But it does not belong to a person according to the character of person without qualification because there are many persons in God, although there are not many essences, as has already been explained and will be explained more fully below.[310] Therefore, concerning unity in the second way, the major premise is true, as was said, and the minor is false. For the unity that is called henad is not greater where there is unity of essence along with unity of person than where it is with a plurality of persons in God, as was said. But the other way around concerning the first unity; the major premise is false, as was said, and the minor is true. But such unity from the side of a person without qualification cannot be the highest in God because it would exclude every sort of plurality that follows upon unity in the second way, and in that way the highest unity is not in God, as the highest simplicity is, because the highest simplicity and unity of simplicity is there according to every [105] character, but the highest unity of discreteness and singularity is not there according to every way because that is incompatible with the highest simplicity. For the highest simplicity of the deity requires that there be a plurality and not a unity of persons in it.

309　See below qu. 9, par. 12 and art. 54, qu. 4.

310　See below art. 54, qu. 4.

QUESTION NINE

Whether There Are in God Three Persons and Not More Nor Fewer

1. With regard to the ninth question it is argued that there are only two persons in God in the first place as follows: In God there is only a person who is not from another and a person who is from another. But it is the case the person who is not from another can only be a single one on account of the perfection that the character of not being from another requires in it, as will now be clear. Hence, since the character of being a person from another does not require less perfection than the character of being a person not from another, therefore, similarly on account of the perfection that the character of not being from another requires in a person, that person that is from another can be only a single one. In God therefore there is only one person that is from another and only one that is not from another. Therefore, there are only two persons in God.

2. It is argued that there are more as follows: It is necessary to maintain in God a reality that generates, as the person of the Father, and a reality that is generated, as the person of the Son, and a reality that is spirated, as the person of the Holy Spirit, and a reality that is neither generated nor spirated, as is the common essence which is only a singular essence of an intellectual nature. And such a reality is only a person; therefore, there are at least four persons in God.

3. It is argued that there are infinite persons in God as follows: In God there are many persons in the same essence on account of its infinity and unlimitedness by which it is communicable in its singularity. But what is [106] communicable on account of its infinity is no less communicable to infinite persons because infinity determines for itself no number. Therefore, and so on.

‹The Resolution of the Question›

4. With the presupposition in this question of what has already been determined,[311] namely, that it is necessary to maintain in God that there are many persons, one must firstly explain how there cannot be only two persons in God, but that it is necessary that there be three, and then that there cannot be more than three, so that according to this there are three and only three, neither more nor fewer.

5. It must therefore be known that, just as 'person' in God is not understood within something absolute, but only in a relative property, and for this reason on account of the nature of a relative property that constitutes a person, a

---

311   See above qu. 8.

plurality of persons and not merely a unity must necessarily be maintained in God, as was established in the preceding question.[312] In that way "person" in God must similarly not be understood within just any relative property, but only within that which pertains to the character of origin and emanation of one person from another. For another relative property in God is not real or distinctive of a person, as will be seen below.[313] On this account the number of divine persons must necessarily be maintained in accord with the character of the divine emanations. For the terminuses of the emanations are the divine persons constituted by the relations. Therefore, in God there are only two ways of a person's emanating from a person, namely, one by the way of nature and the other by [107] the way of will, as will be seen below.[314] And of these the first proceeds from the person who is absolutely not from another, as will similarly be seen below.[315] But the second proceeds at the same time from that one and from another that emanates through that one and terminates in a third person, as will similarly been seen below. Secondly, for this reason there cannot be in God fewer than three persons, as they are in God: a person that is from no one, and a person that is from one, and a person that is from the others.

6. Furthermore, because those two ways of emanating are so singular that they can in no way become many, as will similarly be seen below,[316] and because singular emanations necessarily have singular terminuses, for this reason, thirdly, there cannot be more than three persons, and thus only three, so that there cannot be more or fewer. But because many of these things are still obscure, as Augustine says in book one of *On the Trinity*, chapter two: "*It must be demonstrated whether the faith is in accord with the sacred scriptures. Then it must be explained by clearer arguments*"[317] taken as if from experience. But the Master of the *Sentences* sufficiently introduces authorities of the scriptures of the Old and the New Testament to demonstrate that the persons are three, in book one, distinction two, from the chapter: "We shall set forth therefore in plain sight," up to the end of this distinction.[318] And for this reason it is not necessary to repeat them here.

312　See above qu. 4 and qu. 8, par. 7.

313　See below par. 11 and 12 and art. 54, qu. 4, par. 13–14 and art. 59, qu. 4; Badius 2, fol. 146r–147vZ.

314　See below par. 11 and 12 and art. 54, qu. 4, par. 13–14 and art. 59, qu. 4; Badius 2, fol. 146rN–147vZ.

315　See ibid.

316　See ibid.

317　Augustine of Hippo, *On the Trinity* 1, 2; PL 42: 822; ed. W. Mountain and F. Glorie, p. 31.

318　Peter Lombard, *Sentences* 1, 2, 4; ed. I. Brady, 1, p. 68–77; PL 192: 526–529.

7. He sufficiently introduces through the whole third distinction arguments to demonstrate the same thing taken from a vestige of God in creatures generally and from the character of the image in the rational creatures specifically. [108] And on this account it is not necessary to repeat them here. But Augustine explains one of them specifically that the Master does not explain when he says in question eighteen of the book, *Eighty-Three Questions*: "*In the case of everything that exists, there is one thing by which it is, another by which it is distinguished, and a third by which it is fitting. Its cause is also three by which it comes to be, by which it is this, and by which it is pleasing. But we say that the cause, that is, the author of a creature is God. It is therefore necessary that he be a trinity.*"[319]

8. But this argument and all the other similar ones introduced from a vestige and image of creatures produce probability and no necessity because what is in creatures principally bears witness to those things that are essential in God and common to the three persons, although by appropriation individual ones are adapted to individual persons.

9. But the arguments taken from those things that are in God and pertain to his perfection need to be introduced here to demonstrate the same thing. The first of these is taken from the goodness, love, and charity existing in God, which Richard sets forth in book three of *On the Trinity*, scattered in diverse chapters. He says in chapter eleven: "*In mutual love there is nothing more excellent than that you want another to be equally loved by him whom you love most highly and by whom you are loved most highly. Let us then grant to the most high what is excellent and best. You see therefore how the perfection of charity requires the Trinity of persons.*"[320] For as he says in chapter thirteen: "*In order that charity can be true, it requires a plurality, but in order that it may be perfect, it requires the Trinity of persons.*"[321] And in chapter nineteen he says: [109] "*When one person alone loves another alone, there is certainly love, but not mutual love. There is said to be mutual love when the love of two persons it fanned by the love of a third.*"[322]

10. But a second argument is taken by the same man from the side of happiness and joy, which he puts in chapter seventeen where he says: "*The realization of true and supreme happiness can in no way subsist without the doubling of person.*"[323] And in chapter eighteen he says: And surely "*if in that plurality of persons a third person is lacking, <the realization of true and supreme happiness> would not*

319 Augustine of Hippo, *Eighty-Three Different Questions* 18; ed. A. Mutzenbecher, p. 23; PL 40: 5.

320 Richard of Saint Victor, *On the Trinity* 3, 11; PL 196: 922C–923A; ed. J. Ribaillier, pp. 146–147.

321 Ibid. 3, 19; PL 192: 924B; ed. J. Ribaillier, p. 149.

322 Ibid. 3, 19; PL 196: 927B; ed. J. Ribaillier, p. 154.

323 Ibid. 3, 17; PL 196: 926B; ed. J. Ribaillier, p. 152.

exist in that doubling of person alone."³²⁴ And in chapter twenty he says: "*For the fullness of the highest happiness requires the fullness of the highest joy, the fullness of the highest joy requires the fullness of the highest charity, and the fullness of the highest charity demands the fullness of the Trinity.*"³²⁵

11. But the argument by which it must be proved that in God there are not more than three persons is taken from the nature of such a reality: In God there is a plurality of persons only on account of the personal emanation and relative properties by which he has an order to the acts of the personal emanations, as was said above.³²⁶ Now however there can be only a single person who is not from another and from whom the others are, and there cannot be more characters or modes of emanations than two so that it is necessary that each of them be single and unique, through which there can proceed only two single and unique persons, as all these points need to be explained in what follows.³²⁷ But one single person who is not from another and from whom the others are and two single <persons> that are from another are only three persons. In God, therefore, there cannot be more than three persons.

[110]   <Replies to the Arguments>

12. To the first argument to the contrary that "*on account of his perfection a person who is not from another is unique; therefore, on account of equal perfection that person who is from another has to be unique,*"³²⁸ it must be said that it is not so. For it is the case in all things that have a plurality in the universal nature of things that they have an order to one another in accord with the character of a principle and of what is derived from a principle so that there is one principle of them all from which they have to be derived and to which they have to be reduced, in accord with what we explained extensively in the first question of our sixth *Quodlibet* in describing the hierarchy of the universe.³²⁹ And in that way the first principle in any order requires unity, but what proceeds from a principle does not <require unity> in that way. On this account, although in the order of the divine persons it is necessary that there be a unique person who is not from another, it is still not necessary that the one who is from another be unique; rather, it is quite possible that there be more, and this <is possible> on account of the plurality of emanations, as was said and will be explained below.³³⁰ And the conclusion does not follow because the form of the argument

324   Ibid. 3, 18; PL 196: 927A; ed. J. Ribaillier, p. 153.
325   Ibid. 3, 21; PL 196: 928A–B; ed. J. Ribaillier, p. 155.
326   See above par. 5.
327   See below art. 54, qu. 4, par. 9–21.
328   See above par. 1.
329   See *Quodlibet* 6, qu. 1; ed. G. Wilson, p. 2–31.
330   See above qu. 8 and below art. 54, qu. 4, par. 9–21.

does not hold since it is possible to admit a twofold sort of perfection in God. Although perfection itself is only unique because it belongs to the essential <attributes, there is> one perfection that belongs to God insofar as he is God, and another that belongs to a singular person insofar as he is such a person, for example, to the Father insofar as he is the Father, and to the Son insofar as he is the Son, and to the Holy Spirit insofar as he is the Holy Spirit. But the sort of perfection of God, insofar as he is God, consists in essential and absolute attributes, and [111] in it the Father, the Son, and the Holy Spirit are univocally equal and equally perfect, not three perfect ones, but a single perfect one. And on account of this perfection a person does not have being a person, either a single one or many, but only God, about which there was discussion above.[331] But the character of the perfection of a singular person, insofar as he is a singular person, consists in relative and personal attributes, in which diverse divine persons are neither univocal nor in agreement, that is, the one from which there is another and the one that is from another because the personal property of one is not common to another. For the character of the perfection of the Father or the character in terms of which there is perfection in the Father insofar as he is the Father is proper to the Father and does not belong to the Son nor to the Holy Spirit. For it consists in that innascibility in which he has fecundity such that everyone other and everything other proceeds from him, as will be seen below.[332] But the character of the Son consists in his birth in which he has fecundity in common with the Father so that there proceeds from him one other and everything other. But the character of the perfection of the Holy Spirit consists in his passive procession in which he has fecundity with the Father and the Son so that there proceeds from him everything else. And in that way the character of the perfection of the Father as Father does not belong to the Son nor to the Holy Spirit, nor the other way around, just as it does not belong to the Son that he is the Father or the Holy Spirit, and the other way around. On this account not every personal act that belongs to the Father belongs to the Son or to the Holy Spirit. However, the Son, but not the Holy Spirit, agrees with the Father in some character of perfection, namely, that which consists in their being sources of procession in which they [112] have a common fecundity so that the Holy Spirit proceeds from them. On this account Richard says in book three of *On the Trinity*, chapter fifteen: "*Of course in those divine persons the perfection of one demands union with the other, and consequently in two the perfection of both requires the coherence of the third.*"[333] Therefore, because the person who is not from another but from whom there is another and the

---

331   See above *SQO* art. 42, qu. 1; ed. L. Hödl, pp. 19–31.

332   See below *SQO* art. 57, qu. 1; ed. Badius 2, fol. 117vM–118rQ.

333   Richard of Saint Victor, *On the Trinity* 3, 13; PL 196: 925B; ed. J. Ribaillier, p. 150.

person who is from him do not agree <in this respect> and as a consequence are not univocal in their personal characters of perfections, for this reason it does not follow that, although on account of his perfection one person requires that he be only unique, that another person also similarly requires this, namely, that just as that the person who is not from another and from whom there is another is unique, the person who is from another is similarly only unique, that is, the one who proceeds by the first emanation <is only unique>, although his perfection requires that he be only unique in the character of his personality. For just as the perfection of the Father as he is the Father requires that in God there is only one Father, so the perfection of the Son as he is the Son requires that in God there is only one Son. Nonetheless, just as the perfection of the Father by which he is without qualification not from another does not require that in God there be another who is not from another, whether that other be understood to be a father or not a father, so the perfection of the Son by which he is without qualification from another does not require that in God there not be another who is not from another, whether that other is a son or not a son, in accord with which all these things will be better clarified below.[334]

13. To the second <argument>[335] it must be said that, although in God it is necessary to hold a single reality of the substance and a threefold reality of relation in the persons, that reality of the substance, as it is substance or essence, although it is intellectual, does not nonetheless have the proper character of personality. Because, as was explained above,[336] [113] not every reality that is an essence insofar as it is an essence, whether it is singular or not, has the character of a person unless it has the character of something incommunicable. And for this reason the essence is not counted along with the three personal realities and is not distinguished from them in constituting a person, as Joachim held.[337]

14. To the third argument[338] it must be said that, if there were not in the divine essence one character by which it is communicable and another by which it is communicable to these, then the argument would proceed. But now it is not so. For although it is communicable without qualification on account of its character of infinity and unlimitedness so that for this reason the communication in God proceeds in the singularity of the essence—although it still stops there in creatures, as we have explained more explicitly elsewhere[339]—it is still not communicable except to determinate persons on account of the determi-

---

334   See below art. 54, qu. 4, par. 14 and qu. 6, par. 47.

335   See above par. 2

336   See above qu. 6, par. 12.

337   See above qu. 6, par. 13 and Gregory IX, *Decretals* 1, 1, 1, #1; ed. A. Friedberg, 2, p. 5.

338   See above par. 3.

339   See *Quodlibet* 6, qu. 3; ed. G. Wilson, pp. 42–48

nate number of roots of the divine emanations in the divine essence, such as are intellect and will, as we determined in *Quodlibet* six in the question on the number of persons and will be still further determined below.[340] But the arguments that Richard produces concerning the Trinity that the persons cannot be infinite can all be resolved and produce only probability,[341] just as those by which he proves the Trinity of the persons.

---

340   See *Quodlibet* 6, qu. 1; ed. G. Wilson, pp. 25–28 and below art. 54, qu. 4 and *SQO* art. 59, qu. 4; Badius 2, fol. 146rN–147vZ.

341   See above par. 9 and 10.

[114]　　　　　　　QUESTION TEN

Whether One Person Has Being in Another
Mutually and in the Same Way

1. With regard to the tenth question it is argued that in God one person is not in another mutually and in the same way in the first place as follows: In book four of the *Physics* the Philosopher assigns eight ways of "being in,"[342] and more are not thought to exist. But by none of these ways is one of the divine persons in another, as is seen by examining them. Therefore, and so on.

2. <It is argued> in the second place as follows: That which has "being in" by ever going forth from another never has being in it, because "to be in" and "to go forth from" are contrary relationships that cannot be in the same thing with respect to one. The Son has "being in" by ever going forth from the Father, because it is said in John sixteen: *I went forth from the Father* (Jn 16:28) and in chapter thirteen: *He went forth from God* (Jn 13:3) and in Micah, chapter five: *His going forth was from the beginning, from the days of eternity* (Mi 5:2). And that going forth is explained with regard to the eternal generation by which the Son is always being generated and has always been generated, as will be seen below.[343] Therefore, the Son is not in the Father, nor the other way around by a similar argument, as is clear to one who can see. Therefore, and so on.

3. <It is argued> in the third place as follows: If one person is in another, it is therefore either by reason of the substance or by reason of a relation or by reason of both. It is not by reason of the substance because by reason of the substance they are the same thing, and by the reason by which some things are the same, one is not in another, because "to be in" is a mark of difference or distinction among those things, one of which is in another. For the same thing, insofar as it is the same thing, is not in itself because then something would be in itself firstly and essentially, which is [115] impossible according to the Philosopher in book four of the *Physics*.[344] But they are not distinguished or different by that by which they are the same. <They are> not <in one another> by reason of a relation because they are opposed by reason of a relation, and what is opposite does not have being in its opposite, insofar as it is opposite.

342　See Aristotle, *Physics* 4.3.210a14–24; vet. trans.; ed. F. Bossier and J. Brams, pp. 141–143.

343　See below art. 54, qu. 3, par. 65 and *SQO* art. 58, qu. 1; Badius 2, fol. 123vG–125rT.

344　See Aristotle, *Physics* 4.3.210a33–34; trans. vet.; ed. F. Boissier and J. Brams, p. 143.

Therefore, <they are> not <in one another> by reason of both, according to the author of the *Book of Six Principles*.[345] Therefore, and so on.

4. <It is argued> in the fourth place as follows: If the Father is in the Son, then since the Father is God and the Son is God, God is in God. The consequent is false because there is only one and the same God, and in that way the same thing would be in itself, which is contrary to the Philosopher in book four of the *Physics*.[346] Therefore, and so on.

5. <It is argued> in the fifth place as follows: In the same way it can be argued that the Father is the Son, if the Father is in the Son, and <one can argue> similarly concerning active and passive generation, namely, that passive generation is in the Father so that the Father is generated and that active generation is in the Son so that the Son generates. And if something is in another that is in it, that which is in it is also in that in which it is. If then the Father is in the Son and the Son is in the Father, the Father is in himself, which is impossible, in accord with what has already been said. Therefore, and so on.

6. <It is argued> in the sixth place as follows: If the Son is in the Father, but the Son is only where there is filiation, then filiation is in the Father. But one in whom there is filiation is the Son; therefore, the Father is the Son. The consequent is false; therefore, the antecedent is also.

[116] 7. <It is argued> in the seventh place as follows: As things that are of themselves opposite and contrary cannot be in the same thing, nor <can they be> through something one. For hot and cold can never be found in the same thing through something the same. Hence, because filiation and paternity are opposites, they can never be found in the same thing through something one. Therefore, and so on.

8. <It is argued> in the eighth place as follows: That property that by itself belongs to a person as proper to him cannot be attributed to the essence through the person. For we say that to generate is proper to a person and similarly that to be generated is, and it does not belong to the essence through the person because the essence does not generate and is not generated. Therefore, by the same argument a property that belongs to the essence as proper to it can in no way be attributed to a person through it. "To be in" is such a property, as is clear. Therefore, by the fact that the essence common to the persons is in the persons, it is impossible that a person be in a person. But there is no other argument more basic than this, as is seen from the statements of the saints. Therefore, and so on.

9. <It is argued> in the ninth place as follows: Just as it is a property of the divine essence that it is in the divine persons, so it is a property of it that it is

---

345   See anonymous, *Book of Six Principles* 4, 45; ed. L. Minio-Paluello and B. G. Dod, p. 44.

346   See Aristotle, *Physics* 4.3.210a33–34; trans. vet., ed. F. Boissier and J. Brams, p. 143.

one in number, singular, and the same in them so that it is no more able to communicate to the persons in which it is its property which is "to be in" than its property by which it is "to be one and the same." Hence, because of the unity of the divine essence in the different persons, those persons cannot be said to be one and the same person. And similarly, because the divine essence is in them, one of them cannot be said to be in another.

10. <It is argued> in the tenth place as follows: If the individual persons were mutually in the individual persons, then similarly individual ones of them that are in one of them would be mutually in the individual persons and also in the individual ones that are in them, and the other way around. And in that way in God everything would be in everything, and <there would be> the greatest confusion, just as in bodily things there was the highest confusion in putting everything in everything [117] in accord with the position of Anaxagoras.[347] The consequent is impossible in God because then there would not be the highest discretion and distinction of the persons and personal properties in God. Therefore, and so on.

11. <It is argued> in the eleventh place as follows: If a person were in a person because the essence is in the same, then a person would not be in a person in another way than the essence is in a person, because that which is in something through another cannot be in it in another way than according to its way so that, if that is in it essentially, this is also, and if that is in it accidentally, this is likewise, as is clear from looking at individual cases.[348] Hence, since the essence is in a person as something of the person and denominating him and as that in which he subsists, then similarly, if a person were in a person through the essence, one person would be something of the other person denominating him and in whom he would subsist. The consequent is false, as is clear. Therefore, and so on.

12. <It is argued> in the twelfth place as follows: If many persons or many things are said to be mutually in one another, that is, one of them in another because there is something one in them in common, similarly, if many persons or many things have being in the same thing, then for the same reason one of them will be said to be in the other. But this is false. For we say that white and sweet are simultaneously in one thing, such as milk. Still we do not say that whiteness is in sweetness, or the other way around. Therefore, the first is also false.

13. <It is argued> in the thirteenth place as follows: If in God one thing is in another, if it is not the same as him, it produces a composition with him, as is clear concerning an essence and a property. For when a property is in the essence, if it were not the same as it, it would put composition in God. Hence,

---

347　See Aristotle, *Physics* 1.4.187b29–301 trans. vet,; ed. F. Bossier and J. Brams, pp. 18–19.

348　I have followed the Badius text and other mss. in reading: "as is clear from looking, *ut patet inspiciendo.*"

if one person were held to be in another and one was not the other and not the same as the other, that would put [118] composition in God. Both of these are impossible. Therefore, it is impossible that in God one person be held to be in another.

14. <It is argued> in the fourteenth place as follows: Whatever is in God is God. Therefore, for the same reason whatever is in the Father is the Father. If then the Son is in the Father, the Son is the Father. Therefore, and so on.

15. <It is argued> in the fifteenth place as follows that one <person> is not in another in the same way, and the other way around, because Hilary says in book seven of *On the Trinity*: "*The Father is in the Son because the Son is from him, and the Son is in the Father because the Son is from no one else. The only-begotten is in the unbegotten because the only-begotten is from the unbegotten.*"[349] But these reasons and ways are entirely different because the one is from him and he is from the other. Rather, they are opposite. Therefore, and so on.

16. To the contrary it is argued that those who subsist in something one and simple without being separated or divided are necessarily in one another, or they are absolutely the same because there is no in-between. All the divine persons are such. Therefore, and so on. And this is what the Savior says in John fourteen. *I am in the Father, and the Father is in me* (Jn 14:11).

<The Resolution of the Question>

17. Here one must undoubtedly hold in accord with the authority of the sacred scripture that the individual divine persons are in the individual persons. And since there are only two things in a person: the substance and a relation, in accord with what will be explained below,[350] there is no doubt on this except according to which of them a person can be in a person and how this is possible according to that, if it is according to only one or if it is according to both.

[119] 18. And some[351] say that one person is said to be in another by reason of the essence, and others[352] that it is by reason of the relation. <They say that it is> by reason of the essence because the whole essence of one person is in the other in accord with what Damascene says in book three, chapter six of the *Sentences*: "*We confess that the whole nature of the deity is perfect in each of its persons, whole in the Father, whole in the Son, whole in the Holy Spirit.*"[353] And where there is

---

349   More correctly Hilary of Poitiers, *On the Trinity* 3, 4; ed. P. Smulders, p. 75; PL 10: 78A.

350   See below art. 54, qu. 3, art. 55, qu. 1, and *SQO* art. 56, qu. 4; ed. Badius 2, fol. 116rB–117rK.

351   Rather, Fulgentius of Ruspe, *On the Faith for Peter* 4; PL 40: 754; ed. J. Fraipont, p. 714.

352   Hilary of Poitiers, see below par. 19 and 27.

353   John Damascene, *On the Orthodox Faith* 3, 6; PG 94: 1003A; ed. E. Buytaert, p. 187.

the substance or nature of a person, there is the person also. Therefore, through this natural unity, as Augustine says in the beginning of *On the Faith for Peter*: "*The whole Father is in the Son and in the Holy Spirit, and the whole Son is in the Father and in the Holy Spirit, and the whole Holy Spirit is in the Father and in the Son. None of them is outside of any of them.*"[354] On this Ambrose also says in *On the Letter to the Corinthians*: "*By this the Father is understood to be in the Son and the Son in the Father because their substance is one.*"[355]

19. But others[356] say that one person is in another by reason of the relation because one of those related is understood <to be> in the other. But their statement does not seem to be sufficient. For because the substance of the Father is in the Son, and the other way around, it is only established that the Father is one with the Son, and the other way around. If then on the basis of this the Father were said to be in the Son, and the other way around, then one would be said to be in the other insofar as they are one. But because some things are one, it is not established that one is in the other, but rather the opposite. For insofar as the Father is one with the Son, he is the same thing as he is. But insofar as something is the same thing, it is not in it, because according to [120] the Philosopher in book four of the *Physics*: "*The character of that which is in one thing is other than that which is in this.*"[357] And then since the Father would not be less the same with himself than with the Son, he would similarly be said to be in himself as in the Son, and he would be so through himself and firstly since the Father is through himself and firstly the same with himself, not by something other than himself, and not by something of himself. But this is utterly impossible with regard to bodily things, as the Philosopher proves in book four of the *Physics*,[358] and it is no less impossible in spiritual things, as is seen from the same arguments, since the middle terms are applicable in the same way to spiritual and bodily things, as is clear to one who can see. For the Philosopher argues that if an amphora of wine were through itself in itself, since it would be in itself only because the amphora is in the amphora, and it is the same with the wine because the wine is in the amphora, the amphora, therefore, would not only be the amphora, but would be the wine and the amphora, and similarly the wine would not only be the wine, but also the amphora and the wine.

---

354   Rather, Fulgentius of Ruspe, *On the Faith for Peter* 4; PL 40: 754; ed. J. Fraipont, p. 714.

355   Ambrosiaster, *On the Second Letter to the Corinthians* 5, 19; PL 17: 297D; ed. H. Vogels 2, p. 237. Also Peter Lombard, *Sentences* 1, 19, 4; PL 192: 526; ed. I. Brady, p. 163.

356   Hilary of Poitiers, see below par. 27.

357   Aristotle, *Physics* 4.3.210a13–14; trans. vet; ed. F. Boissier and J. Brams, p. 145.

358   See Aristotle, *Physics* 4.3.210b22-23; trans. vet.; ed. F. Boissier and J. Brams, p. 145.

20. Similarly, in the present case, if the Son, that is, the begotten substance, were in himself through himself, since he would only be in himself because the substance is in the begotten substance, and similarly the begotten or because <he is> begotten is in the substance, therefore, the substance is not only the substance, but <is> the substance and the property, and the property is not only the property, but <is> the substance and the property, Therefore, if according to the stated way of putting it, one person were in another, that is, in terms of the essence alone, for that reason if in God there were only one person, that person would be in himself for the same reason as one person is in another, and that is false. Similarly, from the fact that the Father and the Son are relative to each other, it is only established that one is related to the other and that the understanding [121] of one is not without understanding of the other, not that one is in the other or understood <to be> in the other, in accord with what is seen in related things in creatures.

21. It is clear then that this difficulty is greater than the stated authorities of the saints are seen to explain. And for this reason it must be said that in God one person is in another not by reason of the essence alone and not by reason of a relation alone, but rather by reason of both of them together, that is, of the substance and the relation, and thus not separately, as the stated opinions or explanations hold, but as together. For if in the divine persons there was not the unity of the substance as <there is> not <the unity> of the properties, it is evident that it would no more be said that the Father is in the Son than in creatures. Similarly, if they were not distinct and different in terms of the relative properties, as <they are> not in the substance, one would not be said to be in another, but rather to be the same as him, as has been said.

22. For the understanding of this we must still by beginning further back see how the way of "being in" in God differs from the eight ways of "being in" in creatures that the Philosopher holds in book four of the *Physics*.[359] It must be known therefore that this preposition "in" denotes the circumstance of containment, but that containment necessarily requires some distinction and difference of what is contained from what contains it, and the other way around. For where there is complete identity and lack of distinction, it is impossible that something "be in" <something,> as was said and will now be said more fully. Hence, in order to say that in God one person is in another, identity in substance is not a sufficient reason, but for this it is necessary that there be some otherness through distinction between them.

23. But a distinction between what contains and what is contained can be understood in two ways: either in terms of the whole, namely, of what contains and what is contained, that is, so that nothing of the one belongs to the other, or in terms of a part or as if in terms of a part, that is, so that something that

---

359 See Aristotle, *Physics* 4.3.210a14–24; trans. vet.; ed. F. Bossier and J. Brams, pp. 142–143 and above par. 1.

belongs to what contains does not belong to what is [122] contained. In the first way, something located is in a place, for example, a liquid in a bottle, and form is in matter, and something moved is in the first mover, and that which is for an end is in its end. And in such things the one is in the other, but not the other way around, and this <is> either in no way or not according to the same way of "being in." In the second way this occurs in two ways. For either there is something of that which contains that does not belong to that which is contained, but there is nothing of that which is contained that does not belong to that which contains, the opposite of which is impossible. Or there is something of that which is contained that does not belong to that which contains, and the other way around, and there is something common to both. In the first way a part is in the whole, and a whole is in the parts, and a species is in a genus, and a genus in the species. And neither in this way nor in the preceding does one person in God have being in another, but only in the last way. And thus in accord with the eight ways that the Philosopher holds in books eight and four of the *Physics*,[360] "being in" does not properly belong in accord with one of those ways of "being in," by which one person is in another. For in those eight ways that the Philosopher holds, the reason for "being in" is essentially a diversity between what contains and what is contained, as is clear to someone who runs through the individual ways. But in this case the essential reason for it is the agreement or that in which what contains and what is contained agree, as will now be seen from what will be said. Hence, concerning this way of "being in," Hilary says in book three of *On the Trinity* in the beginning: "*The mind of man does not grasp these matters, nor will a human comparison provide an example for the divine realities.*"[361]

24. For the understanding of this by specifically coming down to the question at hand, it must be known that something or someone can be said to be in another in two ways: in one way through itself and firstly, as that which is in terms of its whole is in another through itself and firstly; in another way as that which is in it in terms of the whole through itself, but not firstly, for example, as that which is "in" is whole in another firstly and by [123] something of it. In the first way in created things, something is in another as something located is in place, but in that way nothing can be in itself, as the Philosopher proves in book four of the *Physics*.[362] But in this way it also does not happen in God that something or someone is in its- or himself, just as it does not in creatures. And on account of the same reasons it is also not possible that in God one person be in another, although it is possible in creatures. Because when some whole is

360   See Aristotle, *Physics* 4.3.210a14–24 and 8.7.261b10–12; trans. vet., ed. F. Bossier and J. Brams, pp. 142–143 and 317. See above par. 1.

361   Hilary of Poitiers, *On the Trinity* 3, 1; PL 10: 76A–B; ed. P. Smulders, p. 73.

362   See Aristotle, *Physics* 4.3.210a33–34; trans. vet.; ed. F. Bossier and J. Brams, p. 143.

in another firstly and through itself, whatever belongs to it is also similarly in it equally firstly and through itself, just as if the whole earth is firstly and through itself in the place of the center, each part of it is firstly and through itself in the center, although not separately. Hence, if the whole person of the Son were through himself and firstly in the Father, and the property of the Son were similarly so that filiation is in the Father firstly and through itself and equally firstly, as the deity of the Son also is, it would denominate the Father as deity also does, and the Father would be the Son by filiation, as he is God by the deity.

25. Besides, if something is in another through itself and firstly, it is impossible the other way around that that other in which it is be through itself and firstly in that which is in it, because the same thing would be what contains and what is contained though itself and firstly with respect to the same thing, and the same thing would be with respect to one thing wholly outside and wholly inside, which is impossible in bodily things in a bodily way and in spiritual things in a spiritual way. And thus if one person were in terms of its whole through itself and firstly in another, so that the Son would be in the Father, the Father could not the other way around be through himself and firstly in the Son in terms of the whole in any way or not at least in the same way. And this is not to be held in God because in God the individual persons must be held to be mutually and uniformly in the individual persons. But that in the second way something is in another, that is, through itself, but not firstly, because it is through something of it [124] that has being firstly and through itself in it, this can be in two ways: either because that something belongs to the one and not to the other or because it belongs to the one in such a way that it also belongs to the other. In the first way in creatures something has being in another, insofar as a bird is said to be in a snare because its foot is in the snare. But in this way it does not happen in God that one person is in another because in the divine persons nothing belongs to one that does not belong to the other, that is, by which one person has being firstly in another, because in the divine persons that which belongs to one and not to another is only a personal property, and the property of one person is not firstly and through itself in another, so that by it a person could be in that person through itself, although not firstly. For filiation is not firstly and through itself in the Father so that through it the whole Son and his divinity are in the Father through themselves, although not firstly. Because the Son is distinguished from the Father by filiation, filiation firstly and through itself, insofar as it is considered from its side, is outside the Father rather than in the Father. And by it the Son <is rather> outside the Father than in the Father, although "inside" and "outside" are not admitted in God in the proper sense. But if something is in another through something of it that it belongs to one of them so that it at the same time also belongs to the other, in this way of "being in" nothing in creatures has being in another, because when two things differ in creatures, nothing in reality is singular and common to

both by which one creature can be in another in any way. And in this way in God one person has being in another in the proper sense, and the whole person is in the whole person, but whole person <is> not in the whole person through itself and firstly, rather through something of itself that it has in common with that in which it is, which is in that through itself and firstly. And through it <the whole person> has being in the other through itself, although not firstly, and this is by reason of that which it has in common with it.

26. I say therefore in drawing the present question to a close that in God one person has being in another in terms of substance and in terms of relation as the same time—according to substance, as in accord with that in accord with which one person principally has being in another. For its substance is in that <person> firstly [125] and through itself, and through that the whole person, which in terms of itself it would not be said to be whole in that according to the common substance, but would rather be said to be one and the same with it, if it were not in it. <One person has being in another> according to the relative property by which <the one> differs from <the other>, as that in accord with that in accord with which one person has being in another, but not firstly, because the property of one person is in that other person only because the substance, which belongs to that person upon which its property is founded, is in that person. For a numerically one and singular substance cannot be in something without whatever is founded on the substance being in it at the same time. And one person is not only in another in terms of this, but the individual persons are mutually in the individual persons.

27. Hence, investigating this more deeply than the other saints who explained that a person is in another only according to substance, as is seen in the first book of the *Sentences*, distinction nineteen, the chapter, "*And from this there follows*," where that material is dealt with, Hilary also explains that one person is in another according to relation in book three of *On the Trinity*, chapter one, where he speaks as follows: "*Therefore, it must be known and understood what those words mean: 'I am in the Father, and the Father in me' (Jn 14:10), at least if we shall be able to comprehend it as it is, so that the character of the divine truth attains what the nature of things is thought to be unable to admit,*"[363] and after a bit he adds: "*What is in the Father is in the Son; what is in the unbegotten is in the only-begotten, the one from the other, and both one. The two are not one, but one is in the other because there is not something else in both.*"[364] [126] See that one is in the other according to substance. And there immediately follows: "*The Father is in the Son because the Son is from him, and the Son is in the Father because the only-begotten Son is in the unbegotten for no other reason than that the only-begotten*

363   Hilary of Poitiers, *On the Trinity* 3, 1; PL 10: 76B; ed. P. Smulders, p. 73.

364   Ibid. 3, 4; PL 10: 78A; ed. P. Smulders, p. 75.

is from the unbegotten."[365] See that one is in another according to relation. And in book seven, chapter nineteen, he says: *"They are in one another since birth is only from the Father."* See, <one is> in <another> according to property. *"For an extrinsic or dissimilar nature does not subsist in another god."*[366] See <one is> in <another> according to substance. Hence, because one person is not in another only according to substance, but also according to the property, so that the whole person is in the whole person, it turns out that one is also in the other by subsisting and subsists in the other. On this account he says at the end of the book that *"'being' and 'being in' do not differ, but 'being in' does not mean 'one thing in another,' as a body is in a body, but 'to be' and 'to subsist' so that he is in one who subsists, but 'to be in' so that he subsists."*[367] Thus in accord with this a person has being in another mutually both according to substance and according to relation, the Father in the Son in no other way than the Son in the Father, although the Father is in the Son with another relation. And this is so for the reason that the substance through which the persons and their properties with them are in one another is in them in the same way insofar as it pertains to the ways of "being in." For although to such an extent the essence is in the persons in accord with a different way because it is in one as communicated by another or by others, but in another as not communicated by another, this makes no difference to the question at hand. But if <the essence> were in them in different ways, the Father would in accord with this be in the Son and the Son in the Father in different ways.

28. And here it must be noted that, although the person that is in and quasi contained in the Father is not in him or contained in him principally by reason of the whole, but by reason of something that belongs to him, as was said,[368] still the person in whom he is [127] and which quasi contains him firstly and principally by reason of the whole that is in him, but not by reason of one of those things on account of which the container, insofar as it contains essentially and firstly, as if exceeds the contained in accord with which it is contained firstly and through itself and the container is quasi outside the contained and contains by something that differs from the contained and exceeds that by which it is firstly and through itself contained. But the contained is conversely quasi within the container and is contained firstly and through itself only by something in which it agrees with the container it and is exceeded by that which firstly and through itself contains it.

29. In accord with this the difficulty that most disturbs the intellect is resolved by understanding that the Father is in the Son and the Son is in the Fa-

---

365   Ibid.

366   Ibid. 7, 31; PL 10: 226A; ed. P. Smulders, p. 298.

367   Ibid. 7, 41; PL 10: 234B; ed. P. Smulders, p. 310.

368   See above par. 22.

ther mutually, in accord with what Hilary says in book three of *On the Trinity* in the beginning: "*The words of the Lord bring obscurity for many when he says: 'I am in the Father, and the Father is in me (Jn 14:10), and not without reason. For the nature of human intelligence cannot grasp the meaning of this statement. For it does not seem possible that something that is in another is itself equally outside of the other. And since it is necessary that those with which we are dealing are not solitary unto themselves, and while preserving the number in which they are, they cannot mutually contain one another so that the one that has something else in itself and remains so, always remaining external, remains always equally internal to that which it in turn has within itself. The human mind does not grasp this, and a human comparison will not offer an example for the divine realities.*" And the reason is that such a way of "being in" cannot be found in creatures, [128] especially in bodily ones. But the intellect in some way attains this in God as Hilary says in book seven, chapter twenty-three: "*The Father is in the Son, and the Son in the Father, God in God, not through a twofold joining of kinds coming together, as is seen in wine and an amphora, nor through the innate nature of a more capacious substance, as is seen in steam and the air, because through bodily necessity internal things cannot become external to those by which they are contained, but through the birth of one living from a living nature. For the reality does not differ since birth does not make the nature of God something less, since nothing else is born but God from God.*"[369] From what has been said the stated difficulty is seen.

<Replies to the Arguments>

30. To the first argument therefore that "*in God a person is not in another in accord with one of the eight ways of 'being in,'*"[370] it must be said that it is true in accord with what has already been explained.[371] For Aristotle lists sufficiently the ways of "being in" that can be found in creatures, and this way that cannot be found in creatures, but only in the uncreated substance, is different from all of them. Still some want that it can be reduced to one of those ways. But <they want> this in different ways insofar as a person has being in a person according to substance and according to relation. In the first way they say that, because the Father is in the Son and the other way around, since the substance of the Father is in the Son and the other way around, the substance has being in the Father and the Son in accord with the way a common form has being in a species. For although [129] in God there is neither genus nor species, each divine supposite still contains as if one species of relation, and the deity, insofar as it is common to the three that differ as if by species, is like the form of a ge-

369 Hilary of Poitiers, *On the Trinity* 7, 39; PL 10: 232C; ed. P. Smulders, p. 307.

370 See above par. 1

371 See Aristotle, *Physics* 4.3.210a14–24; trans. vet., ed F. Bossier and J. Brams, pp. 142–143; see above par. 1 and 22.

nus, although in different ways of commonness,[372] as was touched upon above and will be touched upon further below.[373] But in the second way they say that the Father is the originating principle of the Son and the Son is that which is derived from the principle and originated from him. Therefore, the Son is in the Father as the one originated in the one originating, and the Father is in the Son as the one originating in the one originated, and it is reduced to the way in which something has being in the first mover, or the other way around.

31. Neither of these is sufficient or pertains to the question at hand. The first does not. For although the Father is in the Son and the other way around according to substance, and <this is> so because the same substance is in both, still the Son does not have being in the Father, and the other way around, in the same way in which the substance has being in the Father and the Son, because the substance is in a person as something that pertains to its constitution, but a person <is> not in that way in a person, but as a distinct container is in something distinct that contains,[374] because it cannot be in accord with the way in which a form is in a supposite. Nor, as Hilary says,[375] can an example be found in creatures. Nor is there in them some similar way of "being in" something, by however remote a likeness, to which it can be reduced, as is clear from what has already been said. Similarly, according to what has been said, it does not apply to the present question. For here it is asked about one person's being in another only insofar as one exists as internal to another, but not as emanating from it. Hence, although insofar as one emanates from another, the way of one's being in the other is reduced to the way in which something is in the first mover or the other way around, this is still nothing in relation to the present question. For here there [130] is sought the way in which one has being in another as in something that coexists with it. Hence, even if there were in God two persons, one of which did not proceed from another, as the Son and the Holy Spirit, if they proceeded from the Father alone, one could be in another on account of the identity of the substance, just as now when one proceeds from the other.

32. To the second argument that "one person 'is in' by always going forth from another; therefore, it does not have 'being in it' as in one coexisting with it, which is also contrary to what has already been said,"[376] it must be said that the going forth of one person from another is not to be understood through the

---

372   See *SQO* art. 25, qu. 3; Badius 1, fol. 153rC–vF.

373   See *SQO* art. 44, qu. 1; art. 52, qu. 2, and art, 75, qu. 2; Badius 2, fol. 10vX–11vZ, fol. 57rR–vV, and fol. 296vZ–297rA.

374   I have followed the Badius text that has "*continens*" and "*continente*" instead of "*conveniens*" and "*conveniente*" in the critical edition.

375   See Hilary of Poitiers, *On the Trinity* 3, 1; ed. P. Smulders, p. 73; PL 10: 6A–B. See above par. 29.

376   See above par. 2.

distance of places or of natures, as the heretics understood, when they tried to prove from this the diversity of the natures of the one generating and the one generated, but it is only to be understood through the relative distinction of the one going forth and of the one from whom he goes forth, while in absolutely the same substance. For as Hilary says in book seven of *On the Trinity*, chapter seventeen: "*God is not from God through a lessening or expansion or downward flow, but subsists by birth from the power of nature into the same nature,*"[377] in accord with what will be better seen below concerning the emanation of the persons.[378] In the first way "to go forth from" and "to be in" are contraries and cannot belong to the same thing at the same time. But in the second way they are not contraries, but are necessarily in the same thing at the same time, because what is generated is of the individual substance of the generator and in no way separated from the same.

33. To the third argument that "*one person is not in another by reason of the substance because by reason of the substance they are one and the same thing,* and there *is not 'being in' without a distinction,*"[379] it must be said that it argues correctly that one person is not in another by reason of the substance alone without a relation, but by reason of both in accord with the way explained that one person is in another. And as to the argument that [131] <one person is in another> "not by reason of a relation, because by reason of a relation they are opposed, and insofar as they are opposed, the persons have not being rather than being in one another,"[380] it must be said that it is true principally and firstly. For if they were not firstly and principally in one another according to substance, they would never be in one another through relation. Nonetheless, since they are in one another principally through substance, substance alone without a distinguishing relation would not make them to be in one another, but rather to be the same thing, as is seen from what has been already established.[381]

34. To the fourth argument that "*if the Father is in the Son, God is in God; therefore, the same thing is in itself since there is only one God,*"[382] it must be said that it is necessary that we[383] confess that God is in God, as Hilary says in book seven of *On the Trinity*, chapter seventeen: "*The one, absolute, and perfect mystery of the faith is to confess God from God and God in God, not in bodily ways, but*

377   Hilary of Poitiers, *On the Trinity* 5, 37; PL 10: 154C–155A; ed. P. Smulders, p. 73.

378   See below art. 54, qu. 3, par. 52–57.

379   See above par. 3.

380   Ibid.

381   See above par. 21 and 22.

382   See above par. 4.

383   I have read "we, *nos*" instead of "not, *non*."

by the power of the nature,"[384] and in chapter eighteen: "*Since the only-begotten is himself God and is nonetheless God with him through the unity of the nature and because he is God and God is in him, having in himself both that which he is and that by which he subsists. For as Isaiah says: 'God is in you, and there is no other God besides you'* (Is 45:14); *in that way he foretold the individual and inseparable divinity of the Father and the Son.*"[385] It is nonetheless not necessary to confess that the same one is in himself, although there is only one God, because along with this there are very well many persons that are in one another. For although this name "God" signifies only a nature or essence and does this in common according to the way that an essence is said to be common, it still stands for the supposites from the manner of signifying, just as this name "man" or "animal" does, and in this regard there is not some difference from the side of the essence, although it is unique in many or [132] made many. Hence, although "God" is one and the same on account of the singular one signified, God is quite well in God on account of the different supposites. Still <there is> not one God in another, nor the same in itself, but one in person in another, as was explained.

35. To the fifth argument that, "*if the Father is in the Son and the Son in the Father,* therefore, *the Father is in* the Father,"[386] it must be said that it is true because nothing can be in what is contained without being in the container. But it is not necessary that it is in what is contained in the same way that it is in the container, unless what is contained is in the first container firstly and through itself, and similarly in accord with what is contained in the first contained. For example, if fire is in the heavens and air is in the fire as in a place, therefore, the air is in the heavens as in a place. This is still not in entirely the same way because fire is in the heavens as in its proper and determinate place, but air is in the heavens as in a place that is common and exceeds it. It is therefore true in the present question that, because the Father is in the Son and the Son in the Father, the Father is in himself, but not as the Son is in him and he is in the Son. For the whole Son is in the Father and similarly the whole Father is in the Son through himself, although not firstly in accord with what has been said.[387] But the Father is not in himself entirely through himself. For although he is whole in himself, this is not in terms of the whole as he is whole, but in terms of those things that belong to him as they are something of his and thus quasi accidentally. For just as in bodily things an amphora of wine, which is a composite whole from the amphora and the wine according to the Philosopher

---

384   More correctly, Hilary of Poitiers, *On the Trinity* 5, 37; PL 10: 154C; ed. P. Smulders, p. 191.

385   Ibid. 5, 37–38; PL 10: 155BC–156B; ed. P. Smulders, p. 192–193.

386   See above par. 5.

387   See above par. 19.

in book four of the *Physics*,[388] is in itself accidentally as through its parts, that is, because in the amphora of wine there is the amphora and similarly the wine as parts of it, so in the present case the Father is in himself quasi accidentally, insofar as he is in some way a whole, that is the unbegotten substance, of which according to our way of understanding there are as quasi parts the substance and the property, which is unbegotten. For in the unbegotten substance there is substance and similarly unbegotten, as quasi parts of him, and this singly. For one of them is not [133] in the Father firstly and the other through that as a consequence, but both are equally principally in him. On this account he is in no way through himself whole in himself, but only quasi accidentally. But because one of them, for example, the essence of the Father is in the Son through itself and firstly, and his property is in him through that as a consequence, and through this the whole Father is in him. On this account the whole Father is in some way in the Son. And thus although through something of him he is in the Son and in himself, he is so nonetheless in different ways.

36. To the sixth argument: "*If the Son is in the Father, filiation is in the Father,*"[389] and so on, it must be said that "to be in" is taken very equivocally in God when it is said: "The Son is in the Father;" "The property of the Father is in the Son," "The essence of the Son is in the Son," "The property of the Son is in the Son," "The property of the Son is in the essence of the Son," and "The being of the Son is in his essence." For the Son's having being in the Father is subsistently, and it is similar with the property of the Son being in the Father or the substance of the Son, insofar as it belongs to the Son. But the Son is in the Father subsistently in different ways. For the Son is not in the Father as something of the Father, as his substance and property are, but as subsisting in him because he is in him by subsisting.

37. In order by this to exclude the question hidden in this statement, "The Son subsists in the Father," because that determination can determine "subsists" by reason of the act of being, which is understood in him as material in any verbal adjective, or by reason of the proper act, which is expressed by the participle "subsisting." In the first way that statement is true in this sense: "The Son is in the Father as subsisting." In the second way it is false in this sense: "The Son is subsisting in the Father." For it would be indicated that in subsisting the Son rested upon the Father as upon his foundation in subsisting, [134] as he is said to subsist in the divine essence. And in that way in the first sense "to subsist in" is said subsistently or substantially, but in the second way foundationally. And in that way, when the Son is said to be in the Father, "to be in" is understood subsistently, and <it is> similarly when the property of the Son is

---

388   See Aristotle, *Physics* 4.3.210a31–33; trans. vet., ed. F. Bossier and J. Brams, p 143

389   See above par. 6.

said to be in the Father because the whole Son could be in the Father only if whatever belongs to the Son were in the Father, as the objection proceeds. This is understood subsistently, but the reason is not because the property subsists in the Father, but because it is through himself in the Son who subsists in the Father insofar as he subsists in him. And not only the property of the Son, but also his essence, insofar as it is his and possessed by him as begotten, is in the Father subsistently, although the same essence, as it is the Father's, is in the Father formally, because it is the quasi common form by which he is God, just as the property of the Son is in the Son and the property of the Father is in the Father, although not by inhering as a proper form by which the Son is the Son and the Father the Father. And this property has being in the essence in accord with another way of "being in," namely, foundationally, because the property is founded upon the essence, as has to be explained below.[390] And because the property by which a person subsists has being foundationally in the substance as that upon which it rests, for this reason the whole person is said to be in itself as if accidentally, but in another way than before, namely, as something of it, such as a property, is in something that belongs to it, as in its substance. And this is as in bodily things an amphora of wine is said to be in an amphora of wine, because the wine that is a part of it is in the amphora that is another part of it. And in accord with this way, even "God" taken essentially is said to be in himself because his wisdom and other things of the sort have being in his substance. Therefore, when it is argued further that *"if filiation is in the Father, the Father is, therefore, the Son,"*[391] the equivocation on "being in" is clear. For it would correctly follow [135] if it were in him formally as it is in the Son and as paternity is in the Father. But now it is in him only subsistently, as was said, and what is in another in that way is in him as distinct and separate from him, not as denominating him. And it is the same way with "being generated" and the other things that are in the Son formally and are in the Father subsistently, as was said.

38. To the seventh argument that *"opposites and contraries cannot be in the same thing through one and the same thing,"*[392] it must be said that it is true in creatures where they do not come from the same proximate root. For there they are opposed with respect to the subject. But that is not true in God because all the divine properties arise from the same proximate root, which is the divine essence, and are rooted in it. And on this account and insofar as they are relations, they are opposed with respect to their object so that they cannot be opposed formally in the same thing. But they are still not opposed with respect to the subject in which they are rooted so that they cannot be in the same thing

390   See below art. 55, qu. 6.

391   See above par. 6.

392   See above par. 7.

through it, one of them <in it> formally, but the other <in it> subsistently, as was said.

39. To the eighth argument that *"a property proper to a person does not* belong *to the essence; hence, nor is the converse true,"*[393] it must be said that it is true that it cannot belong in accord with the same way. It can still belong to both in accord with different ways, as in the present question. For although a property does not belong to the essence, as something to which it belongs formally, it still belongs to it as something to which it belongs foundationally. Similarly, although "being in" does not belong to a person formally by denominating that in which it is. It can very well belong to it subsistently, as was said.

40. To the ninth argument that "diverse *persons are not one person,* although *one* essence is *one and the same* with both; therefore, similarly, although one essence is in both, it does not follow from this that *one of them is in the other,"*[394] [136] it must be said that it is not the same because to be one with another denotes absolutely no sort of difference, but pure identity. For where there is greater unity, there is greater identity. On this account it does not at all follow that, if one thing is the same for both, they are the same with one another. For from the fact that they are one and the same in one thing, it does not follow that they are one and the same in all things. But "to be in another" necessarily implies some difference of that which is in from that in which it is, as was said.[395] On this account if something is in the two in which they agree, if those in which they differ are rooted in it, those by which they differ are necessarily understood from the addition to be simultaneously in it. And in that way the whole persons are in the whole persons, as was said.[396]

41. To the tenth argument that *"if individual persons were in individual persons,* this would put the highest confusion of the persons in God"[397] contrary to the statement of Athanasius: *"And not confusing the persons,"*[398] and so on, it must be said that in God individuals are in individuals both in essential and in personal attributes so that through all things, as has already been said, *"there is to be venerated* not only *unity in the Trinity and the Trinity in the unity,"*[399] as Athanasius says, but also the Trinity in the Trinity, that is, by reason of the persons, as Augustine says in book six of *On the Trinity* in the end. *"They are infinite in themselves, and the individuals are in the individuals, and the individuals*

---

393 See above par. 8.

394 See above par. 9.

395 See above par. 22.

396 See above par. 24–25.

397 See above par. 10.

398 See *Pseudo-Athanasian Creed*; ed. Denizer-Schönmetzer, #75.

399 Ibid. p. 38.

are in all, and all are in all, and all are one."[400] Therefore, the unity of the substance is to be venerated in the Trinity of the persons, that is, in the Father, the Son, and the Holy Spirit, and this is like a common form [137] in supposites that have a form, and similarly the Trinity is to be venerated in the unity of the persons of the Father and the Son and the Holy Spirit—in the unity of the essence in which they subsist. And similarly the Trinity is to be venerated in the Trinity, and this is in two ways: either so that the individuals are venerated also in the individuals, and this in six combinations, that is, so that the Father is venerated in the Son and the Holy Spirit, and the Son in the Father and the Holy Spirit, and the Holy Spirit in the Father and the Son or so that all are venerated in each individual and the individuals in all. And this is in nine combinations, so that the Father, Son, and Holy Spirit are venerated in the Father and in the Son and in the Holy Spirit all together, although according to different ways of being each person has in himself and in another, as was said.[401] And although, as was said, the persons are in the persons and through this the personal properties that are in the persons are also in the same ones in which persons are, they are not in one another, as filiation is not in paternity on account of the opposition that they have to each other.

42. Nonetheless, since along with the fact that the essential <attributes> are in the individual persons and their properties, they are also in one another, and this is without any confusion both in the personal and in the essential <attributes>. For along with the fact that they are mutually in one another, they retain their distinctions—personal <attributes> a personal and real <distinction>. And they do this just as if two bodies were placed at the same time in the same place, a glorified and non-glorified one, each of them would be in the other, but still without confusion, because they would be under the same distinction that they would have if they were outside each other. But essential <attributes retain> a rational distinction. Then there would, however, be confusion only if from their being in one another, there were lost the distinction between that which is in and that in which it is, just as there was confusion in chaos. According to Anaxagoras there was no distinction of flesh from bone, from wood, or [138] stone, and other things of the sort. *"Let one who sees this either clearly or through a mirror in an enigma,"*[402] as Augustine says at the end of book six of *On the Trinity, "rejoice knowing God, honor him, and give thanks. But let one who does not see tend through piety toward seeing, not through blindness toward slandering, because God is one, although the Trinity, and one must not*

---

400 Augustine of Hippo, *On the Trinity* 6, 10, 13; PL 42: 932; ed. W. Mountain and F. Glorie, pp. 242–243.

401 See above par. 25 and 26.

402 See 1 Cor 13:12.

understand confusedly him from whom are all things, through whom are all things, and in whom are all things"[403]

43. To the eleventh argument that *"if a person were in a person* through the essence, <a person> would *not be in it otherwise than the essence* <is>,*"*[404] and so on, it must be said that it is true if one person were whole in another through the substance alone and as it is a substance without qualification. For then a person would be only the substance. Or if <a person> were not whole in it, then it would only be in it quasi accidentally and quasi in terms of a part, just as if two bodies were joined under one head, one of them that would have the common head would be in the other in terms of a part and not in terms of the whole, and for this reason because it would be in the other in that way, it would not denominate the whole in which it was, but only that part by which it was in it would. But now because a person is not in a person through the substance alone, although it is firstly and through itself in it through that, but is also in it through a property, although as a consequence, as was said, and through this not through the substance, as it is only a substance without qualification, but specifically as it is under the property of that in which it is. And this is another character with regard to substance than is the character of substance as it belongs to that in which <a person> is. For the Son is only in the Father through substance as that which is under the character or property of "begotten," which, in the Father as the form denominating him, is only in the Father under the character of "unbegotten." For the Father is not wise [139] by begotten wisdom, but by unbegotten wisdom, as was established above.[405] And although substance considered without qualification, as it is considered without qualification, is the primary reason why a person is in a person because it is in them in common as a form denominating them in common, nonetheless, because as such it is not the proximate and complete reason for this, but <is so> only insofar as it is under the character of the property of the person that is in it, and in accord with this character it is not present as a denominating form in the person in which the other <person> is, but only as subsisting in it insofar as it is something belonging to that which subsists in it, as was said.

44. Hence, one person is not in another in another way than the substance is in it, through which it is in it insofar as it is the proximate reason of its being "being in," although it is in it otherwise insofar as it is its first reason. And there can be an evident example of this if we hold that, where Christ now sits bodily at the right hand of the Father, he bodily encloses in his hand a consecrated host. For given this, it is true to say that in the hand of Christ there is the whole

---

403   Augustine of Hippo, *On the Trinity* 6, 10; PL 42: 932; ed. W. Mountain and F. Glorie, p. 243. See Rom 11:36 and 1 Cor 8:6.

404   See above par. 11

405   See *SQO* art. 38, qu. 2 ad 1um; ed. G. Wilson, pp. 166–167.

host in terms of the sacrament and the reality of the sacrament, and the other way around the whole hand of Christ is in the host that is the sacrament so that the dimensions of the hand of Christ in accompanying the sacrament, which is by the power of transubstantiation under the dimensions of the host, are under the dimensions of the host. And it is clear the other way around that the dimensions of the host are under the dimension of the hand of Christ. You see that the substance of the hand of Christ is under the dimensions of the hand firstly in a certain way, as the deity is in the Father under the form of paternity in the Father, and through transubstantiation it is under the dimensions of the host in a certain way, just as through generation the deity is in the Son under the property of filiation and concomitantly through the substance of the hand the dimensions of the hand are under the dimensions of the host in a certain way, just as the paternal property is [140] through the deity in the Son, and the other way around, although not as the dimensions are under the dimensions of the hand, because they are not there through concomitance, as the property of filiation is in the Father. On this account it is not surprising if "the whole *Father is in the whole Son because the Son is from him,* and the other way around because he is from him," as Hilary says,[406] when we see that the whole hand of Christ is under the dimensions of the host through the act of transubstantiation and the other way around the whole dimension of the host with the substance of the hand and its dimensions existing under the host <is> whole under the hand of Christ through the act of grasping it so that through this the whole hand of Christ according to substance and dimensions of the host that it contains also contains the whole of it. Thus no problem is seen if the whole Father containing the whole Son in whom the whole Father is contained contains the whole of himself in the Son that he contains. But it can be more easily answered by means of reason in replying that it is not always necessary that a being in another is in it through something in the way in which that is, because a whole is quite well accidentally through its part in something in which the part is though itself.

45. To the twelfth argument that, "when many things exist in the same thing, *one of them* is not said to be *in another* through that; therefore, they are also not said to be in one another through one thing that exists in many,"[407] it must be said that many things existing in the same thing are not already in one another through that, because that one thing does not belong essentially to both. If nonetheless it did not belong to the essence of both through that one thing, those in which it is[408] would in some way be in one another, as was said about

---

406　See Hilary of Poitiers, *On the Trinity* 3, 4; ed. P. Smulders, p. 75; PL 10: 78A and above par. 15.

407　See above par. 12.

408　I have followed the Badius text in adding "is, *est.*"

bodies joined to one head.[409] And <it is> that way in the present question. Because the one thing that is in the diverse persons is something belonging to both, they are necessarily in each other through that and also in terms of the whole through the concomitance of properties, as was said.

[141] 46. To the thirteenth argument: "what *in God is in another and is not the same as him produces a composition*,"[410] it must be said that "to be in" is used equivocally. For if what is in another foundationally or radically and not subsistently is not the same as it, it produces a composition, as is clear concerning a property and the substance, and this is the case because they are not distinguished relatively from one another. On this account, if they were not the same thing, it would be necessary that this produce a real diversity absolutely, not only by reason, and such a diversity would necessarily put a real composition there. But what is in another subsistently, because it is in another as remaining distinct, as was said according to Hilary,[411] something of the sort is quite well in another and still not the same on account of the relative distinction. And this is the case without any composition because the diversity of relative properties in the same substance does not produce a composition. Hence, <it does> not in those that subsist in it.

47. To the fourteenth argument that "*whatever is in God is God; therefore, whatever is in the Father is the Father*,"[412] it must be said that it is not the same, because "God" is a name of the essence, although it stands for a person. And hence, because nothing in God differs from the divine essence except by reason alone, whether it is essential or personal, for this reason whatever is in God is God, just as whatever is in a being is being. Thus, as being cannot be a genus in relation to diverse beings differing in species, so God cannot be a genus in relation to diverse persons that are distinguished by diverse relations quasi according to species. For in creatures paternity is a relation of supposition and filiation is a relation of supposition, and the former is founded on an active potency, while the latter is on a passive potency. But "Father" both signifies a person and stands for a person. And hence, because one person differs from another in God more than by reason alone [142] and can be in him according to the way already determined, for this reason whatever is in the Father is not the Father, although whatever is in God is God.

48. To the fifteenth argument that "the divine persons are not in one another in the same way since *the Father is in the Son, because the Son is from him*, and *the Son is in the Father*, because he is from the Father, which are completely diverse

---

409   See above par. 43.

410   See above par. 13.

411   See above par. 27.

412   See above par. 14.

ways,"[413] it must be said according to what has already been said that this is not the whole reason for the divine persons' being in one another. On this account Hilary firstly said there: "*One is in another because there is not something else in the two.*"[414] For there is not something else in the other, but one and the same singular substance. And this is the initial reason why one whole person is in another whole person. On this account, although in creatures a son is from a father, the father is not nonetheless in the son because the substance is diverse in the two. Hence, if there were many gods diverse according to substance, in that case one would in no way be the other, according to Damascene in the first book of the *Sentences*, chapter five,[415] and thus one would not be in another. The additional cause or reason for that is that one is from another, and if it were not, the one would not be in the other, but would be entirely the same thing, as was said,[416] because they would not be distinguished by relative properties unless—through what is impossible—there were held to be in the same singular substance of the deity many who were unbegotten, of which one is not from the other. For then one would necessarily be whole in the other because it would be subsistently in the simple substance, and the substance could be in none without any property founded on it being in it, as was said.[417] Hence, on the supposition that many could not subsist in the same singular simple substance distinguished by properties unless [143] one were from the other, Hilary said in implying all this: "*The Father is in the Son because the Son is from him,*"[418] that is, because he is in him through the property by which the Son has being from him. And the other way around, the Son is in the Father because the Son is from him, that is, because he is in him through the property by which he is from him. In that way insofar as it is from the side of the substance, they are in one another through the same thing, but insofar as it is from the side of the properties, they are not in one another through the same thing, and on this account they are in one another as one subsisting in one subsisting.

49. And the otherness of the relative properties, in accord with which they are in one another, does not prevent the uniformity of "being in," because both are "in" through the same thing, that is, through the common essence, as was said, through which filiation by which the Son subsists in the Father is in the Father, who subsists and contains in himself the Son and filiation in the Son, that is, as it is founded in the essence. And similarly, paternity by which the Father subsists in the Son is in the Son subsisting and containing the Father in

---

413   See above par. 15.

414   See above par. 27.

415   See John Damascene, *On the Orthodox Faith* 1, 5, 3; ed. E. Buytaert, p. 23.

416   See above par. 40.

417   See above par. 20–21 and 26–27.

418   Hilary of Poitiers, *On the Trinity* 3, 4; PL 10: 78A; ed. P. Smulders, p. 75.

himself and paternity in him, because it is founded on the same divine essence in accord with the way already determined. And it does not prevent this uniformity that the Father has the essence of the deity in another way, since <he has it> from himself, not from another, but the Son has it only from another, as from the Father. For the character of "to have from" is other than that of "to be in." For although the Son does not have life from himself, as the Father has it, but <has it> from the Father, still, "*as the Father has life from himself, so the Son has life in himself, although the Father gave this to him,*" as John five says.[419] For the Son formally lives through himself, although not from himself as from a principle. And thus although the Father is in the Son and the Son is in the Father through another property and the common substance is had in one way in the Father and in another way in the Son so that for this reason Hilary says: "*The Father is in the Son because the Son is from him,* [144] *and Son is in the Father because he is from the Father,*"[420] still the Father has being in the Son and the Son in the Father uniformly and in one and the same way. And as a consequence, the individual persons are in the individual persons, and all are in the individual <persons>, and the individual <persons> are in all, in accord with the way explained.

50. The argument and the authorities introduced to the contrary[421] are to be granted, and from what has been said it is clear how the argument includes the truth of the authorities and how the truth of the authorities is to be understood.

---

419   See Jn 5:26.

420   Hilary of Poitiers, *On the Trinity* 3, 4; PL 10: 78A; ed. P. Smulders, p. 75.

421   See above par. 16.

ARTICLE FIFTY-FOUR

On the Manner of One Divine Person's Emanating from Another

1. There follows <an article> on the manner of one person's emanating from another. And concerning this ten questions are asked, of which the first is whether it is necessary to hold a person in God that does not emanate from another. The second is whether the person that does not emanate from another is only one. The third is whether in God another person emanates from that person that does not emanate from another. The fourth is whether more other persons than one emanate from that person in God that is not from another. The fifth is whether the two persons that emanate from that one that is not from another emanate from it equally firstly, principally, and immediately. The sixth is whether one of the persons emanating from the one that is not from another emanates from the other. The seventh is whether the person that emanates in common from that one which is not from another and from that one which is from another, as the Holy Spirit does from the Father and from the Son, emanates from them equally firstly, principally, and in the same way. The eighth is whether from each of the three persons mentioned another emanates. The ninth is whether the notional acts of generating and spirating are certain instances of understanding and willing or certain acts of understanding and willing. The tenth is whether the emanations of the notional acts of generating and spirating are founded upon the essential acts of understanding and willing as if presupposing them.

[146]   QUESTION ONE

Whether It Is Necessary to Hold a Person in God That Does Not Emanate from Another

1. With regard to the first question it is argued that in God it is not necessary to hold a person that is not from another, in the first place as follows: A person that does not have being from another, neither with regard to being nor with regard to being a person, exists and subsists by itself alone. But one that exists and subsists by itself alone also exists and subsists absolutely because, as alone, it excludes all help from another. Therefore, and so on.

2. <It is argued> in second place as follows: That which is necessary being is only one. What is not from another is necessary being. Therefore, what is not from another is only one. Therefore, if in God there is a person that is not from another, there is only one person in God. But this is false; therefore, that from which it follows is also, namely, that there is in God a person that is not from another.

3. <It is argued> to the contrary that if in God there is not a person that is not from another, there would not be a person in God at all, because there would not a person in which there is an origin, but one would always be from another that precedes it to infinity. And if there were not a first, there would not be any of those that come after, according to the Philosopher in book two of the *Metaphysics*.[1]

[147]   <The Resolution of the Question>

4. To this it must be said in accord with the statement of Richard in book five of *On the Trinity*, chapter three, in the beginning "that what was *said above concerning the being of God* with regard to the divine *substance*, that is, that it is necessary to hold in the order of the universe of things that some substance, which is God, is from itself and not from another, ought similarly *to be said* concerning the being of God with regard to a divine *person*, that is, that in the order of the divine persons it is necessary to hold some person *that has being from itself and not from another.*"[2] "For," as he says in the same place, "*if this person were from that one and that one from another and so on with the others, the production of such a concatenation would without a doubt go on to infinity.*"[3] Understand: unless we

---

1   See Aristotle, *Metaphysics* 2.2.994a1–b6; anon. trans., ed. G. Vuillemin-Diem, pp. 37–38.

2   Richard of Saint Victor, *On the Trinity* 5, 3; PL 196: 950B; ed. J. Ribaillier, p. 197.

3   Ibid.

hold a circle in the emanation. But then it would follow that the same person would emanate from itself, which is absurd. As Anselm says: "*The intellect does not grasp, nor does nature permit that the one who is from another is the one from whom he is.*"[4] Therefore, lest we extend the number of the divine persons to infinity, it is undoubtedly necessary that we grant that some person exists from himself and does not take his origin from elsewhere.

5. But the argument that Richard sets forth in book one, chapter six up to chapter twelve, concerning the divine substance precedes this deduction if one applies it to the persons as follows: "*Universally all being is distinguished by a threefold distinction. For it will be from eternity and from itself, or the other way around, neither from eternity nor from itself. Or there will be between these two something from eternity that is not nonetheless from itself. For nature does not in any way allow that the fourth exists, which seems to correspond as contrary to this third member.* [148] *For nothing can be from itself that is not from eternity. For as long as it was nothing, it could do absolutely nothing, and it gave being neither to itself nor to another.*"[5] "*But from that which is not from itself, whether from eternity or not from eternity there is inferred by reasoning that there is that which is from itself and for that reason also from eternity. For if nothing were from itself, there would be absolutely nothing from which those things could exist that do not have their being from themselves,*"[6] either from eternity or not from eternity. "*And then there will be no origin,*"[7] and it would go on to infinity, as has already been said.[8] And the last argument proceeded in accord with this.

6. And in this way there can be adduced for the determination of this question almost all the arguments adduced above to prove that there is some substance that is God and subsists as first in the order of the universe,[9] that necessarily has being from itself and not from another, and that is the origin of everything else in itself and from itself, first of all containing and quasi encompassing everything that pertains to the absolute being of the deity, and similarly that which pertains to the character of its personality. And from it all other things, whether they are the divine persons or creatures, have whatever they have in themselves, as was established above[10] and will now be more fully established

---

4   Anselm, *On the Procession of the Holy Spirit* 1; PL 158: 289C; ed. F. Schmidt, 2, p. 182.

5   Richard of Saint Victor, *On the Trinity* 1, 6–12; PL 196: 893D–894A; ed. J. Ribaillier, pp. 91–97.

6   Ibid. 1, 7; PL 196: 894C–D; ed. J. Ribaillier, p. 93.

7   Ibid. 1, 11, p. 96; PL 196: 896C; ed. J. Ribaillier.

8   See above par. 4.

9   See *SQO* art. 21, qu. 3; ed. Badius 1, fol. 125rA–126vI.

10   See above *SQO* art. 53, qu. 10, par. 4.

below.[11] And this is that person that is said to be unbegotten and innascible in God.

\<Replies to the Arguments\>

7. To that, therefore, which is argued in the first place to the contrary that *"a person that does not have being from another exists and subsists by itself alone,"*[12] it must be said that it is true formally, although not efficiently—or that I may speak more properly, although not in the usual way—as [149] productively. For productively a person that is not "from" has being productively neither from himself nor from another, as the divine essence does not, in accord with which this was explained above with regard to the being of God concerning the divine essence,[13] and the same explanations can be applied here to a divine person, as is clear to one who looks. And when it is taken up into the argument that what *"exists and subsists by itself subsists absolutely,"*[14] it must be said that it is not true because something can exist and subsist by itself formally so that it is not from another as from a principle in two ways: in one way because, as it has being and subsisting from no other, so in an essential and natural order it does not have being and subsisting in relation to another. And what is such truly has being and subsisting only absolutely. But in God only the divine essence and what pertains to it has being essentially in that way. Also nothing at all in God has subsisting in that way, as was established above.[15] But \<it is not from another as from a principle\> in another way because, although it has being and subsisting from no other, it still only exists and subsists in an order to another, and that which is such has being and subsisting only relatively. And in this way a person in God that does not have being from another, although \<it has it\> from itself alone, as was said, has being and subsisting personally. This nonetheless belongs to it only in an order to another that has being and subsisting from it, as will now be explained below.[16]

8. To the second argument that *"that which is necessary being is only one,"*[17] and so on, it must be said that this has to be distinguished. For this \<proposition\> *"that which is necessary being is only one"* can be taken essentially or personally from the side of that which is only one. For whether "that which" is taken essentially or personally, if "only one" is taken essentially, it is true in this sense, namely, that, whether [150] it is the essence or a person, that to which

---

11 See below *SQO* art. 54, qu. 3.

12 See above par. 1.

13 See above *SQO* art. 21, qu. 3; ed. Badius 1, fol. 125rA–126vI.

14 See above par. 1.

15 See above art. 53, qu. 10, par. 9.

16 See below qu. 3, par. 32.

17 See above par. 2.

necessary being belongs is only one in the divine essence. But if "only one" is taken personally, it is false in this sense, namely, that to which necessary being belongs, whether it is the essence or a person, is something one in person.

9. And what the argument assumes, namely, that what "*is not from another is necessary being*" is true universally concerning that which is not from another efficiently and only something of the sort. For nothing made or created by another is necessary being. But not only that which is not from another as from a principle is necessary being, as the unbegotten person or the divine essence is, but also that which is from another personally, as the person of the Son and <the person> of the Holy Spirit are. Therefore, when it is concluded: "*Therefore, that what is not from another is only one,*"[18] it is true essentially because there is only one God. But if "only one" is taken personally, it has a twofold reason for its truth because it is either only one in its personality, and in that way it is true if one takes "not from another" as from a principle. For in God there is only one person that is not from another, as will be explained in the following question.[19] Or it is only one in personality without qualification, and in that way it is false, whether "not from another" is taken as from a principle or as an effect, because it holds that there is only one person in God, as the further false conclusion proceeds from false <premises>. For insofar as the premises are true, it in no way follows, and especially not from that <premise> that in God there is a person that is not from another, but rather from that major <premise> that "*what is necessary being is only one,*"[20] if one takes "only one" personally in its false sense and from that first conclusion: "*Therefore, what is not from another is only one*"[21] if one takes "only one" for one in personality without qualification, as is clear for anyone who looks.

---

18 See above par. 2.

19 See below qu. 2, par. 5–6.

20 See above par. 2.

21 See above par. 2.

[151]   **QUESTION TWO**

Whether the Person That Does Not Emanate from Another in God
Is Only One

1. With regard to the second question it is argued that in God the person that does not emanate from another is not only one in the first place as follows: As every production requires a terminus toward which it is produced, so it requires a terminus from which it is produced. Therefore, just as diverse productions require diverse terminuses toward which, as generation and spiration in God require diverse persons that have being from another, namely, the Son and the Holy Spirit, they therefore similarly require two terminuses from which. Just as there is one innascible person that has being from no one and from whom there is the act of generating, so there is likewise another person that has being from no one, from whom there is the act of spirating. And in that way there are at least two persons in God that are not from another.

2. <It is argued> in the second place as follows that in God there is not only one person that is not from another, but that there are many. What is a mark of the dignity and perfection of the divine nature must be held to be in God, but it is not a mark of less dignity and perfection in God that a person is not from another than that it is from another. In fact, <it is> rather a mark of greater dignity and perfection, as will now be seen below.[22] Therefore, that which has more dignity and perfection ought rather to be held to be in God. It is therefore necessary to hold in God many persons that are from another; it is similarly necessary to hold many persons that are not from another, and in that way many innascibilities.

[152] 3. <It is argued> to the contrary: If there were in God many persons not from another, since each person that is not from another is innascible, there would then be many innascibles in God and similarly many innascibilities. Hence, since they would have only one character and would agree in species, but differ only in number, and since the divine essence is one singular nature, there would therefore be in the one singular nature many properties of the same character and species. But this is impossible, whether they are absolute or relative, as is seen in creatures. Therefore, and so on.

4. Likewise, the person in God that is not from another is the first principle of all the others; therefore, there would be two first principles if there were two persons not from another in God. The consequent is false and impossible in

---

22 See below par. 8.

accord with what was determined above concerning the unity of God.[23] Therefore, and so on.

<The Resolution of the Question>

5. It must be said to this that not to be from another in God, according to Richard in book five of *On the Trinity*, chapter three, "*is incommunicable and cannot belong to many.*"[24] And Richard proves this in the same book, chapter four, from the character of the power of being a principle of other things than itself: "Because something of the sort is powerful through its essence, *not through participation, it has the fulness* of this power. Hence, it has in itself *all power*. Hence, *all power is* also *from it* and every other being and every other person, and thus it is necessary that it *alone* be such."[25] Another reason for this is [153] assigned in *Quodlibet* Six from the nature of relation that makes the persons many in God.[26]

6. Hence, just as in accord with what was determined above concerning the oneness of God,[27] it must be held that there is not more than one God in the universe, it must similarly be held here that it is not possible to hold in God more than one person that is not from another. And almost the same arguments by which it was explained there that it is not possible to hold many gods can be here adduced to prove that it is not possible to hold in God many persons that are not from another, such as many who are innascible. For if there were many, they would necessarily have many innascibilities, which are necessarily in different substances of the deity. On this account Hilary excellently states in the book, *On the Synods*: "He who confesses in God two who are innascible confesses two gods. For the nature of the one innascible God requires that God be proclaimed as one."[28]

<Replies to the Arguments>

7. To the first argument to the contrary that, "*as every production requires a terminus toward which, so <it> also <requires> a terminus from which,*"[29] this is true because, as it cannot be without one of them, it also cannot be without the other. Still by the form of the argument it does not further follow that "*as it requires* more and *diverse terminuses toward which,* so it requires more and di-

---

23 See *SQO* art. 25, qu. 2; ed. Badius 1, fol. 148vL–150rR.

24 Richard of Saint Victor, *On the Trinity* 5, 5; PL 196: 952A; ed. J. Ribaillier, p. 199.

25 Ibid. 5, 4; PL 196: 951D–952A.

26 See *Quodlibet* 6, qu. 1; ed. G. Wilson, pp. 2–31.

27 See *SQO* art. 25, qu. 2; ed. Badius 1, fol. 148vL–152rZ.

28 Hilary of Poitiers, *On the Synods* 59–60; PL 10: 521A.

29 See above par. 1.

verse terminuses from which."[30] Rather there is the fallacy of the figure of speech in changing "what" into "who." And it also does not follow from the character of the matter because a greater distinction is required in things derived from a principle than in the principle from which they are derived. For every multitude is able to be produced from unity and to be reduced to it, as was established above concerning the unity of God.[31] Hence, although there are many persons toward which the diverse emanations terminate, as will now be seen below,[32] there can [154] still be one person from which there are many manners of being a principle, as will now be seen.[33]

8. To the second argument that "there being *more* persons in God *that are from another pertains to the dignity and perfection of the divine nature*,"[34] is quite true, as will now be seen, and similarly it is quite true that "*is not a mark of less perfection in God that a person is not from another*."[35] Still it does not follow that it is a mark of more perfection in God that there are more persons not from another, as it is a mark of more perfection that there are many from another. Rather, the form of the argument is faulty in accord with the fallacy of the figure of speech by changing "of what sort" into "how many," as if it one argued as follows: "Just as it is in God a mark of perfection and dignity that a person is from another, so it is a mark of perfection and dignity in God that a person is not from another. Therefore, as it is a mark of dignity and perfection that there are many from another, so it is a mark of dignity and perfection that there are many not from another." And that is not true, just as it would not be a mark of dignity and perfection in God that the divine substance can be multiplied into many gods. Rather, what is a mark of dignity and perfection on the side of the principle need not be a mark of dignity and perfection on the side of what is derived from a principle. Hence, although there is only one dignity and perfection in God, there is nonetheless one character of it as it is in the principle and another as it is in what is derived from the principle. For something is always able to be under the character of greater or equal unity in the principle than in what is derived from the principle.

---

30   Ibid.

31   See *SQO* art. 25, qu. 2; ed. Badius 1, fol. 148vL–152rZ.

32   See below qu. 3, par. 16.

33   See below qu. 3, par. 16.

34   See above par. 2.

35   Ibid.

[155] ## QUESTION THREE

Whether from That Person in God That Does Not Emanate from Another Some Other Emanates

1. With regard to the third question it is argued that in God another person does not emanate from that person that does not emanate from another, in the first place as follows: Necessary being, as was established above in the questions on the unity of God,[36] belongs only to one alone and cannot be multiplied. Hence, since there is nothing in God that is not necessary being, in God the character of necessary being is not therefore more on the side of the essence than on the side of the person. Since therefore it pertains to the character of the essence in God that it cannot be multiplied so that there emanates from it another divine essence, because it is in itself a certain necessary being, as was established above,[37] it similarly pertains to character of the person that is not from another in God, that the person that is not from another cannot be multiplied so that there emanates from it another divine person. Therefore, and so on.

2. <It is argued> in the second place as follows: As was said in the same place,[38] it is impossible that the same thing be necessary being from itself and from another. Hence, since in God there is not a person that is not necessary being from itself, because in that case it could be and not be from itself, there is not therefore in God a person that has being from another.

3. <It is argued> in the third place as follows: If another person emanates from the person that in God is not from another, since it is God and from it another does not emanate except through a production that remains within, because creatures emanate through a transeunt production outside, about which there is no discussion here, that person therefore that emanates from [156] another is either God or is not God. But it is not possible to hold either. Therefore, and so on. <It is> not <possible to hold> that it is not God because the divine production only produces something in the divine substance. But in the divine substance nothing can be produced but God. <It is> not <possible to hold> that it is God because then God would produce God; therefore, he would produce himself as God or a god other than himself. He does not produce himself as God, since Augustine says in book one of *On the Trinity*, chap-

---

36 See *SQO* art. 25, qu. 3; ed. Badius 1, fol. 152rA–157rZ.

37 See *SQO* art. 21, qu. 5 and art. 30, qu. 1; ed. Badius 1, fol. 129rC and 178rQ–vQ.

38 Ibid.

ter one: "*There is nothing that begets itself so that it is.*"[39] And for the same reason it also does not produce itself by some other action so that it is. Similarly, he does not produce a god other than himself because in that way there would not be only one God, which is false accord to what was determined above.[40]

4. Likewise, "*if God produces God, he therefore either produces God who is God the Father or who is not God the Father. If* in the second way, *then* he *who is produced is God who is not God the Father. Therefore, there is not*, as before, *only one God. If* in the first way, then he produces *himself*, which is impossible."[41] Therefore, and so on.

5. Likewise, if the person that does not emanate from another produces God, this is either because he is God or because he is innascible and not produced by another. <It is> not because he is God. For since God, as was said, produces only God, that God produced would for the same reason produce God, and that one produced would similarly, and there would be infinite divine persons. <It is> not because he is innascible, because then he would produce one who is innascible, since the divine production is most perfect, and it is characteristic of such perfection to produce only what is most like itself.

6. Likewise, in God something true is necessary because there is nothing contingent in God. If then this <proposition> is true, "God begets God," it is necessary. Therefore, the negative <proposition> corresponding to it is impossible: "God does not beget [157] God." But this is false because, as that <proposition>, "God begets God," is true for the person of the Father alone, and this <proposition>, "God does not beget God," <is true> for the person of the Son and that of the Holy Spirit.

7. Likewise, if God produced God, then since to produce and to be produced imply distinguishing relations in God with regard to their terminuses, God would then be distinct from God. But this is false; therefore, and so on.

8. Likewise, if God produced God, <he did so> by free will or by nature or by necessity since there are not more ways of acting. <He did> not by nature or by necessity because, since God is the most powerful agent, he has perfect dominion over his action. But this belongs only to one who acts freely and voluntarily, not naturally or necessarily. Similarly, <he did> not by will because the action of producing a person cannot not exist in God, "*because in eternal things being and possibility do not differ.*"[42] Such an action is necessary with the

---

39   Augustine of Hippo, *On the Trinity* 1, 1; PL 42: 820; ed. W. J. Mountain and F. Glorie, p. 28.

40   See *SQO* art. 25; ed. Badius 1, fol. 147rA–157rZ.

41   Peter Lombard, *Sentences* 1, d. 4, c. 1; PL 192:533; ed. I. Brady, 1, p. 78; PL 192: 533.

42   Aristotle, *Physics* 3.4.203b30; trans. vet.; ed. F. Bossier and J. Brams, p 114.

necessity of nature; hence, it is not voluntary because will and nature are distinguished as contraries, as is established in book seven of the *Metaphysics*.[43]

9. Likewise, if God produces God, he produces him either from nothing or from his own substance or from some other substance. <He does> not <produce him> from nothing because then the production of a divine person would be creation, and the person produced would be a creature, not God. <He does> not <produce him> from his own substance because that from which something is generated is in potency in relation to it and goes forth into act through the agent. Since the divine substance that is the substance of the Father is pure form, it is pure act and is therefore in potency to nothing. Therefore, and so on. <He does> not <produce him> from another substance because then he would not be consubstantial with the Father.

[158] 10. Likewise, if God produces God, he produces him either always or not always because there is nothing in between always and not always. It cannot be said <that he does> not always <produce him> because in that way the production would not be eternal since it would have an end, and that is contrary to the character of an immanent divine production. If it is said that God always produces God, then <it is argued> as follows: That the action of producing does not cease is due only to the fact that something is not perfectly produced. This is absurd to hold in God. Therefore, and so on.

11. Likewise, if God produces God, <"God" stands> either for the essence or for a supposite. <It does> not <stand> for the essence because the essence is neither the principle of something by itself, nor is it derived from something else as from a principle, as we said above. <It does> not <stand> for a supposite because there is in God only a relative supposite, which according to the Philosopher in book five of the *Physics* cannot be a principle nor a terminus of an action.[44] Therefore, and so on.

12. <It is argued> in the third place to the principal argument as follows: "*The most noble act is only for the sake of itself, not for the sake of something else,*"[45] according to the Philosopher in books one and ten of the *Ethics*. The action of God that remains in him is most noble because it is with regard to the most noble object, which is the divine essence, whether in understanding or in willing or acting in any other way. Therefore, the divine action that remains within is for the sake of itself and is perfect in itself, not for the sake of something done or produced. But every action by which something is produced is for the sake of that which is produced. Therefore, and so on.

---

43 Aristotle, *Metaphysics* 7.7.1032a12–25; anon. trans., ed. G. Vuillemin-Diem, p. 132.

44 See Aristotle, *Physics* 5.1.225a11–12; trans. vet.; F. Bossier and J. Brams, p 194–195.

45 See Aristotle, *Ethics* 1.3.1097a30–35 and 10.5.1174b17–19; trans. Grosseteste; ed. R. A. Gauthier, pp. 382 and 470.

[159] 13. In the fourth place <it is argued> as follows: Emanation signifies a certain coming to be, whether a motion or an emergence, which absolutely cannot be in God; therefore, and so on.

14. In the fifth place <it is argued> as follows: If in God another person has to emanate from that person that does not have being from another, then it either emanates from it by proceeding from non-being into being or from being into being, and this either from the same being into the same being or from one being into another. <It is> not in the first way because then the person emanating from another in God would have begun to be since everything that proceeds from non-being into being begins to be. <It is> not in the second way because then there would be a change with regard to it. And <it is> not in the third way because then it would have being before it was produced in being, which is impossible. Therefore, and so on.

15. <It is argued> to the contrary that, if in God from a person that is from himself, another did not emanate, since that person could only be a single one, as has already been shown, there would then only a single person in God, and for this reason an absolute one, the contrary of which was shown above.[46]

<The Resolution of the Question>

16. This question only asks whether there is in God some emanation that is a divine action remaining within him, by which one person is able to proceed from another, if one takes procession in a broad sense, as it is common to generation and to spiration. And it must be said that the Catholic faith necessarily has to hold that there is, although it is difficult for it to grasp this mystery, and this <must be held> firstly by an argument taken from the character of a person. For a person in God that is from another is constituted in his personality only from a respect to another from which he is distinguished, and their otherness can be understood only in the character of the origin of one from another, in accord with what has already been determined.[47] But the origin of one from another can only be through the act of one emanating from another, not through an act [160] that passes to the outside, because this is proper to the emanation of a creature. It is therefore necessary to hold in God an act of emanation, and this an immanent act of one person emanating from another, and this must be from that person that does not emanate from another, so that the process does not go on to infinity, as was established above.[48] For if there is an act of emanation in God, that which interiorly emanates through it is necessarily a subsisting person because in the divine essence there can be nothing produced that inheres, and account of the perfection of the divine emanation it is necessary that it be most similar to that which produced it. For *"in accord*

46　See above art. 53, qu. 6, par. ??.

47　See above art. 53, qu. 8, par. 7 and qu. 9, par. 5.

48　See above qu. 1, par. 4.

with the diversity of natures it is necessary that there be a diversity of ways of emanating *in things,* and *to the extent that a nature is higher,* that which emanates in it is more perfect and more *intimate,* as is seen by proceeding from emanation in the lowest inanimate nature, for example, as fire emanates from fire, and up to the generation that is found in the highest beings."[49]

17. The argument taken from the character of the divine nature comes to the same thing because it is supremely active and for this reason supremely diffusive of itself. But supreme diffusion takes place only by sharing through an emanation its own nature with another in the diversity of a person. Hence, looking at emanation in creatures, Richard says in book one of *On the Trinity,* chapter nine: "*Will he who gave the fruitfulness of fecundity to this nature remain sterile in himself?*"[50] as if he would say: "Never!" For Isaiah says in the last chapter: "*Shall I who make others to give birth not give birth myself? Shall I who give generation to others be sterile? says the Lord God?*" Is 66:9).

\<Replies to the Arguments\>

18. To the first argument to the contrary that "necessary being *cannot be multiplied; hence, if the essence cannot be multiplied in God, a person* [161] *similarly cannot,*"[51] it must be said that it is true according to the same character of being, but it is not impossible according a diverse character of being. Hence, because the being of essence can have only one character just as the essence can, but the being of person, if one is speaking not of the being of essence or of existence, but of the being of subsistence, can have many characters. Therefore, although necessary being cannot be multiplied in God from the side of the essence so that there are held to be many gods, necessary being can nonetheless be multiplied from the side of the person so that many persons are held to be in God, not according to one character of person so that there would be many who are innascible or many who are born, but according to many personal characters.

19. To the second argument that "*in God there is not a person that is not necessary being* —and this *from itself; therefore, it does not have it from another,*"[52] it must be said in accord with what has already been said in the questions on the being of God[53] that the statement, "necessary being from itself cannot have necessary being from another," is only true of necessary being that is had by reason of the essence because being from another as from a principle is incompatible with the divine essence. For what has being from another by reason of the essence cannot be God, as was established above in accord with Avicenna in

---

49   Thomas Aquinas, *Summa against the Gentiles* 4, 11; ed. Leonine, 14, 80.

50   Richard of Saint Victor, *On the Trinity* 1, 9; PL 196: 895B; ed. J. Ribaillier, p. 94.

51   See above par. 1

52   See above par. 2.

53   See *SQO* art. 21, qu. 5; ed. Badius 1, fol. 123vB.

the questions on the unity of God.[54] Concerning necessary being that is had by
reason of the person, it is not true. For in that way the Son and the Holy Spirit
have necessary being from themselves formally, although from another [162] as
from a principle, as was explained above with regard to the being of God[55] and
will be explained more fully below.[56]

20. To the third argument that "*a person* produced by that one which is not
from another is either God or not God,"[57] it must be said that it is God. And in
that way it must be granted that that <proposition> is true: "God produces
God." For although the name "God" signifies only the essence without qualification, it still signifies it in the manner of a supposite in common, that is, as what
has the deity in itself, and therefore it stands for a supposite. And in accord
with this it can render the statement true for different supposites in a subject
and in a predicate, as when it is said "God produces God," because God the Father produces God the Son, as the Master explains in book one of the *Sentences*
in forming the question on generation.[58] But we set it forth more generally so
that we include under it both generation and spiration and treat this matter in
summary. Hence, if "God" only stood for the same thing as it signifies only the
same thing, it would be false as this proposition is false: "The essence generates
the essence," because it signifies and stands for only the same thing. And the
arguments of the Master proceed only upon this foundation in book one of the
Sentences, distinction five, in the first four chapters, by which he proves that the
essence neither generates nor is generated.[59] The reason for this is that "essence"
cannot have the character of a supposite either in signifying or in what it stands
for, and it also cannot be extended to the character of a supposite as "light" and
"wisdom" are extended, because from what they signify they maintain a diffusive character, but "substance" or "essence" does not. On this account one cannot
say: "essence from essence," as one can say: "light from light." And to what the
argument assumes, "Therefore, God produces *himself* as God or *a god other than
himself*,"[60] [163] the Master responds in book one of the *Sentences*, distinction
four, chapter one, when he says: "*Neither is to be granted*,"[61] because both are
false and neither follows from the first premise because there is not a division

---

54   See *SQO* art. 25, qu. 1; ed. Badius 1, fol. 147rB–148rE.

55   See *SQO* art. 21, qu. 5; ed. Badius 1, fol. 129rB–129vF.

56   See *SQO* art. 59, qu. 2; ed. Badius 2, fol. 139vA–142rI

57   See above par. 3.

58   See Peter Lombard, *Sentences* 1, d. 4, c. 3; PL 192:533–534; ed. I. Brady, 1, p.
     77–78.

59   See Peter Lombard, *Sentences* 1, d. 5, c. 1; PL 192: 535–540; ed. I. Brady, 1, p.
     192.

60   See above par. 3.

61   Peter Lombard, *Sentences* 1, d. 4, c. 2; PL 192:535; ed. I. Brady, 1, p. 80.

through what is immediate. For there is an intermediate proposition between them on account of which the first is true, namely, that he produces someone other than himself, who is God, yet not another god, but the same God as the one generating him. Hence, some[62] distinguish this proposition: "He produces *another God*," because "another" can be taken as an adjective, and then it is false, because "another" expresses diversity in general, which is determined by the substantive joined to it in denoting otherness in that which is signified by the substantive. And thus in the question at hand it denotes otherness in deity. Or <it can be taken> substantively, and then it is true, because then it allows one to understand a supposite in the place of the substantive and denotes otherness only in personality and falls within the sense that we call intermediate.

21. But this meaning is distorted violently when one makes a subdistinction after "other." Hence, it offers only a false meaning from the force of the language. Nor does the distinction hold for the present question, although it could hold in itself and in [164] another context, where it could offer both meanings without the subdistinction. For if it is argued in this way: "The God who generates is the God who is begotten; therefore, the God who generates is the same as the <God> who is begotten; therefore, by a similar argument the God who generates is not the God who is begotten; therefore, the God who generates is an other than the God who is begotten," because "other" can be taken substantively and denote otherness in person, and in that way this proposition is true: "One is the God who generates, and the other is the God who is begotten," and "other" has to be repeated in this second part of compound sentence, and it follows from the first <proposition>, because the negative part holds true for supposites. Or it can be taken adjectivally, so that its substantive—let it be "God"—denotes otherness in substance, and it is false, as is clear, and it does not follow from the first <proposition>. And in a similar way that conclusion could be distinguished: "The God who generates is the same as the God who is generated," and <it is> true and false in the opposite way, and it follows from the premises in one way, but not in the other.

22. Hence, because in the present question that distinction on the part of "other" does not hold, Praepositinus for this reason says that it expresses otherness both in substance and in person because otherness in substance is not without otherness in person. In that way the sense is: "He produced *another god*," that is, *other* in person and *a god with another deity*."[63] Hence, he established the rule that "*just as the relation* of identity relates through identity *what is signified and what is named*, and on account of this that <proposition> is *false*: 'He produced himself as God,'"[64] because the meaning is: He produced himself as God

62 Bonaventure, *Commentary on the Sentences* 1, d. 4, qu.2; ed. Quaracchi, p. 100A.

63 Praepositinus, *Summa against the Heretics* 4, 4; ed. J. Garwin, p. 217.

64 Ibid.; ed. J. Garwin, pp. 217–218.

in the same personality and in the same deity. As a result of this among the ancients a rule of this sort became traditional: "Complete *union has no place where there is distinction along with union.*"[65] Similarly "*a relation of diversity relates through diversity what is designated and what is named,*"[66] and it denotes [165] a difference in terms of both. On this account "that <proposition> is *false:* 'He produces a God other than himself,'"[67] as was said. But each of these is false in the opposite way for the other part of the compound sentence. The first is false on account of the identity in person that "himself" implies; the second on account of the otherness in substance that "other" implies.

23. On this account, by joining the parts for which the individual <propositions> hold true there is constituted from both the already mentioned third intermediate and true proposition that he produced someone other than himself in person, and this from the second part: "who is God," and this <other> from the first part. And in this way in God an intermediate proposition is to be accepted by reason of the subject matter on account of the identity of the substance in a plurality of persons. And it would not be necessary in another subject matter, as in creatures where a diversity of persons necessarily implies a diversity of substance. For example, if a man produces a man and it is asked whether it is "either himself as man or another man than himself," the latter part is without qualification to be granted: "another man than himself," because he produces another in person and in substance, and the contrary is to be denied at the same time on account of both. Hence, he neither produces himself according to the identity of person nor according to the identity of the substance.

24. On this account an intermediate proposition is not to be accepted in creatures as in God, in whom an intermediate proposition would not have to be accepted, if the division were made through contradictories in asking whether "he either produced himself as God or not himself as God," and it is to be granted: "not himself as God" on account of the diversity in person. Or in asking whether "he, therefore, produced a God other than himself or a God not other than himself," this is to be granted: "Not a God other than himself," on account of the identity of substance. From this another rule of the ancients of this sort contrary to the one already mentioned has become traditional: "Complete *division has no place where there is not union from diverse causes.*"[68]

[166] 25. But Augustine expressed that intermediate proposition to be accepted in God when he said concerning the Father in the Letter to Maximinus: "*He begot*

---

65   Ibid.; ed. J. Garwin, p. 217.

66   Ibid.

67   Ibid.

68   Ibid.

from himself another himself,"⁶⁹ that is, as the Master explains in the first book
of the *Sentences*, distinction four, at the end: "*He begot another, that is, in person
who is what he is*,"⁷⁰ that is, in substance. For although the Father is someone
other than the Son, he is still not something other, but one <with him>, so that
the words that "he is what the other is" is explanatory of "itself (*se*)" so that it is
understood to be in the neuter gender and corresponding to the substance with
regard to the person of the Father in allowing it to be understood with regard to
the substance. Hence, that <proposition> is to be accepted: "The Father begot
someone other than himself," just as this one: "The Father begot him who is
what he himself is." For on account of the identity of the substance he is as if he
himself.

26. On this account that <proposition> that Augustine brings forth in book
fifteen of *On the Trinity* is to be accepted as proper: "*As if speaking himself, the
Father begot the Word*."⁷¹ And in accord with this way in book eight of the *Ethics*,
the Philosopher says on account of the conformity of love: "*A friend is another
self* to a friend."⁷² And the poet pretends that his beloved is he himself where
he says: "*May the gods bring it about without me lest he die as I*."⁷³ In those words
of Augustine,⁷⁴ therefore, the language is proper and true insofar as it is considered from the side of the reality, not insofar as it is considered from [167]
the side of the words. Because, as Simon of Tournai says, "other" is understood
there to be of the masculine gender and therefore personal, but "itself (*se*)" to be
of the neuter gender and therefore essential.⁷⁵ And in that way there is found
an impropriety from the side of the words, just as <there is> in the passage:
"*and to your seed who is Christ*" (Gal 3:16), because the relative pronoun does
not agree with its antecedent in gender. But if we change this masculine "this,
hunc" into this neuter "that, *illud*" and say "The Father begot that which he is,"⁷⁶

---

69   More correctly, Augustine of Hippo, *Letter* 170, 5; PL 33:749; ed. A.
     Goldbacher, p. 625.

70   Peter Lombard, *Sentences* 1, d. 4, c. 2; PL 192:535; ed. I. Brady, 1, p. 80.

71   Augustine of Hippo, *On the Trinity* 15, 14; PL 42:1076; ed. W. Mountain and F.
     Glorie, p. 496.

72   Aristotle, *Ethics* 9.4.1166a30–32; tr. Grosseteste, ed. R. A. Gauthier, p. 594.

73   The editors have not found the source, but refer to Thomas Aquinas,
     Commentary on the Sentences 1, d. 4, qu. 2, art. 2; ed. P. Mandonnet, p. 141.

74   See above par. 25, that is, Augustine of Hippo, *Letter* 170, 5; PL 33:749; ed. A.
     Goldbacher, p. 625.

75   See Simon of Tournai, *Summa*; ed. M. Schmaus, p. 62.

76   Augustine of Hippo, *On the Trinity* 15, 14; PL 42:1076; ed. W. Mountain and F.
     Glorie, p. 496.

in accord with what Augustine says in the sermon on the Symbol,[77] properly speaking, the words are false, because it follows that he would have begotten the divine essence, in accord with which the Master argues in book one of the *Sentences*, distinction five, chapter three.[78] Hence, in order that it may have truth, it needs to be explained and expanded by changing the neuter into the masculine. In accord with this the Master explains when he says: "*The Father begot that which he himself is, that is, the Son who is that which he is. For the Son also is what the Father is, but the Son is not he who the Father is.*"[79]

27. But if we take the relative <pronoun> in the intermediate way that does not refer to the person and the substance at the same time as the pronoun "himself/itself (*se*)" does, but refers only to the substance as "that (*illud*)" does, because it is in the neuter gender, but which can indifferently refer to the one or the other, that <proposition> [168] can be quite correctly accepted. For in accord with what Ambrose says in the *Proslogion*: "*When we say: 'God from God,' we do not understand another God, but the same God from himself.*"[80] But if we change the neuter of the pronoun into the reality named by saying "*the essence from the essence* or *the substance from the substance*," in accord with what Augustine says in books seven and fifteen of *On the Trinity*[81] and as is established in chapter five,[82] properly speaking, the words are without qualification false and extended too far and need to be explained by doing violence to the words in accord with which the Master explains in chapter six: "*That is, the Son, who is the substance* or essence, from the Father, who is the substance or essence.*"[83]

28. And in this or a similar way, all the propositions and statements of the saints have to be explained that imply that the essence is generating or generated, in accord with which the authority of Hilary[84] adduced for this above in chapter five is explained in chapter eight.[85] And when it is taken up in the second subordinate <argument>:[86] "*Either then he produced God who is God*

---

77   See above par. 25, that is, Augustine of Hippo, *Letter* 170, 5; PL 33:749; ed. A. Goldbacher, p. 625.

78   See Peter Lombard, *Sentences* 1, d. 5, c. 1; PL 192:535; ed. I. Brady, 1, p. 81.

79   Ibid. 1, d. 5, c. 2; PL 192:536; ed. I. Brady, 1, p. 82.

80   Anselm of Canterbury, *On the Procession of the Holy Spirit* 14; PL 158:308; ed. F. Schmitt, 2, p. 213.

81   Augustine of Hippo, *On the Trinity* 7, 2 and 6; PL 42:936 and 945; ed. W. Mountain and F. Glorie, pp. 250 and 264 and 15, 20 and 15, 13; PL 42:1076 and 1088; ed. W. Mountain and F. Glorie, pp. 515 and 496.

82   See Peter Lombard, *Sentences* 1, d. 5, c. 1; PL 192: 536; ed. I. Brady, 1, p. 82,

83   Ibid. 1, d. 5, c. 2; PL 192:539; ed. I. Brady, 1, p.88.

84   See Hilary of Poitiers, *On the Trinity* 5, 37; PL 10:155; ed. P. Smulders, p.191.

85   See Peter Lombard, *Sentences* 1, d. 5, c. 1; PL 192:537; ed. I. Bardy, 1, p. 83.

86   See above par. 3.

the Father or who is not God the Father,"[87] the Master of the *Sentences* responds here in a confused manner in distinction four, chapter two. For he makes a difference in the dividing members by adding in the predicate "God" with "the Father" or not adding it when he says: "*God who is the Father* [169] *and who is not the Father*" and by saying: "*Who is God the Father and who is not God the Father*."[88] And he simply denies that affirmative part: "<He produced> God who is the Father," in making no mention at all of it: "<He produced> God who is God the Father," and he concedes that negative part: "<He produced> God who is not the Father," and distinguishes that part: "<He produced> God who is not God the Father." But Praepositinus says in his *Summa*: "*Neither* should be granted because both are false."[89] In their writings the Masters impose multiple distinctions on this.

29. In order that we may unpack the whole matter, it must be known that some[90] distinguish this negative clause: "God who is not God the Father" because "who" can simply refer to "God" by a simple reference to the form or essence or by a personal reference to the supposite. In the first way it is false; in the second way it is true. Just as if one says: "I see a man[91] who is not the most honorable of creatures," if the "who" refers to man by a simple reference to what is signified, it is false. But if it refers to a man by a personal reference, it is true, as is clear. And although at times it is necessary to put such a distinction in familiar or authoritative statements, if, for example, when a certain plant is pointed out in Rome, one says: "This plant grows in my garden," or if one says: "Woman who condemned us has saved us." Although they could not have the truth in a personal designation or reference, the mentioned distinction still does not have a place from the force of the words [170] because every designation and reference is personal from the force of the words, since the statement signifying what is designated or to which the reference is made stands for a supposite, and they are never essential unless the simple supposition is determined in the statement by something added to it, as: "This man is a species and is a universal." And this is clear from designation because a demonstrative pronoun designates only what is its subject, and a relative pronoun refers only to what is put before it and insofar as it is its subject and put before it, because of itself it signifies only a mere substance of which the signification is empty and useless unless it is determined by that which is the subject of the designation and which precedes the reference.

---

87 See above par. 3.

88 Peter Lombard, 1, d. 4, c. 1; PL 192: 537; ed. I. Brady, 1, p. 83.

89 Praepositinus, *Summa against the Heretics* 4, 4; ed. J. Garwin, p. 217.

90 That is, Peter Lombard.

91 The Latin lacks the article, although it seems necessary in a translation.

30. Because, therefore, in the present question, the accusative, "God," when one says: "*God produced God*,"[92] can of itself stand only for a supposite, for nothing but a supposite can determine a personal action, when there is added: "'*Who is not God the Father*,' the 'who' can only refer to him by a reference in this sense: "Who, that is, the God produced, is not God the Father."[93] And Simon of Tournai agrees with this in his *Summa*.[94] But then Master of the *Sentences* says that, when one says: "*Who is not God the Father*," with respect to this verb "is," "Father" can be the principal term in apposition, and this name "God" specifies it. In that way it is true in this sense: "He *who* is of course *God the Father* produced God *who is not God the Father*, and it is the first member of the distinction [171] that the Master holds and he forces it, or the other way around, and then it is false in this sense: "He *who is the Father* produced God *who is not God*." But in the truth of the matter this distinction can have no place here. For since according to the Philosopher, "*words must be sought in accord with the matter*,"[95] and according to Hilary, "*Reality ought not to be subject to words, but words to reality*."[96] Since therefore in the question at hand, neither the words nor the intention of speaking is about anything but divine realities, we ought for this reason to use terms here only as they are determined by the divine realities.

31. Hence, since in God "God" is like a common and general term, as was said above[97] and will be more fully said below,[98] but wherever there is an apposition of a general and a specific term, the specific one ought to be added to the general one, not the other way around, in saying "the animal man," not "man the animal," "so that *foolishness is not produced* in words,"[99] according to the Philosopher. Hence, another sense was entirely forced in the Master in order that he might prove that antecedent: "*God produces God*."[100] And because one must squarely face one's opponent, for this reason even by twisting the sense in order to satisfy the slander and objection of heretics, the Master distinguished that negative <proposition>, as was said, although he perhaps saw quite well that it ought not to be distinguished. But still in that sense in which "Father" is set in apposition to "God," some distinguish that in saying: "He *produced God who*

92   Peter Lombard, *Sentences* 1, 4, 1; ed. I. Brady, 1, p. 78; PL 192: 533. See above par. 4.

93   Ibid. See above par. 4.

94   Simon of Tournai, *Summa* 3; ed. M. Schmaus, p. 62.

95   Aristotle, *Ethics* 2.2.1104a3; trans. Guillemi, ed. R. A. Gauthier, p. 398,

96   Hilary of Poitiers, *On the Trinity* 4, 14; PL 10: 107C; ed. P. Smulders, p. 116.

97   See above art. 53, q. 7 and q. 8, par. 12.

98   See below par. 77.

99   Aristotle, *Rhetoric* 12.1414a24; trans. Guillelmi, ed. R. Schneider, p. 307.

100   Peter Lombard, *Sentences* 1, d. 4, c. 1; PL 192: 533; ed. I. Brady, 1, p. 78.

is not God the Father," it is necessarily understood between "God" and "Father" who is in this sense: "God who is not God who [172] is the Father," and then that <expression> "Who is the Father," can be held implicitly so that the whole <expression>: "'*God the Father*' is taken *linguistically* and *is a circumlocution for one person, just as* this one is said to be *the Holy Spirit,*" as Alexander said in his *Summa,* and in that way it is true, and it is the same to say: 'God who is not God the Father' as to say: 'God who is not the Father.' Hence, the Master implicitly touches upon this when he grants: 'He begot God.' Or it can be held relatively and as spoken, and in that way it is false in this sense: "<He begot> *God who is not the God who is God the Father,*" and it is the second member of the distinction that the Master holds, and heretics twist the sense by which they want to falsify the antecedent main premise.

32. But this distinction really does not hold because, just as in that preceding distinction, the first sense is forced. For by the power of the words, "Father" ought to be in apposition to "God," not the other way around, so in this distinction this second sense is forced because, although the "who" is understood on account of the appositive conclusion that the words presented, it still cannot be understood save implicitly, and thus with the removal of all distinction, it does not make any difference to say: "He produced God who is not God the Father," and to say: "He produced God who is not the Father." Hence, if in that <proposition>: "He produced God who is not God the Father," the heretics had not forced one false sense [173] to destroy that <proposition>: "God generates or produces God," the Master would not have distinguished that <proposition>: "God generates God who is not God the Father," by forcing another true sense to confirm that <proposition>: "God generates God" more than this one: "God generates God who is not the Father," but he would have absolutely granted that one: "God generates God who is not God the Father," and have absolutely denied the contrary affirmative one: "<He generates God> who is God the Father," just as he absolutely grants this one: "<He generates God> who is not the Father," and denies that one: "<He generates God> who is the Father." And in the truth of the matter, if the negative is to be distinguished, the affirmative is also, and this <is so> whether "God" is joined to "Father," or not. And the affirmative and negative propositions are true and false in the opposite way, as is clear if one looks at all the distinctions already given. And this <is so> because <in> the members of that division: "*If God produces God, he produces either God who is God the Father or God who is not God the Father,*"[101] the division is by members opposed as contradictories, because everything that is God is either God the Father or is not God the Father, and in contradictories general rule is: if one is said in many ways, the other is also.

---

101   Ibid. See above par. 4 and 30.

33. Hence, Praepositinus errs much when he says in his *Summa* against the Master that neither of them is to be granted, when he speaks in this way: *"The solution of the argument that is found in the* Sentences *is clear, namely, the Father begot God; therefore, he begot God who is the Father or God who is not the Father, neither is true. This one is false: 'God begot God who is the Father,' because this relative 'who' in the affirmative clause refers to the person of the Son whom this name 'God' stood for, and the Son is not the Father. And this one is false: 'God begot God who is not the Father,' because in the negative <clause> the reference refers to what is signified and named. Therefore, the sense is: He begot God who is not the Father, that is, he begot God the Son who is not the Father* [174] *and whose deity is not the Father."*[102] Hence, he also says that this is false: *"God who is not the Son generates,"* because the *"who"* refers to God, not only to the person of the Father, but also to his deity. But he says that this is true: *"God generates, and he is not generated,"* because neither the person of the Father nor the divine essence is generated. But he supposes something false in his response, namely, that the relative <pronoun> refers to something else in the negative <clause> than in the affirmative because then the negation would deny in another way than the affirmative affirms, and that is false. Hence, if the antecedent does not stand for the deity in both the affirmative and the negative propositions except as it is in the Son's supposite, the relative <pronoun> similarly refers to the deity in both only as it is in the person of the Son, and in that way the negation does not in that case absolutely deny something of the deity and does not in any way have the sense: *"The deity of the Son is not the Father,"* but only this sense: *"The Son is not the Father."* And Simon of Tournai grants this in his *Summa* when he says along with the Master of the *Sentences*[103] as follows: *"God the Father does not generate God who is the Father."*[104] For the accusative *"God"* stands there for the person of the Son, and *"who"* refers to it.

34. In returning to the first claim[105] we say simply and absolutely that God produced God who is not God the Father, that is, who is not the Father, as was explained.[106] And when it is further assumed: *"Therefore, he who is not God* [175] *the Father is God,"*[107] it is certainly true because the Son is he who is not God the Father. And when it is further concluded from this: *"Therefore, there is*

---

102   Praepositinus, *Summa against the Heretics* 4, 4; ed. J. Garwin, p. 217.

103   See Peter Lombard, *Sentences* 1, d. 4, c. 1; PL 192: 534; ed. I. Brady, 1, p.78.

104   See Simon of Tournai, *Summa* 3; ed. Schmaus, p. 61.

105   That is: He produced God who is not God the Father, namely, God the Son, who is certainly not God the Father. See Peter Lombard, *Sentences* 1, d. 4, c. 1; PL 192: 533; ed. I. Brady, 1, p. 78.

106   See above par. 4, 30, and 32.

107   See above par. 4, 30, and 32.

not only one God,"[108] the Master denies this by his words: "*Still he does not generate another God, nor is he who is begotten another God than the Father, but one God with the Father.*"[109] But he does not respond to the inference that is apparent, and he still does not hold it since the consequent is false and its antecedent is true, and according to the rule of the Philosopher, only what is true follows from what is true.[110] Hence, unless the slander and distortion of the heretics had caused this, as was said, where he said: "*But if it is added: 'he generates God who is not God the Father,'*" he ought not to have said: "*Here we distinguish,*"[111] and so on. Rather, he ought to have said: Here we say that it is the same to say: "He generates God who is not the Father," and "He generates God who is not God the Father." For this makes no difference, as was said.[112] And then to respond to the inference and to the form of the argument, he ought to have added: And when it is lastly concluded from this: "*Therefore, there is not only one God,*" we distinguish here because "*There is not only one God,*" can be understood in two ways. For that word "one" can be taken substantively and go with that verb "is," taken personally. In that way it is true in this sense: "Therefore, God is not only one," that is, God is not only one in person, but rather more in persons, [176] that is, God who is the Father and God who is not God the Father, but who is God the Son. And in that way it correctly follows: "*He is God who is not God the Father; therefore, one alone is not God.*"[113] Or the "one" can be taken adjectivally and essentially and determine that substantive "God" in the predicate with the "is" taken non-personally. And in that way it is false in the sense: "*Therefore, there is not only one God,*"[114] that is, there is not one God in essence, but many, so that one God is God in essence who is God the Father and another who is not God the Father, but God the Son, which is what the heretics want. And in that way it does not follow from the first premise because of the fallacy of accident, because "God," that is firstly put in the antecedent when it is said: "He who is not God the Father is God," is taken personally. For otherwise it would not be true, nor would it follow from that premise: "God generates God who is not God the Father." But in the conclusion when it is said: "*Therefore, there is not only one God,*"[115] it is taken essentially. Otherwise, the heretics would not have

---

108 See above par. 4.

109 Peter Lombard, *Sentences* 1, d. 4, c. 1; PL 192:534; ed. I. Brady, 1, p. 78.

110 See Aristotle, *Prior Analytics* 2.2.53b7–8; trans. Boethius; ed. L. Minio-Paluello, p. 94.

111 Peter Lombard, *Sentences* 1, d. 4, 1; PL 192: 534; ed. I. Brady, 1, p.78.

112 See above par. 31.

113 See above par. 4.

114 See above par. 4.

115 See above par. 4.

what they wanted, nor could there be concluded from this the opposite of the first antecedent that the heretics wanted, as is obvious to one who considers this.

35. To that which is assumed in the third subordinate <argument>: "*If God produces God, it is either because he is God or because he is innascible*,"[116] and so on, it must be said that <he does so> by reason of both, that is, by the character by which <he is> innascible God if one looks to the act of production without qualification by a person that in God is not from another, about which the discussion is at present—although in one way by the character by which <he is> God, because the deity elicits all the divine actions, as was established above,[117]—and in another way by the character by which <he is> innascible, because "innascible" stands for the property of the person who is not from another by which the deity is firstly determined for an act of emanation without qualification, as will be explained below.[118] On this account [177] God produces God by reason of the two. Therefore, not everyone in which the deity is present produces God because there is not innascibility in him. Still it does not follow that God who is produced is innascible, as the God who produces is, because the nature of perfect production is similarly such that from the character by which it is production, it does not permit the one producing and the one produced to be the same in person, whether in God or in creatures. But by the character by which there is perfect production in the divine nature, it does not permit the one produced to be completely other than and diverse in nature from the one producing, so that to the extent it is more perfect, it permits less otherness between them, and this <is the case> in creatures, and where it has infinite perfection, <it permits> none at all, as is the case in God alone. Hence, in creatures there is an identity of nature between the one generating and the one generated in something one and common in the same species, but in God there is identity in one singular in accord with the character of an individual. But that it does not permit them to be the same one is by reason of the property that determines the eliciting principle to act. But that it does not allow them to be other, either not completely or in no way, is by reason of the nature that elicits the act. But their distinction is founded upon that non-identity of the one producing and of the one produced, and their likeness is founded upon that identity. On this account it does not follow that, although like produces like in terms of nature, it generates something like in terms of property; rather production without qualification requires a contrary. And in that way the innascible God generates someone like in terms of deity because <he generates> God, but unlike and distinct in terms of innascibility because the innascible

---

116   See above par. 5.

117   See *SQO* art. 39, qu. 4; ed. G. Wilson, p. 196.

118   See *SQO* art. 57, qu. 3; ed. G. Wilson, pp. 196–202.

produces one who is born. And in this way Socrates generates a human being by his humanity because it is humanity without qualification, not because <he is> Socrates, but because <he is> man. But because he is this humanity, he generates a human being other than himself, and he does this because he is Socrates.

[178] 36. To that which is assumed in the fourth subordinate <argument>: "*If that is true for the Father: 'God generates God,' the other is true for the Son and the Holy Spirit: 'God does not generate God'''*[119]—and if we wanted to extend the intermediate argument: "If that <proposition> is true for the Father and for the Son: 'God produces God,' this one is similarly true for the Holy Spirit: 'God does not produce God,'" it must be said that since the truth of a proposition only has being from the force of the terms and in a term only two things are noted, namely, what it signifies and what it stands for, the understanding of this question depends upon what is signified and the supposition of this term "God." For although the truth of a proposition is principally caused by what is signified by a term, still insofar as it stands for what it signifies in diverse ways, either for what it signifies or for what it stands for, it has in accord with this to cause truth in the proposition in diverse ways.

37. It must firstly be known from the side of what is signified that every categorical statement universally signifies the same thing, namely, the reality and the nature that has being in the supposite, either as its quiddity and essence, as humanity has being in Socrates or as an accident of it, as whiteness in Socrates. Hence, this name "God" signifies only the deity that this name "deity" signifies, just as "white" signifies only whiteness, as this name "whiteness" also does. Thus this name "God," insofar as it is considered from the side of the reality signified, does not signify something other than is signified by this name "deity." But they differ only in the manner of signifying because "God" signifies in the manner of a supposite or of something subsisting, as Damascene says: "'God' signifies a nature as in one who has it, and 'deity'"[120] does in the manner of an absolute form,"[121] as "white" signifies the same thing as "whiteness," but "white" [179] does in the manner of something inhering, but "whiteness" in the manner of an absolute form. And although that name "God" signifies in the manner of a supposite, it still does not signify a divine supposite, neither one nor many, because "God" signifies only absolutely and in the manner of something absolute and something absolute. But there is no supposite in God that does not signify a respect and the manner of a respect, as is clear from what has already

---

119 See above par. 6.

120 John Damascene, *On the Orthodox Faith* 3, 6; PG 94: 1002C; ed. E. Buytaert, pp 186–187 and PG 3, 4; PL 94: 998A; ed. E. Buytaert, p. 186.

121 See Peter Lombard, *Sentences* 1, d. 19, c. 9; ed. I. Brady, 1, pp. 167–168..

been determined.[122] And through this there is a difference in what is signified and the manner of signifying from the name "person" because "person" signifies relatively and in the manner of something relative and only something relative, although indeterminately, as is similarly clear from what was determined above.[123] Therefore, <there is> also <a difference> because both stand for the three persons indefinitely, that is, in different ways because this name "person" stands for those three indifferently and not for something common save something intentional in relation to them, as is also clear from what was determined above.[124] However, although "God" stands for the same things, it still firstly and principally stands for what is signified and for the thing signified, which is something common to the three, so that with regard to this what is signified and what is named do not differ in this, but when it is joined to another term in discourse, it is by reason of what is joined to it at times understood for what is signified or for itself and at times for the relative supposite in which it has being. It stands for itself when one says: "God is communicable," and for a supposite when one says: "God generates." Thus, although it always firstly and principally stands for what it signifies and for it, insofar as it is considered by itself, still in rendering a statement true by reason of an addition that determines the understanding for it, it at times firstly and principally stands for one relative supposite or many, in accord with how the addition is able to belong to God principally by reason of the supposite and to itself without qualification by reason of [180] the supposite when one says: "God generates," and universally in the personal acts. But at times it is just the other way around as when one says: "God creates," and <it is> universally in that way in the essential acts, just as in creatures the previously mentioned essential predicates firstly belong to the higher ones and through them to the lower ones, but accidental predicates are just the opposite.

38. Hence, because that nature that "God" signifies and stands for is only one and singular, and there is no proposition in which some term is principally placed in which something is said to inhere or not to inhere, or in which it is said to inhere or not to inhere in something, unless it inheres or does not inhere according to what it principally signifies and stands for, either principally by reason of itself or principally by reason of what it stands for. There is therefore no proposition by which something is said to inhere or not to inhere in God or to belong or not to belong to him, or the other way around, in which "God" is denoted to inhere or not to inhere in something, or to belong or not to belong to it, unless that inheres or does not inhere, belongs or does not belong to God,

---

122   See *SQO* art. 28, qu. 5; ed. Badius 1, fol. 168vB–169rE and above art. 53, qu. 6.

123   See above art. 53, qu. 6.

124   See above art. 53, qu. 6.

or the other way around, by which "God" is said to inhere or not to inhere, to belong or not to belong, except by reason of that one and singular thing that it signifies and stands for, insofar as it is considered firstly and principally by itself. Therefore, if it is true that God creates or generates, this is only because this belongs to God without qualification and absolutely by reason of the singular deity, and although on account of the determination of the understanding that the name "God" makes with regard to this, this belongs to him only in one or more relative supposites. But if it is true "God does not create or does not generate," this is only because this does not belong to God without qualification and absolutely by reason of the singular deity, although this belongs to him insofar as it is in one or more relative supposites.

39. Hence, since something cannot belong and not belong at the same time to the singular deity as it is singular, and the other way around [181] it cannot at the same time belong and not belong to something, for this reason whenever an affirmative proposition is shown to be true in which this name "God" is placed, the negative cannot at the same time be shown to be true, nor the other way around even if it is shown to be true for some supposite. Hence, since this <proposition> is true: "God creates," this <proposition> cannot be true: "God does not create." If this <proposition> is true: "God generates," this <proposition> cannot be true: "God does not generate." If this <proposition> is true: "God is incarnate," this <proposition> is not true: "God is not incarnate." Nor is there some difference on this whether something belongs to God naturally and necessarily in some person, as "to generate" in the person of the Father or belongs to him naturally and necessarily in no person, provided that it nonetheless belongs to him in some person at least in some way, as "to be incarnate" in the person of the Son.

40. Hence, it is not necessary here principally to pay attention to the determination that the predicate can make with regard to the subject, although in this way Praepositinus determines this doubt in his *Summa*, where he holds another view than that we stated concerning the supposition of this name, "God." He speaks there as follows: "*One should note that wherever this* name, 'God,' *stands for the essence, it can stand for a person or persons, but this cannot be converted, because from an addition it can only stand for a person, as when I say: 'God generates.' There it stands only for the Father because the subjects are such as the predicates have permitted. It is the same way in a negative* <proposition>; *hence, this* <proposition> *is false: 'God does not generate.'*"[125] But it is evident that the contrary of his statement is true because in some cases it stands for the essence where it can in no way stand for a person, as when it is said: "God is communicable." But nowhere does it stands for a person without also standing there for the essence unless it is prevented from standing for a person only through what

125 Praepositinus, *Summa against the Heretics* 4, 3; ed. J. Garwin, p. 216.

it immediately implies, if one speaks as follows: "Someone who is God does not generate," for example, the Son or the Holy Spirit. For although because of [182] the addition it does not by what it implies stand only for a person firstly and principally in verifying the truth of the proposition for it, it still at the same time stands for the essence. For it is not true that the Father generates without its being true that God generates, but it stands without qualification for the one simple God, of whom it is true to say that he generates and is generated, spirates and is spirated, although the expression is verified in various ways for the diverse supposites firstly and principally. Hence, this argument does not follow: "Someone who is God does not generate; therefore, God does not generate," on account of the fallacy of the consequent as if by denying universally from the inferior to the superior, just as it does not follow: "Some man is not running; therefore, no man is running," because that <proposition>: "God does not generate" includes this one: "No one who is God generates." And the reason for this is that insofar as this term "God" stands for what it signifies, which is a singular reality, and in that way it has the character of a proper term and produces a singular proposition, although insofar as it is able to stand for relative supposites and as it is common to them by communication, not by multiplication, it in some way has the character of a term that names and in some way produces an indefinite proposition. And with regard to this it would correctly follow: "Someone who is God does not generate; therefore, God does not generate," just as it follows: "Some man or someone who is a man does not run; therefore, man does not run." But in the present question it changes the agreement because the same singular reality is signified by this name "God," because it stands for it uniformly in the negative proposition as in the affirmative one, although for diverse supposites.

41. However, by this name "man" the same universal reality is signified, and it can stand for diverse singular things in the negative <proposition> and in the affirmative one and for diverse supposites, and for this reason by standing for what is signified and for a supposite, this name "man" can stand for a different thing signified in the affirmative than in the negative, as <it can> also <stand> for a different supposite. But although this name "God" can stand for a different supposite, it still cannot stand for another reality signified. [183] Hence, since the proposition that is true for a supposite also requires truth for what is signified so that it is true without qualification, as was said, for this reason "That man is running" and "A man is not running" can both be true at the same time without qualification because <they are true> for what is signified and for a supposite at the same time. But these <propositions> cannot <both be true>: "God generates" <and> "God does not generate," because although they can both be true at the same time for a supposite, they still cannot both be true

for what is signified, as was said.[126] And in that way, by reason of the deity that cannot be multiplied, for which "God" stands and behaves in the manner of something subsisting, this proposition "God generates God" and this one: "God does not generate God," cannot be true at the same time; rather, they are contradictory, just as these two <propositions>: "Socrates is running" and "Socrates is not running." And the negation placed before and placed after makes no difference, so that if the negative <proposition> were true, this would be only because the predicate does not belong to God without qualification by reason of his deity, and in that way it would be necessary that it disagree with the deity in whatever supposite it would be found. Thus it would be false by reason of the essence and of any person, that is, that God did not generate by reason of the deity without qualification nor in some supposite by reason of the deity. For what disagrees with the deity signified without qualification disagrees with it in any person on account of its unity in the many persons contrary to that which is the case in creatures because the essence <of a creature> is multiplied in diverse persons. But if the affirmative proposition is true, this is because the predicate belongs to "God" without qualification by reason of his deity, and it is possible that at the same time it belongs to God as he is in some supposite, although it does not belong to him as he is in others.

42. To what is objected in the fifth place: "*If God would produce God, God would be distinguished,* because active and passive production imply [184] *distinguishing relations between the terms,*"[127] it must be said in accord with what has already been explained[128] that in any term it is possible to consider that which it signifies,[129] and that is only what it signifies, and it is possible to consider what it stands for, and this is only what it renders the statement true. But a term can stand for something else and render the statement true in two ways, either firstly and principally, or secondarily. In the first way this name "God" stands for what it signifies in the manner of a supposite. But in the second way in the question at hand, "God generates God," the name "God" in the subject firstly and principally stands for the relative supposite of the Father, and this name "God" in the predicate stands for the relative supposite of the Son. But in a third way it stands for the essence. Therefore, when it is said that "active and passive production imply *distinguishing relations* between *their terms,*"[130] it is true, but only between those for which the statement is firstly and principally proven true and insofar as it is proven true for them, not for that for which it proves the statement true secondarily and insofar as it is proved true for

---

126 See above in this par.

127 See above par. 7.

128 See above par. 36 and 40–41.

129 I have conjectured "*significat*" instead of "*supponit.*"

130 See above par. 7.

it. Hence, since, as was said,[131] on account of the determination of the act of producing, "God" <in the nominative> stands for the Father in rendering the statement true and "God" <in the accusative> firstly and principally stands for the Son, although secondarily for the essence, it therefore denotes a distinction for the persons, not for the essence. But when it is explained by saying: "*God is distinguished*,"[132] "God" firstly and primarily stands for the essence because "is distinguished" does not denote some person for itself determinately, and in such a statement it always stands for and denotes that the statement is shown to be true for the essence, as it is signified by this name "God" in the manner of a supposite, and even if it signified only in the manner of an action—if one is speaking in terms of grammar, [185] as this verb "to distinguish" signifies—but <signifies> a true action in the manner of an action, as this verb "create" signifies when one says "God creates." On this account it does not follow further that "it denotes a distinction between the terms, and therefore between God and God"[133] so that a distinction is held to be understood with regard to God by reason of the deity; rather, it would be the fallacy of a figure of speech because of the change of supposition. For "God" principally stands for the person of the Father or of the Son or of both at the same time when one says: "God produces God." And the other way around, <it stands> for the essence principally when one says: "God is distinguished."

43. As for what is further argued: "*If God produces God, he does so, therefore, by will or by nature or by necessity*,"[134] and so on, it must be known for the resolution of this that <the proposition> "God produces God by necessity, will, or nature" can be understood in two ways. For "by necessity," "by nature," and "by will" can be taken as nouns or as adverbs. If they are taken as nouns, they are in that way ablatives and express the way of originating the act of production in the one originating it. And in this way God does not produce God by necessity because necessity, which is the manner of producing other things by nature, is only an external principle, which is. called the necessity of coercion. And the heretics understood this concerning such a sort of necessity when they asked whether the Father begot the Son by necessity or whether both produced the Holy Spirit of necessity. On this Hilary says in *On the Synod*: "*If someone says that the Son is generated against the Father's will, let him be anathema. For the Father was not coerced against the Father's will, nor did he beget the Son compelled by natural necessity when he did not will to.*"[135] And Augustine says in question seven of *To*

---

131   See above par. 40

132   Ibid.

133   Ibid.

134   See above par. 8.

135   Hilary of Poitiers, *On the Synods* 58, 25; PL 10: 520C.

Orosius: "*Necessity is not present in God.*"[136] But if the three already mentioned are taken as adverbs so that they are the same as "necessarily," "voluntarily," and "naturally," they in that way express only [186] the manner of production. In that way, in every manner of production God produces God out of the necessity not of some need, in accord with which Hilary says in *On the Synods*, chapter forty: "*The Father did not beget the Son compelled by natural necessity,*"[137] and similarly the two of them did not produce the Holy Spirit by some necessity. And the heretics were also asking about such necessity. But since according to Anselm in book two of *On Free Choice*: "Necessity is of two sorts, namely, *one that precedes and is the cause that a thing exists and a subsequent necessity that a thing produces.*"[138] In both ways the necessity that expresses the manner of production is present in the divine production. But it is called "*preceding necessity from the cause that a thing exists,*"[139] because it is the manner of the act, since as it is the character and principle of the act, just as the heaven is said to be moved necessarily, because it is moved from the necessity of its form, and similarly fire heats of necessity, because it does so from the natural necessity of its hotness. But it is said to be "*a following necessity that the thing produces and that produces nothing,*"[140] because it is the manner of the act, not because it is the reason and principle of the act, but from the condition of the act. And this second can exist where the first does not, as when I say that you are speaking of necessity when you are speaking. For as Anselm says: "*When I say this, I mean that nothing can bring it about that when you are speaking, you are not speaking, not that someone is forcing you to speak.*"[141]

44. But where the first necessity is present, the second is necessarily present. And the first of these can be called the necessity of causality, but the second the necessity of existence. By the first necessity, according to the philosophers, the heaven is said to be moved of necessity because it has a necessary efficient cause of its motion. In the second way the heaven is said to be moved of necessity because it cannot be that there is not motion in the heaven and that someone speaking speaks of necessity [187] when he is speaking because it is not possible that someone is not speaking while he is speaking. In the first way God produces God of necessity, and this necessity is called by some "*the necessity of immutability,*"[142] and it is called by Anselm "*the necessity of immutability in pre-*

---

136   Pseudo-Augustine, *Dialogue of Questions with Orosius* 65, 7; PL 40: 736.

137   Hilary of Poitiers, *On the Synods* 58, 25; PL 10: 520C.

138   Rather, Anselm of Canterbury, *Why God Became Man* 2, 17; PL 158: 424A; ed. F. Schmitt 2, p. 125

139   Ibid.

140   Ibid.

141   Ibid.

142   Bonaventure, *Sentences* 1, d. 6, q. 1; ed. Quaracchi, p. 126.

serving constancy."[143] But insofar as "nature" and "will" are taken adverbially, they both concur in this way in every production of God from God because God naturally and voluntarily generates and similarly spirates God. For because God does nothing except as an intelligent and voluntary nature, whose nature suffers no violence or need, whose intellect does not err through ignorance, and whose will is not impeded by lack of power, and because those pertaining to the essential attributes that precede according to reason are in reality absolutely the same in God as the foundations and principles of the personal acts, it is impossible that in God nature does something that he does not know and understand by his intellect and does not will or consent to it by his will or that he does something by his will from his substance without nature concurring and intellect knowing.

45. But with regard to this there is less doubt in the production of the Holy Spirit from both, namely, that his production is by nature and intellect along with its being by the will, than <in the production> of the Son from the Father, that is, that his production is by the will along with its being by nature and intellect, because that of the Holy Spirit is by the manner of the will and that of the Son by the mode of nature and intellect, as will be seen below.[144] But nature and intellect could by reason be separated from the will and act without it because by a certain order of reason in God nature and intellect [188] precede the will, as has already been seen above and will be seen more fully below,[145] and not the other way around, as Augustine says in *To Orosius*: "*Will cannot precede wisdom.*"[146]

46. On this account authors more carefully affirm that the production of the Son is also by the will along with its being by nature and intellect. For on this point the heretics erred more, as is seen from the Master in the first book of the *Sentences* through the whole of distinction six.[147] On this Hilary says in *On the Synods*: "*The holy Church declares anathema those who say that the Father begot the Son neither with counsel nor by will.*"[148] And Richard says in book six of *On the Trinity*, chapter seventeen: "*For the one producing who is omnipotence itself it is the same to produce another from himself as to will the same from a most ordered cause, but to will from the cause that is more a principle is the same as to generate. For although both ways of proceeding lie in the will, they still differ in accord with the*

---

143   Anselm of Canterbury, *Why God Became Man* 2, 17; PL 158: 422C–D; ed. F. Schmitt 2, 123.

144   See below par. 47.

145   See *SQO* art. 48, qu. l; ed. M. Führer, pp. 37–40 and art. 58, qu. 2; ed. Badius 2, fol. 127rI–128vS.

146   Pseudo-Augustine, *Dialogue of Questions with Orosius* 65, 7; PL 40: 736

147   Peter Lombard, *Sentences* 1, d. 6; PL 192: 539–540; ed. I. Brady, 1, pp. 89–94.

148   Hilary of Poitiers, *On the Synods* 34, 13; PL 10: 507B–C.

difference of the cause. Hence, a more principal way of proceeding exists in the cause that is more a principle. Do you want to hear on this a shortened account? That the unbegotten wills to have someone conformed to himself seems to me to be the same as to beget the Son. For that the unbegotten and the begotten to will to have one loved by them in common seems to me the same as to produce the Holy Spirit."[149] And in chapter eighteen he says: *"It seems to me that for God the Father to beget the Son is the same as to produce a person from his own person naturally and by desire."*[150]

47. But one must note that although both, that is, nature and will, concur in the twofold production of God from God at the same time, they still do not do so in the same way, but in diverse ways insofar as [189] the eliciting principles of those productions differ. For in the principal production, which is generation, which is elicited from the principle that is nature, God produces God naturally firstly and principally, but voluntarily secondarily and consequently. In the second production, which is spiration, the other way around, the power eliciting the act is the will as a free potency, but a natural necessity is still impelling it to act. For in generation the power that elicits the act is intellect as a nature impelling it to act by an natural impulse, but in spiration it is the other way around. But in generation the will is joined to nature as consenting to nature in the act of generation. But in spiration nature is joined to will as inclining it along with the will to the act of spiration. And in that way the one generating firstly and principally generates naturally, but voluntarily concomitantly, while the one spirating spirates in the opposite way.

48. Nonetheless, the will is joined to nature in one way in generation, and nature is joined to will in another way in spiration, because the will is joined to nature in generation, not as compelling, but as pleased with the action. But in spiration nature is joined to the will as inclining free will as if by a natural impulse in its action so that for this reason both actions can be called natural. On this account Richard says in book six of *On the Trinity*, chapter one, that *"in God nothing is in accord with the gift of gratuitous grace, but everything is in accord with property of exigent nature."*[151] And Hilary says in book five of *On the Trinity*: *"From the power of nature upon the same nature the Son subsists by birth. And from the power of nature upon the same nature the Holy Spirit subsists by procession."*[152]

49. Therefore, to that which was introduced into the argument, namely, that *"God does not* produce God by nature or necessity, because he produces him

---

149   Richard of Saint Victor, *On the Trinity* 6, 17; PL 196: 982B; ed. J. Ribaillier, p. 252.

150   Ibid., 6, 18; PL 196: 983B; ed. J. Ribaillier, p. 253.

151   Ibid., 6, 1; PL 196: 969C; ed. J. Ribaillier, p. 228.

152   Hilary of Poitiers, *On the Trinity* 5, 37; PL 10: 155A; ed. P. Smulders, p. 191.

freely,"[153] it must be said that [190] he produces him freely and thus by will, but by a will that consents, not by one that elicits, in the first production, and in this way <he does so> freely, as Richard says in book six, chapter three: *"This undoubtedly will be for him to produce an offspring: to find his pleasure in him in every way."*[154] And by this it is not excluded that <God produces God> by nature and thus also necessarily and naturally, but in accord with the manner of necessity that was said to be found in God. But <God produces God> in the second production by a will that elicits, and by this it is not excluded that <he produces God> by concomitant nature and in this way naturally and necessarily, as is seen from what has already been said and will be explained more fully in the following question.[155] But to the addition that *"nature or necessity and will* are distinguished *as contraries* and do not concur in the same action,"[156] it must be said that the will acts either as absolutely free or as free by choice. In this second way nature or necessity and will do not concur in the same action. But in that way God does nothing by will within himself, but only with regard to creatures. Hilary speaks in accord with this in *On the Synods,*[157] and Anselm says in *Why God Became Man,* chapter two: *"In God there is no necessity of making or of not making."*[158] And in the same place Anselm says: *"In God will alone produces."*[159] But in the first way they both very well concur in the same action, as was determined above concerning the will of God,[160] although not in the same way, as was already explained here.

50. But with regard to the argument introduced that *"God does not produce God by will* or voluntarily *because* such production *cannot not exist,"*[161] one can reply [191] in the way already stated by distinguishing concerning the will regarding the diverse manner that the will concurs for the act of generating and of spirating, while nature does in a contrary way. For regarding this the magisterial teaching is accepted that there is an antecedent will and a concomitant will: the first in spiration, but the second in generation. But as Augustine says in book fifteen of *On the Trinity,* chapter twenty: *"Since the Eunomian heretics*

---

153   See above par. 8.

154   Richard of Saint Victor, *On the Trinity* 6, 3; PL 196: 970A; ed. J. Ribaillier, p. 231.

155   See above par. 39 and below q. 5.

156   See above par. 8.

157   See Hilary of Poitiers, *On the Synods* 34, 12 and 58, 24: PL 10: 507C and 520C.

158   Anselm of Canterbury, *Why God Became Man* 2, 17; PL 158: 442A; ed. F. Schmitt 2, 123.

159   Ibid.

160   See above *SQO* art. 47, qu. 1–5; ed. M. Führer, pp. 5–34.

161   See above par. 8.

were not able to understand and did not want to believe that the Son of God is begotten by nature, they said that he is the Son of the will, intending to assert an antecedent will,"[162] that is, by which he begot the Son as by an eliciting principle. On this account, in distinction six, chapter six,[163] the Master calls it efficient and not merely antecedent in order, as a principle precedes what is derived from a principle, but temporally, in understanding that will not merely antecedently as a origin, but also antecedently in newness either for the one willing, as we at times will what we did not will before, or for the work itself or the reality produced, as God at some time willed to produce a new creature that he did not before will to produce. And they said this to show that the Son of God was a creature. Against them Augustine says in *On the Letter to the Ephesians* on the words of chapter one: *He predestined us* (Eph 1:5): "*This was said concerning our Lord Jesus Christ because he was always with the Father, and the eternal will of the Father never preceded him in order that he might be.*"[164]

[192] 51. To what follows: "*If God produces God, he therefore <produces him> from something or from nothing,*"[165] and so on, it must be said that <he does> not <produce him> from nothing, but from something, and not from another substance, but from the substance of the one producing. It is necessary to hold that everything that is produced in God be produced from something, but one cannot say that something produced in God is produced from nothing, because when something is said to be produced from nothing, "nothing" is taken in three senses according to Anselm in the *Monologion*, chapter eight:[166] <It is taken> in one way negatively. In that way that which absolutely does not have being is said to be from nothing, in accord with which someone silent is said to speak of nothing. In this way, therefore, nothing existing in God or in creatures can be said to be from nothing, nor can that which has being something, whether it is produced or not. For a contradiction would be implied, namely, that it would have being and would not be, and for this reason neither in God nor in creatures can something be said to be produced from nothing.

52. In the second way something is said to be from nothing because there is not something from which it can be said to be, and according to this that is said to be from nothing that does not have a cause of its being. In that way in God the Father or the divine essence can be said to be from nothing because neither has a principle or a cause of its being. But then that proposition "from"

---

162   Augustine, *On the Trinity* 15, 29: PL 42: 1087; ed. W. Mountain and F. Glorie, p. 515.

163   See Peter Lombard, *Sentences* 1, d. 6, qu. un.; PL 192: 540; ed. I. Brady, 1, p. 90.

164   Rather, Jerome of Bethlehem, *On the Letter to the Ephesians* 1; PL 26: 448C–D.

165   See above par. 9.

166   Anselm of Canterbury, *Monologion* 8; PL 158: 156B–C; ed. F. Schmitt, p. 23.

is included under the negation so that it is the same to say "from nothing" or "not to be from something." And for this reason in God nothing produced can be said to be produced from nothing because everything produced in [193] God has something from which it is as from a principle and as if from matter, as will now be seen.[167] But that way of saying that something is from nothing ought not to be used in God because according to the common usage it not only implies a negation of being from another, but the negation of being without qualification. Hence, Anselm says in the *Monologion*, chapter six: "*Although the highest essence does not exist through something that produces it or from some matter, <it is> still not through nothing or from nothing because whatever it is, it is through itself and from itself.*"[168] In that way whatever the Father is, he also from himself and through himself, not from nothing. And thus in these two ways "from nothing" is said negatively.

53. In the third way "from nothing" is said positively,[169] and this in two ways: In one way as if materially so that nothing enters into the substance of the thing, as iron enters into the substance of a knife that is made from iron. Again in that way nothing is produced from [194] nothing because nothing of nothing has being something. In another way in terms of origin because its substance has being after nonbeing, and in that way only a creature has being from nothing, but not something produced in God, because in God there is only what is everlasting, as will be said below.[170] But the heretics said that whatever is produced in God was produced from another substance, but one also created from nothing. Hence, they said that nothing is produced by God but what was a creature and of another substance than the divine substance and was produced after the one producing it, and they said that the Son was the noblest creature created by God, as Hilary says in the beginning of book four of *On the Trinity*: "*The heretics say that the Son is not born from the Father and is not God from his nature, but is from his creation. For as there are many sons of God, so this Son also is, and as there are many gods, so this God also is, still with a more generous disposition both of adoption and naming in him. Thus he is adopted before the others and greater than those adopted sons, and created more excellently than the other natures; he is above the other creatures and created from nothing in the image of that eternal creator and was commanded by a word to subsist from nothing, since mighty God was able to make from nothing a likeness of himself.*"[171] And he says this against the Arians who said that the Son was the noblest spiritual creature before other creatures and received human nature in the Virgin. But Photinus

---

167   See below par. 55 and 56.

168   Anselm of Canterbury, *Monologion* 6; PL 158: 152C; ed. F. Schmitt, p. 20.

169   See ibid., 6; PL 158: 156C–157B; ed. F. Schmitt, pp. 23–24.

170   See below par. 69.

171   Hilary of Poitiers, *On the Trinity* 4, 3; PL 10: 98; ed. P. Smulders, p. 102.

said that he received his beginning in the Virgin when he assumed flesh. And they both said that the Holy Spirit is the noblest creature after the Son and said that both were deified by God with the dignity of grace and that for this reason both are said to be God in sacred scripture. But those who speak in that way, as Ambrose says in book one of *On* [195] the *Trinity*, "*deny that the Son is one in divinity with the Father. Let them therefore do away with the Gospel; let them do away with the words of Christ. For he says: 'The Father and I are one'*" (Jn 10:30). "*The catholic and apostolic Church declares anathema those who say: 'There was a time when he was not,' and 'He was not before he was born' and 'that he was made from nothing or from another substance.'*"[172]

54. Hence, to disprove this error from the text of scripture rather than from the power of natural reason, the discussion of the Trinity by Ambrose and Hilary and other Catholics stands guard, as is clear to one who looks at their books. Hence, we ought to hold that it is so from the statements of sacred scripture that are explained by their discussions, and we ought to investigate how we can understand that "*God produces God from his own substance.*"[173] But as Hilary says in book one of *On the Trinity*: "*When treating of the nature of God or his birth or—or to speak more generally—of his procession, we shall offer examples because the weakness of our intelligence forces us to seek certain forms from lower beings as indications concerning higher ones in order that, guided by our habitual dealing with familiar things from the awareness of our senses, we might be brought to some opinion of an unfamiliar idea.*"[174]

55. It must therefore be known that in the example of natural production it is possible to find those things that we can use for our purpose with regard to the divine production. For it is possible to consider in what is produced three things that somehow differ in reality, namely, the subject matter that is in potency to form, the form itself that the agent brings into act from the potency of the matter, and the composite constituted in being from the two, which is by itself the terminus of natural production. To these three really different elements in the production of [196] a creature, it is possible to find in divine production three corresponding elements differing only according to reason, namely, the divine essence, the personal property, and the supposite or person containing both of them, in accord with what Augustine says in book seven of *On the Trinity*, chapter two, concerning the person of the Son, "who is *wisdom that has been born*, so that through his saying, *born*, we understand the property, but through his saying, *wisdom*, we understand the essence."[175] Hence, as in the production

172 Ambrose of Milan, *On the Faith* 1, 19; PL 16: 556A; ed. O. Faller, p. 51.

173 See above par. 9.

174 Hilary of Poitiers, *On the Trinity* 1, 19; PL 10:38; ed. P. Smulders, p. 19.

175 See Augustine, *On the Trinity* 7, 2; PL 42: 936; ed. W. Mountain and F. Glorie, p. 250.

of a creature, the product itself also has being through the act of production, and as whatever is in it also has being in it through the act of production, so according to the determination of the Philosopher in book seven of the *Metaphysics*,[176] the composite is generated through itself and firstly, but secondly the form in the composite, but the matter as unbegotten and incorruptible has being only in the composite through generation, but is in no way generated in it, unless one is speaking of generation in the widest sense.

56. Similarly, in a divine production whoever is produced in God has his being through the act of production and also whatever is in him. On this account Augustine says that *"generation from the Father gives the essence to the Son,"*[177] as a composite in creatures has its being and whatever is in it through the act of natural generation. For a person is what is constituted in God from the essence along with the property, although without composition, as will be seen below.[178] "And Hilary says that *"the Son has nothing but what was born,"*[179] *"that is, what he received by being born,"* as Praepositinus explains.[180] Still, although we properly say that a person is produced through itself and firstly, [197] it is nonetheless not customary that theologians say that the property and the essence are in any way produced accidentally, but only that they are had through the production in the person produced, although in different ways, because the property not only has being in the person produced through the production, but also has being through it without qualification, because it has being in it without production. But the essence has being in what is produced through the production, but does not have being without qualification through production, because without passive production it has being in the one who produces.

57. On this account it could perhaps in some way be said properly or at least more properly or less improperly than of the essence that the property is produced in the person produced, as that filiation is not generated without qualification in terms of itself, but only in the Son. But in no way could it be properly said that the essence was also produced in what is produced, so that the deity would be generated in the Son, but only that it is had in him through generation and thus that the essence is properly said to be communicated to the Son through generation. Hilary nonetheless grants that the substance is generated in the Son when he says in book two of *On the Trinity*, in the beginning: *"How

---

176   See Aristotle, *Metaphysics* 7.8.1033b17–19; trans. anon., ed. G. Vuillemin-Diem, p. 136.

177   Augustine of Hippo, *On the Trinity* 15, 26; PL 42: 1094–1995; ed. W. Mountain and F. Glorie, p. 528.

178   See below par. 58 and 72 and art. 55, qu. 5, par. 7.

179   Hilary of Poitiers, *On the Trinity* 4, 10; PL 10: 102D; ed. P. Smulders, p. 111.

180   Praepositinus, *Summa against the Heretics* 11, 6; ed. J. Garwin, p. 270, and Hilary of Poitiers, *On the Trinity* 4, 10; PL 10: 102D; ed. P. Smulders, p. 111.

will he be the Father if he does not generate in the Son what he has of the substance and nature?"[181] But we say this less properly and truly, as in creatures matter is less truly and properly said to be generated than the form.

58. Therefore, we say that as in natural production the matter is the subject of generation insofar as it is in potency to form and through this to the composite to be generated from it, so in the divine production, for example, in the generation of the Son and similarly in the spiration of the Holy Spirit, the divine essence itself is the quasi subject of generation and like something in potency, although necessarily always joined to act for generating from it [198] the person constituted from the essence and the property, who is wisdom that is born, in accord with what has been said.[182] Thus "wisdom" names the subject, which in creatures is the matter, but "born" names the property had through generation by which the Son is constituted in the being of one generated and is distinguished from the Father, who is unborn wisdom, and with whom he is in agreement insofar as he is wisdom without qualification and thus absolutely.

59. In that way it must absolutely be said that *"God generates God from his substance,"*[183] that is, from the substance of the one generating, as Augustine says in the sermon, *On the Symbol: "When God begot the Word, he begot that which he himself is, not out of nothing, nor out of some matter already made and created, but from himself,"*[184] that is, from his substance. And in *On the Faith for Peter*, he says: *"The Father, God born from no one, once begot the Son from his nature without a beginning."*[185] The Master of the *Sentences* introduces many authorities for the same point in distinction five, the chapter, "It is also said."[186] But I am speaking about the substance of the one generating with reduplication, that is, "Insofar as he is generating." For although it is the same in the three, it does not have the character of the potency that someone be generated from it except insofar as it has being in the Father, so that by this there is excluded the problem that the Master of the *Sentences* introduced from the stated authority from Augustine's *On the Faith for Peter*, in distinction five, the chapter, "It is also said," where he speaks as follows: *"See, Augustine says here that the Son is born from the nature of the Father. But there is one nature of the Father and of the Son and of the Holy Spirit. If then the Son is born from the nature of the Father, he is born of the nature*

---

181 Hilary of Poitiers, *On the Trinity* 11, 3; PL 10: 52; ed. P. Smulders, p. 39.

182 See above par. 55.

183 See above par. 9.

184 Augustine of Hippo, *On the Faith and the Symbol* 2, 4; PL 40: 183; ed. J. Zycha, p. 7.

185 Fulgentius of Ruspe, *On the Faith for Peter* 2, 10; PL 65: 767C; ed. J. Fraipoint, p. 718,

186 Peter Lombard, *Sentences* 1, d. 5, 1; PL 192: 539; ed. I. Brady, 1, p. 85.

of the Son and of the Holy Spirit, in fact from the nature of the three persons."[187]
On this account the Master replies to the problem [199] and explains it in the
chapter "It is also shown, where he says: "*The Son was born from the substance of
the Father, or the Father begot the Son from his nature or essence, that is, from himself as nature or essence he begot the Son of the same nature or essence,*"[188] and <he
says> this as if "from" could only express the circumstance of a quasi efficient,
not that of a material cause, which one ought not to say.

60. And to what is argued to the contrary, namely, that "*the divine* essence *is
pure act and form; hence, it is in potency to nothing,*"[189] it must be said that something is in potency to something that is absolute and differs from it in reality
and intention and that goes from potency to act through motion or change of
reality or reason, or <it is in potency> to something that is only a respect and
differs from it only by reason, never going from potency to act through any
change, but is always naturally joined to act. In the first way matter in creatures
is in potency to form as to something really different from it and passing from
potency to act through a real change in the matter. And similarly the form of a
genus is in potency to the form of a difference as something differing in intention from it and passing from potency to act through a change of reason. And
the divine essence is not in that way in potency to something, and the minor
premise in the argument has truth concerning this. But <it does> not <have
truth> in the second way; rather, from the nature of the divine form, insofar as
it is pure act, it is the case that it is in potency to many respects. Hence, the divine production from the side of that from which it is produced, not only from
the side of the manner of producing, differs from every manner of production
that is possible to take place in creatures. For as Victorinus says in [200] his
argument against Arius, the eternal generation is without proportion to every
generation.[190]

61. Hence, one who wants perfectly to see the manner of divine production,
and this insofar as it pertains to the present question, ought to look at the
manners of other generations and ascribe to this production whatever there is
of nobility and to deny whatever there is of a lack of nobility and then show
how there is in it some nobility that can be found in none of the others, as is
explained in the *Gloss* on the Letter to the Hebrews, chapter one, on the words:
Since he is the splendor of the glory (Heb 1:3).[191] The divine production therefore
differs most highly from any other production because any other production

---

187   Ibid.

188   Ibid., 1, d. 5, 2: PL 192: 539; ed. I. Brady, 1, p. 88.

189   See above par. 9.

190   See Victorinus, *On the Generation of the Divine Word for Candidus, an Arian*
      30; PL 8: 1034C–1036A.

191   See *Ordinary Gloss on Hebrews* 1, 3; ed. 1634, 6, fol. 7 94F–795B.

passes through change to perfection, and in it potency is distant from act, but in this <divine production, it does so> in no way. It differs in particular from the natural production that is generation because that is from something substantially imperfect, but this is from a perfect substance. And in this respect it agrees more with the production that is alteration because in it the subject that is in potency is something existing in act, but it differs insofar as in alteration the subject is in potency to something absolute that is really different from it. In the divine production, however, <the subject is in potency> in no way. And in this respect the divine production agrees more with the production of a species from a genus because in this production the genus, which is like the subject and matter, is in potency to something absolute, as to a difference that differs from it only in intention. But here the subject is in potency to something relative that differs from it only by reason. And [201] although this production is more like the divine than the other, it still differs from it in many other ways because the production of a species from a genus through a difference moves from something incomplete to something complete by taking on the determination of a complement so that in terms of things different in reality it descends into different species, and there is only one common element in terms of reason. But in the divine production the subject is not something incomplete determined by an assumed property, but one and the same singular thing in reality has being through production in diverse relative persons under diverse relative properties, and it is common not in terms of reason, but in terms of communication.

62. Hence, since that common element is one and the same singular thing, for this reason this <proposition> is true: "The three persons are one God and one substance," and because in the constitution of a person it has with it the characters of the properties that differ from it only by reason, for this reason the converse is true: "The one God is three persons or the Trinity." In accord with this the Master proves it by authorities in book one of the *Sentences*, distinction four, the chapter: "Some, nonetheless."[192] But on account of the two of them together, all the propositions are granted in which concrete nouns are predicated of concrete nouns, such as; "The Father is God," or abstract nouns <are predicated> of abstract nouns, such as: "Paternity is the deity," or conversely, abstract nouns <are predicated> of concrete ones, such as: "The paternity is the Father," or <conversely>: "The Father is the deity," as was said, although they are not always equally proper, and this is so everywhere where "*the opposition* or *disparity of a relation* is not opposed."[193] For that prevents predication and does this either principally or because of an addition. <It does so> principally: either by reason of the signification of the terms, on account of which one does not say:

---

192   See Peter Lombard, *Sentences* 1, d. 4, c. 2; PL 192: 534–534; ed. I. Brady, 1, pp. 79–80.

193   See Anselm of Canterbury, *On the Procession of the Holy Spirit* 1; PL 158: 288; ed. F. Schmidt, 2, p. 181.

"Paternity or the Father is filiation or the Son," or by reason of the manner of signifying on account of which one does not say: "The essence generates or is generated." [202] However, although it is said absolutely: "The essence is the Father," because of an addition it is still not said: "The essence is the Father of the Son." For although Master Alexander distinguishes in his *Summa*,[194] when he says that "Father" can be taken adjectively or substantively, and if it is taken substantively, it is true in that way, because it then stands for the whole person who has the Son in this sense: "The essence is the person who is the begetter of the Son," just as conversely this proposition is true: "The Father of the Son is the essence," that is, the person who generates the Son is the essence. But if it is taken adjectivally, it is in that way false, because it says that the property by which the Father is related to the Son as generating him belongs to the essence. Master Praepositinus nonetheless says in his *Summa* that [203] "it is true without qualification and that *'Father'* is only taken substantively, as in this case: *The essence is the Father.*" And he proves this because there follows: "*The Father of the Son is the essence; therefore, the essence is the Father of the Son.*" The first is true because *Father* is taken *substantively*; hence, the second is also. Likewise, *the essence is the Father; this is true because 'Father' is taken substantively. Therefore, it is either the Father of someone or of no one. If of no one, it is not the Father at all. If it is the Father of someone, this is only of the Son.*"[195]

63. But in the truth of the matter that <proposition> is false: "*The essence is the Father of the Son,' and 'Father'" is taken only adjectivally,*"[196] because names that are imposed from active and passive potency, as are "teacher and student," "father and son," "builder and <building>" are adjectives by their signification only, and this is from the relation that they have to something else to which the potency from which they are imposed has a respect. But this is so because when something has the character of an addition or adjective from a respect to something else, the more the respect is determinate, the more it has the character of an addition, and it has it less, the more the respect is indeterminate, as is seen from the infinitive mood that the grammarians say can stand for more than any other mood because the others express a finite relation (*inclinatio*) to a supposite, but this expresses an infinite one. And similarly an adjective is made into a substance in the neuter gender rather than in the masculine or feminine gender. Hence, although "Father" in saying: "The Father of the Son," has a finite and explicit relationship, <it is> not so when it is put by itself. For this reason, although it could be taken substantively when one says: "The essence is the Father," it still <can> only <be taken> adjectivally when one says: "The essence is

---

194　Rather, Bonaventure, *Sentences* 1, d. 4, c. 1; also see Alexander of Hales, *Gloss on the Sentences* 1, d. 4, art. 5; ed. Quaracchi, p. 163A.

195　Praepositinus, *Summa against the Heretics* 4, 5; ed. J. Garwin, p. 218.

196　Ibid. See above par. 62.

the Father of the Son." And in that way <that proposition>, "The essence is the Father of the Son," is false without qualification, as was said. But this one, "The essence is the Father" is true.

[204] 64. If it is objected: "The essence is the Father and is only the Father of the Son; therefore, the essence is the Father of the Son or is not the Father,"[197] it is clear that it is a figure of speech, because in the first proposition, "Father" by itself stands for the whole person, in the second when "the Father of the Son" is said, it unites the property only with regard to the subject "Father." Therefore, the first argument of Praepositinus is not valid: "*The Father of the Son is the essence; therefore, the essence is the Father of the Son,*"[198] because it would have to be converted as follows: "Therefore, something that is the essence is the Father of the Son," just like that proposition: "An individual is man" is not converted as follows: "Therefore, man is an individual," but as follows: "Therefore, something that is a man is an individual."

65. Similarly, when it is argued: "*The essence is the Father; therefore, either of someone or of no one,*"[199] it does not follow because of a figure of speech. For as soon as there is added: "*of someone or of no one,*" it joins otherwise than it previously stood for, and it must be said: "of no one," that is, "is not the father of someone." And it does not follow from this that the essence is not the Father on account of a figure of speech, but there only follows: "Therefore, the property of paternity does not belong to it." For the deity, as was said,[200] or the divine essence has the character of something common, although through communication alone, and the person has the character of something proper, and in that way the essence has a certain character of a whole, and the person has the character of a quasi part—although neither part nor whole are truly in God, as was established above[201]—and on this account such a proposition is to be granted as proper and true: "The Son is of the divine substance or of the substance of the Father," by a quasi participative inclusion in this sense: "The Son is someone of the substance of the Father," that is, someone subsisting in the substance of the Father. But he is not something, as we say [205] that Socrates is something of the substance of man because in diverse human beings there is a true division of humanity. In this way there is also granted that the Father, the Son, and the Holy Spirit are of one substance, that is, persons whose substance is one. But if that genitive "of the substance" is understood to be construed in the usual way as if of a material cause, as that from which something or some-

---

197 See above par. 62.

198 Praepositinus, *Summa against the Heretics* 4, 5; ed. J. Garwin, p. 218,

199 Ibid.

200 See above par. 31.

201 See above *SQO* art. 28, qu. 1; ed. Badius 1, fol. 165rN–vR and art. 43, qu. 4; ed. L. Hödl, pp. 63–69.

one is produced, this <proposition> is granted as follows: "Christ is the Son of the substance of the Father or of the deity," as Augustine says in book fifteen of *On the Trinity*: "*The expression 'the Son of his love'* (Col 1:13) *is understood as nothing other than 'the Son of his substance'. And this is so because he is born from his substance*,"[202] just as we say that an image is a statue of bronze, because it is formed from bronze. But in that way we cannot say that the unbegotten is the Father of the divine substance because he is not produced from that as if from matter. On this account Augustine says in book seven of *On the Trinity*: "*We say the three persons are of the same substance or are one essence, but we do not say that three persons are from the same essence*."[203]

66. Still that proposition: "Christ is the Son of the divine essence"[204] ought not be generally granted unless the circumstance of a quasi material principle is expressed because, according to the common usage of such a construction, it is usually understood in the circumstance of an agent cause so that the divine substance itself is understood to have produced the Son. On this account the Master explains such a quasi improper proposition in the previously mentioned chapter, "It is also shown," when he says: "*Explain those words: 'The Son of the substance of the Father,' that is, <the Son> of the Father, who is the substance and with whom the Son is the same substance*."[205] But it is not necessary to explain it in that way; rather, it has a true and proper sense. For otherwise this <proposition>: "*The unbegotten is the Father of the substance of the Son*" would be equally true and proper, as that one: "Christ is the Son [206] of the substance of the Father," if one explains it in that way, that is: "<Christ is> the Son who is the substance and with whom the Father is the same substance." And that is not true, because if one construes that genitive "of the substance" in the usual manner of a quasi material principle, that <proposition> is true and proper: "Christ is the Son of the substance of the Father," but in no way is that <proposition> true and proper: "The unbegotten is the Father of the substance of the Son," as was said.[206]

67. But some say that in such propositions: "The Father begot the Son of his essence," and "The three persons are of one essence," that genitive in all such propositions is construed from the force of a designation of the essence, just as it is said: "A woman of outstanding form," that is, "A woman having an outstanding form." And it is not necessary to say this here, as was seen, nor should it be, because such a construction is used among the grammarians only in ac-

---

202   Augustine of Hippo, *On the Trinity* 15, 19; PL 42:1087; ed. W. Mountain and F. Glorie, p. 514.

203   Ibid. 7, 6; PL 42: 945; ed. W. Mountain and F. Glorie, pp. 264–265.

204   See above par. 65.

205   Peter Lombard, *Sentences* 1, d. 5, c. 2; PL 192: 539; ed. I. Brady, 1, p. 88.

206   See above par. 65.

cidental forms, but not in substantial ones. But all those propositions in which
the substance or essence is put as the terminus from which or as the terminus
toward which of a personal act ought to be explained in that way, as Hilary
does in book nine of *On the Trinity*: "*And we do not preach that the Father is in
the Son by bodily insertion, but that the nature born from him of the same nature
naturally had in himself the begetting nature*, that is, we do not *preach* that *the
Father is in the Son* by a bodily *insertion*, that is, as something located is in [207]
a place. Rather supply: *We preach the nature born*, that is, that the Son who is
the nature born had in himself from him, that is, from the Father, *the nature of
the same kind that naturally begets*,"[207] that is, which is the Father who naturally
begets.

68. And it should be noted here for the fuller understanding of what has already been said that if the three prepositions "by (*a*)," "from (*ab*)," "of (*de*)," and
"out of (*ex*)"[208] are used in their proper sense, they name diverse circumstances
and relationships, although they are often used for one another, since the preposition "by (*a*)" denotes the circumstance of an efficient cause or of an originating principle, on the basis of which that proposition "The Son is <produced>
by the Father," is accepted, but not this proposition "The Son is <produced>
by the substance of the Father." But "from" denotes the circumstance of an effect or of something derived from a principle, and on this account "being from
another" in God belongs only to a person who proceeds. But "of" and "out of" in
common denote the circumstance of a material or an efficient cause or as if <of
such a cause>. Hence, these propositions are accepted without difference: "The
Son is of the Father," or "out of the Father" or "of the substance of the Father" or
"out of the substance of the Father." But they differ a little both in the material
circumstance and in the circumstance of an efficient cause or as if <of such a
cause>. For they differ in the material circumstance because "of" indifferently
and equally properly denotes the circumstance of matter that is really something other than the form of that which is produced from it and of that which
is not really something other than it. Hence, it is said properly and equally that
the knife is of iron and that a species is of a genus. But "out of" properly denotes
the circumstance of matter in the first way, not the second. Hence, it is more
properly said that the knife is out of iron than a species is out of a genus. And
in accord with this we more properly say in God that the Son is of the essence
of the Father than that he is out of the essence of the Father. As Augustine
says in book seven of *On the Trinity*: "*We do not say three persons out of the same
essence as if* [208] *there is one thing in God that is the essence and another that is*

---

207   Hilary of Poitiers, *On the Trinity* 9, 51; PL 10: 322; ed. P. Smulders, p 429.

208   "A" and "ab" are the same preposition; hence, Henry speaks of three prepositions, and yet he distinguishes them as if they were four.

the person."[209] Still we assign another reason for this. They differ also in the circumstance of an efficient or originating cause because a thing is said to be out of something, whether it is of that substance or not. For it is correctly said that a son is out of a father and that a house is out of a builder. But "of" is only said when one is of the substance of the other; hence, it is properly said that a son is of a father, but not that a house is of a builder. Augustine makes that distinction in *On the Nature of the Good*,[210] and it is found in distinction thirty-six of the first book, the chapter: "That also."[211] But besides those manners, "of" and "out of" are taken only as ordinals, as noon comes to be out of or from morning. But this has nothing to do with the present question on God.

69. But to that which is further argued: "If God produces God, he therefore produces him either always or not always,"[212] and so on, it is necessary here firstly to explain that a divine production that is terminated internally is eternal, always persisting without beginning and without end, and then to grant one member of the division in the argument and deny the other. The first member is explained in two ways, namely, in one way by reduction to what is impossible, in the other way by ostension. <It is explained> in the first way that, if it had a beginning or an end of duration, then it would not be before it was or after it was, and that could not be without some change in the deity at the same time from the side of that which is produced, of that which produces, and of that from which it is produced, if it did not exist before it existed. For an agent doing an action that does not regard something external does not act newly without being differently disposed toward the action than before, nor can a production be new after not being unless what is produced has being after not being, and there would be [209] a new disposition in that from which it is produced that previously did not exist. But change absolutely cannot be present in God, as was shown above.[213]

70. By the ostensive path the same thing is seen because production does not begin or cease unless the agent stands in different ways with regard to the subject from which it produces or the subject <does> with regard to what produces it. For if the agent exists in that disposition in which it is able to act and if the subject exists in that disposition in which it is able to receive its action in itself and if they are close, it is impossible that the action not exist. But in

209   Augustine of Hippo, *On the Trinity* 7, 6; PL 42: 945; ed. W. Mountain and F. Glorie, p. 265.

210   Augustine of Hippo, *On the Nature of the Good* 27; PL 42: 560; ed. J. Zycha, p. 868.

211   Peter Lombard, *Sentences* 1, d. 36, c. 5; PL 192: 621; ed. I. Brady, 1, pp. 262–263.

212   See above par. 10.

213   See *SQO* art. 30, qu. 6; ed. Badius 1, fol. 184rZ–vD.

God the person that is in no way from another is pure act and always perfectly fecund for producing, and the divine essence is in him from eternity, and in that way they are not merely quasi close, but united in the highest way. Hence, <that person> is always fecund so that the Son is produced from him. Therefore, it is eternally necessary that God produces God so that the one produced is coeternal with the one that produces, in accord with what the Master of the *Sentences* explains in book one, distinction nine, in the beginning, by means of many authorities.[214] And in that way it must be granted that God always produces God.

71. And to what is assumed in the argument that *"the action of producing does not cease is only due to the fact that something has not been perfectly produced,"*[215] it must be said that there is a certain production in which what is produced receives through the production being after nonbeing with nonbeing preceding being by nature or by duration. There is also a production in which what is produced receives being, but not after nonbeing that precedes by nature or duration. In the first production a thing has being only through some becoming by which it acquires being. For when being is acquired through becoming, it in no way naturally has being from itself, as will now be said. And concerning such production it is true that it does not cease because something is not [210] perfectly produced in it, as is seen in production through natural motion. For according to the commentators on the Philosopher, Averroes and others,[216] every natural form that is reduced from potency to act by a natural agent, insofar as it moves to act through a natural change that is motion, is divided in terms of different ways of being since the motion to form is only the acquisition of one part of form after another. Thus, although the same thing according to reality and substance in a nonrational animal is something living, breathing, and sensing, if it is produced in being through motion, it is after the second being extended into something living, and then from something living into something breathing, and finally from something breathing into something sensing, and the middle of the change is not at the same time as the beginning and the end. For although they at the same time have their being constituted in substance, they still do not have at the same time the diverse beings of substance received through motion, which are completely had only in the last one. For one proceeds from the other according to the path of continuous generation so that what is before is always in potency to what is later, according to Averroes.[217] But if the production is instantaneous, as is the true generation of

---

214 See Peter Lombard, *Sentences* 1, d. 9, c. 2; PL 192: 546–547; ed. I. Brady, 1, pp. 103–104.

215 See above par. 10.

216 See Averroes, *Commentary on the Physics* 2, com. 26; ed. Juntas 4, fol. 58vbK–59rb13.

217 See Averroes, *Commentary on the Physics* 7, com. 9; ed. Juntas 4, fol. 312rbF.

completely indivisible substances and of those whose production is at the end of motion, as the illumination of the medium, according to the Philosopher in book seven of the *Physics*,[218] the production immediately stops there because something is immediately perfectly produced, and then the agent only acts for the conservation of what is produced so that there is another [211] action by which the thing is produced and conserved, although the agent is the same. On this account Averroes says on book two of the *Physics*, a twofold agent is distinguished: one which is the cause only of the thing's coming to be, which acts once and immediately stops, as a human being does in generating a child, but another that is not only the cause of the thing's coming to be and being, but also of the conservation of both, and this never ceases, as the sun <does not> in generating a human being. For if it ceases from the act of generation, it still does not cease from the act of conservation.[219]

72. Hence, since production is such in all things that have being after non-being either by nature or by duration, for this reason every such nature has a beginning of its being. For since that production is simple and indivisible, it necessarily has being firstly in some indivisible point and thereafter <it has> nonbeing, while what is produced remains in itself through an act of conservation. Thus in accord with this, the position of Avicenna,[220] by which he says that the world has being from eternity from another and nonbeing from itself that precedes by nature, implies what is impossible. But if that production were composite, it would similarly necessarily be finite and have begun because otherwise the parts would be infinite in the thing produced through that production. But if there is a production in which what is produced through the production receives being from another, but not after nonbeing that precedes by nature or by duration, in such a production the thing does not have being through some becoming because a becoming that is ordered to being is with regard to a subject and matter that does not have being from itself, but only potency for the being that is acquired for it in what is produced through becoming. Hence, because in a divine production that which is the quasi [212] subject and matter from which the production is made, as was said above,[221] is the divine essence, which has being in act from itself that does not in any way exist in potency to being, as was established above,[222] although it is, as was es-

---

218   See Aristotle, *Physics* 8.2.245a21–24; trans. vet.; ed. F. Bossier and J. Brahms, p. 264.

219   See Averroes, *Commentary on the Physics* 2, comm. 26; ed. Juntas 4, fol. 58vbK–59rbI.

220   See Avicenna, *Metaphysics* 4, 2; ed. S. Van Riet, p. 210.

221   See *SQO* art. 39, qu. 2; ed. G. Wilson, pp. 179–181.

222   See *SQO* art. 32, qu. 5; ed. R. Macken, pp. 79–84.

tablished above,[223] in some way in potency to the person to be produced from it, for this reason such a production is not the coming to be of some thing and its being, but is only the communication of the being and essence and of the reality to which having relative being from another is communicated. For what is produced in personal relative being has being from another and has essential being communicated to it from another through production. And concerning such production it is not true that it ceases, although someone is produced perfectly and perfect in it, just as its having being from another does not cease, as the coming to be by which it has its being ceases in the previously mentioned production. And in that way it is not necessary that it cease to have its being from another, as it is not necessary that it begin to have its being from another.

73. For to have its being from another is not incompatible <with eternal production,> and it does not assert a beginning of being in duration nor that another precedes from which it has its being, in accord with what the heretics say. And the Master explains this well by the authorities of the saints in the previously mentioned ninth distinction concerning that production that is generation and birth.[224] And the philosophers also correctly admit this in creatures. For they hold that the world has being from another, but from eternity without beginning and without end, while not holding that from itself the world has nonbeing that precedes its being either by nature or by duration, as [213] Avicenna held in accord with the way previously mentioned,[225] but <they hold> that from itself the world had from eternity only the potency for being and that along with this it is quite compatible that it has being from another from eternity. But this cannot be maintained. For that which of itself has only the potency for being from itself and from its essence implies no being because in that case it would be necessary to receive that being from another. Therefore, although it is held to have being from another from eternity, it must held be held, in accord with the position of Avicenna, that it has from itself nonbeing that precedes by nature or by duration and in that way has being acquired through coming to be and has a beginning and an end, as was said.

74. Hence, only in God is someone able to have being from eternity and from another and <have> this without any coming to be. And the proper reason for this is that the subject existing in a divine production as if matter has absolute being from itself communicable to another to which its relative being belongs from eternity through production, just as the one from whom he is produced has from eternity the opposite relative being, lest he be held to be mutable. As Ambrose says; "*Tell me, you heretic, did almighty God exist when*

---

223   See *SQO* art. 32, qu. 5; ed. R. Macken, pp. 96–97.

224   See Peter Lombard, *Sentences* 1, d. 9, c. 2; PL 192: 546–547; ed. I. Brady, 1, pp. 103–104.

225   Avicenna, *Metaphysics* 4, 2; ed. S. Van Riet, p. 210; see above par. 72.

he was not the Father and was God? For if God began to be the Father, he existed firstly and afterwards began to be the Father. How then is God immutable"[226]—as if he would say: In no way! But if he is always the Father and is only the Father by generating the Son, and generation on the part of the Father and the birth of the Son are simultaneous without anything in between, and the birth of the Son and his being are similarly simultaneous because his birth is most perfect, the Father therefore simultaneously has from eternity being because he is the Father and the Son <has being> because he is the Son, which it is impossible to hold with regard to any creature, by whatever it is held to be produced. And the Master explains this well in the previously mentioned distinction nine [214] at the end by the authority of Hilary.[227] And in that way production in God does not cease or begin, but is, was, and will be always present, and what is produced does not begin to be nor cease to be, but always is, was, and will be. But as it was said above that the present tense is most fitting for eternity, although it can be perfectly explained through no tense,[228] so if production and what is produced are explained in their duration in terms of themselves, they are more properly explained by saying the production always is and similarly what is produced <always is>. Similarly, if their duration explained together, it is still certain that it is explained less properly by the pure past in saying the one produced was always being produced, or was always produced, or always will be produced, or always is going to be produced, lest we understand through the past tense its failing and through the future its expectation. As Augustine says on the words: *"Today I have begotten you"* (Ps 2:7): *"In eternity there is not something past as if it has ceased to be, nor something future as if it is not yet."*[229] But it is also not most properly explained by *"the present alone"* in saying: "It is *always* being produced,"[230] lest the production be understood to be in coming to be. For just as cessation of the past is incompatible with eternal production as well as expectation of the future, so the coming to be of the present is incompatible.

75. Hence, although it cannot be perfectly explained, the manner is better expressed by which the perfection of the production is explained without the expectation of something and its presence without the cessation of something and the permanence of both without becoming or succession. And this is done by changing this active proposition: "God produces God," [215] into the passive and saying: "God is always produced by God," so that on account of the past tense that it consignifies, "produced" pertains to the perfection of the

---

226   Ambrose of Milan, *On the Faith* 1, 9; PL 16: 564B–D; ed. O. Faller, p. 25.

227   Peter Lombard, *Sentences* 1, d. 9, 4; PL 192: 549; ed. I. Brady, 1, p. 109.

228   See *SQO* art. 31, qu. 3; ed. R. Mackin, p. 19.

229   Augustine of Hippo, *Homilies on the Psalms* 2, 7; PL 36: 71; ed. E. Dekkers and F. Fraipont, p. 5.

230   Ibid.

production by which God was produced as perfect without the expectation of something. And because "is" is the present of the substantive verb, it pertains to the presence of what is produced without a lapse into some failure, and because "always" includes every difference of time, it pertains to the eternity of both without becoming and succession. Still, in his explanation Gregory refers those two, "produced" and "is," to the perfection of the person produced,[231] as is clear from his authority that the Master cites on this in the previously mentioned distinction nine in that chapter: "Here it can be asked," where you will find many authorities on this matter.[232]

76. To the last argument with regard to the previously mentioned subordinate argument: "If God produces God, 'God' stands either for the essence or for a supposite,"[233] it must be said in accord with what has been already determined, that it stands for a supposite, or rather for supposites because to be the principle and the terminus of a personal actions belong only to supposites. And what is assumed against this, namely, "that in God there is only a relative supposite,"[234] which according to the Philosopher in book five of the *Physics*: "can be neither the principle nor the terminus of an action,"[235] it must be said that <the Philosopher's statement> is true by itself by reason of the relation. But <our statement> still can be <true> by reason of that on which it is founded, such as the divine essence is, which under the character of one relative property is [216] the principle "by which" quasi formally and under the character of another relation is the principle "of which" quasi materially, and the relative property is the character of the supposite in the manner of the principle of individuation in creatures, which is the condition and manner of existing by which the supposite has the character of a singular.

77. To that which is brought in the third place against the main <argument> that "*every divine action is most noble* and thus exists *on account of itself, not on account of what* is produced,"[236] it must be said in accord with what was explained above in speaking about divine action in general that an act that is properly an action and one that is properly an operation differ.[237] And as they differ, so they have different perfections. For as the perfection of an operation consists in an

---

231 See Gregory the Great, *Moral Commentaries on Job* 29, 1; PL 76: 477B; ed. M. Adriaen, p. 1434.

232 See Peter Lombard, *Sentences* 1, d. 9, c. 4; PL 192: 547–549; ed. I. Brady, 1, pp. 106–109.

233 See above par. 42.

234 See above par. 42.

235 See Aristotle, *Physics* 5.1.225a11–12; trans. vet., ed. F. Bossier and J. Brams, pp. 194–195.

236 See above par. 12.

237 See *SQO* art. 39, qu. 1; ed. G. Wilson, p. 173.

action with regard to a most perfect object, as is seen in the operation that is happiness, so the perfection of an action taken in the proper sense is that it has something perfect perfectly produced. And for this reason, although a divine act that is properly an operation, such as to understand, is on account of its own perfection, not on account of something else that comes from it, still an act that is properly an action, such as to generate and to spirate, can on account of another sort of its perfection quite well be on account of something else or on account of someone else that comes from its action.

78. To the fourth argument that "*emanation* implies a *motion* of coming to be or an *emergence* for someone,"[238] of which sort there is nothing in God, it must be said that it is true through the full proper sense in accord with which we use these terms in creatures. Still they are truly said to be in God through some transference, as Hilary says in [217] the beginning of book four of *On the Trinity*: "*We are not unaware that for explaining divine realities neither the language of human beings nor a comparison with human nature can suffice. That which is ineffable does not have the boundary or limit of some signification, and that which is spiritual is different from the appearance and example of bodies. Nonetheless,*" as he says, "*when the discussion is about heavenly natures, those things that are attained by the perception of minds must be expressed by common usage both of nature and of speech. We are of course not going to say things befitting the dignity of God, but ones that we sense and understand and are necessary for the weakness of our mind.*"[239] And as he says in book one: "*If in discussing the nature and birth of God, we bring forth any examples for comparisons, let no one suppose that they absolutely attain in themselves the perfection of reason. For there is no comparison of earthly things to those that are divine, but the weakness of our intelligence compels us to seek from lower things certain indications* concerning *higher ones, so that as our habitual dealing with familiar things admonishes us from the consciousness of our idea, we may be brought to an idea of an unfamiliar perception.*"[240] And as he says in book two; "*The character of what is said will have to be understood from the mind of the speaker.*"[241] Therefore, although "emanation," "procession," and such names taken from creatures signify in them motion, coming to be, bodily emergence, and the other things that are not of dignity with regard to God, when they are transferred to God, they are used only insofar as those names signify something that is of dignity and perfection without qualification, even with regard to creatures in accord with the manner explained above.[242] [218] Hence, concerning the

---

238   See above par. 13.

239   Hilary of Poitiers, *On the Trinity* 4, 2; PL 10: 97; ed. P. Smulders, pp. 101–102.

240   Ibid, 1, 19; PL 10: 38; ed. P. Smulders, p. 19.

241   Ibid. 2, 31; PL 10: 71A; ed. P. Smulders, p.66.

242   See *SQO* art. 32, qu. 2; ed. R. Macken, p. 36.

emergence of a person from a person that emanation implies, Ambrose says in book one of *On the Trinity*: "*If we are seeking the proper sense of his generation, 'he went forth from God.' For since in our usage that is said to go forth which already is and what is said to go forth is seen to emerge from external hidden places, we attend to the proper sense of the divine generation, although with limited language, so that he is not thought to have gone forth from some place, but that God <went forth> from God.*"[243] And in book two he says: "*And when he goes forth from the Father, he does not as if leave some place, nor is he separated as if from a body.*"[244] But the heretics have interpreted "emanation," "emergence," and other such terms in accord with the way we use them in bodily matters without attending to their spiritual interpretation, as Hilary says in the beginning of book two of *On the Trinity*: "*Many have arisen who have taken the simplicity of the heavenly words in accord with the sense of their choosing, not in accord with purity of the truth, interpreting them otherwise than the force of the statements demands; for heresy comes from their understanding, not from the scripture.*"[245] Hence, they formed all their arguments against the spiritual understanding of the holy fathers on the bodily understanding of the words, and they interpreted in a bodily sense the statements of scripture that have to be interpreted spiritually so that, because birth in creatures gives being to one who was not previously, so <it did> in God also and other such things. In accord with this, Damascene says in book one, chapter eight: "*The Father never was when the Son was not, but the Son was simultaneous with the Father, born from him. And in that way he begets without being acted upon, without time, without change, and without intercourse, nor does he have a beginning.*"[246]

[219] 79. To the last argument that "*if one person emanates from another* in God, he is therefore produced in being by that other,"[247] and so on, it must be said that it is the case that there is a person that does not emanate from another, because he has being from himself formally, that is, from his form, which is his essence, because it is being or rather is necessary being. But he does not have either his essence or his being from another as from a principle, and on this account he is not produced in being. But on the contrary, a person that emanates from another as from a principle has from another his essence and all the being he has, and on this account it is true to say that he is produced in being by another. But this can be understood in two ways: In one way because being is communicated to him

---

243 Ambrose of Milan, *On the Faith* 1, 17; PL 16: 876D–877A; ed. O. Faller, p. 47.

244 Rather, Ambrose of Milan, *On the Holy Spirit* 1, 11; PL 16: 733A; ed. O. Faller, p. 67.

245 Hilary of Poitiers, *On the Trinity* 2, 3; PL 10: 51; ed. P. Smulders, p. 39.

246 John Damascene, *On the Orthodox Faith* 1, 8, 2 and 4; ed. E. Buytaert, pp. 30 and 33.

247 See above par. 14.

from that other, but in another way because being is acquired for him from that other. In the first way in God being is communicated to a person emanating from another, because he has all that he has—both his essence and his being—from him, insofar as, in producing him, the other communicates to him his essence from which he produces it and in the essence communicates to him his being and all that he has except his property by which he is distinguished from the person produced by him. On this account the person produced has being from himself formally, that is, from his form, which is his essence, just as the person who produces does, because in chapter seventeen of John he says: "*As the Father has life in himself, so he also gave to the Son that he have life in himself*" (Jn 5:26). But in the second way a person emanating from another in God is in no way produced in being by the other, because what is produced in being by another in that way does not have being from himself formally, that is, from his form, which is his essence, but receives being in his essence from another who exists. On this account it is necessary that it is something other in essence than that by which it is produced. But such is the essence of the whole of creation that even the philosophers who held that the world existed from eternity held that it had being from another through acquisition, because [220] it does not have being from its essence, since of itself it is not being nor necessary being, but only possible being. On this account, although it had being from another from eternity, it would never be said to be eternal.

80. And when it is further asked in the argument: "*If a person emanating from another is produced in being by him, therefore, he is either produced in being from nonbeing or produced in being from being*,"[248] it must be said that "from" can express either the circumstance of a quasi material principle or the circumstance of order with regard to what is produced. In the first way, when in God a person is produced from the divine essence, which is being itself that is communicated to the one produced, it is true to say that he is produced from being into being and in no way from nonbeing into being. And then what is further asked in the argument; "*Therefore, from the same being into the same being or into some other*,"[249] it must be said that it is not from one being into another, as the minor premise for this proves, but from the same being into the same, but in a different sense as from it and as into it. For it is from the same being as that of the Father, but into the same being as it is communicated to the Son by the Father. And for this reason it does not follow that this person had being before he was produced or did not have it through production, because that being is not his insofar as he is produced from it, but insofar as it is in him. But in creatures no production is possible in this way from being into being, because what produces never communicates its own being to a creature.

---

248   See above par. 14.

249   See above par. 14.

81. But if "from" denotes a circumstance of order, no person in God is produced in that way from nonbeing, because the one who produces produces only from his own substance, which is being itself and which is also the substance of the one produced. But nothing can be produced from nonbeing into being, whether nonbeing is held to precede being itself by nature alone or also by duration, unless it is [221] such that its substance is in potency to being and nonbeing so that from itself only nonbeing belongs to it, but being belongs to it only from another, as Avicenna held with regard to the essence of a creature.[250] Hence, some others of those philosophizing who held that the created world was of itself in potency for being, but in no way for nonbeing, and that from the necessity of nature it had being from God from eternity, just as he himself was eternal, said that the created world would be produced into being, but not from nonbeing. Similarly, in accord with this way in which "from" denotes the circumstance of order, no divine person is produced from being into being, neither from the same being nor from another. He is not produced from another, because then there would be change with regard to the person produced, just as when it denotes the circumstance of a quasi material principle with regard to the essence from which he is produced. Nor is he produced from the same being, because he never had this being without the one produced, and it would still be without its production into being, if it were so.

---

250   See Avicenna, *Metaphysics* 4, 1; ed. S. Van Riet, p. 186.

QUESTION FOUR

Whether from That Person That in God Is Not from Another More Persons Than One Emanate

1. With regard to the fourth question it is argued that from that one person in God that is not from another there do not emanate more other persons than one in the first place as follows: Where there is only one simple principle of emanating a person, there is only one simple emanation, and so there is also only one thing that emanates because from the same thing insofar as it is the same there proceeds only the same thing. In that person that in God [222] is not from another there is only one simple principle of emanating, as is the divine essence, in which there is no diversity except according to reason alone, as was established above.[251] Therefore, there is in God only one simple emanation and an emanating person. And if there is some diversity in them, it will be only according to reason, which does not suffice for the difference or distinction of persons, as will be said below.[252] Therefore, and so on.

2. <It is argued> in the second place as follows: The characters of the principles of any two emanations differ from one another only insofar as the characters of the terminuses <differ>. But of two emanations, that is, through the manner of nature and will, the characters of the principles are in the same person, that is, the one that is not from another. Therefore, similarly the characters of the terminuses can also be in the same person that is from another, that is, the one that is emanating in the manner of nature and of will. And for the same reason, however many are the principles and characters of emanating in the person that is not from another, only one person can emanate from it whether by a single emanation or by many.

3. <It is argued> in the third place as follows: Those things that differ only by reason cannot be principles of things that differ really because, since there are many attributes in God differing only by reason, as was established above,[253] by the same argument there then would be in terms of any of the divine attributes something emanating that differs really from that from which it emanates, and that is false. Hence, since all the things that are in the person that is not from

---

251 See *SQO* art. 28, qu. 4; ed. Badius 1, fol. 167vT–168rV.

252 See below art. 55, qu. 6 and *SQO* art. 68, qu. 5; ed. Badius 2, fol. 229vP–232vC.

253 See *SQO* art. 28, qu. 4; ed. Badius 1, fol. 168rX–vY; also *SQO* art. 32, qu. 4; ed. R. Macken, pp. 57–73; art. 35, qu. 8; ed. G. Wilson, pp. 80–88; art. 36, qu. 1; ed. G. Wilson, pp. 93–94; and art. 51, qu. 1; ed. M. Führer, pp. 216–223.

another differ from one another only according to reason, <they cannot be the principle of things that differ really,> therefore, and so on.

4. <It is argued> in the fourth place as follows: A diverse way of emanating according to nature in the same species does not diversify that which emanates according to species, [223] as Ambrose says in the book, *On the Incarnation of the Word*: "*I shall bring forth an example from the Scriptures that in many things there are diverse beginnings and one substance.*"[254] Therefore, although the emanation in the manner of nature and of will is diverse, that which emanates will not on this account be diverse in species. But in God, as will be seen below,[255] there is a diversity of those that emanate only in species or quasi <in species>. Therefore, and so on.

5. <It is argued> in the fifth place as follows: One nature has only one way of communicating it. For according to the Commentator on book eight of the *Physics*: mice that are generated, one from propagation, another from putrefaction, are not of the same species.[256] The divine nature is only one. Therefore, and so on.

6. <It is argued> in the sixth place as follows: It belongs to the character of the person that is not from another that it is only one; therefore, <it> similarly <belongs to> the character of a person that is from another.

7. But <it is argued> that at least three emanate in the first place as follows: Because we see in creatures three principles of emanations and ones that elicit acts, which are nature, art or intellect, and will; hence, since these three are in God and two of them, namely, nature and will, are held to be principles of emanations, and through this two persons emanate from the one that is not from another, a third will similarly emanate from the art that is in him.

8. <It is argued> in the second place as follows. Nature and will in God do not differ more than nature and intellect. Therefore, if will in the person that is not from another is a principle productive of another person than nature <is>, then the intellect is similarly.

[224]   <The Resolution of the Question>

9. It must be said that according to Richard in book five of *On the Trinity*, chapter five, that "*to be a person from another is not an incommunicable existence.*"[257] Otherwise, since to be a person not from another, but from oneself,

---

254   Ambrose of Milan, *On the Incarnation of the Word* 9; PL 16: 879A; ed. O. Faller, p. 273.

255   See below par. 14.

256   Averroes, *Commentary on the Physics* 8, comm. 14; ed. Juntas 4, fol. 387E and *Commentary on the Metaphysics* 12, comm. 13; ed. Juntas 8, fol. 35D.

257   Richard of Saint Victor, *On the Trinity* 5, 5; PL 196: 952A; ed. J. Ribaillier, p. 200.

as has been shown,[258] is an utterly incommunicable existence, there would be in God only two persons, only a single one that has being from another, just as there is only a single person that does not have being from another. And in that way it is not contrary to that manner of being by which a person has being from another that there are many from another in God. And in that way it is not possible that many persons in God do not have being from another, the reason for which was established above.[259] It is nonetheless possible that many persons in God be from another, the reason for which is common with regard to both, namely, that unity belongs to the character of the first and the principle, but not to the character of that has being from the principle, as Dionysius says in chapter four of *On the Divine Names*: "*Every dyad is not a principle, but the monad is the principle of the whole dyad.*"[260] "*For,*" as he says in chapter five, "*Every number already exists in the monad, but to the extent that it goes forth from the monad, to that extent it is distinguished and multiplied.*"[261] And these are multiplied and distinguished either by an absolute difference of realities as there is creatures or by a difference of real relations as there is in the divine persons or by a difference of reasons alone as there is in the divine attributes.

10. There is a threefold plurification existing in a certain order among themselves and to the first unity. For the plurification of creatures presupposes [225] the plurification of the divine persons by an order of duration, and that <plurification of the divine persons presupposes> by a certain order of reason the plurification of the divine attributes, to whose number intellect and will belong, and they are the two principles of operation of every intellectual nature, which along with all the other essential attributes pertain to the divine essence. That person in God that is not from another embraces and contains them in himself, and they have being in others in a certain order from him. For from him, as Richard says in book five of *On the Trinity*, chapter four: "*There is everything that is; from him is all being, all existence, every person human, angelic, and divine.*"[262] For because he contains both those principles in himself, from himself, and not from another, he has them in himself in full and unexhausted fecundity for the production of the two persons within himself so that it is not only possible that a person in God be from another, but it is also necessary on account of the two principles of emanations in God, which are in that <person>, that

---

258   See above qu. 2, par. 5.

259   See above qu. 2, par. 8 and below art. 53, qu. 9.

260   Pseudo-Dionysius, *On the Divine Names* 1, 4; PG 3: 722C–D; trans. Scotus Eriugena.

261   Ibid., 1, 5; PG 3: 831B; trans. Scotus Eriugena.

262   Richard of Saint Victor, *On the Trinity* 5, 4; PL 196: 951D–952A; ed. J. Ribaillier, p. 199.

two other persons emanate from that one, one through the principle that is intellect, but the other through the principle that is will.

11. For the understanding of this it must be known in accord with what was determined in the first question of *Quodlibet* seven[263] that in an intellectual nature intellect and will have their perfection only in a twofold manner of action, of which one is the essential action of intellect and will, but the other is their personal or notional <action>. For no matter how much it is perfected by the essential act of understanding, the divine intellect does not have its perfection until there is conceived in it the Word proceeding from it through its notional act of speaking. Similarly, the will is not perfected through the essential act of willing until there is produced in it love proceeding from its notional act, as we have explained more explicitly in that question and more extensively from that part: "It must, therefore, be known as [226] from a principle," and so on, up to that part: "But it must be further noted."[264]

<Replies to the Arguments>

12. To the first argument to the contrary that "in the person that is not from another *there is only one simple principle of emanating*," as the divine essence is; hence, <there is> only one simple emanation,"[265] and so on, it must be said that, although the divine essence, which is a unique form, is simple in essence, it is multiple in power. And for this reason insofar as it is utterly the same and in accord with the same character, diverse emanations do not proceed from it, but <they do so> only under diverse characters of diverse properties without which there is not the proximate reason for eliciting some emanation productive of a person, although from itself it is the first reason of all the divine emanations, as was said above and will be explained more fully below.[266]

13. To the second argument that "*of two emanations* of which the principles are intellect or nature and will, the terminuses from which *are in* one and the *same person that is not from another; therefore, the terminuses to which* or the characters of the terminuses to which are similarly <in one and the same person>, because the terminuses from which or the characters of the same do not differ more than the terminuses to which,"[267] it must be said that it can be understood in two ways that some things differ more or less: either in terms of form or in terms of subject. For those that differ more in form can agree in subject more than those that agree in form. For whiteness and sweetness differ more than two whitenesses, but the former can be in the same subject, the latter cannot

---

263   See *Quodlibet* 7, 1; ed. G. Wilson, pp. 6–8.

264   Ibid; ed. G. Wilson, pp. 13–21.

265   See above par. 1.

266   See *SOQ* art. 39, qu. 4; ed. G. Wilson, pp. 196–202 and below qu. 6 and art. 55, qu. 6.

267   See above par. 2.

not. Therefore, although [227] the characters of the terminuses of the emanations do not differ more than those of the principles, it is quite possible that the characters of the principles are compatible with one another in the same thing, but the characters of the terminuses are not. The reason for this is that the character of a principle always tends toward unity, but the character of what is derived from a principle <tends> toward plurality so that, since it is necessary that there be one principle of all things and that the first principle has to have in itself the characters that are the principles of all the other things that receive being from it, it is necessary that in the first principle that is not from another there be at the same time the first principles of the first emanations, although the characters of the terminuses are not. And this is so for the reason that an emanation that is for a terminus in accord with one character, as to what is produced under the character of filiation, proceeds principally from the principle that is intellect or nature, but with an addition from the principle that is will, and not the other way around. And the other way around, the emanation that is for a terminus in accord with the character of spiration principally proceeds from the principle that is will with only an addition from the principle that is nature, and not the other way around. And in that way it is impossible that one person having in himself two characters of the terminuses proceeds or emanates in accord with those two emanations, just as it is impossible that he principally proceeds in accord with both emanations and in accord with none, but in accord with both from an addition.

14. To the third argument that *"in the person that does not proceed from another* nature and will *differ only by reason; therefore, they cannot be the principles of* many emanations *that differ really,"*[268] and so on, it must be said that nature, which is intellect, and will can be considered in two ways in that person that is not from another: <They can be considered> in one way without qualification and absolutely, and in that way they are principles only of the essential actions that are to understand and to will, and <they can be considered> in another way as with relative properties. In that way they are the proximate principles of notional actions that are to speak and to spirate. In the first way it is true that they differ [228] from each other only by reason, and in that way they cannot be the proximate principles of diverse personal emanations differing by the reality of a relation, although they are the remote principles. But in the second way it is not true that they differ only by reason, that is, this whole, the intellect with one relative property and the will with another; rather, they differ really because of the relations. For they are diverse real disparate relations, although not opposed relatively insofar as they are in the person that is not from another, as will now be said.[269] Nor is it similar regarding the other attributes

---

268   See above par. 3.

269   See below qu. 6.

because their characters do not at all express proper principles of some actions, as nature, intellect, and will do. On this account, despite their differing only by reason, they can be the proper principles of essential actions, and under the characters of the relative properties they can also be principles of the notional actions, as will now be seen.

15. To the fourth argument that *"a diverse manner of emanation in terms of species does not diversify that which emanates according to species,"*[270] it must be said that, in taking "diversity in terms of species" in the broad sense, we hold that in God the two manners of emanation and the diverse manners of being of the divine persons differ in species, in accord with what Ambrose says shortly before the authority introduced. *"Since the Father is not from another and the Son is not from himself, the species is seen to be diverse here; the species is certainly distinct, but the divinity is not distinct."*[271] We shall now also say that the persons also differ in species in accord with the same manner. But since *"diversity or distinction according to species comes from form,"* according to the Philosopher [229] in book eleven of the *Metaphysics*,[272] insofar as form is twofold or, to speak more properly, insofar as there are two characters of form, namely, abso-lute <form> that belongs to the essence, and relative <form> that belongs to the property. In terms of the first there is no distinction in God according to species; rather, God is one species in one singular nature that cannot become many. And <the heretics> nonetheless argued that this distinction is in God if it is necessary to hold that the unbegotten and the begotten are in him, because they were unable to understand that both were of one substance in terms of number. Hence, against such people Ambrose states the proposition that was assumed, namely, that *"there are diverse beginnings in many "*[273] in accord with a diverse manner of having and of receiving, where there is nonetheless only one nature that is had or received. And he explains this in creatures concerning one common nature that is produced in diverse ways in diverse <beings>. And in accord with this he explains concerning the text of Genesis. And at the end of the explanation he concludes: *"Therefore, we note that those things that belong to the same genus began to be in a diverse way, some from water, some from earth, and some from generation by male and female, and are still of one nature. Therefore, if this can occur in these beings that are mortal, how do they impose a law of any*

---

270 See above par. 4.

271 Ambrose of Milan, *On the Incarnation of the Word* 9; PL 16: 842D–843A; ed. O. Faller, p. 273.

272 Aristotle, *Metaphysics* 10.9.1058b1–3; anon. trans.; ed. G. Vuillemin-Diem, p. 204.

273 Ambrose of Milan, *On the Incarnation of the Word* 9; PL 16: 843A; ed. O. Faller, p.273.

necessity upon the divinity of the Father, and the Son, and the Holy Spirit?[274]—
that is, diverse beginnings. But in terms of relative form there is in God quite
well a distinction according species or as if <according to species>. For just as
paternity and filiation are relations quasi diverse in species, so the Father and
the Son constituted by them as persons are persons quasi diverse in species,
but containing in the single individuals their whole species that cannot become
many in others, as will be said below.[275] And a mode of emanation diverse by
such a diversity according to species, as are generation and spiration, is correctly
distinguished as emanating according to species.[276]

[230] 16. To the fifth argument that *"one nature has only one way of communicating it,"*[277] one must reply by distinguishing both from the side of the way of
communicating and from the side of the nature communicated. From the side of
the nature communicated it must be said that a nature is communicated in two
ways: through an act of production or of emanation. In one way as that which
has being through production not merely in what is principally produced, but
also in accord with what it is. In another way as that which has being in accord
with what it is without production, although not in what is produced. In the
first way all the forms of a creature have being through production because not
only what has form has being through production, but the form itself <does>,
because from itself it does not have being at all. In the second way the form of
deity has being through production because <it has it> in what is produced, but
not in itself, because from itself it has being also in the supposite produced. On
this account it was said above[278] that the form of the deity is in no way produced,
just as matter is also not in natural beings, but is only had through production.
But a natural form is generated in some sense. But in the first way the personal
property of the person produced has being in a certain way through production,
as was said above. But it is in no way able to be communicated, neither in itself
because it is singular, in which it agrees with the deity, nor in diverse supposites,
and in this respect it differs from the same. But from the side of the way of communicating, it must be said that the way of communicating the nature can be said
to be one or diverse: either only from the side of that which communicates and
produces that to which it is communicated or only from the side of the act of
producing it, or in both ways. In this third way one nature quite well has diverse
ways of communicating in creatures, as is seen from the examples of Ambrose
already stated concerning the production of the same bird in terms of species

---

274   Ibid.; PL 16: 843B and 843A; ed. O. Faller, pp. 274 and 273.

275   See *SQO* art. 59, qu. 5; ed. .Badius 2, fol. 147vA.

276   I have conjectured "distinguitur" instead of "distinguunt," but the sense still
        eludes me.

277   See above par. 5.

278   See above qu. 3, par. 55.

now from water, now from earth, and now from the union of [231] male and female.[279] But this does not occur in those ways that do not naturally come to be in creatures without sexual intercourse except where the agent is supernatural. In God one nature also very well has diverse ways of communicating, for example, of the deity by the Father to the Son through generation and to the Holy Spirit by both through spiration. In the first way the same nature still has diverse ways of communicating in creatures, and this either by another agent supernaturally or by both naturally.

17. Concerning the first Ambrose gives the example from the truth of the nature of human flesh that in Christ and in us *"arose from diverse principles,"*[280] although there was one way of forming it. For the Holy Spirit supplied what the male seed could have done, and in this way, insofar as was in her, the Virgin was a natural mother. But if <it is brought about> by an agent acting naturally in both ways, in that way <there is produced> whatever is generated from propagation by a male and female. If by the power of the sun alone, the stars, and the heavenly bodies, the same proportion of mingling could be produced in terms of hot, cold, moist, and dry, and if such power as is poured out in the seed by those generating naturally, the same in terms of species could be produced by the power of the sun, the heaven, and the stars without the union of male and female. And this <is so> because from the side of the agent producing within and of the production itself, this manner of production is the same as that which is through propagation.

18. But the philosophers would deny that it is possible and for this reason <would deny> that the same nature can be communicated by propagation and without it. On this account [232] Averroes[281] says that a mouse generated from putrefaction and without it is not of the same species, which is perhaps not true at least in the lower species. But if in the already mentioned way there is a diverse way of communicating only from the side of the act of producing, if the agent is supernatural, it can very well communicate the same nature according to diverse manners of producing it, either from preceding matter or through creation out of nothing. But if it is a natural created agent, <it can> in no way. And through this manner the Father communicates the same nature of the deity to the Son and to the Holy Spirit in accord with diverse productions, the reason for which is the fecundity and perfection of the two principles, that is, of nature and of will in God, although in creatures there can only be the fecundity for communicating a nature in accord with the principle that is nature, but not

---

279   See above par. 15.

280   Ambrose of Milan, *On the Incarnation of the Word* 9; PL 16: 843C; ed. O. Faller, p. 274.

281   See Averroes, *Commentary on the Physics*, 8, com. 46; ed. Juntas 4, fol. 387E and *Commentary on the Metaphysics* 12, com. 13; ed. Juntas 8, fol. 298vaG–299vbK.

in accord with another principle, even through the principle that is will is in it, and this is on account of its natural imperfection.

19. To the sixth argument that *"the person that is not from another is only one; therefore, that which is from another* is <only one>, <it must be said that> there is no parallel. And it is clear how there is no parallel, and as a consequence the solution of the argument <is clear> from the side of those things already said for the body of the question[282] and in the resolution of the second argument of this question[283] and also from the resolution of the first argument for the ninth question of the preceding title.[284]

20. To the seventh argument that *"there are three principles of emanation, nature, art, and will;* therefore, *at least* three emanations and three persons proceed from [233] that <person that is not from another>,"[285] it must be said that in intellectual beings art and intellect are the same principle, but nature and will are not. And the reason is that through an object present to it the intellect elicits its act by a certain impulse or by a certain immutability of natural necessity, just as an absolute, non-intellectual nature does. But will <does> not <do so> in that way, but is freely borne to it, in accord with what will be more fully explained below.[286]

21. To the eighth argument that *"intellect and nature differ no less than nature and will; therefore,* as nature and *will* are diverse principles of emanations, nature and *intellect* are *similarly,"*[287] and so on, it must be said that although nature and intellect do not differ less than nature and will in terms of reality, they still differ less in terms of the manner of operating. On this account as has already been said, nature and will are diverse principles of emanations, but nature and intellect are not.

---

282   See above par. 9–10.

283   See above par. 13.

284   See above art. 53, q. 9, para. 12.

285   See above par. 7.

286   See below qu. 6, par. 46, 51, and 69 and qu. 10, par. 6–7.

287   See above par. 8.

[234]   QUESTION FIVE

*Whether the Two Persons That Emanate from That Person That Is
Not from Another Emanate Equally Firstly, Principally, and Immediately*

1. With regard to the fifth question it is argued that the two persons that
emanate from that person that is not from another emanate equally firstly,
principally, and immediately in the first place as follows: Emanations whose
principles have equal potency and fecundity in the same person emanate from
it equally firstly, principally, and immediately because when there is no prerog-
ative among the principles, <there is> also not among those that proceed from
the principles. The principles of the emanations, which are nature and will in
the Father, are such because otherwise there would not be perfect equality in
them, nor as a consequence in the persons produced by them. Therefore, and
so on.

2. <It is argued> in second place as follows: Dionysius says in *On the Divine
Names*, chapter two: "*The Father is the fontal deity, but the Son and the Holy
Spirit are fruits of the begetting deity, if one may say so, germinated for God and
like flowers and superessential lights.*"[288] There another translation says: "*Sprouts
of the divine nature and like flowers and superessential lights.*"[289] But in two flowers
and lights [235] proceeding from the same <principle>, both proceed equally
firstly, principally, and immediately. Therefore, and so on.

3. <It is argued> in the third place as follows: If from the person that is not
from another both persons do not emanate equally firstly, principally, and immediately, this would only be because there would be something in it through
the first emanation through which it would proceed to the second emanation.
But this is impossible because then with respect to the emanation that emanates from it that person would not be firstly and principally in potency before
<it was> in act. But this is impossible. Therefore, and so on.

4. To the contrary <it is argued> that two emanations that stand in such
a way that the terminus of the one is the principle of the other do not proceed from the same <principle> equally firstly, principally, and immediately.
The two previously mentioned emanations are such. For the terminus of the
emanation that is generation is the Son, who along with the Father is the one
principle of the emanation that is spiration, as will be seen below.[290]

---

288   Pseudo-Dionysius, *On the Divine Names* 1, 2; PG 3: 671A; trans. Scotus
       Eriugena.

289   Ibid., trans. Sarraceni.

290   See below qu. 6.

<The Resolution of the Question>

<Art. 1: Whether the Persons Proceed Equally from the First>

5. It must be said to this that, in accord with what was said and determined above[291] according with the authority of Dionysius, *"Every number comes from the monad,"*[292] so that it is necessary to reduce in an orderly way every plurality and number to some single first in such a way that two do not have to be reduced to the first one through equality. Hence, the Philosopher also holds in book ten of the *Metaphysics* that in the first differences of the proper genera it is always necessary to hold one [236] more noble extreme of contrariety that firstly and more principally partakes of the character of the genus and <to hold> another of less nobility that partakes of the nature of the genus through some falling away from it.[293] In the deity therefore it is necessary to reduce all plurality to unity in an orderly way so that no two have to be reduced to the first one through complete uniformity. On this account, since there is in God a plurality of persons, it is necessary to reduce that <plurality> to the unity of the deity in such a way that there are many persons, but only one God, but not by being in relation to the deity through a complete uniformity, but in a certain order so that there is one first person that has in itself from itself, not from another, everything that belongs to the deity, and all the others <have it> from that one. And through this <it has it> firstly so that the other persons have to be reduced to it as to their first and principle, and in this way only by a certain order so that there is one first principle that in itself has from itself, not from another, everything that belongs to the deity, and all the others have it from it, and for this reason firstly so that the other persons have to be reduced to this one as to their first and principle, And for the same reason this <is so> only by a certain order so that one of them is the principle of the other, and <the latter> has to be reduced to it as to its principle, and so on thereafter, as will now be seen. For if two persons are held to be from one without an order, there would be in that one the characters and properties for originating those two equally uniformly and without order. And in that way either both of them would be constitutive of that person or neither would—for example, either that by which one has its emanation from it in one way or that by which it has its emanation from it in another way. For because it is common, not proper, the common character by which the others have emanation from it can be constitutive of no person. But it must not be said that it is neither or none of them, neither one nor both, because persons in God are constituted only by the

---

291   See above qu. 4, par. 5 and 9.

292   Pseudo-Dionysius, *On the Divine Names* 5; PG 3: 831B.

293   See Aristotle, *Metaphysics* 10.4.1055a3–29; anon. trans, ed. G. Vuillemin-Diem, p. 193.

property by which one is related to another in accord with the character of its origin, as will be stated below.[294]

6. It is therefore necessary to say that both of them are constitutive of the person that is not from another in God. Hence, since, as has been already said in the preceding question,[295] those two characters or properties of the emanations [237] do not have one character, but one of them is in the manner of nature and the other in the manner of will, there would not be a single person not from another, but two, not only two in accord with the same character, as two innascibles, or two unable to proceed, but according to diverse characters, as two unable to be produced, from one of which one person would have to be produced in the manner of will, but another from the other in the manner of nature, and this would necessarily further argue against the oneness of the one God. For according to Hilary, if many were innascible, although according to the same character of the property, there would be many gods.[296] In that way for much better reason, if there were many unable to be produced according to diverse characters of the properties, there would many gods. Thus, just as the oneness of God requires the oneness of the innascible, and the one innascible indicates that there is one God and a plurality indicates a plurality, so the oneness of God requires the oneness of the one unable to be produced so that there is one unable to be produced in accord with one singular character and one manner of the inability to be produced, and one unable to be produced in accord with one character indicates that there is one God and a plurality <indicates> that there is a plurality. Hence, for this reason it is entirely unsuitable and impossible that from that one person that is not from another there emanate two others equally firstly, principally, and immediately.

7. In accord with this, in coming down to the question, I say to the first argument of the question concerning *"equally firstly"* that because the one production of them necessarily—if one may speak in that way—presupposes the other, and not the other way around, for this reason those two do not emanate equally firstly from that one that is not from another, but by a certain order of nature so that *"firstly"* and similarly *"secondly"* explain the disposition of those ordered in accord with a natural order of origin. For in that way one may express those things in God ordered in such [238] an origin as was established above.[297] But because Richard says in book five of *On the Trinity*, chapter seven: *"In that plurality and true eternity of persons nothing there precedes something else; nothing there follows upon something else, and nothing there is earlier in time, nothing is later in time. But what cannot be temporally earlier can be earlier causally*

---

294 See below *SQO* art. 56, qu. 3; ed. Badius 2, fol. 114eL–115vZ.

295 See above qu. 3, par. 43 and qu. 4, par. 11.

296 See Hilary, *On the Synods* 64, 27; PL 10: 523C.

297 See *SQO* art. 52, qu. 4; ed. Badius 2, fol. 59r O–60rR.

and for that reason naturally. For perfection of one person demands the company of another and in that way it turns out that one is the cause of the other."[298] And from this it is seen that he wanted that things ordered naturally in accord with the characters of their origins can not only be explained in accord with the state of their order through those that are first, second, and third, by which they can undoubtedly be explained, but through those that are earlier and later, which is regarded as absurd because the saints deny this latter, but hold the former. In the end of book twelve of *On the Trinity*, the second last chapter, Hilary speaks in this way in talking about the birth of the Son: *"Let the birth testify that God is the author; let it not signify something in reverse order from the author. And by common confession the birth is second from the author because it is from God."*[299] And in the last chapter he says: *"The Son is true God from you, God the Father, and born from you in your unbegotten nature thus to be confessed after you as with you because you are the eternal author of his eternal origin. And since he is from you, he is second from you."*[300]

[239] 8. If "before" and "after" of themselves really expressed only the circumstances of those characters by which things ordered differ from one another insofar as they have an order, and this indeterminately in relation to the things ordered in any order so that their circumstance is determined in accord with the manner of the order and of the things ordered by which they are joined so that, if they are joined to those things that are ordered according to place, they would express "before" and "after" in terms of place. If <they are joined to those things that are ordered> according to time or duration or according to nature, they would express "before" and "after" in terms of time or duration or in terms of nature.. But if <they were jointed to things that are ordered> in terms of origin or in terms of reason only, <they would> similarly <express> "before" and "after" in terms of origin or in terms of reason alone.

9. And Richard undoubtedly understood it in this way, and he indicates it quite well by what he said: *"That which cannot be prior temporally can be prior causally and for that reason naturally."*[301] And he takes "causally" and "for that reason naturally" there in a wide sense for "in terms of origin." For by the fact that he is so in terms of origin, he is so naturally. Hence, in book six, chapter seven, he says: *"We want 'before' and 'after' to be understood here not by a succession of times, but by the order of nature,"*[302] and this in accord with the manner

---

298   Richard of Saint Victor, *On the Trinity* 5, 7; PL 196: 953D–954A; ed. J. Ribaillier, p. 203.

299   Hilary of Poitiers, *On the Trinity* 12, 31; PL 10: 466; ed. P. Smulders, p. 621.

300   Ibid., 12, 54; PL 10: 468; ed. P. Smulders, p. 624.

301   Richard of Saint Victor, *On the Trinity* 5, 7; PL 196: 954A; ed. J. Ribaillier, p. 203.

302   Ibid., 6, 7; PL 196: 972A–B; ed. J. Ribaillier, p. 234.

by which an order of nature is to be held in God, as we have determined above in the questions on the order of the attributes.[303] And in that way I have also not found a saint who expressly denies that "before" and "after" are held in an order with regard to God insofar as they note the circumstance of that order. But what they deny is most of all insofar as they denote the circumstance of things ordered by time or duration or by one of the other manners of order that are not found [240] or accepted in God, which the heretics nonetheless held in him, and this <is found> in the article on the present question. Because, as the Master says in book one of the *Sentences*, distinction twelve: Arius argued as follows: "*If the Holy Spirit proceeded from the Father, he therefore did so either after the Son was already born or when the Son was not born. If <he proceeded> when the Son was already born, the Son was born before the Holy Spirit proceeded. But if <he proceeded> when the Son was not born, he proceeded before the Son was born.*"[304] And Hilary also expresses this well in what he adds after his previously mentioned statement in the second last chapter when he says: "*Therefore, the only pious language here about God is to know the Father and along with him the Son who is from him. And may I never come to that point of folly and impiety that I presume that you were ever without your wisdom, power, and word, the only-begotten God, my Lord Jesus Christ. For although a word, wisdom, and power in us needs our interior activity, with you nonetheless the generation of perfect God who is your word, wisdom, and power is absolute so that he who is born from you under these names of your eternal properties is inseparable from you.*"[305] Likewise, after the already mentioned statement, he speaks in the last chapter as follows: "*But since he is yours, you are not separable from him because you are not to be confessed to have at some time been without your <Son> lest you be proven either to be imperfect without generation or superfluous after generation.*"[306] Augustine also expresses the same thing well when replying to the previously mentioned argument of the heretics in book fifteen of *On the Trinity*, where he says: "*In that highest Trinity that is God there are no intervals of time by which it can be shown <or even asked> whether the Son was firstly born from the Father and the Holy Spirit proceeds from both afterwards.*"[307] Then, [241] after the insertion of some things, he says: "*These things of course cannot be sought there where nothing begins in time so that it continues in the following time.*"[308] Therefore, when <Arius> asks whether

---

303 See *SQO* art. 52, qu. 3; ed. M. Führer, p. 259.

304 Peter Lombard, *Sentences* 1, d. 12, c. 1; PL 192: 553; ed. I. Brady, 1, p. 118.

305 Hilary of Poitiers, *On the Trinity* 12, 51–52; PL 10: 466–467; ed. P. Smulders, pp. 621–622.

306 Ibid. 12, 54; PL 10: 468; ed. P. Smulders, p. 624.

307 Augustine of Hippo, *On the Trinity* 15, 26; PL 42: 1092; ed. W. Mountain and F. Glorie, p. 524.

308 Ibid. 15, 26; PL 42: 1094; ed. W. Mountain and F. Glorie, pp. 527 –528.

the Holy Spirit proceeded when the Son was already born or when the Son was not yet born, neither is to be granted. But by looking at before in time in accord with his understanding, both are to be denied, and that proposition is to be granted: "He did not proceed when the Son was already born," because in the simultaneity of eternity they both proceeded at the same time, although the procession of the Son was first in terms of origin and the procession of the Holy Spirit second, as was said.[309]

10. Hence, since "before" and "after" in God with regard to those things in which it is possible to find some order are not at all understood in accord with the manner of that order, that is, of reason or of origin, as we have determined in the question on the uniformity of the divine acts,[310] this occurs more from our usage than from the nature of the matter. And the reason for this usage is what I expressed above in a certain question on the order of the attributes,[311] namely, that "earlier" and "later" or "before" and "after" are in common usage founded upon things ordered not by reason of a relation that they have between one another, but by reason of the things they signify, one of which has a posteriority in order with respect to the other, as was explained there in creatures. And this cannot be the case in God because it cannot be by reason of the substance—for it is a single one—nor by reason of a relation since "*relative things are by nature simultaneous,*"[312] and there cannot be many realities in God upon which they are founded.

11. But if one looks more interiorly at the notional relations in the divine persons, it is possible to find something in them on account of which the character of earlier and later can be founded on them. For a notional relation can be considered in God [242] in two ways: in one way absolutely as it is a relation, in another way as it has the character of origin, that is, as it is the character by which from another one is, such as paternity, or by which one is from another, such as filiation. Hence, in accord with the first manner of considering them, that is, as they are absolute relations, the relations are simultaneous by nature, and "earlier" and "later" cannot in any way be founded on them. And it is not surprising that in that way the relations do not have an order of origin or of causality between one another because, according to the Philosopher, "*relative things are by nature simultaneous,*"[313] and neither is the cause of the other's existence. But in accord with the second manner of considering them, that is, as they pertain to origin, they are not in that way simultaneous by nature, that is, by a natural understanding, in which they do not have a difference between

---

309   See above par. 7–8.

310   See *SQO* art. 39, qu. 7; ed. G. Wilson, pp. 228–237.

311   See *SQO* art. 52, qu. 3; ed. M. Führer, pp. 263–264.

312   Aristotle, *Categories* 7; trans. Boethius, ed. L. Minio-Paluello, p. 24.

313   Ibid.

the first and the second, just as <they do> not in accord with before and after without having between one another a natural order of origin, and as such, they are not simultaneous by nature, that is, in the nature of originating, in which in accord with the same manner they have a difference in terms of first and second and, according to the statement of Richard, a difference in in terms of before and after,[314] so that in the way that the Son is said to be second after the Father, because he is from him, he is also said to be posterior to him, that is, posterior in origin, not in time or duration or the like.

12. And in accord with this to the previously mentioned question of Arius whether the Holy Spirit proceeded when the Son was already born or when the Son was not already born, it could be replied: "When the Son was already born" so that the Son might be understood to be born before the Holy Spirit proceeded, not because the birth of the Son preceded the procession [243] of the Holy Spirit in time, but only by natural origin, as has been said.[315] Nonetheless, because the heretics understood "before" and "after" in the other ways, the Church for this reason denied without qualification with regard to those other ways that they exist in God, and common usage still twists "before" and "after," "earlier" and "later" back to those manners. And on this account the Church denies without qualification that they are in any way accepted in God. Nonetheless, I do not see that, insofar as lies in the nature of the reality and of the circumstances that they imply, both "first" and "second" cannot be accepted in God in accord with the way in which order has being in him, nor do I nonetheless defend that it ought to be done in that way.

13. In that way, therefore, in returning to the present question, I say that the two previously mentioned emanations of persons from that one that is not from another do not emanate "*equally firstly*," but one <emanates> firstly and the other secondly because they emanate by an order of nature. For although one emanation does not proceed from another, one of them still naturally presupposes the other, and not the other way around, as was said.[316] Thus in accord with this there is another character of the order of the Father to the Son and of both to the Holy Spirit, and of one emanation to the other. Richard gives this argument in another way in book five of *On the Trinity*, chapter seven, when he says: "*Duality is naturally prior to trinity. For the former can be without the latter, but the latter cannot be without the former. Therefore, that procession*

314 See Richard of Saint Victor, *On the Trinity* 5, 7; PL 196: 953D–954A; ed. J. Ribaillier, p. 203.

315 See above par. 5.

316 See above par. 7.

that can subsist in a duality of persons is naturally prior to that which cannot exist without the Trinity of persons."[317]

<Art. Two: Whether They Proceed Equally Principally>

14. Through this the reply to the second part of the question is seen. For just as those emanations do not proceed *"equally firstly"* from that person that is not from another, because the second requires the first, and not [244] the other way around, but that which is required by another for its being is more principal than that which requires it, so the emanations do not proceed equally principally, nor do those persons, but that emanation proceeds more principally that is in the manner of nature, and similarly the person that is produced by it <proceeds more principally>. But Richard gives this argument. For speaking of that first emanation and of first person and of the second emanation and of the second person in this way, he says in book six of *On the Trinity*, chapter seven: *"That first one can consist in a duality of persons alone, but the latter one absolutely cannot be without the Trinity of persons. But duality is prior to trinity with regard to the order of nature. For where there is a trinity, a duality cannot be lacking. But a duality can be even where it happens that a trinity is lacking. Therefore, insofar as it pertains to the order of nature that procession is more principal in which the cause of proceeding is more principal."*[318] Likewise, he gives the same argument from the side of the manners of emanating in chapter eight, when he speaks as follows: *"But the procession of that one is more principal in the manner of nature which clearly proceeds from the innascible alone."*[319] And in chapter seventeen he says: *"The Father produces both the Son and the Holy Spirit from himself, but both exist as consubstantial with him. And yet both cannot be said to be his Son because the production of both is not uniform. For if both were uniform, one would not have been more principal than the other. Among all the manners of proceeding it is clear that the manner of proceeding which is that of the Son from the Father has the first place and is more principal than the others. For where he has not preceded, none will have a place of existing at all."*[320] Understand: He has preceded by the order of natural origin, not of some duration, so that this principality does not express some level of dignity, but the manner of one placed in an order of origin, as the Father is said to be the more principal person in the Trinity, as will now be said in accord with Richard.

[245]   <Art. Three: Whether They Proceed Equally Immediately>

15. But to the third article of the question whether both emanations of the persons proceed equally immediately, one must firstly see how the two persons

317   Richard of Saint Victor, *On the Trinity* 5, 7; PL 196: 953D; ed. J. Ribaillier, p. 202.

318   Ibid. 6, 7; PL 196: 972B; ed. J. Ribaillier, p. 235.

319   Ibid. 6, 8; PL 196: 972D; ed. J. Ribaillier, p. 235.

320   Ibid. 6, 17; PL 196: 981C–D; ed. J. Ribaillier, pp. 250–251.

proceeding from that person that is not from another both immediately proceed from it and then <see> the principal goal of how they proceed equally
immediately. With regard to the first, therefore, it must be known that in God
the person that proceeds firstly from the person that is not from another proceeds immediately, as Richard says in book five of *On the Trinity*, chapter eight:
"*It is necessary that there immediately proceed from that most principal existence
some one <person>; otherwise, it would be necessary that he remain alone*,"[321] and
this <can be> only immediately because there is no other from which it could
proceed, whether mediately or immediately. As he then continues, "*For clearly
there can be no other that does not proceed from it immediately or mediately.*"[322]
And this <is so> because, if that one immediately proceeds from the second,
it has from itself the power of producing other than from the first so that it is
necessary that the third also immediately proceeds from the first. In that way
it would be true concerning the diverse persons produced not only that, where
there is not an immediate production, there cannot be a mediate <one>, but
also concerning the same person produced, that if there is not some one person
immediately produced by it, there cannot be one mediately produced by it. And
in that way in God there can be an immediate production that is in no way mediated and does not require another mediated one, but the other way around,
there can be no mediated production without the same being immediate. And
along with this it requires the other immediate one. But whether there is some
mediate <production> pertains to the following question,[323] and for this reason the rest of this article will be reserved until that one.

16. But insofar as it pertains to the present question "whether *the two persons
that are from another* proceed *equally immediately from the one that is not from
another*,"[324] [246] it must be said that because immediateness consists in the
denial of an intermediate, although mediateness can be multiple in accord with
the plurality of intermediates, immediateness still consists in what is simple
and indivisible in which it is possible to admit only equality. On this account it
must absolutely be held that two persons proceeding from that one that is not
from another proceed from it equally immediately from it. For in <the Father>
the will is equally as fecund as nature and does not requite an intermediate to
produce a person through the manner of will more than nature does to produce a person through the manner of nature. On this account Richard says in
book six of *On the Trinity*, chapter eight: "*In the divine nature you will find one
procession that is immediate and principal, but another that is immediate but not*

---

321   Ibid. 5, 7; PL 196: 954A; ed. J. Ribaillier, p. 202.

322   Ibid.

323   See below qu. 6, par. 35.

324   See above par. 1.

principal."[325] And as a result of this that one that is absolutely immediate is more principal than the one that is at the same time mediated and immediate, as Richard says in book six of *On the Trinity*, chapter two: *"That procession of a person from a person is absolutely immediate in accord with the principal order of proceeding and in accord with the operation of nature."*[326]

<Replies to the Arguments>

17. To the first argument to the contrary that *"the principles of both emanations are equally fecund; therefore, they emanate equally firstly, principally, and immediately,"*[327] it must be said that equal fecundity very well leads to equal immediacy, as was said,[328] but not to equal primacy and principality for the reason that the fecundity of the principle of the second emanation is as if dependent upon the fecundity of the principle of the first emanation and not the other way around, as was said and will be more fully said below.[329]

[247] 18. To the second argument from Dionysius it must be said that his language in that statement is metaphorical and was said through a likeness with regard to those things that emanate, but not with regard to the manners of emanating in favor of which the argument proceeds. For there is a likeness insofar as the persons that proceed in God represent the paternal beauty and brilliance and on this account are like *"flowers and lights"* proceeding from him. But there is not a likeness with regard to the principles of the two flowers or lights that in no way depend on one another in bodily things, from which the metaphor is taken, as the principle of the emanation of the second production quasi depends on the principle of the first production, as was said.

19. To the third argument that *"there is no reason why both emanations of the persons do not emanate equally firstly, principally, and immediately except because there is something in the second emanation through the first,"*[330] it must be said that for the action of emanation from the will the act of emanation from the intellect is required not so much because the action of the will requires knowledge of what is willed as because the will is a fecund principle for personal emanation from it only if the production is communicated by an action of emanation from the intellect in accord with which it will be explained in the next question to follow. But as to what is assumed in the same argument, namely, that *"nothing is required for the action of emanation from the will on account

---

325   Richard of Saint Victor, *On the Trinity* 6, 8; PL 196: 973C; ed. J. Ribaillier, p. 236.

326   Ibid. 6, 2; PL 196: 969C; ed. J. Ribaillier, p. 230.

327   See above par. 1.

328   See above par. 12 and 13.

329   See above par. 12 and below qu. 6

330   See above par. 3.

of which *a person does not emanate* from it *equally firstly* as <it does> from the intellect, since it would otherwise be *in potency* for the second emanation *before it was in act*,"[331] it must be said that it is true if it required it as something not always possessed in the order of duration, but <it is> not <true> when [248] it requires it not as something possessed from itself and its own operation, but as something always necessarily possessed with itself, but in a certain order of priority, if it is permissible for us to speak in that way it was for Richard.

---

331 See above par. 3.

QUESTION SIX

Whether of the Persons Emanating from the One That Is Not from Another One Does Not Emanate from the Other

1. With regard to the sixth question it is firstly argued that of the two persons that emanate from that person that is not from another, one of them does not emanate from the other, because the Holy Spirit who does not emanate by the principal emanation does not emanate from the Son who emanates by the principal emanation, in the first place as follows: For Damascene says in book one of the *Sentences*, chapter ten: "*We believe in one Holy Spirit, God who proceeds from the Father and comes to rest upon the Son.*"[332] Therefore, it is the Son in whom the procession of the Holy Spirit terminates. But the principle from which he emanates and the terminus in which he terminates are not the same. Therefore, and so on.

2. Likewise, <it is argued> in the second place as follows: In chapter eleven he says: "*We say that the Holy Spirit is from the Father and we call him the Spirit of the Father, but we do not say he is from the Son, though we call him the Spirit of the Son.*"[333] [249] Likewise, in the letter, *On the Trisagion*, at the end he says: "*The Spirit is the subsisting procession and emanation of the Father, but of the Son, and not from the Son, as the enunciating breath (spiritus) of the mouth of God the Word.*"[334] But if he emanated from the Son, he would be said to be from him. Therefore, and so on.

3. Likewise, <it is argued> in the third place as follows: In book one, chapter seven, he says: "*It is necessary that the Word have breath (spiritus), for even our word is not without breath that at the time of utterance is the sound of the word revealing the force of the word in itself. For in the divine nature the Word of God does not fade away like our word, but is subsisting as the Word of God, and in that way we understand the Spirit of God as following along with the Word and abiding as his operation, proceeding from the Father, resting upon the Word, and revealing his existence.*"[335] But between that which enunciates or manifests something else and that which it manifests there is not naturally an order of origin. For the two

---

332   John Damascene, *On the Orthodox Faith* 1, 8, 12; PG 94: 822B; ed. E. Buytaert, p. 38,

333   Ibid.1, 8, 18; PG 94: 831B; ed. F. Buytaert, p. 47.

334   John Damascene, *On the Hymn, Trisagion*; PG 95: 59.

335   John Damascene, *On the Orthodox Faith* 1, 7, 1; PG 94: 903C–806B; ed. E. Buytaert, pp. 25–25.

can stand in relation to each other so that neither is nonetheless from the other. But in God there is not an order of origin between some persons without its being between them from the necessity of nature. Therefore, and so on.

4. Likewise, <it is argued> in the fourth place as follows: If the Holy Spirit proceeds from the Son, this is only because the action of the will presupposes the action of the intellect. But it is not proven on this account that it is necessary to hold that the Holy Spirit proceeds from the Son because for the action of the will there is required in the intellect only the knowledge that is to understand or to know, which the action of speaking a word also quasi presupposes because *"a word is knowledge from knowledge."*[336] If then both require the same knowledge, they both can produce their emanations equally firstly according to the order of nature, despite that objection. Therefore, and so on.

[250] 5. Likewise, <it is argued> in the fifth place: Since the Father spirates immediately, as was established above,[337] he has by himself alone the full power of spirating the Holy Spirit. But it is superfluous that many do that which a single one can equally do. But in God nothing is to be held superabundant or superfluous. Therefore, and so on.

6. <It is argued> in the sixth place as follows: If the Holy Spirit proceeded from the Son, since nothing can proceed from the Son unless he already exists, but <the Son> only exists after he has already been born, the Holy Spirit would therefore proceed after the Son was already born, which Augustine denies, as has been already said.[338] Therefore, and so on.

7. <It is argued> in the seventh place as follows: If the Holy Spirit proceeds from the Son when he also proceeds from the Father, he proceeds from both either insofar as they are one or insofar as they are two. <He does> not <proceed from them> insofar as they are one, because they in no way concur in the unity of some person. Besides, if <he proceeded from them> insofar as they are one, then it would fittingly be said that the Father and the Son are one spirator, but in no way that they are two spirators. The consequent is false, as will be seen below.[339] Therefore, and so on. Nor <does he> likewise <proceed from them> insofar as they are two because the Father and the Son are two in some respect only insofar as there occurs the relative opposition of born and unborn, according to Damascene in book one, chapter two.[340] "But in spirating

---

336 Augustine of Hippo, *On the Trinity* 9, 11; PL 42: 970; ed. W. Mountain and F. Glorie, p. 307.

337 See above qu. 5, par. 9.

338 See Augustine of Hippo, *On the Trinity* 15, 26; PL 42: 1092; ed. W. Mountain and F. Glorie, p. 524 and above qu. 5, par. 9.

339 See below par. 65–66.

340 See John Damascene, *On the Orthodox Faith* 1, 1, 3; PG 94: 791C–D; ed. E. Buytaert, p. 14.

the Holy Spirit there is no such opposition, [251] as Anselm says in *On the Procession of the Holy Spirit*: "The Holy Spirit is from the Father and the Son insofar as they are one, that is, from God, not from that by which they are other than each other."[341] Therefore, and so on.

8. <It is argued> in the eighth place as follows: If the Holy Spirit proceeds from both, then <he proceeds from them> either insofar as they are one or insofar as they are many. <He does> not insofar as they are many, because then the substance of the Father would be other than that of the Son. <He does> not insofar as they are one, because they are one only in substance, and that same substance is in the Holy Spirit. Therefore, for the same reason the Holy Spirit would proceed from himself, which is impossible.

9. <It is argued> in the ninth place as follows: If he proceeded from both, <he would> therefore <proceed> either as from one principle or as from many. <He does> not as from one because <he does> not by reason of a person since they are not one person, nor <does he proceed> by reason of the substance since then he would be a principle of himself along with them. Nor <does he proceed> by reason of some property that is common active spiration because, if <he did> on account of the unity of such a property, which is the reason for eliciting the act, the two would be said to be one principle. For the same reason on account of two properties that are the reasons for eliciting two acts, as are paternity with respect to generation and spiration with respect to spiration, insofar as both are in the Father, the Father would be said to be two principles of the Son and of the Holy Spirit because <he would be> one principle of the Son and another of the Holy Spirit. The consequent is false; therefore, the antecedent is also.

10. Besides, if they were one principle, they would therefore either be the one that is the Father, and in that way the Son would be the Father, or <they would be the one> that is not the Father, and then the Father would not be the Father, and both are false. Therefore, and so on.

11. <It is argued> in the tenth place as follows: If the Holy Spirit proceeds from both, he therefore either <proceeds> as from one spirator or <as> from two. He <does> not <proceed> as from one, because "spirator" is a denomination from an act as it emerges from a supposite. But supposites are denominated many from an act in the plural, as many who spirate. Therefore, and so on. He <does> not <proceed> as from two because to be a spirator implies the character of a principle, and they do not spirate as two principles. — Likewise, they do not create as two creators, but as one. Hence, they do not spirate <as two either>. Similarly, <he does> not <proceed> from them as they are two principles, because there is in them [252] only one single common character of

---

341   Anselm of Canterbury, *On the Procession of the Holy Spirit* 14; Pl 158: 318B;
       ed. F. Schmitt 2, p. 12.

spirating the Holy Spirit on account of which there belongs to them the character of a principle with respect to the Holy Spirit.

12. It is argued that the Son also does not emanate from the Holy Spirit in the first place as follows: The Holy Spirit proceeds in the manner of the will, but the Son <proceeds> in the manner of the intellect. But what belongs to the will presupposes what belongs to the intellect, not the other way around, as Damascene says in book two, chapter twenty six: "*The voluntary is that whose principle is in the knower.*"[342] And Augustine says in *To Orosius*: "*The will cannot precede wisdom.*"[343] But that from which something else emanates is in some way prior to it, as was said above. Therefore, and so on.

13. It is argued that it is necessary that one of them proceed from the other as follows: Richard says in book five of *On the Trinity*, chapter ten: "*If two persons proceeded from only one, neither would immediately cling to the other,*"[344] and as he says in chapter twelve: "*If neither immediately clings to the other, they would surely be united by a mediated kinship.*"[345] And in that way there would not be among the divine persons the highest and equal kinship, which is impossible.

14. But it is argued through Augustine that the Son emanates from the Holy Spirit in book nine of *On the Trinity*, the last chapter: "*Desire precedes the mind's giving birth.*"[346] The Holy Spirit proceeds by the desire of the will, as was established, but the Son or the Word <proceeds> by the mind's giving birth. Therefore, and so on.

15. But that the Holy Spirit proceeds from the Son is said in the Creed of Athanasius: "*The Holy Spirit from the Father and the Son, not made, nor created, nor begotten, but proceeding.*"[347]

[253] <The Resolution of the Question>

16. This question touches on the controversy concerning the procession of the Holy Spirit. For those who say that the Holy Spirit does not proceed from the Son say that neither of the persons emanating from the person that is not from another emanates from the other, because those two persons that emanate are the Son who emanates in the manner of nature and the Holy Spirit who emanates in the manner of will. But concerning the Holy Spirit no one

---

342 John Damascene, *On the Orthodox Faith* 2, 38, 3: PG 94: 954C–D; ed. E. Buytaert, p. 146.

343 Pseudo-Augustine, *Dialogue with Orosius*; PL 40: 736.

344 Richard of Saint Victor, *On the Trinity* 5, 10; PL 196: 957C; ed. J. Ribaillier, p. 208.

345 Ibid. 5, 12; PL 196: 958D; ed. J. Ribaillier, p. 210.

346 Augustine of Hippo, *On the Trinity* 9, 12; PL 42: 972; ed. W. Mountain and F. Glorie, p. 310.

347 Pseudo-Athanasian Creed, in *Enchiridion Symbolorum*, ed. H. Denzinger and A. Schönmetzer, #75.

has ever doubted whether the Son proceeds from him. For from the beginning of the faith all have denied this, and they undoubtedly did not introduce this because sacred scripture does not teach it in some statement by ascribing some authority to the Holy Spirit over the Son of the sort that ought to belong to the one from whom another proceeds over the one who proceeds from him. For what it is written in Isaiah forty-eight that Christ said: *The Lord and his Spirit sent me* (Is 48:16), he is understood to have been said concerning his mission to preach and with regard to his human nature over which the Holy Spirit has the authority to send.

17. With regard to this question therefore there is only a doubt with regard to the procession or emanation of the Holy Spirit from the Son. And the Master says in distinction twelve of book one that *"many heretics have denied this."*[348] And there are some who say that the whole church of the Greeks is heretical on this because they do not agree on this with the church of the Latins on all things. And this seems harsh to many on account of John Damascene and very many other teachers of the Greeks. On this account they say that there is no opposition in the statements of the Greeks to the statements of the Latins with regard to the procession of the Holy Spirit insofar as it is from the side of the reality. And some show this from the side of the word by which the Greeks express their intention. But others show this from the side of the manner of speaking and expressing their intention.

[254] 18. The first ones say that among the Greeks "to proceed" not only expresses the emanation of a person and its emergence from the one from whom it emanates, but also expresses its going forth into another as into one in whom the one emerging and emanating comes to a rest. Hence, although they understood that the Holy Spirit emerges and emanates from both, they still could not in terms of the proper sense of the word among them say that he proceeded from the Son because, although he goes forth from both, he still goes forth from the Father into the Son, and not the other way around, and this <is so> insofar as in the emanation of the Holy Spirit the spirative power has being from the Father in the Son, and not the other way around. But John <Damascene> is against this in what he says, as has already been established: "*We do not say that the Holy Spirit is from the Son.*"[349] Therefore, as the Greeks do not say that the Holy Spirit proceeds from the Son, so they also do not say that he is from the Son by any manner of emanation. And this is true for many of them. Still, as those who have seen their books say, some of them say that he proceeds from the Son. For Cyril, as they say, in speaking of the Son says: "*The Spirit of the truth*

---

348   Peter Lombard, *Sentences* 1, d. 11, c. 1; PL 192: 551; ed. I. Brady, 1, p.114,

349   John Damascene, *On the Orthodox Faith* 1, 8, 18; PG 94: 831B–834A; ed. E. Buytaert, p. 47. See above par. 2.

flows forth *from* him, just as he ultimately does from *God the Father.*"[350] And Didymus says in the book, *On the Holy Spirit:* "*Nor is the substance of the Holy Spirit another apart from that which is given to him by the Son.*"[351] In the same place the same man says, as it is said in the last chapter of the *Decretals:* "*The savior is not from himself, but is from the Father and me.*"[352] And in accord with this the Master introduces many authorities in the *Sentences,* distinction twelve.[353]

[255] 19. For this reason others say in order to excuse those who also do not say that the Holy Spirit is from the Son that, although the Greeks do not say that the Holy Spirit is from the Son, they still do not deny this. The reason why they do not say this is that, as John Damascene says in the beginning of his *Sentences* on behalf of himself and of his people: "*We accept and venerate and know everything that has been handed down to us both through the law and the prophets and through the apostles and evangelists, seeking nothing beyond these things. Let us love these things, abide in them, and not cross the eternal boundaries, and let us not go beyond the divine tradition.*"[354] And on this he agrees with Blessed Dionysius who says: "*One should not dare to say something about the* substantial divinity *besides those things that have been expressed by God for us from the sacred words.*"[355] Hence, since it is not expressly contained in the sacred words concerning the Son that the Holy Spirit proceeded from him, as it is expressly contained concerning the Father in John fifteen: *The Spirit of the truth who proceeds from the Father* (Jn 15:26), for this reason then they do not say that the Holy Spirit proceeds from the Son, and <they do not say> this especially because the general synod of Nicaea expressed this concerning the profession of faith that was established where we read as follows: "*We believe in the Holy Spirit who proceeds from the Father to be adored with the Father and the Son,*"[356] and also because it is found to have been forbidden in certain councils under penalty of anathema that anything be added to the symbol decreed in the councils. Likewise, in the time of the apostles it is said to have been written [256] in a certain legend of Blessed Andrew: "*Peace to*

---

350   Cyril of Alexandria, *Letters* 17; PG 77: 118C. See also Jerome, *Interpretation of the Book of Didymus on the Holy Spirit,* PL 23: 134A, and Peter Lombard, *Sentences* 1, d. 11, c. 2: PL 192: 553A; ed. I. Brady, 1, p. 117.

351   Didymus, *On the Holy Spirit* 36; PG 39: 1065A; also Jerome, *Interpretation of the Book of Didymus on the Holy Spirit;* PL 23, 135A.

352   Peter Lombard, *Sentences* 1, d. 11, c. 2; PL 192: 553A–B; ed. I. Brady, 1, p. 117.

353   Ibid.

354   John Damascene, *On the Orthodox Faith* 1, 1, 2; PG 94: 791A; ed. E. Buytaert, pp. 12–13.

355   Pseudo-Dionysius, *On the Divine Names* 1, 1; PG 3: 587C; trans. Saracennae; see also Thomas Aquinas, *Summa of Theology* 1, qu. 36, art. 2, ad 2um.; ed. Leonine, 4, p. 376A.

356   *Nicene–Constantinopoletan Symbol;* in *Enchiridion Symbolorum;* ed. H. Denzinger–A. Schönmetzer, #150.

all who believe in one God the Father and in his one Son and in the one Holy Spirit proceeding from the Father and abiding in the Son."[357] Nor do the Greeks expressly deny that the Holy Spirit proceeds from the Son except those who among them were expressly heretical.

20. But is it enough for John Damascene and those like him not to say this and on this point to hold it as doubtful and imply that it is false, since the apostle says in the Letter to the Romans, chapter ten: *In the heart it is believed unto righteousness, and on the lips confession is made unto salvation* (Rom 10:10)? Before this was actually determined and expressed by the Church and later men, it was sufficient to confess that the Holy Spirit proceeded from the Father without saying or professing that he proceeds from the Son, because it is permissible to hold contrary opinions about the divine notions and other matters of faith up to the point that they have been discovered by veridical reason or by the authority of the Church, as it has been discovered thus far that the Holy Spirit proceeds from the Son. For it was ordered that this be professed and added in the Symbol of the Council of Nicaea as follows: *"And in the Holy Spirit who gives life,* who proceeds from the Father and the Son."[358] And the expression: *"And from the Son"* was added by the authority of the Council of Ephesus in the first book of the *Decretals* in the second last chapter concerning the Holy Spirit where it is said: [257] *"He is called the Spirit of the truth, and the truth is Christ. Hence, he also similarly proceeds from him, as* <he does> *from God the Father."*[359]

21. Nor did the holy fathers decree this merely as their will moved them, but on the basis of veridical reason showing and explaining this to them. For there are certain arguments for this that are reductions to what is impossible or unsuitable, but the ostensive argument is stronger. One argument that leads to what is unsuitable, which accord to Anselm *"is impossible in God,"*[360] is the argument of Richard already touched upon, that the Son and the Holy Spirit would not be joined by the highest kinship.[361] Hence, in order that their kinship might be perfect, it is necessary that each person be immediately joined to each so that from the first there are two and from the two there is the third and the one in between is from one and the other from it. In that way there is full

---

357   *The Martyrdom of Saint Andrew;* PG 2: 1217; 2, 1; *Acta Apostolorum Apocrypha;* ed. M. Bonnet, p. 2.

358   *Nicene–Constantinopolitan Creed* in *Enchiridion Symbolorum;* ed. H. Dinzinger–A. Schönmetzer, #151.

359   Gratian, *Decretals* 3; ed. A. Friedberg, p. 1194.

360   Anselm of Canterbury, *Why God Became Man* 1, 20; PL 158: 375C; ed. F. Schmidt, 2, p. 86; see also his *On the Incarnation of the Word* 10; PL 158: 276C; ed. F. Schmidt, 2, 26.

361   Richard of Saint Victor, *On the Trinity* 5, 12; PL 196: 958D; ed. J. Ribaillier, p. 210.

equality in the Trinity like a triangle enclosed by three lines to which nothing can be added or taken away, that is, so that from the first point there proceed single lines to the second and to the third point, and one line from the second to the third. But this argument does not sow that the Holy Spirit proceeds from the Son more than the other way around that the Son <proceeds> from the Holy Spirit.

22. But others have another argument and, as it seems to them, leading to what is impossible of this sort: If the Holy Spirit does not proceed from the Son, there can be no distinction of the Son and the Holy Spirit, because in God there is a distinction of persons only according the characters of origin, which are only because one is from another. Therefore, if one of them is not from another, there is no distinction of them, and they are not diverse persons. In that way to hold that the Son is another person than the person of the Holy Spirit and that neither of them proceeds from the other is [258] to hold not only what is impossible, but what is also self-contradictory, namely, that one person is distinct and not distinct from another. This argument does not show that the Son proceeds from the Holy Spirit rather than the other way around, just as the preceding one <did not>. But the former argument is more efficacious because that to which it leads is truly unsuitable and correctly follows from the position, but the unsuitable conclusion to which this latter argument leads does not follow from the position. For if the Holy Spirit is held to proceed from the Father and the Son without qualification and neither <proceeds> from the other, the Son would still be distinguished from the Holy Spirit, although otherwise and not so properly as now, as will be seen below.[362] For there are certain relations of origin and ones that are opposed, as those that are in diverse persons, one of which proceeds from the other, and certain disparate ones, as those that are in the same person, from which diverse persons proceed in diverse ways or in diverse persons proceeding in diverse ways from the same person. In the first way there are diverse relations in the Father and the Son; in the second way <there are diverse relations> in the Father with respect to the Son and the Holy Spirit and in the Holy Spirit and the Son with respect to the Father. And this diversity of relations is sufficient in them, even if neither proceeded from the other.

23. And this is explained by reducing it to what is impossible by granting the opposite. Because if the Son and the Holy Spirit were distinguished from each other only because the Holy Spirit proceeds from the Son, by the same reason, therefore, by which the Holy Spirit proceeds from the Father in another way than the Son proceeds from him, the Holy Spirit is not distinguished from the Son, and if that is so, therefore, for the same reason neither is the emanation by which the Holy Spirit proceeds from the Father, as he proceeds from

362   See *SQO* art. 59, qu. 4; Badius 2, fol. 146rN–147vZ and 60, 2; ed. Badius 2, fol. 162vB–163rE.

him, [259] distinguished from the emanation by which the Son proceeds from the Father. And furthermore nor is the power to spirate by which the Holy Spirit emanates from the Father distinguished from the power to generate by which the Son proceeds from the Father, and thus insofar as both the Son and the Holy Spirit proceed from the Father, they are not distinct persons, but a single one. Nor similarly are the emanations of generation and of spiration diverse emanations, but a single one. And similarly the generative power and the spirative <power> are not distinct powers, but a single one, except perhaps according to reason alone. And in that way the Son and the Holy Spirit would proceed equally principally, firstly, and immediately from the Father because this primary principality and immediacy is founded only on diverse characters of originating in the order of nature, as was said.[363] But the contrary of this was shown and determined in the preceding question.[364]

24. Furthermore, if the spirative power as it belongs to the Father were not distinguished from the generative power, neither would spiration <be distinguished> from generation. Hence, since the Son has the spirative power only from the Father and not as more distinct from the generative power than insofar as the Father has it, similarly, the emanation of spiration as it is from the Son would not be distinguished from the emanation of generation, nor as a consequence would the Holy Spirit be from the Son, which is completely false.

25. Therefore, the Son and the Holy Spirit are be sufficiently distinguished by disparate relations, if neither proceeded from the other, just as their processions also <would be>, which are not otherwise distinguished, nor similarly are the principles that elicit them, as they are under the personal respects, so that according to this it is necessary to reduce the distinction of the persons of the Son and of the Holy Spirit from opposing relations when they proceed from one another to the distinction of the emanations and further to the distinctions of the principles of emanating through the disparate relations, so that if there were not this distinction of [260] disparate relations, nor <would there be> that of opposition. On this account the diverse disparate relations can also be in the same person that is the principle of them, although not in the same person that is proceeding from a principle, as was said above.[365]

26. Therefore, the distinction of these two emanations is not to be sought in another way. For although between the persons there is a distinction by relations not only disparate and quasi different in species, as will be said below,[366] but also by opposing ones, that is, insofar as one of them proceeds from another, still a distinction is not to be sought among the emanations except through

---

363   See above qu. 5, par. 11.

364   See above qu. 5, par. 11.

365   See above par. 22.

366   See below par. 31.

disparate relations in accord with a diverse manner of proceeding, not through ones opposed relatively, because one procession does not proceed from another and is not said to be relatively to it, whether the second procession emanates from a single person or from two. But there is nonetheless an order of nature between them insofar as one quasi presupposes the other, even if the second procession were not from the Son, as was said. Thus in accord with this the order of nature among the processions is in different ways, but <it is> in other way among the persons, so that we absolutely ought not at all to seek a similar manner of distinction among the processions of the sort we see in the persons.

27. Augustine clearly teaches this manner of the distinction of the emanations and no other in book fifteen of *On the Trinity*, chapter twenty-seven, in determining that on account of such a distinction of the emanations the Son is distinguished from the Holy Spirit insofar as the one is called the Son and the other is not, when he speaks as follows: *"In that eternal, equal, incorruptible, and ineffably immutable Trinity it is difficult to distinguish generation from procession."*[367] And below he says: *"Raise your eyes to this light and fix them there if you can. For in that way you will see how the birth of the Word of God differs from the procession of the gift of God. And on this account the only-begotten Son [361] said that the Holy Spirit proceeds, but is not born from the Father. Otherwise he would be his brother."*[368] And after interposing an explanation of these things on the word that proceeds from our understanding and on the love <that proceeds> from the will, he adds: *"And in that way there is conveyed in this intelligible reality a certain distance between birth and procession."*[369] And Anselm explains this more clearly in the beginning of *On the Procession of the Holy Spirit*: *"Therefore, this is the sole cause of plurality in God, namely, that Father and Son and Holy Spirit cannot be said of one another, but they are other than one another, because in the two previous mentioned ways God is from God, and this whole can be said to be a relation. For because the Son is from God by being born and the Holy Spirit <is from God> by proceeding, they are related to each other by the diversity of birth and of procession so that they are diverse and other than each other."*[370] And below he says: *"And if the Son and the Holy Spirit were not many through something else, they would be diverse through this alone."*[371]

28. But because the previously mentioned men hold in their argument that to hold that the Son is distinct from the Holy Spirit if he does not proceed

---

367 Augustine of Hippo, *On the Trinity* 15, 27; PL 42: 1095; ed. W. Mountain and F. Glorie, p. 529.

368 Ibid.; PL 42: 1097; ed. W. Mountain and F. Glorie, p. 532.

369 Ibid.; PL 42: 1097; ed. W. Mountain and F. Glorie, p. 533.

370 Anselm of Canterbury, *On the Procession of the Holy Spirit* 1; PL 158: 287; ed. F. Schmitt, 2, p. 179.

371 Ibid.; PL 158: 292; ed. F. Schmitt, 2, p. 185.

from him is to hold what is self-contradictory, it must be said that it is not true, just as to hold that a human being would differ from an animal if he were not risible is not to hold something self-contradictory, namely, that he would differ and not differ from an animal by risibility or that he would be a human being without risibility. And similarly in the present case there is only proposed as something impossible, namely, that the Son does not differ from the Holy Spirit if <the Holy Spirit> does not proceed from him by active spiration or would not be the Son if he did not spirate the Holy Spirit. It still does not follow that he does not differ from him at all, just as it does not follow that if a man is not risible, he does not differ from an animal [262] at all; rather, even if he were not risible—if one holds that this was the case, albeit impossible—he would still differ from an animal by rationality. So in the present question the Son would differ from the Holy Spirit by nascibility, even if the Holy Spirit did not proceed from him, if one holds that this is so, albeit impossible.

29. For the understanding of this it must be known that something is only then held to be impossible, when it is held along with that which principally asserts its contradictory, and that only happens when that removes something that pertains to its signification and essence, as if it were said: "If a man were not rational, he would differ from an animal," because if "rational" were removed, there remains only what he has in common with an animal. But when it does not imply that which belongs to the signification and essence of what is asserted, then it does not assert its contradictory principally, but only as a consequence. And for this reason only such an assertion is held as impossible. For example, if he is said to be a man and that he is not risible. For because "risible" is an accident of "man," it lies outside what it signifies. It is that way in the present question in asserting that he is the Son and that the Holy Spirit does not proceed from him. For active spiration lies outside of what "son" signifies and is like a consequence of his person in a certain order, as is seen from what has been said.[372] And for this reason, just as it is true to say that, if a man were not rational, he would not differ from an animal, because he differs essentially by "rational," which is not removed except as a consequence by the removal of "risible," so it is true to say that, if a man were not risible, he would still differ from an animal, because he differs essentially by "rational," which is not taken away except as a certain consequence by the removal of "risible," and that consequence is still to be denied, because it is opposed to what is asserted.

30. However, something opposed to what is asserted that lies outside its essence and meaning, must always be denied in false assertions, according to the art of the [263] Philosopher in book eight of *Topics*.[373] And similarly it is true

---

372   See above qu. 5, par. 5 and 7.

373   See Aristotle, *Topics* 8.3–5.159a3–b35; anon. trans.; ed. L. Minio-Palluello and B. G. Dod, pp. 295–297.

to say in the present question that, although the Son does not spirate the Holy Spirit, he still differs from the Holy Spirit by birth, according to the manner stated, because not to spirate does not remove birth from the Son except by a certain consequence, as is seen from what has already been said. Besides, let it be that to spirate belongs to the essence and the signification of the Son, so that it is self-contradictory to assert <that he is> the Son and that the Holy Spirit does not proceed from him, still it pertains to the person of the Son only as something that is common to him along with the Father, and birth belongs to him as something proper by which he differs from the Father, just as to be animal is something common to a man and to a brute, but <to be> rational by which <a man> differs from a brute is proper to him. Just, therefore, as it is true to say that although a man were not animal, but only rational, he would still differ from a brute, because a brute is non-rational, so it is true to say in the present question that, even if he did not spirate the Holy Spirit, the Son would differ from the Holy Spirit because the latter is not born, despite the self-contradictoriness implied in both cases. But it would be false to say that, although the Holy Spirit is not spirated, he would differ from the Son, because to be spirated is a property constitutive of the person of the Holy Spirit by which he differs from the Son, and self-contradictories are implied.

31. But against this it is argued in accord with those upholding the contrary position as follows: A relation distinguishes in God only insofar as it is real and by the character of its quiddity. But the character of its quiddity and reality in accord with which one is other than another is only taken from the fact that through it a supposite is related to its opposite. If then the Holy Spirit did not proceed from the Son and thus would not be distinguished from him in accord with the opinion of others, neither would generation and spiration in the Father be distinguished as disparate except in terms of reason alone, just as the Son also would be distinguished from the Holy Spirit only by reason alone. And it must be said that what they assumed as a principle is false, namely, that the reality of a relation in accord with [264] which one is from another is taken only from a relation to its opposite, because the reality of a relation is not at all taken from a relation to its opposite, but from its foundation, as has often been said in other questions and will be said more fully below.[374]

32. To show the present issue more effectively, that is, that the Holy Spirit proceeds from the Son there is an ostensive argument explaining the reason for such a position. For according to what was said above in the beginning of the resolution of the preceding question,[375] it is impossible that many proceed from the same principle through complete equality without any order. For this is the

---

374 See *SQO* art. 34, qu. 2 and art. 34, qu. 5; ed. R. Macken, pp. 181 and 205 and below art. 55, qu. 6, par. 15–19

375 See above qu. 5, par. 5.

case only in things that differ in terms of matter and only numerically, as one craftsman produces two knives and not one by means of the other, or as one light produces many rays.

33. But to apply that more clearly to the present question, by beginning a little more deeply, it must be known in accord with what was determined far above[376] that being is the first and more proper of all those things that belong to God. And in terms of its concept it presupposes nothing before itself in God, but everything else is included in its concept of it. On this account Dionysius says in chapter five of *On the Divine Names:* "*Being is set before the other attributes of God, and it is by itself the greatest. God is therefore rightly praised as being more principally than by the others,* as by what is more excellent *and more worthy than his other gifts,*"[377] so that for this reason somehow by a certain order of our reason and understanding, living proceeds from being as from what is the first and the principle, and understanding <proceeds> from living, and willing <proceeds> from understanding. But [265] in their proceeding understanding from living and living from being have a different sort of proceeding than willing has from understanding, because the former three are related among themselves in their being one from another as if through a certain informing. For understanding is a certain living, and living is a certain being. But understanding and willing are not related among themselves in that way, but rather as if through a certain distinction. For willing is not a certain understanding, nor the other way around.[378] And it is similarly with regard to intelligence and will, and this is due to the fact that they have a certain order of reason between themselves, that is, although both are quasi natural potencies of an immaterial, living nature, the action of the will still quasi requires an action of the intellect, and not the other way around. For we can understand what we do not will, but we cannot will what we do not understand or know,[379] according to Augustine.[380] And on this account, as in accord with our understanding intelligence stands quasi more immediately in relation to life than will does, as they proceed by a certain quasi order of reason from life, and just as there is such an order of reason in them as they have being in the person that is not from another with regard to their essential acts, which are willing and understanding, so there is in

---

376 See above qu. 5, par. 5 and *SQO* art. 27, qu. 1; ed. Badius 1, fol. 157vG–158rH and 36, 1; ed. G. Wilson, pp. 93–94.

377 Pseudo-Dionysius, *On the Divine Names* 1, 5; PG 3: 819A–B; trans. Saracennae.

378 See *SQO* art. 45, qu. 2; ed. L. Hödl, pp. 105–109 and art. 61, qu 6; ed. Badius 2, fol. 178vF–179rL.

379 See *SQO* art. 8, qu. 2 and art. 24, qu.1; ed. Badius 1, fol. 64rG–65rM and 137rB–137vE.

380 See Augustine of Hippo, *On the Trinity* 10, 2, 4; PL 42: 974; ed. W. Mountain and F. Glorie, p. 315.

them an order of nature with regard to their notional acts, which are speaking or generating and spirating. For just as the perfection of the will with regard to its quasi first essential act requires the previous perfection of the intelligence with regard to its quasi first and essential act, so its perfection with regard to its notional quasi [266] second act, by which it is consummated in perfection, as was stated above, requires the quasi second perfection of the intelligence, namely, with regard to its notional act. But the quasi second perfection of the intelligence consists in the production of the Word, while the quasi second perfection of the will consists in the love that proceeds, which is the Holy Spirit, in accord with what will be explained below.[381]

34. Necessarily, therefore, by the order of nature the procession of the Holy Spirit quasi presupposes the production of the Son. Hence, Damascene also says in book one, chapter seven: "<We have learned of> *the Holy Spirit following with the Word. Nor is the Father ever lacking to the Word, nor the Spirit to the Word.*"[382] But one can understand that expression: <the Holy Spirit> as following not the Word, but <as following> the Father along with the Word. And this cannot stand because the Father producing the Word by the work of intelligence communicates everything that is his to him except his property of origin by which he generates and stands in relative opposition to him, as Augustine says in book fifteen of *On the Trinity*, chapter fourteen: "*The Word of God, the only-begotten Son, like and equal to the Father in all things, is absolutely everything that the Father is, and is yet not the Father, because this one is the Son, that one the Father.*"[383] And there follows after a little: "*Therefore, as if speaking himself, the Father begot the Word equal to himself in all things, and he would not have entirely and perfectly spoken himself if there were something more or less in the Word than in himself.*"[384] The Son therefore has from the Father communicated to him through generation whatever is in the Father except his property relative to the Son by which he is the Father and generates the Son or speaks the Word. Hence, <he> also <has> his will fecund with the power to spirate. Hence, since the same action proceeds in common from both in whom there is the same common active power that is the principle of action, [267] therefore, just as the Father spirates the Holy Spirit by that power so that he proceeds from him, the Son also <spirates him> so that he proceeds from him, just as <he does> from the Father, so that he follows the Word in the way in which he follows the Father. And this is what Richard says in book five, chapter eight:

381 See *SQO* art. 60, qu. 3 and art. 61, qu. 6; ed. Badius 2, fol. 163vK–167rH and 178rE–180rS.

382 John Damascene, *On the Orthodox Faith* 1, 7, 1; PG 94: 806B; ed. E. Buytaert, pp. 26–27.

383 Augustine of Hippo, *On the Trinity* 15, 14; PL 42: 1076; ed. W. Mountain and F. Glorie, p. 496.

384 Ibid.

"If the same common power belongs to both, it follows that the third person in the Trinity both has received being and has existence from both."[385] And after some things inserted after this, he says: *"He gave to the one immediately existing from himself whatever could truthfully be given by one who is omnipotent. There is therefore common to them that being from which there is the being and the power of all the rest. Therefore, from that twofold existence there is every essence, every existence, every person; therefore, there is also that which is the third person in the Trinity. And as the perfection of the one is the cause of the other, so also the perfection of the two is the cause of the third person in the Trinity."*[386] On this account the Son says of the Holy Spirit in John, sixteen: *He will glorify me because he will receive from what is mine* (Jn 16:14). And lest it be said: *"It is true that he will receive it but only from the Father,"* he adds: *Everything that the Father has is mine* (Jn 16:15), in which there is included the authority as a principle and spirative power that the Son has from the Father and as common with the Father, and through that he implies he has it from himself from what is his own.

35. From this there is seen what was omitted in the preceding question,[387] namely, that because the first person has from himself the power by which the third <person> is produced, he immediately produces it along with the second <person>, because the second <person> has that power from the first so that the second also immediately produces the third through that power and so that the third person proceeds not only immediately, but also mediately from the first. Still it is not possible that a person in God be produced only mediately, as was said there. On this account Richard says in book five [268] of *On the Trinity*, chapter six: *"In human beings a person at times proceeds only immediately from a person and at times only mediately, but at times both mediately and immediately. Both Isaac and Jacob proceeded from the substance of Abraham, but the one only mediately, the other only immediately."*[388] But the divine processions do not correspond to these processions, but rather that one does by which Eve immediately proceeds from the substance of Adam, and Seth immediately proceeds from the substance of the two, and <proceeds> mediately from the substance of Adam through Eve, so that in that way Seth proceeded both immediately and mediately. Hence, as he concludes in chapter nine: *"It is necessary that one existence be immediately joined to the innascible and the other <be joined to it> both mediately and immediately, but none only mediately."*[389] And as he concludes

---

385   Richard of Saint Victor, *On the Trinity* 5, 8; PL 196: 954D–955B; ed. J. Ribaillier, p. 204.

386   Ibid; PL 196: 955B–C; ed. J. Ribaillier, p. 205.

387   See above qu. 5, par. 15–16.

388   Richard of Saint Victor, *On the Trinity* 5, 6; PL 196: 933A; ed. J. Ribaillier, p. 201.

389   Ibid. 5, 9; PL 196: 955D; ed. J. Ribaillier, p. 205.

in chapter ten: "*If there could have been a fourth person in the deity, it would undoubtedly have to draw its origin immediately from the other three. And if there could have been a fifth person, it would for a similar reason immediately proceed from the other four, and in that way in the following ones however far this series of processions might be extended. For as in the two persons there is that common power, from which it is clear that the third draws its origin, so there would be that power common to the three, from which the fourth would have to be, if a fourth had place in the deity. Otherwise the two would selfishly keep for themselves what could be given to the third with no impairment to the property of the two. And you will undoubtedly find in the following what we have stated in these. For such a difference of properties consists in the number of those producing.* [269] *For the first has being from no other; the second only from one, but the third from two, and if the number went on to more, it would be necessary to find the same sort of progression in all.*"[390] In that way it is clear by a veridical argument that from the necessity of the divine nature that it is necessary that the Holy Spirit proceed from the Son, whatever the Greeks may say.

36. Nor does it help them that, according to Dionysius: "*One should not dare to say concerning the deity something beyond what is expressed in the sacred writings.*"[391] It is true <that one should not dare to say anything beyond what is expressed> either mediately or immediately. For although there is expressed immediately by the sacred writings only that which the words were imposed to signify by themselves, still there is expressed mediately by the same words whatever can be elicited and understood by a veridical argument through what the words firstly signify. On this account Augustine says in that sermon, "Because most profoundly," "*Concerning the assumption of the Blessed Mary, the Mother of God, matters that are great must be handled with greater caution to the extent that they cannot more particularly be clearly supported by the testimonies of authorities. But because,*" as he goes on to say, "*sacred scripture leaves certain matters to be investigated by the pursuits of true studies, they should not be regarded as superfluous when they are set forth by true investigation. For the authority of the truth is fecund, and when it is carefully examined, it is known to bring forth from itself that which it is. For when it is examined, it often begets a true* understanding *that the plain words concealed.*"[392] And he concludes from these words after a bit: "*What is to be said when the divine scripture endorses nothing but that one must seek by reason what agrees with the truth, and the truth itself becomes the authority without which it is necessary that the authority is useless?*"[393]

---

390   Ibid. 5, 10: PL 196: 936D–937A; ed. J. Ribaillier, p. 207–208.

391   Pseudo-Dionysius, *On the Divine Names* 1, 1; PG 3: 587C.

392   Rather, William of Saint Theodoric, *Sermon on the Assumption* 2; PL 40: 1143-1144.

393   Ibid.; PL 40: 1144.

37. Therefore, although it is not expressed through the words of scripture as their immediate sense, it is still expressed by them as their [270] mediate sense to be drawn out by veridical reason from the sense that is immediately expressed. For since scripture says that the Holy Spirit proceeds from the Father, and he cannot proceed from him unless <the Father> quasi previously by the order of nature communicates to the Son that power through generation that reason dictates by the pursuit of a true investigation. And from this it follows, as is clear from the argument set forth, that the Holy Spirit also necessarily proceeds from the Father. In this way Augustine concludes from the words of scripture in book fifteen of *On the Trinity*, chapter twenty-five, that the Holy Spirit proceeds from the Son, where he speaks as follows: "*The Holy Spirit proceeds from both because the holy scripture says that he is the Spirit of both.*"[394] For he is said to be the Spirit of the Son in Romans, eight: *If anyone does not have the Spirit of Christ, he does not belong to him* (Rom 8:9) and in Galatians, four: *God sent the Spirit of his Son into our hearts* (Gal 4:6). For he is said to be the Spirit of the Father in Matthew, ten: *For it is not you who speak, but the Spirit of your Father* (Mt 10:20). Likewise, he is proven to proceed from both because we read that he is sent by both since one who sends is none other than one who has authority over the one who sends. For the Son says of the Holy Spirit in John, fifteen: *The Paraclete will come whom I shall send to you from the Father* (Jn 15:26) and in John, sixteen: *Whom the Father will send in my name* (Jn 14:26).

38. Hence, on account of this mediate sense of sacred scripture, it is to be held generally that what is said of one person is understood of the others, where "*an opposition of relation does not prevent this.*"[395] And there is much need to look to this rule frequently because as the Master of the Sentences says: "*When Christ says that the Holy Spirit proceeds from the Father,*[396] *he does not add: 'alone,' and for this reason he also does not deny that he proceeds from himself because he usually attributes to <the Father> what he himself is because he has it from him.*"[397] Hence, Augustine says [271] in chapter twenty-seven: "*Therefore, if the Holy Spirit proceeded from the Father and the Son, why did the Son say: 'He proceeds from the Father,' unless it was as he was accustomed to attribute to him what belongs to him from whom he himself is? Hence, there are also his words: 'My teaching is not mine, but that of him who sent me'* (Jn 7:16). *If then the teaching in this case is understood to be his, which he still said is not his, but the Father's, how much more ought it to be understood in the former case that the Holy Spirit proceeds*

---

394   Augustine of Hippo, *On the Trinity* 15, 26; PL 42: 1095; ed. W. Mountain and F. Glorie, p. 524.

395   Anselm of Canterbury, *On the Procession of the Holy Spirit* 1; PL 158: 288; ed. F. Schmitt 2, p. 181.

396   See Jn 15: 26.

397   Peter Lombard, *Sentences* 1, d. 1, 1; PL 192: 552; ed. I. Brady, 1, p. 116.

from him, where he says in that way: 'He proceeds from the Father,' since he did not say: 'He did not proceed from me.'[398] Hence, the apostles too subsequently held this manner <of interpretation>.

39. Nor should one absolutely deny that scripture expressed in the proper and immediate sense that the Holy Spirit proceeds from both, although in metaphorical language, where John says in the Apocalypse, chapter twenty-two: *He showed me a bright river of living water going forth from the face of God and of the Lamb* (Rev 22:1). That water is the Holy Spirit; that throne of God and of the Lamb is the concordant will of the Father and the Son. Through this it is seen that the mere mention in the Creed of the Nicene Council that the Holy Spirit proceeds from the Father does not help them. For through this, as was said,[399] we are given to understand that he also proceeds from the Son.

40. And the addition that *"the Council forbids under anathema to add to the Creed* or subtract from it,"[400] is true because it is not permitted to add what does not lie hidden in the understanding of the words, and that is not to add but to explain what is implied, which is not something else, but the same thing. But the Nicene Council also correctly forbids adding to the Creed what is something else, and it says at the end of the Creed that [272] is sung at Mass: "*Let one who teaches something else or preaches something else, that is, something contrary or in a contrary manner, be anathema."*[401] And in accord with this the Master of the Sentences explains how the Apostle says in Galatians, five: *If anyone announces to you another gospel than you have received, let him be anathema* (Gal 1:8). And on this Augustine says in the *Homilies on John*, part two, sermon forty-three, on the words: *I still have many things to say to you, but you cannot now bear them* (Jn 16:12): "*He does not say: 'More than you have received, but besides what you received.' For if he said the former he would have spoken against himself since he desired to come to the Thessalonians in order to supply what was lacking to their faith.*[402] *But one who supplies what was lacking does not take away what was present."*[403] Understand this "supply" not with respect to the immediate, but with respect to the mediate sense. For when what lies hidden in the immediate sense is supplied, there is not taken away what was present, nor is something added in the proper sense, but it is explained. Hence, to whatever extent a sen-

---

398   Augustine of Hippo, *On the Trinity* 15, 27; PL 42: 1095; ed. W. Mountain and F. Glorie, p. 529.

399   See above par. 17–38.

400   See above par. 19.

401   See Peter Lombard, *Sentences* 1, d, 11, c. 1, n. 3; PL 192: 552; ed. I Brady, 1, p. 115.

402   See 1 Thes 3:10. Henry seems to attribute to John what Paul wrote to the Thessalonians.

403   Augustine of Hippo, *Homilies on John* 98; PL 35: 1884; ed. R. Willems, p. 581.

tence is pronounced against those who add or take away something, it does not touch those who add in this way for the explanation and clarification of what was implied, unless such a clarification was expressly forbidden in a sentence as it was forbidden under excommunication of a sentence already pronounced[404] in the explanation of the rule of the Friars Minor promulgated by Pope Nicolas.[405] On this account, while respecting the sentence pronounced in that council about not [273] adding something to the Creed that the holy fathers handed down in the Nicene Council in the time of the Constantine Augustus, they later: *"under Theodosius the Elder gave form to the Creed and showed that the Holy Spirit is consubstantial to the Father and to the Son, condemning Macedonius who denied that the Holy Spirit was God,"* as <is seen> in the Decretals, 1, d. 15, c. 1.[406]

<Replies to the Arguments>

41. To that which is firstly argued to the contrary from Damascene,[407] it must be said that although the procession of the Holy Spirit terminates in the Son, because the spirative power is had in the Son from the Father, it cannot through this be excluded, but necessarily must be included that he proceeds from the Son on account of the same power, as was said.[408]

42. To the second argument from the statement of the same man: *"We do not say that the Holy Spirit is from the Son,"*[409] it must be said that John Damascene is believed to have existed in the beginning when the opinion of the Latins began to be spread that the Spirit proceeds from the Son, and the Greeks did not want to affirm this because they did not have this expressed in scripture, as was said.[410] On this account, he would not as a Greek have seen the truth perfectly, but left in doubt, he did not deny without qualification that it is so, but he said: *"We do not say,"* and he immediately adds what scripture expresses. Hence, the Latins prove that [274] the Holy Spirit proceeds from the Son when he says:

---

404   There aere two types of excommunication, one by sentence prounounced (*latae sententiae*), the other by sentence to be pronounced (*ferendae sententiae*). The former was more or less automatic, that is, if you do X, you are excommunicated. The latter required a judgment to be passed upon a particular action done.

405   See Nicolas IV, "The Sower Went Out to Sow" 14 August 1279; ed. C. Cenci 2, pp. 404–416.

406   Gratian, *Decretals* 1, d. 15, c. 1; ed. Ae. Friedberg 1, p. 34.

407   See above par. 1

408   See above par. 34.

409   John Damascene, *On the Orthodox Faith* 1, 8, 18: PG 84: 831A–B; ed. E. Buytaert, p. 47. See above par. 2.

410   See above par. 19–20.

"*But we call him the Spirit of the Son.*"[411] But he immediately says the contrary of this, as was objected,[412] in the letter, *On the Trisagion*, where he says: "*But of the Son, and not from the Son.*"[413] And it must be said that he had perhaps written that letter long before when he was firm in that opinion before the church of the Latins opposed the Greeks on this.

43. To the third argument that "the Holy Spirit" according to Damascene "is the one who speaks and reveals the Son, but such a one does not necessarily proceed from him whom he speaks and reveals,"[414] it must be said to the form of the argument, although not to the intention of Damascene, that a person speaks and reveals a person by himself internally in the divine nature or externally through an effect in a creature. That which in the first way speaks and reveals a person proceeds from him. And in that way according to the Latins the Word reveals the Father and the Holy Spirit reveals both. But that which reveals only in the second way in no way <proceeds from both>. And Damascene and the Greeks held that the Holy Spirit reveals and speaks the Son only in that way because he proceeds from him and is sent, according to them, to creatures. And only in this way, according to them, does he have authority over him on account of the order of their processions. Hence, Damascene says in chapter ten: "*We believe in one Holy Spirit,*"[415] and so on, "*like the Father and the Son in all things, proceeding from the Father and handed on through the Son and received by every creature.*"[416] Hence, in book fifteen of *On the Trinity* Augustine contradicts the Greeks on this when he says: "*The Spirit, however, does not proceed from the Father into the Son and proceed from the Son to sanctify* [275] *a creature, but proceeds from both together, although the Father gave this to the Son so that, as the Spirit proceeds from the Father, he also proceeds from the Son.*"[417]

44. To the fourth argument that "*The Holy Spirit proceeds from the Son is only because the action of the will presupposes the action of the intellect,*"[418] it must be said that it is true according to the manner already determined.[419] And it is argued against this that the same action of the intellect precedes its notional ac-

---

411 John Damascene, *On the Orthodox Faith* 1, 8; PG 94: 831A; ed. E. Buytaert, p. 47.

412 See above par. 2.

413 John Damascene, *On the Hymn Trisagion*; PG 95: 59–62.

414 See above par. 3.

415 John Damascene, *On the Orthodox Faith* 1, 8, 12; PG 96: 806B; ed. E. Buytaert, p. 38.

416 Ibid.; PG 96: 806B; ed. E. Buytaert, p. 39.

417 Augustine of Hippo, *On the Trinity* 15, 27; PL 42: 1095–1096; ed. W. Mountain and F. Glorie, p. 530.

418 See above par. 4

419 See above par. 33.

tion and that, on that supposition, the intellect and the will are capable equally firstly of the actions productive of the persons so that we can perhaps in accord with that understand what Damascene says in book one, chapter ten: "*The generation of the Son from the Father is like the procession of the Spirit.*"[420] And it must be said that the action of intellect that is required as if preceding the emanation of the Word is only the essential act of understanding, in which the operation of understanding is not perfected, as was seen above.[421] And that is really required for the essential act of willing in which the act of willing is not perfected, as was seen above.[422] For will proceeds from knowledge, as Augustine says in book fifteen of *On the Trinity*, chapter twenty-seven: "*No one wills what he does not at all know what or of what sort it is.*"[423]

45. And basing themselves on this, the Greeks say that this essential act of understanding is sufficient as previous to each emanation so that, given it, both emanations proceed equally firstly, and it is not necessary that one emanation be previous to the other nor that the power productive of the Holy Spirit be communicated to the Son, just as conversely the power productive of the Son is not communicated to the Holy Spirit. But this is contrary to what has been said and shown in the beginning of the resolution of the preceding question and of this one. Nor does the action of the intellect that is essential understanding suffice to produce [276] the notional action of the will because, as for the essential action of the will without qualification there is demanded the essential action of the intellect, so for the complete action of the will that consists in the action of the emanation of the Holy Spirit there is required the complete action of the intellect that consists in the action of the emanation of the Word. And in that way, as was said,[424] it is necessary that the power productive of the notional action of the will be communicated to the Son quasi previously by the order of nature and that in that way the Holy Spirit be produced by him along with the Father, as Richard says in book one of *On the Trinity*, chapter seven: "*In the goodness of the highest wisdom the flame of love burns neither otherwise nor more than the highest wisdom dictates.*"[425]

46. And along with this one can add in saying that this is necessary because, as the will is fecund for spirating the Holy Spirit, it is necessary that it be not

---

420   John Damascene, *On the Orthodox Faith* 1, 8, 12; PG 94: 822C; ed. E. Buytaert, p. 40.

421   See above par. 33.

422   See above par. 33.

423   Augustine of Hippo, *On the Trinity* 15, 27; PL 42: 1097; ed. W. Mountain and F. Glorie, p. 532.

424   See above qu. 5, par. 5–6 and 10.

425   Richard of Saint Victor, *On the Trinity* 3, 7; PL 196: 919D; ed. J. Ribaillier, p. 141.

only the will by which one loves without qualification, but that it be the concordant will by which one loves by the will concordant with the will of another so that in that way the spirative will is a certain union of the two into one active principle if it has to spirate a love flowing from both as the union of both into one derived from both as its principle. For otherwise essential love in the will is not perfectly fecund for producing the proceeding love that is the Holy Spirit. On this account Richard says in book three of *On the Trinity*, chapter sixteen: "*Between the delights of charity and wisdom this is especially wont to be the difference, namely, that the delights of wisdom can and are wont to be drawn from one's own heart. But the delights of intimate charity are drawn from another's heart. For one who loves intimately and desires to be loved intimately is not so much delighted as worried if he does not draw from the heart of his beloved the sweetness of the love he feels.*"[426]

[277] 47. To the fifth argument that "neither of the persons proceeding from another proceeds from the other because both proceed sufficiently from the Father through immediacy,"[427] it must be said that, although both proceed sufficiently from the Father through immediacy, the condition of their order of nature requires that one of them be from the other, as was said,[428] and along with this the nature of the will that can only be fecund as it is concordant and of the two <requires this>, as has already been touched upon.[429] And in that way the fact that the Holy Spirit proceeds from the Son is not on account of some imperfection of the Father, but on account of the condition of nature by which it is necessary that the Son share in the character of that perfection by which he spirates the Holy Spirit.

48. To the sixth argument that "*if the Holy Spirit proceeded from the Son, he would proceed after he was born,*"[430] it is true by a certain order of natural origin, but not <in an order> of some duration, in accord with which it has been sufficiently explained above.[431]

49. To the seventh argument that "*if the Holy Spirit proceeded from the Son when he proceeds from the Father, <he proceeds from them> either insofar as they are one or insofar as they are two,*"[432] it must be said that some distinguish here, saying that the "as" has the force of reduplication and in that way determines the act of proceeding placed in the predicate in a certain respect and

---

426   Ibid. 3, 16; PL 196: 925D; ed. J. Ribaillier, p.151.

427   See above par. 5.

428   See above par. 26 and 33.

429   See above par. 39 and 46.

430   See above par. 6.

431   See above qu. 5, par. 6.

432   See above par. 7.

comparison with the subject, which is the Father and the Son. The "as" then can determine the act of proceeding as it refers to the subject in the character by which it is acting or in the character of the power of acting that is in it. [278] In the first way they say that they spirate as many, in the second way that they spirate as one, as will now be seen.⁴³³ But they in no way spirate as one, as the minor premises brought against this member prove.⁴³⁴ But that this distinction is impossible for that first member is seen from the fact that an agent in the character by which it is an agent as it is eliciting expresses the one eliciting the act, but not the character of eliciting as by which it elicits it. But now the reduplication with regard to the predicate reduplicates only the cause or character of the predicate that it has in the subject by which it has inherence in it, but not the whole subject, as is seen from book one of the *Prior Analytics*.⁴³⁵ Although therefore there are many from which the Holy Spirit proceeds, as Anselm says in *On the Procession of the Holy Spirit*: "*because the God from whom the Holy Spirit is is the Father and the Son, for this reason he is truly said to be from the Father and the Son, who are two, but not as they are two,*" that is, as eliciting in some way as they are two connoted with regard to the character of eliciting, as will now be said.⁴³⁶

50. To the eighth argument that "*he proceeds from them as they are one or as they are two,*"⁴³⁷ it must be said that <he> in no way <proceeds from them> as they are two, as the minor premise against this argument shows,⁴³⁸ but as they are one—not the one that is the essence insofar as it is something purely absolute, as the minor premise adduced against this member proves, nor the one that is the common relative notion insofar as it is a pure relation because it cannot be an eliciting principle of an action, as was said above,⁴³⁹ but in an intermediate manner, that is, as they are one essence not merely under the character of the essence, but as it is will, and not as it is will absolutely, but as it is will under the character of the common relative notional property. But it is still not as the essence is completely one under such a character because then the Father and the Son would not have the character of a union or of being connected in spi-

---

433   See below par. 50.

434   That is, they in no way spirate as one because they in no way agree in the unity of some person.

435   See Aristotle, *Prior Analytics* 1.38.49a11–b3; trans. Boethius; ed. L. Minio-Paluello, p. 79.

436   See below par. 50.

437   See above par. 8.

438   The minor premise is that the substance of the Father would be other than that of the Son.

439   See above par. 49.

rating [279] the Holy Spirit, as will be seen in what follows.[440] But it is rather as the will is one that connotes the distinction of many, namely, of the Father and the Son, with regard to that unity so that in that way the Father and the Son are said to spirate the Holy Spirit as they are one in essence considered under the character of a common relative property, and as they are connoted as many with regard to that one, although not as they are many distinct as principles eliciting the act, as it has already been said in the resolution of the preceding argument.[441] And in accord with this, although they do not spirate as many, they are distinct as principles and elicit the act on account of the character already mentioned; they still spirate as they are connoted as many distinct with regard to that in which they are one, which is the character of eliciting the act and as many united in one spirative character. I understand that they are united by the connotation with regard to one character of acting, on account of which connotation they necessarily concur in that one action.

51. For the understanding of this, it must be known that, in accord with what will be determined below,[442] essential acts are previous by a certain order of reason and the foundations of notional acts and quasi complements of their eliciting power or character under the character of a respect, as the character of speaking the Word or the speaking power in the Father is the divine essence in the Father insofar as it is the intellect informed by essential wisdom in the actual act of understanding under the character of a notional respect that the Father has toward the Son. But the character of spirating the Holy Spirit or the spirative power in the Father and the Son is the same divine essence insofar as it is the will informed by essential love in the actual act of willing or loving, and <it is> this under the character of the common notional respect that the Father and the Son have in common toward the Holy Spirit. [280] But in this it is different on the side of the intellect as it is fecund for speaking the Word and on the side of the will as it is fecund for spirating the Holy Spirit because the intellect can have perfect fecundity for the production of the Word as it exists in one person. But the will cannot have perfect fecundity for the production of the Holy Spirit unless it exists in two persons, and this <is so> because the fecundity of the intellect consists in the fulness of perfect wisdom, which can exist in a single <person>, as Richard says in book three of *On the Trinity*, chapter sixteen: "*Nothing contrary to nature is defined if the fulness of wisdom is said to be able to subsist in the singleness of a person. For as it seems, even if there were only one*

---

440   See below par. 67 and 68.

441   See above par. 49

442   See *SQO* art. 60, qu. 1; ed. Badius 2, fol. 154rQ–P and below par. 75 and qu. 8, par. 6 and 15, and qu. 10, par. 2

person in the deity, he could still have the fulness of wisdom."[443] But the fecundity of the will consists in the fulness of perfect love that can only exist in at least two, as Richard says in the same place and was already established above:[444] *"The fulness of charity or of love is not drawn save from another's heart."*[445] As he says in the same book, chapter two: *"As long as one loves no one other than himself, that love which he has for himself is proven to be private love because it has not yet attained the highest level of charity."*[446] *"Therefore,"* as he says in chapter three, *"it cannot a joyous love unless it is mutual."*[447] Hence, since in essential love the will cannot have the highest fecundity unless love is supremely perfect and joyous, it is necessary that the will be fecund because love is mutual so that, as he says in chapter three: *"There is one who gives love and one who returns love,"*[448] because as he says in chapter seven: *"For one who loves in the highest way it is not enough unless the one loved most highly returns the highest love."*[449]

[281] 52. And according to this, as was already said above,[450] in order that the common will of the Father and the Son may be fecund for spirating the Holy Spirit, it is not enough that it be one common to both and that there be the common essential love in it by which both together will and love, but it is necessary that there be the concordant and mutual will of the two by which one offers the other the highest love and the other in turn returns it. And when it exists, the will is fecund so that it is necessary that the love that is the Holy Spirit emanates from it, as Richard says in chapter seventeen: *"In mutual and very fervent love there is nothing more excellent than that by the one whom you love in the highest manner and by whom you are loved in the highest manner you will that another be equally loved. In those, therefore,"* as he says, *"who are mutually loved the perfection of the two requires someone to share the love shown in order that it may be consummated,"*[451] and this is through the spirative power, which is the will concordant in mutual love for producing the Holy Spirit, not only as <the Father and the Son> are one in that will or love, but also as they are many distinct from one another.

---

443   Richard of Saint Victor, *On the Trinity* 3, 16; PL 196: 925D–926A; ed. J. Ribaillier, pp. 151–152.

444   See above par. 46.

445   Richard of Saint Victor, *On the Trinity* 3, 16; PL 196: 925D; ed. J. Ribaillier, p. 151.

446   Ibid. 3, 2; PL 196: 917A; ed. J. Ribaillier, p. 137.

447   Ibid. 3, 3; PL 196: 917D; ed. J. Ribaillier, p. 138..

448   Ibid.

449   Ibid. 3, 7; PL 196: 919D; ed. J. Ribaillier, p. 142.

450   See above par. 46.

451   Richard of Saint Victor, *On the Trinity* 3, 11; PL 196: 922C–923A; ed. J. Ribaillier, p. 146.

53. And this distinction is connoted by the fact that the will is said to be concordant and mutual love. For there can be a concordant will and mutual love only of many insofar as they are many. For the inseparable prefix "con" implies an association that can only be of many who are distinct. On this account it is correctly said in the plural that the Father, the Son, and the Holy Spirit are three coeternals, although this <proposition> is nonetheless denied: "The Father and the Son and the Holy Spirit are three eternals." Also because this will is the concordant and mutual love of the two, although it is one and the same, its character is still not the same as it is in the Father given to the Son and conversely returned to the Father by the Son because, as [282] Richard says in book three, chapter nineteen: "*When two mutually love each other and offer each other loves of the highest affection, the love of the latter runs to the former and that of the former to the latter and tends to quasi diverse <beings>*," and because "*it tends to quasi diverse <beings>*,"[452] it is somehow diverse in character. But this diversity of character is and consists in what is purely essential, and despite this there exists in that concordant will and mutual love a fecundity utterly one and the same in which the Father and the Son are entirely one and in complete uniformity spirate the Holy Spirit, who "*is concordantly loved by the two, and the love of the two is melted into one by the fire of the third love*,"[453] as Richard says in the same place. And in accord with this in the spiration of the Holy Spirit the distinction of the Father and the Son is to be considered in two ways: in one way as they are expressed as eliciting the act, in another way as they are understood to be concordant in will and in mutual love with regard to the character of eliciting the act. From the distinction of them[454] considered and expressed in the first way they are in no way to be said to spirate as many. For although there are many who spirate, they still do not spirate on account of the plurality that is in them as a principle, but only from their distinction connoted in the stated manner. And in that way the Father and the Son do not spirate the Holy Spirit as they are many in the action of eliciting, although they concur in one character by which they elicit the act, but as many in one will, which is the reason for eliciting the act by being concordant and in mutually giving their love in it, as will now be more fully explained.

54. To the ninth argument that "*he either proceeds from them as from one principle or as from many*,"[455] it must be said that in such matters it is especially necessary to look at what is signified by the term. It is therefore to be understood on account of what is signified by this name [283] "principle" that in God there is a name that purely signifies the pure essence and in the manner of "essence

---

452 Ibid. 3, 19: PL 196: 927B; ed. J. Ribaillier, p. 154.

453 Ibid.

454 I have conjectured "of them, *eorum*" instead of "of it, *eius*,"

455 See above par. 9.

and stands only for the essence, as does this name "deity." And there is another name that signifies the essence, not in the manner of the essence, but in the manner of a supposite and stands for a supposite, as does this name "God." But there is a third name that signifies a pure relation in the manner of a relation and stands only for a relation, as does this name "paternity." There is a fourth name that signifies in an intermediate way, that is, the essence principally, but under the character and manner of a respect or relation, as this name "potency" and this name "principle," but in different ways, because "potency" signifies the substance principally under the character of a respect to an act, but this name "principle" does so principally under the character of what is produced. And again "potency" signifies the substance under the character of a respect and in the manner of a respect insofar as it is from the formal character from which the name is imposed to signify.

55. On account of this we determined above regarding this[456] that potency is not a substance, but a relation, not because it signifies a pure relation like this name "paternity," but because, although it signifies a substance and stands for a substance, it still signifies it under the character and manner of a respect. But similarly "principle" principally signifies a substance and under the character of a respect, but in the manner of a supposite; hence, it also stands for a supposite. Hence, both this name "potency" and this name "principle" signify a substance principally, but under the character of a respect, and <they do> this under a certain indifference and indetermination, just as this name "person" principally signifies a supposite but under a certain indifference and indetermination. And this indetermination is made determinate by [284] what is added, and along with this this name "principle" stands for a supposite under a certain indifference and indetermination, as this name "God" does. Because therefore this name "principle" principally signifies the essence, although under the manner of a relation and by this expresses concerning what it signifies an elicitive character rather than the supposite in which it is, since it elicits its act through it, although it also stands for it, but the essence is one in God and the first reason for eliciting all the divine acts, as was established above,[457] and the character of a principle is attributed most of all to what is first, because to the extent that something has the character of the first, to that extent it has the character of a principle—for "*the first* and *the principle are the same*," according to the Philosopher in book one of the *Posterior Analytics*,[458]

56. For this reason I say that in God there is only one character of "principle" taken in the most proper sense, and it is said only in the singular. And this is so

---

456   See *SQO* art. 35, qu. 8; ed. G. Wilson, pp. 78–79.

457   See *SQO* art. 39, qu. 4; ed. G. Wilson, pp. 196–202.

458   Aristotle, *Posterior Analytics* 1.2.72a7; trans. Jacobi; ed. L. Minio-Paluello and B. G. Dod, p. 8.

whether it renders a statement true by signifying the essence under the character of one respect or many and whether it stands for one supposite in rendering a statement true or for many, two or three at the same time, although if "principle" is not in this way taken in the proper sense, that is, for what is unqualifiedly first and remote, but for what is near and immediate to the proper act, principles are said to be many, just as potencies are also said to be many. For it happens in opposite ways in the character of a principle and in the character of a potency, because each thing has the character of a principle more to the extent that it has more the character of what is first and removed from what is derived from a principle, as has already been said. But everything has the character of a potency to the extent that it has more the character of what is proximate and immediate to what is derived from a principle. On this account according to the Philosopher in book nine of the *Metaphysics*: [285] Vinegar is not properly wine in potency, but water existing in the vine is.[459] Hence, the Father is said to be the one principle of the Son, of the Holy Spirit, and of creatures, because the divine essence is one, which in him is the one reason for originating them all, although it is under the character of one respect in originating the Son and under another in originating the Holy Spirit and under a third in originating creatures. Similarly, the Father and the Son are one principle of the Holy Spirit and of creatures, although under one respect in originating the Holy Spirit and under another in originating creatures and although they are diverse supposites. And this <is so> because the one divine essence in them is the first reason for eliciting them, and it does not matter in some respect that they are said to be one principle of the Holy Spirit, even if under many relative characters in the Father and the Son, the essence was the reason for being the principle and origin of the Holy Spirit, just as it does not matter in the Father that he is said to be one principle of the Son and of the Holy Spirit, although the essence in him is the reason for originating them under diverse relations. And in that way the precise reason why the Father and the Son are said to be the one principle of the Holy Spirit is the essence under the character of a respect and relation without qualification, which they have to the Holy Spirit in producing him. I do not mean under the character of one relation that is the common notion of the two. For it is the case because it is one. For, as was said, if it were not one but many, they would nonetheless be said to be one principle of him on account of the one essence that has the character of the first principle.

57. And from this four things are seen: first, that the unity of the principle is taken through itself and precisely from the unity of that which is the first reason for originating, although only as it is considered under a character of respect or relation to that of which it is the reason for originating. On this account, although the same essence is in [286] what is derived from the principle,

---

459 Aristotle, *Metaphysics* 8.5.1044b34–35; anon. trans., ed. G. Vuillemin-Diem, p. 165.

the same character of a principle is still not because it is not in it under the character of the same respect. The second thing is that the Father and the Son are said to spirate the Holy Spirit in different ways as they are one and as they are one principle because they spirate the Holy Spirit as they are one in essence and under one character of a common relation by which they are in common related to the Holy Spirit, but they spirate the Holy Spirit as they are one principle in the essence and distinct by the proper characters by which they are related to each other. On this account the third thing is seen, namely, that they do not correctly say that the same notion is in the Father and the Son in accord with which they are said to be one principle of the Holy Spirit. For this is the case, as was said, although immutably. On this account Augustine says in book five of *On the Trinity*, chapter fourteen: "*The Father is the principle for the Son because he begot him.*"[460] And from this the Master of the Sentences concludes in book one, distinction twenty-nine, the chapter "Then": "*By the notion by which he is the Father, he is said to be the principle of the Son, that is, by generation.*"[461] And in the chapter, "But one," he speaks as follows: "*It can of course be understood that both the Father and the Son are said to be the principle of the Holy Spirit by the same notion or relation.*"[462] And there is much on this matter through the whole distinction. The fourth thing is that, when it is said that "*the Father and the Son* spirate the Holy Spirit as they are one, that is, as one God,"[463] although in the book, *On the Holy Spirit* Anselm says this,[464] there is not expressed the precise character of the unity of the Father and the Son in spirating the Holy Spirit. For if that in which they are one is expressed precisely, it is necessary that it be expressed under the character of the respect that belongs only to the Father and to the Son. [287] But although "God" stands for the relative supposites, it still does not signify something under the character of relation, and along with this it does not signify the essence as it precisely belongs to the Father and the Son, but signifies it as it also belongs to the Holy Spirit. On this account when it is said that they spirate as one, that is, as one principle, the precise character of their unity in spirating the Holy Spirit is also not expressed because although "principle" signifies the essence under the character of a relation, it does not signify it precisely under <under the character of> that <relation> by which the Father and the Son are related to the Holy Spirit, but does so generally <under the character> by which the Father is related to the

460   Augustine, *On the Trinity* 15, 14; PL 42: 920–921; ed. W. Mountain and F. Glorie, p. 222.

461   Peter Lombard, *Sentences* 1, d. 29, 3; PL 192: 601; ed. I. Brady, 1, p. 218.

462   Ibid. 1, d. 29, 4; PL 192: 602; ed. I. Brady, 1. p. 219.

463   See Anselm of Canterbury, *On the Procession of the Holy Spirit* 7; PL 158: 305B; ed. F. Schmitt, 2, p. 198.

464   Ibid.

Son, and both are to the Holy Spirit, and the whole Trinity is to creatures, and also one creature to another. Hence, because Anselm holds the precise reason for spirating the Holy Spirit in the Father and in the Son <is> that they are one God, he proves through this that it is necessary that the Holy Spirit be from the Son or the other way around with the same necessity by which the Father is from the Son and the other way around, and similarly that the Holy Spirit is from the Father or the other way around. And it is evident that it would not hold from the form of the argument. For if someone would say that the Holy Spirit does not proceed by reason of the deity without qualification, but only as he is under the character of a relative notion, and that it is held to be in the Father alone, just as the notion of active generation is, and if along with this he says that those two notions in the Father have no order among them, such a person can grant that it is necessary that the Son and the Holy Spirit proceed from the Father still in such a way that neither proceeds from the other, despite the arguments of Anselm, as it is clear to someone who looks.

58. Hence, if similar questions were raised concerning the Father with respect to the Son and the Holy Spirit, namely, whether he produced them as one or as many, one must answer as before that he who produced them would be one. But if it were asked whether he produced them as he is one or as he is many, it must be said that <he produced them> as he is one essence, as before, but as under the characters of diverse relations or properties. But if it is asked whether they proceed from him as from one principle or as from many, it must be said that they proceed as from one by reason of the unity of the essence, although under the diverse characters [288] of the relations so that, if the Father were said to be many principles, a plurality of divine essences would be implied to be in him. Hence, Anselm says in *On the Procession of the Holy Spirit* concerning the unity of the principle of the Father and of the Son with respect to the Holy Spirit: *"Just as we do not believe that the Holy Spirit is from that because of which the Father and the Son are two, but from that in which they are one, so we do not say that he has two principles, but one, at least if God should be said to have a principle. For only something that begins to be seems to have a principle."*[465] On this account he indicates that in God all things are not taken univocally in accord with the manner they are used in creatures, but in a more eminent manner. Hence, he adds: *"Still if it is understood in a certain ineffable manner, because it cannot otherwise be spoken of, he can be called a principle not inappropriately."*[466] But those words of Anselm, *"from that in which they are one,"*[467] must not be understood absolutely, but only by reason of a respect. For on this account the

---

465 Anselm of Canterbury, *On the Procession of the Holy Spirit* 10; PL 158: 311C and 312A; ed. F. Schmitt, 2, pp. 205 and 206.

466 Ibid.; PL 158: 312B; ed. F. Schmitt, p.206.

467 See above n. 131.

name "principle" implies a respect in accord with what Augustine says in book five of *On the Trinity*, chapter thirteen: "'Father' is said relatively, and likewise 'principle' is said relatively."[468] And in chapter fourteen he says: "*It must be said that the Father and the Son are the principle of the Holy Spirit, not two principles, but as the Father and the Son are one God. And in relation to a creature he is said to be one creator and one God. In that way* <they are said to be> *one principle in relation* [289] *to the Holy Spirit, but the Father and the Son and the Holy Spirit are said to be one principle in relation to a creature, just as he is* <said to be> *one creator and one God.*"[469]

59. As for that which is argued in accord with this: "*If* the Father and the Son *were one principle* of the Holy Spirit, *therefore,* <they would be> *the one principle that is either the Father or that is not the Father*,"[470] it must be said that, if one is speaking precisely and separately, both must be denied, as the objection proceeds. But both must be granted if taken together, because the Father and the Son are one principle of the Holy Spirit, which is the Father for one and which is not the Father for the other, because the relation that is included in the name "principle" is not determined to one singular or common <person> or to many, and "principle" does not stand determinately for one of the supposites, as was said,[471] although it may be determined by an addition.

60. To the tenth argument that "*if the Holy Spirit proceeds from both, he proceeds as from one spirator or as from two,*"[472] it must be said that on this article not only are diverse people opposed to one another, but even from among the great teachers the same man is opposed to himself. For he said on book one of the *Sentences* that "*an act takes is number from supposites. But an act is signified in a verb, in a participle, and in a verbal noun. And for this reason we cannot say that the Father and the Son spirate the Holy Spirit or that they are the one spirating or that they are the spirator, but that they spirate and [that] they are the ones spirating and are the spirators, although there is one act by which they spirate.*"[473] But in the first part of his *Summa* he returns to the same opinion when he says: "*Although the Father and the Son are one principle of the Holy Spirit, they are still two spirators on account of* [290] *the distinction of the supposites as* <they are> *two spirating*

---

468   Augustine, *On the Trinity* 5, 13; PL 42: 920; ed. W. Mountain and F. Glorie, 220.

469   Ibid. 5, 14; PL 42: 921–922; ed. W. Mountain and F. Glorie, 223.

470   See above par. 10.

471   See above par. 55.

472   See above par. 11.

473   Thomas Aquinas, *Commentary on the Sentences* 1, d. 11, 1; ed. P. Mandonnet, p. 284.

because the acts are referred to the supposites."⁴⁷⁴ But revoking his statement on this, he immediately states the opposite in adding: "*But it seems better to say that because 'spirating' is an adjective, but 'spirator' a substantive, we can say that the Father and the Son are two spirating on account of the plurality of the supposites, but not two spirators on account of the one spiration.*"⁴⁷⁵

61. But afterwards a certain other man came along, who detested the stated contrariety on book one of the *Sentences* and wrote as follows: "*On this question the same men contradict themselves. For although they had firstly said that the Father and the Son are many spirators, they later said that it is better to say that the Father and the Son are one spirator.*"⁴⁷⁶ And there he immediately adds and says correctly "*that the whole reason why we hesitate to grant that the Father and the Son are many spirators is that, just as there is one potency for spirating in the Father and the Son, so there is one potency for creating in the three persons, but on account of the unity of the potency for creating, all three persons are said to be one creator, therefore, on account of the unity of the potency for spirating, the Father and the Son ought therefore to be said to be one spirator.*"⁴⁷⁷ But he adds the reason for this variance, namely, that the three persons are said to be one creator, but the two are not said to be one spirator, when he says: "*Because just as the three persons do not create insofar as they are many, but insofar as they are united in something absolute, that is, in the deity, so the Father and the Son do not spirate insofar as they are many, but insofar as they are united in something absolute, but this is in different ways. For insofar as the three create, they are one in the deity so that the deity creates, but the two are not one in the deity so that the deity spirates.*"⁴⁷⁸ Therefore, as he says: "*By reason of the deity to which it belongs to create, but not to spirate, the many persons could be said to be one creator, but not one spirator.*"⁴⁷⁹

[291] 62. But it is evident from what has been determined above concerning the divine actions in general⁴⁸⁰ that the principle of a divine action, as the agent from which it emanates, cannot be the divine essence, but only a subsisting supposite, although <the divine essence> is the reason for eliciting them all,. For the form of a thing does not act, but what has the form acts through the form. Hence, the Philosopher did not attribute the act of understanding, concerning which more is seen, to the soul that is united <to the body>, but to the composite. For it is no different, according to what he says, "*to say that the soul understands and weaves*

---

474   Thomas Aquinas, *Summa of Theology* 1, qu. 36, a. 4 ad 7um; ed. Leon. IV, p. 384b

475   Ibid. 1, qu. 36, a. 4; ed. Leon. IV, p. 384b.

476   Giles of Rome, *Commentary on the Sentences* 1, d. 11, 4; ed. Venice, fol. 67rA.

477   Ibid.

478   Ibid.

479   Ibid.

480   See *SQO* art. 39, qu. 3 and 4; ed. G. Wilson, pp. 184–186 and pp. 196–202.

or builds."[481] But although the many as many do not create or spirate, but only as they are united in something one, namely, in the deity, still <they do> not, as has been already explained,[482] in <the deity> as completely absolute, but under the character of some respect. Still the act of creating will no more be able to be attributed to the divine essence in saying that the essence creates than the act of spirating will in saying that the essence spirates, although the evidence is made stronger concerning "to create" because the essence is the reason for creating in the three persons, but the reason for spirating is only in the two. Hence, on this account if it is found somewhere that the essence is the creator or is said to create, the words are to be explained so that "essence" stands in the improper sense for that to which it belongs. It is therefore necessary to assign another reason for the diverse predication of "creator" in the singular of the three and of "spiration" in the plural of the two, which not only shows the reason why this can be so, but why it must be so and not otherwise.

[292] 63. For the understanding of this it must be known that although verbal nouns signify the same act as verbs and participles, for example, "builder" and "building," "creator" and "creating," "spirator" and "spirating," they signify it in diverse ways because a verb and a participle signify it as it emerges from the agent in act, but the verbal noun signifies it only as only as it emerges from him habitually. For a builder is one suited for building, although he is not building in act, but he is not someone building unless he actually builds. And similarly in God, although there an act as it is within does not differ from the habit, still from its character a verbal noun indicates only one as acting habitually. And in accord with this as one spirating is only one from whom the act of spirating emanates in act, although a spirator is always spirating in act, this noun still indicates one spirating only habitually. And in accord with this the verb and the participle are differently related to one who is supposed to act or otherwise regard him and the verbal noun. For since, as has been determined above,[483] an act as it is in acting belongs through itself to a supposite, a verb and a participle name an act as being through itself with regard to a supposite as it is a supposite. On this account plurality in predication generally follows upon the plurality of the supposite in the consignification of the plural number of the verb and participle, as will be explained below in speaking of the manner of speaking about God.[484] But because a verbal noun signifies the act as a habit that through itself is with regard to the power that elicits the act, but not the supposite—for "builder" signifies only one who has the power and potency for building insofar as he is

---

481   See Aristotle, *On the Soul* 1.4.408b11–13 in Albert the Great's *Commentary on On the Soul*; ed. F. S. Crawford, p. 85.

482   See above par. 51, 54, 55, and 58.

483   See *SQO* art. 39, qu. 3; ed. G. Wilson, pp. 184–186.

484   See below par. 65.

suited to elicit such an act—for this reason plurality in the consignification of the plural number of such nouns does not generally follow upon the plurality of the supposite, but does so at times and does not at others.

[293] 64. But in order to know when it does and when it does not, one must take note from the side of the power or of the character of acting that elicits the act. For it is either diverse in subjects that are diverse, and then a verbal noun is generally predicated of them in the plural, as Socrates and Plato are two builders. Or it is the same in subjects that are diverse, as is the case in God with respect to all the actions that belong to many persons. But this happens in two ways. For they are either entirely one in that power or character so that it elicits the act in accord with entirely the same manner or character of eliciting as it is in one and the other without any connotation of distinction of the supposites and some diversity of them in the manner of acting through it. Or although they are completely one in it, it is still not elicitive of the act entirely according to the same manner or character of eliciting it as it is in one and in the other, but connotes a distinction of the supposites and some diversity in the manner of acting through it. A verbal noun that regards the eliciting power in diverse supposites in the first manner is predicated of them only in the singular because, although they are many that elicit, they still elicit the act on account of such an eliciting power insofar as they are completely one in it and not insofar as they are many in terms of themselves. Thus the reduplication implied by "as" determines the act with respect to the persons eliciting it without denoting the condition of those eliciting it, that is, insofar as they are eliciting it, but <that> of the eliciting power insofar as the character of eliciting is entirely the same with respect to many in eliciting the act and the precise reason why one and the other elicit the act so that, although the persons are diverse, they still do not at all elicit the act insofar as they are diverse, but only insofar as the character of a person belongs to them and they have unity in the active power in the manner stated so that if there were only one of them, it would elicit the act no less than all would together. Such a verbal noun is the noun "creator, because in the diverse supposites it refers to the creative power that is in the divine essence under the character of a respect to creatures, as that in which they are all one, and it is the character eliciting the act as [294] it is in the one and in the other without any connotation of the distinction of the supposites with regard to it and of their diversity or divergence of the manner of acting through it. And on this account it is predicated of them only in the singular in saying: "They are only *one creator* in the way they are said to be *one God*," as is seen from the statements of Augustine already cited above.[485] For although there are many creatures, <the divine persons> still elicit the act of creating on account of such a power as they

---

485 See above par. 58.

are entirely one in it and not as they are many in terms of themselves, and so on in accord with the manner already stated.

65. But a verbal noun that is with regard to the eliciting power in diverse supposites in the second way is predicated of them only in the plural. For on account of such an eliciting power they elicit the act not only as they are one in it, but along with this as they are many and distinct so that the reduplication by "as" determines the act with respect to the persons eliciting it while connoting at the same time the condition of the elicitive power insofar as it is the character of eliciting and of those who elicit it as they are distinct. And although that power is the same in many such, the precise character is not completely the same by which one and the other elicit the act. Hence, those persons elicit the act insofar as they are distinct and diverse, not only because the character of a person belongs to them without qualification and they have unity in the eliciting power in the manner stated so that if there were only one of them, it would in no way elicit the act without the other. Such a verbal noun is [295] this noun "spirator" because in diverse supposites it refers to the spirative power that is the divine essence under the character of the common respect to the Holy Spirit in accord with the manner already stated, as that in which they are entirely one, but the elicitive character is not entirely the same as it is in the one and as it is in the other without any connotation of their distinction with regard to it from what is connoted with regard to the eliciting power, in accord with what was said in part above.[486]

66. There is also some divergence of them in the way of acting and of eliciting the act through it, as will now be seen, on account of which it is predicated of them in the plural in saying that "they are *many spirators*."[487] For on account of something of the sort connoted and the manner of eliciting the act they do nor elicit the act only as they are entirely the same in the spirative power, but also as they are many in terms of themselves, and so on, according to the way already stated. And thus, although in creating the Father and the Son and the Holy Spirit are many, still because they are absolutely without any difference of character and distinction connoted, they create totally as they are one, not as many, and they are one creator, not many creators, since the "as" determines the act of creating as it refers to the character of acting and in no way to the agents. But in spirating because along with the fact that the Father and the Son are many in themselves, they have in the spirative power some difference of character and some distinction connoted, although they are really entirely one in it, they do not totally spirate as they are one nor totally as they are many, but as many insofar as their distinction is connoted in the spirative power and they have some difference of character in it, but <they spirate> as one insofar

---

486   See above par. 53.

487   See above par. 11.

as they are really one in it and further united in one common [296] fecundity, and on account of that distinction and difference of character they are said to spirate as two and to be two spirators. Nonetheless, on account of the unity in which they are one—with every distinction, expressed and connoted, and difference of character reduced to it—they are also said to spirate as one and to be one spirator as the "as" determines the act of spirating and is referred to the agents and is referred to the character of acting. Nonetheless, because they spirate as one in that in which the spirative power is realized, they are better said to spirate as one than as many and that they are one spirator than that they are many, as the previously mentioned Master said in correcting himself,[488] still not without it being correctly said that they are many.

67. And he seems to deny this because he explains the authority of Hilary that says that "the Holy Spirit *proceeds from the Father and the Son as authors*,"[489] in saying that "*there the substantive is used in place of the adjective.*"[490] And it is not necessary to say that because there are correctly said to be two spirators because they are many in the spirative power on account of what is connoted and they are one on account of what is principally signified so that in accord with this they are many united. And furthermore, because on account of the difference of character they are mutually joined to each other in mutual love by the bond of love, for this reason the Holy Spirit proceeds from them as joined to each other and insofar as the love of the two is conflated into one by the fire of love, that is, by one fecundity of those joined together in producing the Holy Spirit, the Holy Spirit is said to be the union of the two and to proceed as the union of the two, that is, in which the two are perfectly united, so that the character of this [297] union becomes what proceeds from the two, not only because they are one in the spirative power—for in that way a creature would rather be said to proceed from the whole Trinity as their union, because it proceeds from the three insofar as they are one without connoting a distinction with regard to that unity, as was said[491]—but along with this because as they are many. For if in accord with the manner stated he did not proceed from them as they are one and as they are two, he would in no way be said to proceed from them in the manner of a union.

68. Further, because he proceeds from them as they are united in that way and concordant in will and mutual in love, will and love also have through this the fecundity of eliciting a love that proceeds so that, if there were not such an

---

488   See Thomas Aquinas, *Summa of Theology* 1, qu. 36, a. 4; ed. Leon. IV, p. 384b; see above par. 60.

489   Hilary of Poitiers, *On the Trinity* 2, 29; PL 10: 69A; ed. P. Smulders, p. 64.

490   Thomas Aquinas, *Summa of Theology* 1, qu. 36, a. 4, ad 7um; ed. Leon. 4, p. 384b.

491   See above par. 46 and 50–51.

association and concurrence of many in such a will and love, they would not have such fecundity, and such a connection and association can in no way exist with regard to such a will as it is existing in the person of the Father alone. For this reason it is clear that it would be impossible for the Holy Spirit to proceed from the Father alone with the exclusion of the Son. Hence, it is not only necessary to hold that the Holy Spirit proceeds from the Son because, on account of the natural order of processions, it is necessary that the will be communicated to the Son by the Father by which he necessarily has to spirate the Holy Spirit, in accord with which the argument set forth above proceeds,[492] but it is also necessary that he proceed from the Son if he has to proceed from the Father. For although the will is in the Father alone, still because it would not be mutual, it would not be fecund so that it is not only impossible to exclude the Son from the production [298] of the Holy Spirit and to hold that he can proceed from the Father alone, as the Son proceeds; rather, it is also impossible because it is not only impossible that the Son be excluded from the act of spiration, but given this despite its impossibility, it would along with this be impossible that the Holy Spirit be held to be spirated by the Father alone.

69. And all this results from the condition of wisdom from which there proceeds the Son "whose perfection *is drawn from his own heart* and <from the condition> of love, whose perfection *is drawn only* from *another heart*,"[493] as was already said according to Richard. But it does not take place in the act of creating as it does in the act of spirating. For the precise reason for creating is the divine essence alone as it is the will free in choice without any connotation of a distinction and plurality of persons. And this <will> has being uniformly in the individual persons and in the three, on which account if, despite its impossibility, two persons were excluded from the act of creating, it is not self-contradictory to hold that the third person creates by himself alone, and the reason is that to create does not belong to a divine person by the reason by which it is one or more, but by the reason by which it is a divine person without qualification. Thus, if only one absolute person were understood to be in God, as the Jews and the gentiles understand, it would be necessary to hold that he creates. And on this account certain men say that the whole Trinity and any person in it create, not because it is such <a person>, but because it is God.[494] And the reason is not only that in God they are one in [299] substance because to create does not belong to the substance, as was said,[495] but because "God" stands inde-

---

492   See above par. 32.

493   Richard of Saint Victor, *On the Trinity* 3, 16; PL 196: 925D; ed. J. Ribaillier, p. 151.

494   See Giles of Rome, *Commentary on the Sentences* 1, d. 11, 4; ed. Venice, fol 67rA.

495   See above in this par.

terminately for a person along with signifying the substance. Therefore, to that which is argued against the members of the division in the argument that "the Holy Spirit proceeds from the Father and the Son *as from one* spirator, because 'spirator' is a denomination of an act as it emerges from a supposite,"[496] and so on, it must be said that it is true but not by reason of the supposite as the act emerges from it, but by reason of the elicitive power and character by which it emerges. Hence, because it is one, although it connotes a plurality of supposites with regard to itself, as was said,[497] there is correctly said to be one spirator.

70. Similarly, to the argument that <he proceeds> *"not as from two spirators, because 'spirator" implies the character of a principle and they do not spirate as two principles,"*[498] it must be said that it is not the same with the name "spirator" as with the name "principle," although both are taken from the same thing, namely, from the common power elicitive of the act, because the character of a principle is taken precisely from the elicitive power as it is elicitive. But now, as was said, that power is elicitive in the full sense as the supposites have unity in it. For many as many can in no way at all be the principle of one simple effect. But the character of spirator is not taken precisely from the elicitive power as it is elicitive in the full sense and the supposites have unity in it, but as their distinction and plurality is connoted with regard to such unity. Because, as was said,[499] that power that is the will quasi informed by actual love cannot be the precise reason of eliciting the act of spirating because the will is also the love of the two, but because the will is concordant and mutual love so that for this reason, although "spirator" includes in itself the character [300] of a principle, it still adds in what it signifies an order to the persons as they are distinct, not as eliciting the act, but as concordant and mutual in the elicitive character, and on this account "spirator" can be predicated in the plural, but "principle" cannot, as was said.[500]

71. It is also seen in relation to that which was assumed in accord with this concerning the concerning the creator that it is not the same in accord with what has already been said.[501]

72. To that which is argued that "*the Holy Spirit proceeds from the Son,* not the other way around,"[502] it must be granted that that argument correctly explains the reason for it because, if there were not that order of the two emanating

---

496 See above par. 11.

497 See above par. 59.

498 See above par. 11.

499 See above par. 34, 46–47, and 52.

500 See above par. 55–56 and 66.

501 See above par. 11.

502 See above par. 12.

principles, there would not be a reason why the Holy Spirit would proceed from the Son rather than the other way around. But in *On the Procession of the Holy Spirit* Anselm explains another reason for this that is a reduction to what is impossible and a posteriori. For as he says: "*If the Son proceeded from the Holy Spirit, he would be his son,*"[503] which would undoubtedly be true if the will preceded the intellect in this order by which the intellect precedes the will. For then the person that is not from another and that one that is from him by the will would be the Father of the Son by the common notion, just as they are now the spirator of the Holy Spirit by a common notion.

73. According to the same way the argument of Richard must be granted that one of them necessarily proceeds from the other and this by the already stated [301] ostensive argument that demands it, but not on account of the arguments of Anselm[504] and Richard[505] except on account of those that show it would be unsuitable if it did not come about in that way, as has been said.[506]

74. To the last argument that "*according to Augustine in book nine of On the Trinity that desire precedes the mind's giving birth,*"[507] it must be said that Augustine is speaking there literally concerning the mind's giving birth through preceding discursive reasoning and inquiry. For, as he says there, "*Inquiry is the desire to discover that proceeds from and depends on one who is seeking, and it does not come to a rests in the end aimed at unless that which is sought is joined as something found to the one seeking. For it can be called will because everyone who seeks wills to find, and if that which is sought pertains to knowledge everyone who seeks wills to know.*"[508] And then there follows: "*Therefore, desire precedes the mind's giving birth, and in that way the knowledge itself that we will to know by seeking and finding is born as an offspring.*"[509] But this desire is an imperfect love of the will, as it also exists with imperfect knowledge. But there is another perfect love that is joined to perfect knowledge that is called "*an offspring.*"[510] And concerning it he immediately adds: "*And the same desire by which one longs to know something becomes the love of it known when it holds and embraces the beloved child, that is, the knowledge, and unites it to the one begetting, and it is a certain image of the*

---

503   Anselm, *On the Procession of the Holy Spirit* 2; PL 158: 294B; ed. F. Schmitt, 2, p. 186.

504   See above par. 14.

505   See above par. 13.

506   See above par. 21.

507   See above par.14.

508   Augustine, *On the Trinity* 9, 12; PL 42: 972; ed. W. Mountain and F. Glorie, p. 310.

509   Ibid.; PL 42: 971–972; ed. W. Mountain and F. Glorie, p. 310.

510   Ibid.

Trinity, namely, the mind itself, and [302] *its knowledge, and love as the third.*"[511] But such a process does not exist in God as Augustine says in book fifteen of *On the Trinity*, chapter twenty-six: "*We cannot, can we, ask whether the Holy Spirit had already proceeded from the Father when the Son was born or had not yet proceeded and proceeded from the two after he was born where there are no times, as we could ask where we find times whether the will firstly proceeds from the human mind so that, when what is sought is found, it is called an offspring? And when it is already born or begotten, that will is perfected, coming to rest in that end, so that what had been the desire of one seeking is the love of one enjoying, and it now proceeds from both, that is, from the begetting mind and the begotten knowledge, as from parent and child. These things certainly cannot be sought where nothing begins in time so that it is completed in a later time.*"[512] And briefly in that way according to Augustine in book fifteen of *On the Trinity* that statement of his in book nine of *On the Trinity* cannot be applied to the divine emanations to prove that the will precedes knowledge and that as a consequence the Holy Spirit precedes the Son so that he proceeds from him.

75. It must nonetheless be understood that for all those things that are found in us from the side of the intellect and the will through discursive reasoning in time, there are found in God corresponding ones in the permanence of eternity. For there is a certain essential knowledge in the Father as there is in us a first incomplete knowledge of something that precedes all desire and love and firstly arouses the desire of love to seek a perfect knowledge of what is known. "*For no one,*" as he says in book fifteen, chapter twenty-seven, "*wills anything when he does not at all know what or of what sort it is.*"[513] To this love in us there corresponds the essential love in the Father that is delighted at the conception of the Word from the paternal mind quasi [303] informed by actual essential knowledge, and this delight corresponds to the desire in us that seeks perfect knowledge, and when it has been attained, that will is perfected and becomes the love of one who enjoys and that proceeds from the begetting mind and the begotten knowledge, to which there corresponds in God the proceeding love that is the Holy Spirit. And in that way in God desire proceeds in a certain order the mind's giving birth, that is, the desire of essential love in the Father as it is the Father's alone. That nonetheless is not the love that is the Holy Spirit, as the preceding love is also not perfect love except because that personal love has in itself the essential love, just as it also has all other essential attributes, and that perfect love in us contains in itself that love that was firstly imperfect, as has been said.[514] And in that way there is never love unless it proceeds from

511   Ibid.
512   Ibid. 15, 26; PL 42: 1094; ed. W. Mountain and F. Glorie, pp. 527–528.
513   Ibid. 15, 27; PL 42: 1097: ed. W. Mountain and F. Glorie, p. 532.
514   See above par. 33 and 46.

a knowledge corresponding to it, that is, essential love from essential <knowl-edge> and personal <love> from personal <knowledge>, so that personal love also cannot proceed except from previous personal knowledge, from which it is elicited, as was established above.[515]

76. But it must be understood that it can be understood in two ways that love is elicited from someone: in one way as from one eliciting the act, in another way as from that which is the reason for eliciting the act. In the first way love proceeds from knowledge, and this is from the unborn knowledge that is the Father and the born knowledge that is the Son. And in that way the Son is knowledge from knowledge, that is, born knowledge from unborn knowledge, as Augustine says in book fifteen of *On the Trinity*, chapter twenty-seven con-cerning the procession of these in us: *"When we speak what we know* from that which we know, *our knowledge is formed, and there is produced in the keen edge <of the mind> of one thinking an image most like that thought that we retained in memory, while will or love as a third,* which he shows *proceeds from knowledge, joins these two, that is, as parent and offspring."*[516] In the second [304] way love proceeds from personal will by the mediation of essential will, just as knowl-edge born proceeds from the intellect by the mediation of essential knowledge.

---

515   See above par. 33, 45, and 50.
516   Ibid.

QUESTION SEVEN

Whether the Person that Proceeds in Common from that Person That Is Not from Another and from That Which Is from Another, as Holy Spirit <Does> from the Father and the Son, Emanates from Them Equally Firstly, Principally, and in the Same Way

1. With regard to the seventh question it is argued that the person that emanates in common from the one that is not from another and from that one that is from another, as the Holy Spirit <does> from the Father and the Son, does not emanate from them equally firstly, because what belongs to a principle and to what is derived from a principle belongs to them in an order of natural origin, as it is clear from what was established above.[517] To spirate the Holy Spirit belongs to the Father and to the Son as to a principle and to what is derived from a principle because it belongs to the Father from himself, but the to the Son from the Father, as was likewise established above.[518] Therefore, and so on.

2. <It is argued> that he does not proceed equally principally because Augustine says in book fifteen of *On the Trinity*, chapter twenty-six, that "*the Holy Spirit principally* [305] *proceeds from the Father*."[519] — Likewise, Jerome says that "*the Holy Spirit properly proceeds from the Father*,"[520] as the Master shows by a threefold authority in book one of the *Sentences*, distinction twelve, in the chapter, "From the same one."[521] But he is not said properly to proceed from the Father except for some difference because he does not proceed properly in that way from the Son. But when something proceeds from two, from the one properly and from the other not properly, it principally proceeds from that one from which it proceeds properly. Therefore, and so on.

3. It is argued that <he does> not <proceed> equally immediately because he proceeds "*from the Father through the Son*," as the Master shows by many authorities of Hilary in the distinction mentioned in the chapter, "Perhaps."[522]

---

517 See above art. 52, qu. 1; ed. M. Führer, pp. 243–246.

518 See above qu. 6, par. 34.

519 Augustine of Hippo, *On the Trinity* 15, 17; PL 42: 1081; ed. W. Mountain and F. Glorie, pp. 503–504.

520 Pseudo-Jerome, *Letter 17: An Explanation of the Faith for Cyril* 1; PL 30: 176D.

521 See Peter Lombard, *Sentences* 1, d. 12, c. 2; PL 192: 554; ed. I. Brady, 1, p. 119.

522 See Peter Lombard, *Sentences* 1, d. 12, c. 2; PL 192: 554; ed. I. Brady, 1, pp. 119–121.

But nothing proceeds equally immediately from two when it proceeds from one through the other. Therefore, and so on.

4. <It is argued> that <he does> not <proceed> equally through himself, because that which belongs through itself to something does not belong to it from another. But to spirate belongs to the Son from another, just as being from the Father does, but <it belongs> to the Father through himself. Therefore, and so on.

5. It is argued that <he does> not <proceed> in the same way in the first place as follows because he proceeds from the Father as love proceeding to the Son, but from the Son the other way around as love proceeding from him to the Father, as was said above.[523] But love is the manner of producing the Holy Spirit from the two, but this manner and that other are not the same. Therefore, there is not the same manner of the Holy Spirit's proceeding from both. But where there is not the character of entirely the same manner, there is also not the same manner of proceeding. Therefore, and so on.

[306] 6. <It is argued> in the second place as follows: A primary and a secondary cause do not produce their effect in the same way, according to proposition one of the *Book of Causes*.[524] The Father is the primary cause in the production of the Holy Spirit, and the Son is the quasi secondary cause because the Son has it from the Father that he produces the Holy Spirit. Therefore, and so on.

7. <It is argued> in the third place as follows: "*That on account of which each thing is such is more such.*"[525] If therefore the Son spirates on account of the Father from whom he has this, the Father spirates more; hence, he does not <spirate> in the same way.

8. To the contrary <it is argued>: Whichever things are one without qualification in doing some act act equally firstly, principally, immediately, through themselves, and in the same way because the opposites of these have no place in what is simple and the same. The Father and the Son are one without qualification in spirating the Holy Spirit, as was established above.[526] Therefore, and so on.

<The Resolution of the Question by Replying to the Arguments>

9. It must be said to the first argument in accord with what has been said at the beginning of the resolution of the question prior to the last[527] that, just as it is necessary that a multitude proceeding from one be reduced in a certain order to the one from which they both proceed so that the many cannot for this

---

523   See above qu. 6, par. 53.

524   See anonymous, *Book of Causes* 1, 1; ed. A. Pattin, p. 46.

525   Aristotle, *Posterior Analytics* 1.2.72a29–30; trans. Jacobi; ed. L. Minio-Paluello and B. Dod, p. 9.

526   See above qu. 6, par. 51.

527   See above qu. 5, par. 5.

reason proceed equally firstly from the one, in accord with what was explained there, so it is necessary from this side that a plurality from which one proceeds be reduced in a certain order to the one from which both proceed, that is, the one that <proceeds> from both and similarly the other of them from [307] which that one proceeds so that one person absolutely cannot for this reason proceed from many equally firstly. Nonetheless, <it is> otherwise in this case than in that. For in that case two in no way proceed from one equally firstly without there being some order, as was explained there.

10. But in this case <they proceed> somehow in that way and somehow not <in that way>. For in accord with a certain distinction set forth in the preceeding question,[528] namely, that "equally firstly" can determine the act of spirating as it refers to the agent as it is acting and precisely eliciting the act, if one understands that the potency of spirating from the side of the act is also included under that determination, or as it refers to the agent eliciting the act by the spirative power if one understands the spirative power from the side of the agent not included under that determination. In the first way I say that the Father and the Son do not spirate equally firstly, but in a certain order, that is, in which they have the spirative power, namely, the Father from himself, the Son from the Father. For in that way to spirate belongs to the Father firstly and to the Son secondly, and this is not by reason of the act itself, but by reason of the spirative power understood with regard to the act which the Father and the Son have in a certain order because the Son is from the Father, just as, according to Hilary,[529] the Son is second from the Father, insofar as he has being from the Father. In the second way I say that the Father and the Son spirate equally firstly without any order because they are one principle in the origin of spiration, as was said above. The argument introduced against this proceeds only in the first member of the disjunction, as is clear to one who takes a look. [308] 11. To the second argument concerning "*principally*,"[530] one must distinguish by the distinction already set forth, and it is true and false in the same way. Hence, Augustine says in chapter seventeen, adding why he said "*principally*": "*For this reason I added 'principally' because the Holy Spirit is found to proceed from the Son, but the Father also gave this to him.*"[531]

12. And since "being a principle" is said in four ways, namely, (a)[532] by power as a father, not a mother, principally generates, as <is the case> in creatures; (b)

---

528   See above qu.6, par. 66.

529   See Hilary of Poitiers, *On the Trinity* 12, 55 and 56; PL 10:470 and 472; ed. P. Smulders, p. 626 and 627. See above par. 3.

530   See above par. 2.

531   Augustine of Hippo, *On the Trinity* 15, 17 and 26; PL 42: 1081 and 1095; ed. W. Mountain and F. Glorie, pp. 503–504 and 529.

532   I have added the letters for clarity.

by action, as the form of fire principally generates fire, not its heat, (c) by dignity, as the primary and universal cause principally acts with respect to a secondary and particular one, and (d) by authority, as a prince principally commands
with respect to a bailiff. In God and in the present question "being a principle"
is taken only in this last way, although not in the same way in every respect, as
will be explained below.[533] And in that way being a principle belongs only to the
Father, not only in spirating, but in every action that he does in common with
another person, whether one or more, because the name "author" only belongs
to someone with respect to another if he has it from himself that the other
proceeds from him, as Hilary says in book four of *On the Trinity*: *"That the
Father is said to be the author of the one whom he begot is shown in using the name
by which he is understood not to have come forth from another and from whom we
are taught that he who was born subsisted."*[534] Hence, if the Father had being from
another, he would not be said to be principally the author of the Son. And for
this reason in accord with what was said above,[535] the Son is wont to ascribe
those things that belong to him to the Father.

13. Still, by extending the name "author," Hilary says that the Holy Spirit
proceeds from the Father and the Son as authors in calling [309] everyone an
author from whom another has being, and in that way the Holy Spirit is said
to be an author only with respect to creatures. And because in this manner of
<being> an author the authority of dignity is not present, as it is in a prince
with respect to a bailiff, in God the subordinate authority in one does not for
this reason correspond to the authority in another person, in accord with what
will be explained below,[536] in the way in which subordinate authority in a bailiff
corresponds to the authority in a prince. And this <is so> because in a bailiff
the power of a king is received in a lower level than it is in the king, but in God
an entirely equal power is received from the author in the one who is from him.
And in that way it is clear that statement of Augustine proceeds in the first
member of the previously mentioned distinction, and the statement of Jerome
can be distinguished in a similar manner,[537] and they proceed in the sense of
the same member.

14. "Properly" is nonetheless said in three ways: in one way as it is distinguished over against "by participation," as God is said to exist properly because
<he exists> essentially and all other things <exist> by participation. In anoth-
er way it is distinguished over against "common," as risibility is said to be proper
to man, because it is not something common to him with another <being>. In

---

533   See *SQO* art. 60, qu. 9; ed. Badius 2, fol. 171rR–172vA.

534   Hilary of Poitiers, *On the Trinity* 4, 9; PL 10: 102; ed. P. Smulders, p. 110.

535   See above qu. 6, par. 38.

536   See *SQO* art. 57, qu. 2; ed. Badius 2, fol. 120vK–121rN.

537   See above par. 2

a third way it is distinguished over against being from another, as he is said to reign properly who has being a king from himself by having the royal power from no other, but not that one who has and holds his royal power from another. And in all these ways it expresses a special way of having something, but in God it is understood only in accord with the third way of "properly." And in that way only the Father is said to spirate the Holy Spirit properly because he has it from himself, not from another that he spirates him, but the Son <is> not <said to spirate him properly>, because he has this from the Father.

[310] 15. To the third argument concerning "*equally immediately*,"[538] it must be said in accord with the already stated distinction that if it refers to the agents by reason of the power in them, in that way he equally immediately proceeds from both because that <power> is only one and equally simple in both, and no mediation can be found in it. But if <it refers to them> by reason of their being agents, it is in that way possible to speak of them in two ways: in one way insofar as each of them has the power of spirating in himself, and in that way both spirate equally immediately. <It is possible to speak of them> in the other way, insofar as the Son has it from the Father that he spirates; in that way the Father spirates through the mediation of the Son, and in accord with this they do not spirate equally immediately, and there is no contradiction or contrariety because it is in accord with diverse characters and considerations. And although a means is found in many ways, the means in the present question is only a means in a natural order because the Son has from the Father the power of spirating in such an order, as is seen from what has been determined above.[539] Hence, even though someone is said to work through another in many ways, as we have explained above in the question on the uniformity of the divine actions,[540] in the present question in accord with which the Father is said to spirate by the mediation of the Son, he is also said to spirate "*through the Son*,"[541] as the Master confirms in the already mentioned distinction twelve of the *Sentences* by the authorities of Hilary[542] in the chapter, "Perhaps," so that the Father is said to spirate through the Son because the spirative power under the precise character by which it belongs to the Father in spirating the Holy Spirit also belongs to the Son in spirating the same <Spirit> except that the Father has it from himself and the Son has it from the Father, as is seen from what has already been determined and will now be further explained.[543] And it is not a problem that from one person another in

---

538   See above par. 3.

539   See above qu. 6, par. 18, 34, and 41.

540   See above *SQO* art. 39, qu. 7; ed. G. Wilson, pp. 221–251.

541   Peter Lombard, *Sentences* 1, d.12, 2; PL 192: 554–555; ed. I. Brady, 1, p. 120.

542   See Hilary of Poitiers, *On the Trinity* 12, 55 and 56; PL 10: 470 and 472; ed. P. Smulders, pp. 626 and 627.

543   See above qu. 6, par. 18, 34, and 41.

that way proceeds mediately and immediately. For this is according to a diverse manner since the same [311] spirative power that he gives to another by means of whom he spirates, he also retains for himself so that he can immediately spirate. And through this the reply is seen to the argument to the contrary.[544]

16. But it must be understood for the understanding of this proposition, "The Father spirates or does something through the Son," that this preposition "through" with regard to its occurrence denotes some character of causality over the act it determines, but at times it denotes that causality over the act as it flows from the agent, and in that way <it> also <denotes> some causality with regard to that through which it acts. And this is either final as when an artisan is said to work through the love of gain, or formal as when he is said to work through art, or efficient as when a bailiff is said to do something through the king, or material, as when a human being is said to be acted upon through a passive potency. And the Father acts through the Son in none of these ways because the Son has no causality over some act as it has its emergence from the Father so that he is the reason, cause, or principle of an act's emerging from him; by no means, <does he act> in this way as if in accord with the genus of efficient cause. On the contrary, the Son is said to do whatever he does through the Father, as was explained in the question already dealt with,[545] because the Father is the reason or principle that any act emerges from the Son because <the Son> has the power for this from him. But at times it denotes that causality over the act only as it passes into the effect or into what is derived from the principle. And this happens in three ways. For at times that through which the other acts has some power of acting from itself that is strengthened through the power of the other. In that way a king is said to act through a bailiff. But at times it has no power in acting from itself, but from the other. And this happens in two ways because it either receives the power flowing from it and another <power>. In that way an artisan produces a knife through a hammer. Or it receives the same <power>. In this way the Father works through the Son, and <he does so> [312] in the same ways in which something is said to act through another and by means of it and in accord with the same kind of cause, as is clear to one who looks.

17. To the fourth argument concerning "through himself," it must be said that "through" can be taken in the present question in terms of language so that "himself" is a reflexive pronoun, both in terms of grammar and of signification in itself, or <it can be taken> in terms of grammar as it is a certain adverbial circumlocution determining the predicate in relation to the reason or cause of the inherence of the predicate in the subject, and "himself" is not a significative expression in terms of itself, but only a part of speech. If it is taken in the first

---

544   See above par. 8.
545   See *SQO* art. 39, qu. 7; ed. G. Wilson, pp. 221–251.

way, it must be said that the Father and his Son spirate the Holy Spirit through themselves, although not both equally from themselves, because each of them spirates him through the divine essence that is his, and in that way <each does so> through himself, although the Father has <the essence> from himself, but the Son has it from the Father, and for this reason it is said that the Father spirates from himself, but the Son does not <spirate> in that way. And according to this way the Father equally spirates and generates through himself insofar as he immediately does both, although <he does not do both> in that way insofar as he does one of them through the other, as he spirates through the Son, just as the Father does not generate and spirate equally principally insofar as he spirates through the Son, as was established above according to Richard.[546] But if "through himself" is taken in terms of speech, it must be said that since, as it was said [313] in the previously mentioned question,[547] "through" is understood in many ways and in terms of many kinds of cause, as has also been now explained in the ways of speaking, "through himself," can be understood in terms of every kind of cause, as is clear from book one of the *Posterior Analytics*.[548] But in the present question it pertains only to the way of <understanding> "through itself" in terms of the genus of formal cause, because "through itself" is the condition of the means or of the reason of the inherence of the predicate in the subject, and in the present question this is the spirative power, as was established.[549] And something is said to act through itself because it has in itself essentially as something of itself that by which it acts, and those things that have that equally essentially in themselves are said to act equally essentially on account of that "through itself," so that the distinction touched upon and applied to the previously mentioned articles[550] does not have a place here.

18. Hence, since the Father and the Son have in themselves equally essentially the power spirative of the Holy Spirit, just as is said in John five: *As the Father has life in himself, so he has also given to the Son to have life in himself* (Jn 5:26), so it can be said: "As the Father has the spirative power in himself, so he has given to the Son to have the spirative power in himself," and this equally essentially in both cases. And in accord with this Augustine explains the quoted words in *On John*, sermon twenty-two, where he says: <he has life "*in himself so that he does*

---

546 See above qu. 5, par. 14, and Richard of Saint Victor, *On the Trinity* 6, 8; PL 196: 972D and 981C–D; ed. J. Ribaillier, pp. 235 and 250.

547 See *SQO* art. 39, qu. 7; ed. G. Wilson, pp. 228–232.

548 See Aristotle, *Posterior Analytics* 1.4.73a35; tran. Jacobi, ed. L. Minio-Paluello and B. Dod, p. 12.

549 See above par. 15.

550 See *SQO* art. 39, qu. 7; ed. G. Wilson, pp. 228–232.

not live by participation, but so that he lives in common <with the Father>,[551] *and he is entirely life. What is the difference? The one gave; the other received.*"[552] On this account the Father and the Son spirate the Holy Spirit equally and through themselves, [314] and this is in accord with the second way of saying "through himself," just as that <proposition>: "The Father is God through himself," is in accord with the first way of saying "through himself." Still none of those <propositions>: "The Father is God," "The Father spirates," "The Son is God," or "The Son spirates," is through himself and firstly because the reason of the inherence of the predicate in the subject is not proper to one of them, but common to both, and in that way it belongs to each "through himself," just as in demonstratives a common being acting upon by a common cause belongs to many, just as a changeable proportion belongs in numbers and magnitudes, as the Philosopher says in book one of the *Posterior Analytics*.[553] But only something common of the sort that is common to both of them is predicated firstly and through itself of that, if there is something of the sort. For this proposition is through himself and firstly: "The Father generates," and on this account although the Father generates and spirates equally immediately, as was already said above,[554] he still does not generate and spirate equally through himself, insofar as "through himself" is taken in terms of language.

19. To the objection to the contrary that *"what belongs to something through itself does not belong to it from another,"*[555] it must be said that something belongs to something from (*a*) itself or of (*ex*) itself formally, or effectively, or principally. In the first way it belongs to each of them of himself that he is God and that he spirates because <they do so> through that which is an essential form in them. And what in that way belongs to something of itself, but only from another, does not belong to it through itself. But in the second way nothing belongs to the Son of himself because he only has what he has from the Father, but what he has from another as from a principle, he very well has formally of himself and in that way through himself.

20. To the fifth argument[556] concerning the same way, it must be said that the previously mentioned distinction does not have place here because the manner of the action regards only the manner of emanating <the action> from the power of the agent. But one must here [315] distinguish concerning the

551   Augustine has "immutably, *incommutabiliter*," which makes much better sense than "commonly, *communiter*."

552   Augustine of Hippo, *Homilies on John* 22; PL 35: 1479; ed. R. Willems, p. 229.

553   See Aristotle, *Posterior Analytics* 1.10.76a43–b2; trans. Jacobi, ed. L. Minio-Paluello, p. 23.

554   See above qu. 5, par. 15–16.

555   See above par. 4.

556   See above par. 5.

action itself because its manner can be considered in two ways in accord with the twofold relation it has: in one way insofar as <the action> emanates from it through the power of the agent, in another way insofar as it passes into the terminus or the effect. In the first way there is no difference from the side of the action in God where the persons act with an immutable necessity in accord with the manner of their power, unless there is some diversity in the power by which they act. But this power in the action of spirating, which is the concordant will of the two in mutual love for each other, as was said above,[557] can be considered in two ways: in one way by reason of what is principally signified by will and love, in another way by reason of what is connoted from the side of the will through the fact that it is understood to be concordant and from the side of love through the fact that it is mutual. In the first way since will and love are in them both by reason of what is essential in them and by reason of the notional respect under which they are the reason for spirating, they are one and the same in the Father and the Son, and the Father and the Son are one principle in accord with this, as was established above,[558] and from the same thing, insofar as it is the same, one action is able to proceed only in one and the same way. I mean that the Father and the Son spirate the Holy Spirit in absolutely one and the same way, as Augustine says in book fifteen of *On the Trinity*, chapter twenty-seven: "*The Holy Spirit proceeds from the two at the same time, although the Father gave it to the Son that, as he proceeds from him, he also proceeds from the Son.*" And adding the reason for this, he says: "*As the Father has life in himself and also gave it to the Son to have life in himself, so he gave him that the life, which is the Holy Spirit, proceeds from the Son as he proceeds from him.*"[559] And in book six of *On the Trinity*, Richard speaks as follows: "*Of course, he proceeds* [316] *both from the Father and from the Son* in entirely one and the same way, since in both there is one and the same character in every respect."[560]

21. But if the character of spirating is considered in the second way by reason of what is connoted with regard to the will, insofar as it is said to be concordant, since concordance lies only in uniformity, with regard to this both again spirate in one and the same way, and on this account the Holy Spirit is not spirated more or less or to a greater degree by one than by the other. But if it is considered by reason of what is connoted with regard to love, insofar as it is said to be mutual, along with the character by which mutual love regards both terms, because insofar as it is mutual it is of the Father for the Son and of the

---

557 See above qu. 6, par. 46.

558 See above qu. 6, par. 56.

559 Augustine of Hippo, *On the Trinity* 15, 27; PL 42: 1095–1096; ed. W. Mountain and F. Glorie, p. 530.

560 Richard of Saint Victor, *On the Trinity* 6, 9; PL 196: 973B; ed. J. Ribaillier, p. 236.

Son for the Father, with regard to this they do not spirate entirely uniformly or in the same way. But this difference consists in the character of spirating only as it is in those who spirate and love each other mutually, but not as it regards the act. And for this reason it does not redound upon the act of spirating so that it in some way becomes many on account of them, just as the plurality of those who spirate also does not.

22. But if the act of spirating is considered as it passes into the object, this can be in two ways: in one way as it passes into the object that is the terminus of the action constituted by it, in another way as it passes by means of it into the object that is only the terminus of the action and not constituted by it. In the first way the Holy Spirit is the terminus of the act of spirating proceeding from it as a person subsisting in himself, and in this way he proceeds uniformly and in the same way from them, because <he does> not <proceed> more fully or more perfectly from one than from the other. In the second way the Father and the Son who mutually spirate for each other as they mutually love each other are the terminus of the act of spirating. For through the act of spirating, the Holy Spirit proceeds as a person subsisting in himself and in that way as the terminus of the act constituted by it. He also proceeds from the Father into the Son and from the Son into the Father as into the terminus of the action that is [317] only the terminus, not constituted by it. And this is for the reason that he proceeds through the manner of mutual love, and he is the love that proceeds in which their mutual love is perfected as in him by whom they mutually love each other, and in that way he proceeds from the Father into the Son as one by whom the Father perfectly loves the Son and he proceeds from the Son into the Father as one by whom the Son perfectly loves the Father, and in that way he is the union of the two by whom they mutually love each other perfectly. For love only exists if it tends toward another. In this way then, insofar as they spirate the Holy Spirit mutually, one into the other, they do not spirate in entirely the same way. But this difference does not reflect on the one spirated or on the act of spirating because it only exists on the side of the terminuses, namely, of the Father and of the Son insofar as they mutually spirate for each other the Holy Spirit, as was said.[561]

561　See above par. 20 and above in this par.

QUESTION EIGHT

Whether from Any of the Three Mentioned Persons Some Other Emanates

1. With regard to the eighth question it is argued that from any of the three mentioned persons some other emanates as follows: It stems from the character of the perfection of a person in God that another person emanates from him, as was said above.[562] But there is equal perfection in any of the divine persons, even when another person [318] has emanated from him. For the person emanating takes nothing away from the power of the one from whom he emanates. Therefore, from any of the divine persons another emanates, even though another has emanated from the same.

2. <It is argued> in the second place that from any of the persons emanating another entirely like him emanates because from a person from whom another emanates his substance is communicated to the person who emanates, as was established above.[563] But the substance is not communicated unless its power and potency are communicated at the same time. However, by the same power and potency it is possible that something similar emanate from the one in which it is. Therefore, and so on.

3. And this is confirmed by what the Apostle says in Hebrews, chapter one, concerning the Son of God: *Since he is the splendor of glory bearing in himself all things by the word of his power* (Heb 1:3), and so on. There is therefore some word of the power of the Son by which he bears all things. But a word by which all things are borne can be only an infinite, uncreated, and eternal word. There is therefore some infinite, eternal, and uncreated word of the power of the Son. But such is only a personal word proceeding from the power of the Son. But there is not a word in God if it is not a son. Therefore, in God a word proceeds from the Word, and a son from the Son. And in the same way it can be argued from the side of the Holy Spirit in producing another Holy Spirit.

4. <It is argued> in the third place as follows: The Son either can generate another son or he cannot. One should not say that he cannot because he is omnipotent. And Richard says in book three of *On the Trinity*, chapter four: "*The omnipotent cannot be excused through impossibility.*"[564] And Augustine likewise says in *Answer to Maximinus*, [319] book one, chapter thirteen: "*The Son did*

---

562   See above qu. 3.

563   Ibid.

564   Richard, *On the Trinity* 3, 4; PL 196: 918A–B; ed. J. Ribaillier, p.139.

not generate, not because he could not, but because he ought not to have."⁵⁶⁵ But this would not be true unless he were able to generate. For if he could not generate, it would be true that he did not generate because he could not. If therefore he could generate, he therefore generated because *"in* eternal beings potency and act do *not* differ."⁵⁶⁶ And also in them potency is impeded by nothing except perhaps by the will, and in that case if the Son could generate but did not generate, this would be because he did not will to, which is impossible, because this would be a great *"lack of good will,"*⁵⁶⁷ according to Richard where <he was quoted> above, and the Father would have a will in act that the Son would not have.

5. <It is argued> in the fourth place that in God from any person from whom one person emanates, another similar to him in person can emanate. For in God the one emanating from another, by the fact that he emanates from him, takes away by his emanation none of the potency through which he emanates in the person from whom he emanates. And if this is so, for the same reason by which he produces one person through that potency, the one produced produces another similar to him, just as we see in a human father that after one son has been produced through his generative potency, he can still produce a second, and for the same reason in God when the second person has been produced, he can produce a third, and so on to infinity. Therefore, and so on.

6. <It is argued> in the fifth place as follows: The same act of understanding that belongs to the Father belongs to both the Son and the Holy Spirit; hence, that similarly does which is founded upon that act of understanding for the production of another person. Hence, since upon the essential act of understanding, as was said above⁵⁶⁸ and will be more fully [320] explained in the following question,⁵⁶⁹ the notional act of speaking is founded, the notional act of speaking therefore uniformly belongs to the three persons, as the act of understanding also does, and in that way, as the Father brings forth the Word, which is his Son, by the act of speaking, the Son and the Holy Spirit also similarly do. Hence, according to Augustine in the beginning of *On the Trinity:* *"Nothing brings forth or produces itself,"*⁵⁷⁰ the Son therefore produces a son other than himself in speaking a word other than himself, and the Holy Spirit

565   Augustine, *Answer to Maximinus* 2, 12, 3; PL 42: 768; ed. P. M. Hombert, p. 564.

566   Aristotle, *Physics* 3.4.203b30; trans. vet.; ed. R. Bossier and J. Brams, p. 114; also see *Aristotelian Authorities*; ed. J. Hamesse, 2, p. 103.

567   Richard of Saint Victor, *On the Trinity* 3, 4; PL 196: 918B; ed. J. Ribaillier, p. 139.

568   See above qu. 6, par. 51 and *SQO* art. 39, qu. 7; ed. G. Wilson, pp. 248–249.

569   See below qu. 9.

570   Augustine, *On the Trinity* 1, 1; PL 42: 820; ed. W. Mountain and F. Glorie, p. 28.

similarly does, because otherwise he would produce the one by whom he was produced, which is impossible. For the same reason one can argue concerning spiration with regard to willing to prove that the Holy Spirit produces another holy spirit, and this would be to infinity in both cases.

7. <It is argued> specifically in the sixth place as follows that a person emanates from the Holy Spirit as follows: The Father and the Son together in producing the Holy Spirit do not have less efficacy than the Father alone has through himself in producing the Son. But in producing the Son through his efficacy, the Father gives to him the ability to produce another person along with the Father. Therefore, on account of the efficacy that they both have in producing the Holy Spirit, they will give to him the ability in common with both of them to produce yet another person, and in that way for the same reason thereafter <persons will be produced> to infinity.

8. To the contrary there is the Catholic faith that if there is some other person emanating from those mentioned in God, there is not exactly a trinity of persons in God.

<The Resolution of the Question>

9. This question seeks that the reason be explained why in God there are three persons and only three, which was stated above in summary and in general in a certain question on this raised in the preceding article.[571] [321] And to the present question it must be said that from one of three mentioned persons, of which the first does not emanate from another, but the second emanates from him, and the third emanates from the two together, it is not possible to understand that some other emanates except through some way of emanation other than those already mentioned, which are by the way of nature and of the will, either through one of those two ways or through both of them.

10. But in the first way, which principally pertains to the already mentioned question, some other person does not emanate from one of those three persons because according to what was determined above,[572] it is not fitting to maintain in God some other way of emanation. Because if some other were also possible, some person would proceed in accord with it, and if there were many other ways, many others would proceed in accord with them, and this <would be> not only from one of them, but from all of them together, because in accord with what has already been determined,[573] there can be diverse ways of emanating only if they have a certain order of origin among one another so that, according to the determination reached above, from a single person that is not from another the second person would proceed through the first emanation and through this there would be communicated to him all the other

---

571   See above art. 53, qu. 9.

572   See above art. 53, qu. 9, par. 5.

573   See above qu. 5 and *SQO* art. 52, qu. 2, par. 12; ed. M. Führer, 256.

ways by which one person is able to emanate from another, and for this reason through the second way of emanating from the person that is not from another and from that which is from the other together, a third would emanate by a second emanation, and for the same reason a fourth from those three, and so on thereafter.

11. Also in the second way that principally pertains to this question some other person does not emanate from one of those three persons because from one way of emanation only one person can proceed in God, however many ways of emanations are held to be in God, [322] whether only the two already mentioned ways or finite or infinite many, as Richard says in book five of *On the Trinity*, chapter ten: "*In accord with any difference it is impossible that there be more than one person. For from one person alone there can be only a single person. Similarly, the person that is only from the two can be only a single one*,"[574] and so on thereafter if there were more than two in the divine emanations. And in God from only one person two persons cannot proceed, but only a single one and according to a single way of emanating, and similarly from only two persons only a single one can proceed and according to one other way of emanating. And from this he concludes, adding further: "*Just as therefore in the divinity there can be only one person that is from himself, so there can be only one person who is from only one person, and only one other that is from the two.*"[575]

12. Hence, since in God there are only the two sorts of emanations through which there emanate only two persons, and besides them there is, according to what has already been determined,[576] only one person that is not from another, it is for this reason irrefutably concluded that there are only three persons in God, one that emanates from no one, one that emanates from that one alone that does not emanate from another, and a third from which no one emanates and that emanates in common from the one that emanates from no one and from the one that emanates from the other. For that conclusion, that is, that from only one person there can be only a single person, Richard in the same place gives an argument that leads to what is impossible. "*For*," as he says, "*if two proceeded only from one, surely neither of those proceeding would immediately cling to the other, which is impossible,*"[577] and <it would be> similarly, if two proceeded only from [323] two. "*Because,*" as he says there, "*if there could be a fourth person in the deity, it would undoubtedly be necessary that it take its origin immediately from the other three. Otherwise, it would not cling to one of the others except by*

574   Richard of Saint Victor, *On the Trinity* 5, 10; PL 196: 937B–C; ed. J. Ribaillier, p. 208.

575   Ibid.; PL 196: 937C–D; ed. J. Ribaillier, p. 208.

576   See above qu. 2 and art. 53, qu. 9, par. 5.

577   Richard of Saint Victor, *On the Trinity* 5, 10; PL 196: 937C; ed. J. Ribaillier, p. 208.

mediated kinship. And if there could be a fifth person there, it would for a similar reason immediately proceed from the other four, and so on in the others, however far the series might be drawn out in an intelligible way."[578] And this argument proceeds in common, whether two persons are held to proceed from one person alone, whether according to one way of proceeding or according to many, and so on with the rest.

13. But on that which specifically pertains to the present question, namely, that in God two persons cannot proceed according to one and the same way of proceeding, whether from one person or from many, there are other specific arguments for this. For it is clearly impossible that according to one singular way of proceeding or emanating—for instance, according to one singular way of generating—there would emanate two persons, that is, two sons, because a numerically one and singular action <tends> toward only one numerically singular terminus, as this whitening <tends> only toward this whiteness, according to the Philosopher in book five of the *Physics*.[579]

14. Similarly, it is also absolutely impossible that according to a specifically same, but numerically diverse way of emanating—for example, according to diverse generations or spirations—numerically diverse persons are held to emanate in God, that is, two sons or two holy spirits. [324] And this is explained in two ways: in one way from the side of that which is as if the matter or the subject or the foundation upon which the acts of emanation are founded and with regard to which they have being and from which the emanating persons have to be produced and upon which the properties of the emanating persons have to be founded. But the other is from the side of that from which the acts of the emanations proceed and are elicited.

15. In the first way <it is explained> as follows: Whatever is essential in God is only one, singular, and simple. For the divine essence is singular and unique. Similarly, the divine intellect and will are, and <so are> to understand and to will, upon which all the personal and notional <attributes> are founded and with regard to which they have being. For the notional acts, such as to speak or generate and to spirate, are founded upon the essential acts that are to will and to understand, as will be explained in the following question.[580] They also have being with regard to the divine essence as with regard to a subject and quasi matter, and from it the persons have to be produced, as was established above,[581] and upon it the personal properties, paternity, filiation, and spiration,

---

578   Ibid.; PL 196: 936D–937A; ed. J. Ribaillier, p. 207.

579   See Aristotle, *Physics* 5.4.227b9–10; trans. vet.; ed. F. Bossier and J. Brams, p. 203.

580   See below qu. 9, par. 4–11.

581   See above qu. 3, par. 58 and *SQO* art. 35, qu. 3; art. 39, qu. 2, and art. 39, qu. 4; ed. G. Wilson, pp. 25–29; pp. 179–181, and pp. 198–200.

have to be founded. Hence, since that which is founded upon something or has being with regard to something or has its being produced from it cannot be made many numerically at the same time and in the same instant under the same species unless that is made many upon which it is founded and with regard to which and from which it has being. For example, in creatures, since the act of seeing color is founded upon the act of sight being changed by color, if the change is only one and simple, there can at the same time and in the same instant be only one simple <act of> seeing. Similarly, when the act of whitening is with regard to a body, if the body is only one numerically, there can at the same time in the same thing be only one whitening with regard to it. Similarly, when something becomes white from non-white, if the non-white subject is numerically one, there can come to be from it only one white thing and by only one act of whitening. Similarly, when whiteness is founded upon a body and a likeness <is founded> upon whiteness, if that body is numerically one, the whiteness founded upon it cannot be numerically many, and if the whiteness is numerically one, the likeness founded on it is also, even if it is related to many through it, as one father can very well be related to many sons by one paternity. It is necessary therefore that, as the essential acts of understanding and willing in God, upon which the notional acts are founded, are singular and simple numerically and unable to be made many, and similarly as the one divine essence is singular and simple with regard to which the acts of speaking, spirating, and understanding have being as with regard to a subject or quasi matter, it is necessary that the acts themselves similarly be singular, simple, and only one. Similarly, it is also necessary that the persons that have their being produced from it, according to the way determined above,[582] be singular and only one in number as well as the personal properties that have their being founded upon the divine essence so that in that way it is no more possible that there be in God many generations, many sons, or many filiations than that there be numerically many changes in numerically the same matter in the same instant under the same species or <that there be> in the same man numerically many filiations or that one and the same man be many sons for this reason. And this <is> especially <so> in one and the same instant, just as whatever things are in God have being at the same time in the same instant of eternity.

[326] 16. In the second way[583] the same point is explained as follows. In any emanation of a divine person the whole fecundity in producing the person is entirely exhausted in the production of a single person so that fecundity remains neither in the one producing nor in the one produced for producing another emanation of a similar person. Otherwise, that second similar person would be produced without fecundity of production, and what is produced would be

---

582   See above par. 11–13.
583   See above par. 14.

derived from a principle without the character of being its principle in the one who is its principle, which is entirely impossible.

17. But that is seen from the side of the intellect in the production of the Word in that way, and it is in a similar way understood from the side of the will in the production of the Holy Spirit. For because the Word that is produced in God always remains, and the act of producing and the one producing it likewise always exist uniformly, once it has been produced, there cannot remain fecundity for producing another word unless there could be two productions of entirely the same manner and of the same character at the same time emanating from the same principle and existing entirely uniformly with regard to it, since every production of a word in God is necessarily of the same character, just as every word that can exist in God <is>, and just as every act of understanding and every production of sons in the same nature <are>, and all sons, and all filiations are even in creatures. But that is entirely impossible. For it is impossible that two productions of entirely one and the same character exist entirely uniformly with regard to the same thing, as the preceding argument showed,[584] especially <as produced> by the same agent that always exists uniformly. For that is also impossible by diverse agents, as it is impossible in creatures that one and the same nature numerically that exists uniformly be moved at one and the same time, whether by the same agent or by many diverse motions of the same species. It is impossible therefore that [327] in God there be many productions or many who are produced of the same character. And in that way many persons cannot proceed in God entirely according to the same way of producing, in accord with which all these matters were handled more fully in a certain question of a *Quodlibet*, namely, whether there are in God three persons and only three.[585]

<Replies to the Arguments>

18. To the first argument to the contrary that "*equal perfection is in the indi-vidual persons, therefore, the emanation of a person is from the individual per-sons both equally and uniformly*,"[586] it must be said that in God the perfection and the character of the perfection differ. For a perfection belongs to purely essential attributes, and on this account it is the same concerning the individual persons. But the character of the perfection is the manner of having it in accord with which it is limited to that which is personal, which is not always common to many, in accord with what was explained above.[587] Hence, the fact that the Son and the Holy Spirit do not generate does not come from imperfection, but from the condition of their perfection. For the three have the same perfection

---

584 See above par. 16.

585 See *Quodlibet* 6, qu. 1; ed. G. Wilson, pp. 2–31.

586 See above par. 1.

587 See above par. 15.

as they have the same deity, and it comes from the same perfection and from the diverse condition of the perfection that the Father generates and is not generated, that the Son is generated and does not generate. For only the Father has that <perfection> for generating because <he has it> under the property of innascible primacy, but the Son has it for being generated because <he has it> under the property of nascibility.

19. To the second argument that "*a person from whom another emanates communicates* his own substance and therefore also his power to the one that emanates,"[588] and so on, the reply to this depends upon what is signified by this name "power" or "potency" in God. And for the understanding of this it must be known that if one takes what the name signifies in a broad sense, something is signified [328] in two ways: in one way as that from which the imposition of the name is made, and in the other way as that on which it is made. In the first way "potency" formally signifies only a respect or a relation and includes in what it signifies in a quasi material way that upon which such a respect is founded. And in this way we said above in speaking about the potency of God in general[589] that it signifies only a respect. But in the second way, if one is speaking about what potency signifies and this in particular about the potency that in God is with regard to the notional acts of the persons, it must be known that, since in the divine persons there are only the substance and the real relations, "potency" can only signify the substance alone or a relation alone or both together. <It does> not <signify> in this last way because that which signifies the substance with a property is only a person, and "potency" does not imply a person from what it signifies.

20. It can only be understood to signify the substance alone in two ways: either in terms of itself or under the character of some respect. In the first way it cannot be said to signify the substance because in terms of itself "substance" denotes no relationship to act, and "potency" necessarily denotes that, as was sufficiently explained above in speaking of the potency of God in general.[590] Therefore, if it signifies the substance, this is necessarily under some respect to an act, and it is necessary to hold this, namely, that it signifies the substance as that upon which the name is imposed and only the substance, and <it does> this as it is under the character of a respect and only as it is under the character of a respect. <It signifies> only the substance because potency is only that by which an agent elicits an act or that from which it is elicited. But this is only the form by which an agent acts and the nature by which the one acted upon is acted upon. And <it is> not under the character of a respect in such a way that the respect itself is [329] the potency, but <it is> that without which a

588   See above par. 2.
589   See *SQO* art. 35, qu. 2; ed. G. Wilson, pp. 15–20.
590   See ibid.

substance does not have the character of a potency. On this account although the substance is the same under diverse respects, it is not entirely the same as the potency, but rather as <it is> under a respect, that is, because under such a respect it is a potency without qualification. Thus because it is under diverse respects, it is diverse potencies, and thus it is, as we have determined elsewhere,[591] that, although the soul is one substance, it is still diverse potencies, and a potency is nonetheless only the substance of the soul, and the substance of the soul is its potencies, just as it is with regard to prime matter that, although it is one substance, it is still many potencies. And the Philosopher speaks in this way when speaking of matter in book twelve of the *Metaphysics*: "When the agent is one, if the matter were one in terms of potency, the species is one in terms of substance, <and> what is generated from it would be only one."[592]

21. But others,[593] considering that a potency is only the substance and not attending to the fact that it is a potency only as it is under a certain respect, think that, as the substance is one, so the potency is one. And they say that in God there is only one potency in the three, just as there is only one [330] substance, and as it seems, it is the position of the Master of the *Sentences* in book one, distinction seven, the chapter "The Same."[594] Hence, these men reply to the argument from the side of the power or potency, just as it was already replied from the side of the perfection, when they say that *"the potency of the Father and the Son is the same* as the deity is," and that *"it is from the same potency* that the Father generates and the Son is generated,"[595] so that the Father has no potency that the Son does not have. But the Father has the same potency to generate as an active potency that the Son has to be generated as a passive potency, and this because <they have it as> joined to another respect in the Father and in the Son. And in that way they say that the Father communicates to the Son his power or potency by which he generates, as <he communicates> his nature, but the Son cannot generate by it, but only the Father, because the Father has it under another respect than the Son does.

22. But as was said, it ought not to be said that it signifies something entirely absolute, but <does so> only under the character of a respect so that, as the essence is the potency to generate under the respect of the Father and to be generated under the respect of the Son, so it is potency for an act indeterminately as the essence, and so <it is> the potency to generate only under the respect of

---

591 See *SQO* art. 43, qu. 4; ed. L. Hödl, p. 65.

592 Rather, Averroes, *Commentary on the Metaphysics* 8, comm. 11; ed. Juntas 8, fol. 219rbH and 12, comm. 11; ed. Juntas 8, fol. 297vaH.

593 See Giles of Rome, *Commentary on the Sentences* 1, d. 11, 4; ed. Venice, fol. 67rA.

594 See Peter Lombard, *Sentences* 1, d. 7, 2; PL 192: 542; ed. I. Brady, pp. 93–94.

595 Ibid.; ed. I. Brady, p. 94.

paternity and the potency to be generated only under the respect of filiation. Hence, there are different potencies insofar as there are different respects. And in that way there is not the same potency in the Father to generate and in the Son to be generated and in both of them to spirate and in the Holy Spirit to be spirated, unless we understand the same <potency> insofar as it is of itself indeterminate, because <it is> under an indeterminate respect and is not in the Son the potency to generate or by which he actively generates and is not in the Father the potency to be generated or [331] by which he is passively generated, and similarly regarding the potency of both with respect to the Holy Spirit and the other way around.

23. Therefore, one must reply in another way to the argument that says that "the person communicating his substance also communicates along with it his power."[596] It must be said that it is true with regard to that which is the power or potency itself, which is only the substance, as was said,[597] but not with regard to the potency according to the character of potency. For he no more communicates his potency or the substance under the character of his potency than he communicates his property under which the substance has the character of his potency determined to him.

24. But one can reply in another way by distinguishing that there is a certain substance that from itself has a determinate respect to an act and <there is> a certain substance that <has a determinate respect> only through something that belongs to that in which it is. Concerning substance in the first way it is true that, when the substance is communicated, its potency is also communicated. In this way every created substance has a potency determined for it to a certain act, according to the Philosopher at the end of book four of *Meteorology*,[598] and this <is> on account of the limitation of a created substance. But on account of its unlimitedness the uncreated substance has from itself potency without determination to something for all the essential acts, but for the notional acts only through a determination to act under some property. Therefore, in God a person that communicates his substance communicates the potency for all the essential acts, but not the potency for all the notional acts, because it [332] is only from of an addition in the person to whom it is communicated. And on this account it can only be communicated if together with the communication of the substance there is communicated the addition on account of which it has that potency. And for this reason because the person from whom another emanates does not communicate to him his property under which his substance has the potency determined to that act of emanation,

596   See above par. 2.

597   See above par. 19.

598   See Aristotle, *Meteorology* 4.12.390a10–11; trans. Henry Aristippus in Albert the Great, *Meteorology*, ed. P. Hossfeld, 6, 1, p. 298.

on this account, although he communicates to him his substance, he still in no way communicates this potency. Thus, just as the Father does not communicate to the Son his substance under his property, so he does not communicate to him his potency by which he generates.

25. And as to what was confirmed *"concerning the Son* that he would have *a word* because according to the Apostle *"he bears all things by the word of his power* (Heb 1:3)," it must be said according to the Gloss that in that case *"word"* is not taken for some concept of the mind, but for the command of the will. For it speaks as follows: *"In commending his power he says: The Son is the one who bears, that is, who contains and governs all things by his word, that is, by the command of his might alone, that is, of his power and goodness. And note,"* he says, *"that it was said through a likeness. For in saying this he wanted to point out the facility of containing through a metaphor for those who without any labor move or do something by a word or finger."*[599]

26. To the third <argument> that *"the Son either can or cannot generate a son,"*[600] it must be said that by treating the character of potency in the way already stated in which some[601] hold that potency signifies the substance absolutely, it is quite important to ask whether the Son can generate or whether there is in the Son the potency for generating [333] because to be able when signified by a verb signifies a potency as applicable to an act insofar as it is in the one to whom being able is attributed. But potency signified by a noun signifies a potency as it is an absolute reality in terms of what is said and the manner of signifying with regard to the act as applicable without qualification to an act as in some supposite, although not determinately in that to which it is attributed. Hence, it must be said according to those men that it is true that "in the Son there is from the Father the potency to generate," not by which the Son himself generates, but by which someone in God generates, so that in accord with this it is different to say: "In the Son there is the potency that is for generating," and "In the Son there is the potency so that he generates." And according to those people this <proposition> is true without qualification: "In the Son there is the potency that is for generating," but this one is false without qualification: "The Son can generate," and that opposite one is true: "The Son cannot generate," at least if one distinguishes in accord with them, as will now be said.[602]

---

599   Peter Lombard, *Comments on Hebrews* 1, 1; PL 192: 406A–B.

600   See above par. 4.

601   See Giles of Rome, *Commentary on the Sentences* 1, d. 11, 4; ed. Venice, fol. 67rA.

602   See below par. 28 and 29.

27. And as for that which is argued by Richard that "*The omnipotent cannot be excused through impossibility,*"[603] it must be said that it can be understood in two ways that someone is excused from acting through impossibility insofar as that impossibility can be caused in two ways or from two causes. <It can be caused> in one way and from one cause because of the lack of a potency that can be ordered to the act; in another way because of its inapplicability to the act as it is in someone.[604] In the first way, as they say, the statement of Richard is true. Hence, after he said: [334] "*The omnipotent cannot be excused through impossibility,*" he immediately adds: "*But it is clear that it is not because of the lack of potency.*"[605] And in this way the Son cannot be excused through impossibility from being able to generate because, as was said, he has the potency that is ordered to this, although in another person. But in the second way the statement of Richard is not understood and is not true. For in that way the Son is excused through impossibility from being able to generate because the potency that is in him for generating is not applicable to the act of generating actively insofar as it is in him because it is not in him so that he generates nor under the property by which it can be determined to this, as was said.[606] And in that way this impossibility in the Son does not express something as a privation. For this would be a lack in the Son, not a condition of the person. But it expresses something only negatively. For although it is a lack if there is not in someone that which is able to be in him from his condition, as sight in an animal, the sort of lack "privation" names, it is still not a lack if there is not in someone that which is not able to be in him from his condition, as will be explained below.[607]

28. And in that way it is argued against this argument that, if the Son cannot generate and the Father can generate, therefore, the Father can do something that the Son cannot do. The Master touches upon this argument in distinction seven of book one of the *Sentences* in the beginning of the distinction. And it must be said that it does not follow because in accord with what the Master of the *Sentences* says: "*To be able to generate the Son is not to be capable of something, but for something*"[608] because in God generation is not [335] something, but for something, similarly, the Son is not either. And therefore, to be able to generate is to be able for something, and to be able to generate the Son is not to be

---

603   See Richard of Saint Victor, *On the Trinity* 3, 4; PL 196: 918A–B; ed. J. Ribaillier, p. 139. See also above par. 4.

604   See Thomas Aquinas, *Commentary on the Sentences* 1, d. 44. qi. 1., art. 4;ed. P. Mandonnet, p. 1024.

605   Richard of Saint Victor, *On the Trinity* 3,4; PL 196: 918A–B; ed. J. Ribaillier, p. 139. See also above par. 4.

606   See above par. 27.

607   See below par. 31.

608   Peter Lombard, *Sentences* 1, d. 7, c. 1; PL 192:541; ed. I. Brady, 1, p. 91.

able to generate something. It is not a problem that the Father is capable for the action of some respect of which the Son is not capable and can produce someone that the Son cannot produce, and this is not because of the impossibility of a lack and condition, as was said and will be more fully said,[609] so that one cannot conclude from the already stated manner that "there is therefore some potency in the Father that is not in the Son," but only that the potency that is the same in the Father and in the Son is for producing some action or person in the Father for which it does not exist in the Son.

29. As for what is argued on the basis of the statement of Augustine: *"That the Son does not generate is not because he could not* generate, *but because he ought not to have,"*[610] it must be said that that negation where it is said: *"He could not,"* can be understood purely as a negation or as a privation. If <it is understood> as a negation, in that way it must be said that <the proposition>, *"The Son did not generate, not because he could not,"* has a twofold interpretation. Because when "he could" includes the potency as ordered or able to be ordered to the act in the person to whom it is attributed, that negation when one says: *"he could not,"* can deny the potency for generating actively by reason of the potency and its application to act at the same time or by reason of its application to act alone. In the first way it is false because it denies that there is in the Son the potency by which he is generated or by which someone is generated, and the heretics were looking for that sense. Hence, in book three of *Against Maximinus*, chapter twelve, Augustine sets before the words quoted: [336] *"Heaven forbid that you somehow think that the Father is more powerful than the Son because the Father begot the creator, but the Son did not beget the creator. For he was not unable to,"*[611] and so on. And in this way that <proposition> is true, not because he could not, if one explains in this sense the statement of Augustine: *"He did not generate, not because he could not, but because he ought not to have,"*[612] that is, not because he did not have the potency by which the Father generates, but because he ought not to have <generated>, and this for the reason that <the potency for generatng> was sufficiently realized in act and entirely exhausted in the Father's having generated through it. Hence, explaining why he ought not to have, Augustine immediately adds, saying: *"For the divine generation would be without limit if the begotten Son generated a grandson for the Father because, unless the grandson himself begot a great grandson for his grandfather, he would be said to be impotent according to your amazing wisdom, and unless that one begot a grandson for his father and a great grandson for his great grandfather, he would not be called*

---

609 See above par. 27 and below par. 31.

610 Augustine of Hippo, *Answer to Maximinus* 2, 12, 3; PL 42: 768; ed. P. M. Hombert, p. 564; see above par. 4.

611 Rather, ibid. 2, 12, 3; PL 42: 768; ed. P. M. Hombert, p. 564.

612 Ibid.

omnipotent by you, and the series of generations would not be completed if one were
always born from another, nor would anyone complete it if one did not suffice."[613]
Hence, if the Father did not pour out the whole potency of active generation in
one act in generating the only Son, the Son would generate a son unto infinity,
and upon this our argument above was founded in showing more than one Son
cannot be born from the one Father.[614]

30. But from the fact that it is denied in that way of the Son that he could
not generate by saying: "*not because he could not*," it does not follow, although it
seems to follow, that he could have generated. For the sense of that <proposi-
tion> is: "<he could> not because he did not have the potency [337] by which
he is generated as applicable to generating, as it is in himself, both by reason
of the potency and by reason of its applicability; rather, he had the potency by
which he is generated. And from this it does not follow that he could generate
because, as was said above,[615] "he could" expresses not only the potency, but
its applicability to the act in him to whom it is attributed. But to have such a
potency in no way implies such applicability, and in that way that <proposi-
tion> is true: "*The Son did not generate, not because he could not,*"[616] that is, not
because he did not have the potency by which he is generated. Rather, he had
it, although not as applicable to that act as it is in him, as was said.[617] But if
that negation, "*he could not,*"[618] denies of the Son the potency to generate, not by
reason of the potency itself by which the one who generates generates, but only
by reason of its applicability to the act, it is in that way true under this sense:
"The Son does not have the potency as applicable to generate," and that <prop-
osition>, "*The Son does not generate, not because he could not,*" is false under this
sense: "<He does> not <generate,> not because he could not generate, that is,
not because he did not have the potency in himself as applicable to generate.
On the contrary, he had it in that way, '*but he ought not to have,*'[619] because he
willed not to," because the Father generated the Son who is sufficient. According to this way some[620] are accustomed to say that the Son can generate, but
does not generate, by reducing his potency to act on account of the problem
that follows, namely, the generation of sons to infinity, which was [338] already

613   Augustine of Hippo, *Against Maximinus* 2, 12, 3; PL 42: 768; ed. P. M.
      Hombert, p. 564.

614   See above par. 15 and 16.

615   See above par. 27 and 29.

616   See above par. 4 and 29.

617   See above par. 29.

618   See above par. 4 and 29.

619   Ibid.

620   See Thomas Aquinas, *Commentary on the Sentences* 1, d. 7, q. 2, a. 2; ed. P.
      Mandonnet, p. 184.

introduced in accord with Augustine.[621] But this is nothing, since "*in eternal* <*realities*>," according to the Philosopher, "*being and potency do not differ.*"[622]

31. Hence, it is impossible that whatever is not in God be in him, and it is impossible that whatever is in him not be in him because, according to Anselm, "*In God the least unsuitableness is the highest impossibility.*"[623] Hence, if something unsuitable follows from holding that the Son is able to generate, it is the highest impossibility; rather, "if he could generate, he did generate,"[624] in accord with which the reasoning of the argument proceeds. But if that negation, "He could not generate," is held in the sense of a privation, it is in that way false under this sense: "The Son could not generate," that is, he was powerless in lacking the potency for generating that he was still able to have, either by not at all having the applicability of it to act or <by not having> a perfect applicability on account of some defect or impediment. For a negation and a privation differ in this way: For negation expresses the removal of something from something else absolutely, but a privation denies the possibility of the being of that which is removed from the subject from which it is removed, according to the Philosopher in book four of the *Metaphysics*.[625] And in that way again the statement of Augustine is true: "*The Son did not generate because he could not,*"[626] under this sense that the Master of the *Sentences* holds in book one: "*It was not because of his powerlessness* [339] *that the Son did not generate*"—which the reasoning of the argument clearly shows—"*but because he ought not to have,* that is, *it was not suitable for him,*" that is, because it was not suitable for his property, and for this reason he ought not to have, "*just as the Son* cannot be *the Father,* certainly not *because of some powerlessness, but because of the property of his being born, because of which he ought not to be the Father,* but only the Son."[627] Hence, in God that something ought not to be or is done unfittingly or is not suitable that it be done is the same as that it ought or is fitting that it not be done, and so that it is impossible that it be done.

32. But if one holds that potency is not substance nor the other way around except under the character of a respect so that under different respects the same substance is very well a different potency, it makes no difference to say that the Son can generate and that there is in him the potency that is for gen-

621 See above par. 29.

622 See anonymous, *Aristotelian Authorities*; ed. J. Hamesse, p. 103.

623 Anselm of Canterbury, *Why God Became Man* 1, 10; PL 158: 375C; ed. F. Schmitt, 2, p. 86.

624 See above par. 4.

625 See Aristotle, *Metaphysics* 4.2.1004a16–17; trans. anon.; ed. G. Vuillemin-Diem, p. 62.

626 See above par. 4 and 29.

627 Peter Lombard, *Sentences* 1, d. 1, 7; PL 192: 542; ed. I. Brady, 1, p. 93.

erating, and it makes no difference to ask whether the Son can generate and whether in the Son there is the potency for the act of generating because if one is speaking about such a potency, *"To whatever its potency belongs the act corresponding to it also belongs,"*[628] nor is the potency in something unless its applicability to act is in the same one. And in that way there is no difficulty with regard to what was stated in the argument because, as the Son is not able to generate, but to be generated, so there is also not in him the potency that is for generating, but that which is for being generated, and the Father has some potency that the Son does not have. Nor *"is there entirely the same potency in the Father by which the Father was able to beget* and in the Son *by which the Son was able to be begotten,"*[629] just as [340] to beget and to be begotten are also not the same, so that one ought not to say that *"the same potency that is in the Father is also in the Son,"*[630] although <it is> for another act, because to be for another act under another respect is to be another potency. For the fact that *"potencies are distinguished by acts,"*[631] according to the Philosopher, only means that the potency is other, that is, is for another act.

33. But one must reply to the form of the argument as before[632] in accord with the Master of the *Sentences*. And in that way, just as it is nothing unsuitable that there is some potency that is not in the Son, it is nothing unsuitable that there is some property of the Father that is not the Son's, as will be seen below.[633] And similarly, this <proposition>, *"The Son does not have the potency for generating that the Father has,"*[634] should not be distinguished because he does not have the potency to generate as the Father does, nor is it the same potency by which <the Father> can beget and <the Son> be begotten, as was said,[635] although the Master distinguishes them in distinction seven of the *Sentences*.[636]

34. Hence, in the already mentioned argument the Master of the *Sentences* replies that a relation is changed into a substance. Still if one argues in this way: "If the Son cannot generate, there is therefore some potency not in the Son that

---

628   Aristotle, *On Sleeping and Waking* 1.454a8; see *Aristotelian Authorities*, ed. J. Hamesse, p. 201.

629   Peter Lombard, *Sentences* 1, d. 7, 2; PL 192: 542; ed. I. Brady, 1, p. 94.

630   Ibid.

631   Aristotle, *On the Soul* 2.6.415a16–21; ed. F. Crawford, p. 179.

632   See above par. 31.

633   See below art. 55, qu. 1.

634   Peter Lombard, *Sentences* 1, d. 7, c. 2; PL 192: 543: ed. I. Brady, 1, p. 94.

635   See above par. 32.

636   See Peter Lombard, *Sentences* 1, d. 7, 2; PL 192: 543; ed. I. Brady, 1, p. 94.

is in the Father,"[637] the Master would say in accord with the already mentioned opinion that it does not follow, but that this correctly follows: "Therefore, the potency [341] is not in the Son for the same act for which it is in the Father;"[638] still the same potency that is in the Father is in the Son. And this cannot stand. For since, as was said,[639] <a potency> is only a substance as it is for an act, it is also a determinate potency only as it is for a determinate act. Therefore, although the same substance that is in the Father is in the Son, still if it is in the Father for the act that is to generate, that is, so that the Father generates by it and for this reason is a determinate potency in the Father, but it is in no way in the Son for the same act, but rather for the opposite, there is not therefore in the Son the same potency that is in the Father. In fact, it would be useless in him. Therefore, the move that was mentioned correctly involves going from relation to substance.

35. For although substance is not a relation, still because the name "potency" does not belong to it except as it is under a respect that is a relation, potency is a relation and also signifies the substance along with this. For just as to be substance under one respect is not to be it under another respect, so although the substance is absolutely the one and same substance, it is not one potency as it is under one respect and under another, but is different <ones>. For, according to some, substance is drawn to a relation, although it is not principally a relation. And according to this manner of potency the Son is excused by impossibility from being able to generate, not <an impossibility> that is a defect, if one takes impossibility in the sense of a privation, for the omnipotent can be excused from no act by such impossibility, but <he can be by an impossibility> that is a condition of the nature, if one takes impossibility in the negative sense. For although the Son does not [342] at all have the potency for generating actively, this is not because of some powerlessness or defect in him, but because it is not at all suitable; rather, it is contrary to his manner of being, as was said.[640] But how it is not opposed to the omnipotence of the Son that there is not in him some potency that is in the Father will be seen below.[641]

36. But in speaking in this way about potency in the statement of Augustine: "*The Son did not generate, not because he could not,*"[642] the negation in the words: "*he could not,*" is held only in the sense of a privation. For in that way this

---

637   See above par. 28.

638   See Peter Lombard, *Sentences* 1, d. 7, 2; PL 192: 543; ed. I. Brady, 1, p. 94.

639   See above par. 32.

640   See above par. 31.

641   See *SQO* art. 58, qu. 1, ad 3um; ed. Badius 2, fol. 125vZ.

642   See above par. 4 and 29.

<proposition>, "The Son could not generate," is false, as was already said.[643] But in the sense of a negation that <proposition>, "The Son could not generate," is true without qualification, and it only has a single sense because it denies the potency without qualification, as was said.[644] And in that way in the sense of a privation that <proposition>, is true without qualification: "*The Son did not generate, not because he could not, but because "he ought not to have,*"[645] as was said.[646]

37. To the fourth argument that "the person *emanating takes nothing away from the potency of him from whom he emanates,* and in that way after the emanation of one person another similar one can emanate,"[647] it must be said that it is not true, nor does this comes from some lessening of the potency of the one from whom he emanates, in accord with which the objection nonetheless proceeds. But it rather comes from the perfection of the potency by which it pours itself out once into a perfect permanent act and into the perfect production of a person through it. For that acts are repeated from the same potency happens only because of a lack of potency, that is, because it [343] does not perfectly pour itself out into act at one time so that what does not follow in a single act follows in many. And by the same argument that things produced in the same nature are multiplied comes only from the defect of what is produced, that is, insofar as it does not fully contain in itself what pertains to its nature and character. For on this account alone many individuals are produced under the same species, according to the Commentator on book one of *On the Heaven and the World.*[648] Therefore, where a potency perfectly at one time pours itself out in a perfect act that produces something perfect, there is only one action in accord with one character and only one product, in accord with what was explained in the *Quodlibet* already mentioned.[649]

38. To the fifth argument that "*the same essential acts of understanding* of the three and similarly of their willing are common, *hence, the notional acts founded* upon them are *also* common to the three,"[650] and so on, it must be said that such essential acts can be considered in two ways: in one way in terms of themselves and absolutely, in another way as they have being in this or that person. In the

643   See above par. 33.

644   See above par. 28.

645   See above par. 4 and 29.

646   See above par. 28.

647   See above par. 5.

648   See Averroes, *Commentary on On the Heaven and the Earth* 1, comm. 4; ed. Juntas V, fol 4vG–H.

649   See *Quodlibet* 6, qu. 1; ed. G. Wilson, p. 2.

650   See above par. 6.

first way the notional acts are not founded upon them because in that way they would be common to all the persons to whom these acts belong, as the objection proceeds, but they are founded upon them in the second way. For the notional act of speaking is founded upon the essential act of understanding only as it has being in the Father. For in the Father alone by reason of his innascibility and primacy, by which he does not have being from another, but everything else and everyone else <has being> from him, there is fecundity for the first act productive of the first product, and it is the fecundity of the wisdom and understanding of the Father essentially existing in the act of understanding for speaking [344] or producing the Word, by which the whole essential divine intellect is perfected both in itself and as it is in each of the three persons, so that the Father quasi in place of all speaks the perfect Word so that it is not necessary that another of the persons speak the Word, and in this way it is impossible that there be in God another word, as was explained above.[651]

39. Similarly, the notional act of spirating is founded upon the essential act of willing only insofar as it has being in common in only the Father and the Son. For in them alone by reason of their common inability to be spirated, by which they do not have being from another through spiration, although that is not held to be a notion, as will be seen below,[652] but from them the one spirated has being, there is the fecundity for the second productive act. And it is the fecundity of the love and will of the Father and the Son existing in the act of willing essentially for spirating the love that is the Holy Spirit, by which the whole essential divine will is perfected both in itself and as it is each of the three persons. Thus, in that way the Father and the Son as if in place of the whole Trinity spirate the single perfect love so that it is absolutely not necessary that the Holy Spirit spirate some love, and on this account it is impossible that in God there is another spirated love or another holy spirit.

40. To the sixth argument that *"by his efficacy the Father gives to the Son* whom he generates that he produces *another person, therefore, both give* the same thing to the Holy Spirit,"[653] it must be said to this in accord with Richard in book four of *On the Trinity*, chapter eleven, that *"just as it is necessary that there be some* person *who does not have being from another, so it is necessary that there be there some person from whom there is not some other; for both of them are proven by the same argument. [345] For if in that true deity there were not some person from whom another did not proceed, but each that proceeds from another had one proceeding from him, such a line of argumentation would go on to infinity."*[654] And

---

651 See above par. 28 and 37.

652 See *SQO* art. 60, qu. 10, ad 1um; ed. Badius 2, fol. 173rH–vK.

653 See above par. 9.

654 Rather, Richard of Saint Victor, *On the Trinity* 5, 11; PL 196: 958A; ed. J. Ribaillier, p.209.

as he says in chapter twelve, this person, *"from whom no person proceeds, has this as proper to himself,"*[655] so as there can be only one person in God who is from no one and from whom another or the others are, and only one who is from another and from whom there is another, so it is necessary that the one that is from another and from whom <there is> no other be only one. For, as he says, *"if there were two such, they would be united by no immediate kinship."*[656]

41. But the more essential cause of such is had from what has already been determined,[657] from which it is also clear that it does not come from some lack of potency or an imperfection of such a person that no person proceeds from him, but from the property of his condition, because it ought not to have <proceeded>, since the whole fecundity of the divine nature is exhausted and realized in the twofold production in accord with what has been already determined.[658] Nor does it come from some lack of efficiency of the Father and the Son in spirating the Holy Spirit that they produce such a person who cannot further produce another, although the Father produces a person who goes on to produce another, but it comes from the condition of those producing and produced. For that the Son receives from the Father the power productive of a person is due to the fact that he is produced by the first production that has an order to the second. And on this account the productive power in accord with that production is also communicated to him so that with the Father he produces the third person, as is seen from what has already been determined above,[659] and when that person has been produced, there does not remain further <power> on account of which no productive power is communicated to him, because there is no more, nor ought there to be nor can there be, as is clear from what has been determined above.[660]

---

655   Ibid. 5, 12; PL 196: 958C–D; ed. J. Ribaillier, p. 210.

656   Ibid.

657   See above qu. 6, par. 34

658   See above par. 16.

659   See qu. 6, par. 34.

660   See above par. 28.

[346]   QUESTION NINE

Whether the Notional Acts of the Emanations of Generating and Spirating Are Certain Instances of Understanding and Willing or Certain Acts of Understanding and Willing

1. With regard to the ninth question it is argued that the notional acts of the emanations of generating and spirating are certain instances of understanding and willing or certain acts of understanding and willing in the first place as follows: Of one potency there is only one essential operation because, according to the Philosopher, "*potencies* are distinguished *by acts.*"[661] But to generate and to spirate are operations of the intellect and of the will that are certain potencies of God, according to the manner determined above,[662] and they are singular and unique in God because in something one there can be only one potency of one character, and the proper operations of these potencies are to understand and to will. Therefore, and so on.

2. <It is argued> in the second place as follows: Augustine says in book fifteen of *On the Trinity*, chapter fifteen: "*If there can be in* a mind *some everlasting knowledge, and if the thinking about the same knowledge cannot be everlasting, and if we do not speak our true inner word except by our thinking, God alone is understood to have an everlasting Word.*"[663] He holds therefore that we speak our word by thinking. Therefore, to speak in us is a certain thinking, but thinking is a certain understanding. Therefore, and so on. Therefore, in a similar way although the speaking of God is not a certain thinking, [347] as he says in chapter seventeen,[664] thinking in us corresponds to it. Speaking will be a certain understanding, and just as it is with regard to speaking from the side of the intellect that it is a certain understanding, for the same reason spirating from the side of the will is a certain willing. Therefore, and so on.

3. To the contrary it is argued that if the notional acts of the emanations of generating and spirating were certain instances of understanding and willing, then in God there would not be another potency by which the Father generates and spirates than that by which he understands and wills, and the acts of

---

661   Aristotle, *On the Soul* 2.6.415a16–21; ed. F. Crawford, p. 179.

662   See *SQO* art. 36, qu. 2; ed. G. Wilson, pp. 95–100 and 45, 2; ed. L. Hödl, pp. 105–109.

663   Augustine of Hippo, *On the Trinity* 15, 15; PL 42: 1078; ed. W. Mountain and F. Glorie, p. 499.

664   Ibid., 15, 17; PL 42: 1080–1082; ed. W. Mountain and F. Glorie, pp. 502–507.

generating and spirating would be essential acts common to the three, just as the potency of understanding is. The consequent is false. Therefore, and so on.

<The Resolution of the Question>

4. In order that we may see the difference of the notional acts of generating and spirating from one side and of the essential acts of understanding and willing from the other, it is necessary to see how these acts have to be formed in the intellect and the will—and firstly from the side of the intellect and then from the side of the will through what is like those that we see in the intellect. For those things that we experience from the side of the intellect are clearer to us than those from the side of the will. And there is a certain order of those that are in the intellect to those that are in the will, in accord with what has been already determined and is to be determined more fully below.[665] And because, as Richard says: *"In created nature we gather those things that we ought to perceive concerning the uncreated nature,"*[666] let us here firstly look at the formation of those acts in our intellect in order that this may become a ladder for us for seeing that in the divine intellect, and let us consider the way our intellect is informed by beginning in what is like it from the way our sensory vision is informed in the eye as from the way in which our most familiar sense is formed, [348] in accord with the procedure of Augustine in book eleven of *On the Trinity* and from there on.

5. But in the formation of bodily vision in the eye the first principle is the form of the visible body from which, according to Augustine in book eleven of *On the Trinity*, chapter two, *"The species or form is imprinted on the sense that is called sight, and from that abstracted species of the body there remains a likeness of a body in sensory memory to which the keen edge of the imagination turns interiorly in order that it may be interiorly formed from it, just as the sense is formed exteriorly from the sensible body presented to it."*[667] And as he says in chapter seven: *"We call this species that is in memory the quasi parent of that which is produced in the imagination of the person thinking. But that is not a true parent; hence, neither is this a true child, but from this we see more exactly and more truly those things that are more interior and truer."*[668] And this <is seen> in the intellectual mind itself in knowing itself for, according to the determination of Augustine through the whole of book ten of *On the Trinity*[669] and as he repeats in book fourteen,

---

665   See SQO art. 39, qu. 7; ed. G. Wilson, pp. 221–251 and art. 60, qu. 3; ed. Badius 2, fol. 162vK–167rI.

666   Richard of Saint Victor, *On the Trinity* 1, 9; PL 196: 895B; ed. J. Ribaillier, p. 94.

667   Augustine of Hippo, *On the Trinity* 11, 2; PL 42: 988; ed. W. Mountain and F. Glorie, p. 339.

668   Ibid., 11, 7; PL 42: 993; ed. W. Mountain and F. Glorie, p. 499.

669   See ibid. 10; PL 42: 971–983; ed. W. Mountain and F. Glorie, pp. 311–329.

chapter four, at the end: "it knows *itself.*" And <it does> this not by taking from elsewhere the species by which it is informed in knowing because "*the mind knows nothing as much as what is present to it, and nothing is more present to it than itself.*"[670] Hence, as he says in chapter five: "*One should believe that* the mind *of an infant knows itself, but cannot think of itself,*"[671] as it is for itself "*memory of itself so that the gaze of the one thinking is formed.*"[672] And it begets in the intellect knowledge of itself because, as he says [349] in chapter seven: "*A word cannot be there without thought. For we think everything that we speak when our thought is formed by those things that were present to memory, but were not thought about.*"[673] And as he says in book fifteen, chapter eleven: "*There is born from the knowledge that remains in the mind that knowledge that is spoken interiorly.*"[674] And as he says in chapter fourteen: "*This word is the truth because whatever is in that knowledge from which it is born is also in it in an enigma like to the Word of God that is God, when it is also born in that way from our knowledge, as that Word is born from the knowledge of the Father.*"[675]

6. But however the truth may be regarding what Augustine intends, namely, that our mind always knows itself, the truth nonetheless undoubtedly consists in the fact that in all our intellectual knowledge concerning something about which a word is able to be formed, there is firstly some simple knowledge or awareness created in the intellect, not by the work of the intellect, because with respect to such awareness the created intellect is only passive, but from an intelligible object that produces in the intellect its species, which is a certain awareness of it that remains in memory. And from that simple awareness or knowledge existing in memory, when the intellect formed in that way turns back upon itself as it is intellect without qualification and moves itself informed by itself in that way as by an intelligible object, there is born a thinking awareness or knowledge that is a word in the intelligence. But I mean according to Augustine in book fourteen of On the Trinity, chapter seven: "*The intelligence by which we understand* [350] *when we are thinking.*"[676] And this, as he says in the same place, "*by the interior word,*" which, as he says in chapter fifteen, "*we say that we understand most of all.*"

7. And from this one must note that there is a twofold act of understanding in the intellect: one of simple intelligence concerning something intelligible as

---

670   Ibid., 14, 4; PL 42: 1040; ed. W. Mountain and F. Glorie, p. 429.
671   Ibid.
672   Ibid., 14, 6; PL 42: 1042; ed. W. Mountain and F. Glorie, p. 432.
673   Ibid. 14, 7; PL 42: 1943; ed. W. Mountain and F. Glorie, p. 434–435.
674   Ibid., 14,11; PL 42: 1072; ed. W. Mountain and F. Glorie, p. 488.
675   Ibid., 14, 14; PL 42: 1077; ed. W. Mountain and F. Glorie, p. 496 and 497.
676   Ibid., 14, 7; PL 42: 1044; ed. W. Mountain and F. Glorie, p. 435.

it is presented in terms of itself before the formation of a word, but formed
through the action of something presented, as a result of which there remains
in memory a simple awareness, and another thinking act formed concerning
the intelligible object after the formation of the word as it is presented in the
word. And the formation of the word is in between the two acts of understanding because one entirely precedes the formation of the word in us, but the other
follows <upon it>. And in that way the act of speaking by which the word is
formed is intermediate between the two acts of understanding. For since, as he
says in chapter fifteen: "*We toss about some object of our mind with this and that
changing thought, thinking now this, now that, as it is discovered or comes to mind;
then a true word is formed, that is, when what I said is tossed about by changing
thought comes to that which we know and is formed from it, receiving its complete
likeness.*"[677] But it is formed from that which we know by simple intelligence as
if from memory.

8. For when our intellect runs through the diverse differences under a genus
in investigating concerning something known by simple intelligence what its
quiddity is, which investigation he calls changing thought, and when the ulti-
mate difference is attained by the completed investigation of it, which Augustine calls: "arriving *at that which we know,*" because then the interior contents of
the thing known are firstly uncovered so that then we are firstly said to attain
or [351] to arrive by the eye of our gaze at the knowable object itself in truly
knowing it, and when we think of this, immediately this knowable object, as
it is actually known and existing in memory by simple intelligence, generates
from itself and as if suddenly, when all the differences have been gathered together with the genus, the quiddity. And in the intelligence this is a certain
distinguishing and dividing or explicating awareness that we call a word, in
which the existing thing itself as explained by its parts moves the intelligence
so that it understands by thinking, not by a changing thinking of the sort that
existed before the formation of the word, but by a stable thinking by which the
thing is perfectly known and grasped. For the second awareness that is in the
word not only knows and understands the thing so that it knows that it knows
and understands it by a second act of understanding turned back upon the first
act of knowing or understanding. And in that way the act that is to speak or to
generate is not the same as either the first or the second act of understanding
because to speak is a true action that proceeds from memory or from the simple
awareness existing in it or from the thing presented as it is in memory. And in
that way it is a certain action or operation of the intellect informed by simple
awareness by which it forms in itself an explanatory awareness most like that
simple awareness. But to understand is a being acted upon in the intelligence

---

677   Ibid.

by the thing intelligible in itself as it is in terms of itself something confused or in its quiddity as it is distinct by its parts in simple awareness.

9. In applying this to the question at hand, we say that by his act of understanding of simple awareness, God the Father knows his essence, which is a certain awareness in him as if in memory concerning which there is naturally formed an explanatory or explicative awareness of his quiddity that is already known by the simple awareness, which is called the Word, as Richard says in book six of *On the Trinity*, chapter twelve: "*A word is usually* [352] *indicative of the meaning and wisdom of the one speaking. Therefore, he is rightly called the Word through whom the knowledge of the Father, who is the fountain of wisdom, is revealed because the Word is born from his heart, and the intention of the speaker is brought forth by him. In the Father there is the conception of all the truth; in the Word there is the utterance of all the truth.*"[678] And in chapter thirteen, he says: "*The Son of God is called the Word because he speaks the paternal brightness, and through him there is revealed of what sort and how great it is.*"[679] But in that way from simple awareness there is formed in God revelatory awareness, not through discursive thought as in us, but at once and from eternity along with the simple, essential awareness. And in this respect the formation of our word differs from the formation of the eternal Word, as Augustine says in book fifteen of *On the Trinity*, chapter sixteen: "*He is said to be the Word of God in such a way that he is not said to be the thinking of God lest there be believed to be something quasi changing in God that receives form in order that it may be the Word. Our thinking, of course, that arrives at what we know and is formed from it is our true word. And for this reason the Word of God must be understood to be without thinking in order that it may be understood to be a simple form, not having something able to be formed that could be unformed,*"[680] and this <Word is> subsisting in that in which it is formed, not inhering in it as happens in our word, and yet he from whom it is formed understands in it, just as we do in the word formed by us.

10. We say therefore in coming down to the question that the emanation of the notional act of speaking the Word or of generating the Son, which is the same thing, is not some act of understanding. But in us it is intermediate between two acts of understanding that are really different, of which one is perfect and complete, but the other imperfect and incomplete. But in God between [353] the Father's two essential acts of understanding that differ only by reason, of which each one is equally complete, because they are really one and

---

678 Richard of Saint Victor, *On the Trinity* 6, 12; PL 196: 976B and 977A; ed. J. Ribaillier, pp. 141 and 142.

679 Ibid. 6, 13; PL 196: 977D; ed. J. Ribaillier, p. 244.

680 Augustine, *On the Trinity* 15, 16; PL 42: 1079; ed. W. Mountain and F. Glorie, p. 500.

the same and differ only by reason,[681] that is, because the one reveals and makes manifest, and this awareness is the quasi thinking of that which is known by the other by quasi simple awareness.

11. Hence, it is true that the act of speaking or of generating in God is an act of the intellect, not under the character by which it is mere intellect or bare intelligence—for under this character the Word is not conceived in him through the act of speaking—but it is an act of the intellect under the character by which it is memory containing in itself simple awareness and in it the object by which it elicits the act of speaking the Word, as was said.[682] And in that way to speak is not some act of understanding that consists in contemplation, but is rather a certain producing that consists in the explication of something contemplated, in accord with what will be more fully explained in the following question.[683] And as this has been said about speaking or generating from the side of the intellect with respect to the act of understanding, it may similarly be understood with regard to some things concerning spiration from the side of the will with respect to the act of willing, although it is different in many ways, in accord with which all these things from the side of the will have to be explained below in speaking of the property of active spiration in the Father.[684] And in accord with this one must concede the argument introduced for this side.

[354]   <Replies to the Arguments>

12. To the first argument introduced for the opposite side that "*the operation or action of the intellect and of the will is only to will and to understand*,"[685] and so on, it must be said that in God intellect can be considered in two ways: in one way as it is intellect under the character of intellect, in another way as it is a nature and under the character of memory, in accord with the way already stated.[686] In the first way its operation is only to understand and consists in contemplation and is completed in the manner of being acted upon, that is, by which its awareness is quasi informed by an intelligible object. But in the second way its operation consists in production. For the intellect existing in the act of understanding of simple awareness is already perfect and is fecund for producing the Word, not as it is intellect and in being acted upon, but as it is nature that produces and is in acting. And it is in a similar way concerning the will and its twofold act except for the fact that the will in the simple act of

---

681   See *SQO* art. 40, qu. 7; ed. G. Wilson, pp. 282–299.

682   See above par. 7–8.

683   See below qu. 10.

684   See *SQO* art. 60, qu. 2; ed. Badius 2, fol. 162vA–163vK.

685   See above par. 1.

686   See above par. 10.

willing is active in moving itself to the object in the act of willing, although the intellect is still purely passive in the simple act of understanding in receiving motion from the object, as has been said.[687]

13. To the second argument that *"we speak a word by thinking,"*[688] it must be said that this does not mean that thinking is the act by which a word is produced as from a principle, but that it is not produced without actual thinking quasi firstly, in accord with what the following question will explain.[689]

---

687   See *SQO* art. 1, qu. 1; ed. G. Wilson, pp. 10–17, 4, 1; art. 4, qu. 1; ed. G. Wilson, pp. 101–103, 40, 7; ed. G. Wilson, p. 283–287; and art. 45, qu. 1; ed. L. Hödl, pp. 105–109

688   See above par. 2

689   See below qu. 10, par. 4.

[355]   QUESTION TEN

Whether the Emanations of the Notional Acts of Generating and
Spirating Are Founded upon the Essential Acts of Understanding and
Willing As If Presupposing Them

1. With regard to the tenth question it is argued that the emanations of the
notional acts of speaking or generating and of spirating are not founded upon
the essential acts of understanding and willing as if presupposing them in the
first place as follows: The essential acts of understanding and of willing are
common to the Father, to the Son, and to the Holy Spirit, who are produced
through the notional acts of generating and of spirating. But the persons doing any acts of understanding precede the acts according to reason, and those
produced through the acts follow them. Therefore, the notional acts, to generate and to spirate, precede according to reason the persons of the Son and
of the Holy Spirit that are produced by them, and the same persons precede
the essential acts. Hence, the notional acts also likewise precede the essential
acts, and thus are not founded upon them. For otherwise the persons of the
Son and of the Holy Spirit would exist and act before they were produced and
would precede themselves and would be the reason of their own production,
and these are all false. Therefore, and so on.

2. <It is argued> in the second place as follows: In the intellect there is the
character by which it is an intellect and the character by which it is a nature,
and it is in a similar way in the will.[690] And according to this, different [356]
operations belong to them, namely, the essential operation of understanding
and of willing insofar as they are intellect and will and the notional operation
of generating and of spirating insofar as they are nature, as was said in the
preceding question.[691] But according to the manner of understanding, the character by which it is a nature is prior in it to that by which it is intellect or will
because, insofar as intellect and will are potencies in nature, <they are> also in
that way quasi naturally determining the character of the nature. Therefore, the
operation of understanding proceeding from them as they are nature is prior
according to reason to that which they are as intellect and will, and in that way
the same thing follows as before.

---

690   See *SQO* art. 1, qu. 4 and art. 40, qu. 6 and 7; ed. G. Wilson , pp. 101–107; pp.
       277–279, and pp. 284–288.
691   See above qu. 9, par. 10, 11, and 13.

3. To the contrary it is argued that essential <attributes> precede notional ones according to reason, as has often been explained.[692]

<The Resolution of the Question>

4. It must be said that the person of the Father has in himself all the essential <attributes> from himself, not from another, just as he does not have being from another. On this account he is called by Dionysius *"the fontal deity,"*[693] and by Augustine *"the principle of the whole divinity."*[694] But by reason of the fact that he exists in act in terms of the essential acts of understanding and willing, he is in complete fecundity for the first acts productive of something, and the notional acts productive of the persons within the divine essence are such. And since there is necessarily a certain order, in accord with what was determined above,[695] of the essential acts in themselves and also similarly of the notional acts, because the act of understanding is in some way prior to the act of willing, and the action of speaking to the action of spirating, hence because the Father is firstly existing in act in accord with the act of understanding, he is by reason of his primacy as if [357] firstly in complete fecundity for the first notional act, which is to generate or to speak, which proceeds from the Father as existing in act through the essential act of understanding, and in accord with this the notional act of generating or of speaking is said to be founded upon the essential act of understanding, and by a certain order of reason quasi presupposes it. And as this is the case concerning the act of generating and of understanding with respect to the Father and the paternal intellect, it is similarly concerning the act of spirating and of willing with respect to the Father and the Son and the will of both.

<Replies to the Arguments>

5. To the first argument to the contrary that *"essential acts are common to the three persons,"*[696] it must be said that it is true; nonetheless, by a certain order of reason, although simultaneously in eternity and similarly by a certain order of reason the Son and the Holy Spirit are produced by the notional acts, and similarly the essential acts are also from them. For the essential acts of understanding and of willing can be considered in two ways: in one way without qualification and absolutely, in another way as they belong to the diverse persons under diverse properties. In the first way all the essential <attributes>

---

692   See above qu. 6, par. 51 and *SQO* art. 52, qu. 2; ed. M. Führer, pp. 250–253.

693   Pseudo-Dionysius, *On the Divine Names* 1, 2; PG 3: 671A; see above art. 53, qu. 3, par. 2.

694   Augustine of Hippo, *On the Trinity* 4, 20; PL 42: 908; ed. W. Mountain and F. Glorie, p, 200.

695   See above qu. 6, par. 33.

696   See above par. 1.

have a certain order of reason to the personal attributes, according to the form and character by which they are essential in accord with what was determined above,[697] because the personal attributes are founded upon the essential ones. But in the second way the essential attributes belong to the different persons by a certain order of reason, insofar as they belong to the Father quasi firstly, because <he has them from> himself, and <they belong> to the Son secondly, because <he has them> from the Father, and to the Holy Spirit thirdly, because <he has them> from both, although simultaneously in eternity. And according to this, if one looks at the diverse persons, the essential acts of understanding and of willing have a diverse order of reason to the notional acts of generating and spirating. For to understand and to will, as they belong to the Father, are quasi prior to generating and spirating. But as they belong to the Son, according to [358] the manner of understanding, the notional act of generating quasi precedes the essential acts of understanding and of willing, which nonetheless, as they belong in common to the Father and to the Son, are prior according to reason with respect to the act of spirating, and the act of spirating is quasi prior with respect to the essential acts of understanding and of willing, as they belong to the Holy Spirit. And in that way it must be said for the explanation of the question and the resolution of the argument that the notional acts of generating and of spirating are not founded upon the essential acts of understanding and of willing, as they are considered without qualification, but only insofar as they have being in a determinate person. For the act of generating is only founded upon the act of understanding as it belongs specifically to the Father because generative fecundity is rooted in it only insofar as it has being under the property of the primacy of the Father, and similarly the act of spirating is only founded upon the act of willing as it belongs in common to the Father and to the Son because spirative fecundity is rooted in it only insofar as it has being under the common character of the principle that the Father and the Son have with respect to the Holy Spirit. Hence, the act of generating is in no way founded upon the act of understanding, as it belongs to the Son or to the Holy Spirit, nor is the act of spirating founded upon the act of willing as it belongs to the Holy Spirit. For otherwise the difficulties included in the argument would follow, as is clear to one looks.

6. To the second argument that "*the character by which the intellect or the will is a nature is prior to the character by which it is the intellect or the will,*"[698] and so on, it must be said that, as was determined above,[699] intellect and will are in God as certain potencies. But a potency is related to two things: both to the

---

697   See above par. 3–4 and *SQO* art. 39, qu. 7; ed. G. Wilson, pp. 222–225, and above art. 54, qu. 6, par. 51.

698   See above par. 2.

699   See above qu. 6, par. 33 and qu. 9, par. 1.

subject in which it is rooted and to the act that is elicited through it. Therefore, the intellect and the will in God can be considered in relation to their quasi subject or to an act. If <they are considered> in the first way, the intellect and the will in that way are in God as certain natures because the natural potencies of God are in God founded naturally upon his divine essence, which is a nature insofar as it is [359] a certain natural reality. And if one is speaking of this naturalness, it is true that the character by which the intellect is a nature is prior to that by which it is an intellect, and similarly that by which the will is a nature is prior to that by which it is a will, because they agree in being in such a way, that is, as nature, that is, by reason of the unity that they have in the subject. But concerning this manner of nature there is nothing for the present question because, according to this manner of nature, they are not principles elicitive of some acts since they are not related to acts at all, as was said.[700]

7. But if they are considered in the second way, that is, in terms of being related to acts, there is in that way still one character in those potencies by which they are intellect and will, but another by which they are a nature insofar as they are related to two acts: to one as they are intellect and will, but to another as they are a nature. For in God there are two acts of such potencies, one that is properly said to be the operation by which they are perfected in themselves absolutely, the other that is properly said to be the action by which they are perfected in relation to another. The acts by which the intellect and the will are perfected in the first way are essential acts, namely, to understand and to will, but the acts <by which they are perfected> in the second way are the acts of generating and of spirating. The first acts belong to the intellect and will in accord with the character by which they are intellect and will. But the second ones belong to them in accord with the character by which they are nature, that is, active principles naturally eliciting acts productive of the persons. For the intellect as intellect is perfected absolutely in knowing the truth, and the will as will is perfected absolutely in willing the good. But the intellect as a nature is perfected in speaking the Word, but the will as a nature is perfected in spirating mutual love from the side of the will. And in that way in relation to another, both from the side of the intellect and from the side of the will, [360] the difference of these acts is seen—from the side of the intellect in a bodily example, and from the side of the will it may be understood through the same from a similar <argument>. For if a seal that has in itself a shape were of an intellectual nature, by the character by which it was an intellect, it would be perfected in making specific its figuration in itself, and it would come to a stop in this. But insofar as it is a nature, it would by itself impress a similar shape on some matter and, if it were possible, on the same matter in which its own shape exists. Through this manner the divine intellect is in some way perfected

---

700   See above qu. 6, par. 31.

by the act of understanding itself and its essence, and this as if by the known essence, which under the character of a knowable object produces knowledge of it in the intellect.

8. But as the divine intellect is perfected specifically in the Father through such an act of understanding his essence, which <the essence> causes to be in his intellect as it is quasi in potency to essential awareness, it is according to that manner of understanding fecund with natural fecundity for producing from itself another similar to itself to which <that intellect> is quasi in potency by reason of the fact that it is in act under that essential awareness. For as the intellect is a certain essential awareness according to act, it is a nature and active principle by which the Father forms from the same intellect as it is pure intellect and only intellect and from a passive principle the awareness that is the Word, which in terms of reality is the same awareness as that from which it is formed, differing only from it insofar as it proceeds from it as manifesting and revealing it, as has often been said. And in the same way we ought to understand that the word is formed in us. For something known firstly impresses its simple awareness on our intellect in presenting itself to it as purely passive and under the character by which it is intellect. But the intellect [361] perfected in that way through simple awareness by the object that it contains in itself has become expressively fecund and an active principle as a nature in itself as it is only intellect and a passive principle for forming in itself explanatory awareness from simple awareness. Thus according to this when a word is said to be formed by the intellect and that the intellect is active in the formation of the word, this is understood of the intellect formed in act by simple awareness. For through this it is a principle, and its character by which it is intellect and passive is necessarily prior to that by which it is a nature and active, and the notional act that it produces as it is a nature is founded upon the essential act that is produced in it as intellect.

9. And as these were explained from the side of the intellect in the act of speaking and in the formation of the word, so let them be understood from the side of the will in the act of spirating and in the production of love that is spirated because the intellect is passive with respect to the act of understanding that belongs to it as it is intellect, but active with respect to the act of speaking that belongs to it as it is a nature. But the will is active with respect to both acts of willing and of spirating so that in that way the act of speaking and the act of spirating are acts and natural emanations in the manner of nature.

10. There is nonetheless some difference in this in producing in the manner of nature from the side of the act of speaking and of spirating because both processions are according to the operation of nature and in the manner of nature. Still one of them is more principal than the other because the act of speaking proceeds in accord with a more principal manner of [362] proceeding than the manner of nature, according to Richard in book six of *On*

the Trinity, chapters two, eight, and nine,[701] so that for this reason the acts of speaking and of spirating are said to be necessary in God not only with the necessity of immutability by which it is impossible that he be otherwise—for whatever is in God is in him by such necessity, as the essential or notional and personal <attributes> are—but also with the necessity of naturalness by which it is impossible that God not elicit such acts through a principle that is a nature in him and that through the same principle he not produce from his substance by the same acts that which remains in it, so that in accord with this such acts proceed according to an operation of nature because <they proceed> in the manner of natural necessity. But how the action of speaking is according to a more principal manner of nature and in the manner of intellect or of intellectual operation, but the action of spirating is not according to a more principal manner of nature and in the manner of the will or of voluntary operation will be explained below.[702]

701   See Richard of Saint Victor, *On the Trinity* 6, 3; 6, 8, and 6, 9; PL 196: 968D–969D; 972D–973C, and 973D–974B; ed. J. Ribaillier, pp. 229–230; 235–237, and 237–238,

702   See below *SQO* art. 60, qu. 4; ed. Badius 2, fol. 167rI–168vO.

ARTICLE FIFTY-FIVE

On the Properties of the Persons in General in Terms of Themselves

After what concerns the persons has been established, there follows an article on their properties that are commonly called notions. And first of all concerning them in general; secondly in particular, insofar as they belong to individual persons in a proper sense. And with regard to the first, two questions are asked, of which the first concerns them in terms of themselves, the second concerns them in relation to the persons.

With regard to the first of these, six questions must be asked, of which the first is whether in the divine persons it is necessary to hold properties of the persons; the second is whether they are many; the third whether there are only five; the fourth whether they are all notions; the fifth whether they are relations; the sixth whether they are all real relations.

QUESTION ONE

Whether in the Divine Persons It Is Necessary to Hold Properties of the Persons

1. With regard to the first of these it is argued that in God it is not necessary to hold some properties of the persons in the first place as follows: A property is always something outside of the concept of that of which it is a property, as "risible" is something outside the concept "man." For it is possible to understand "man" without at the same time understanding "risible." But in God there is nothing outside the concept of the persons because in God, in accord with what was determined above,[1] there are only substance and relation, and both belong to the concept of a person, as will be seen below.[2] Therefore, and so on.

2. <It is argued> in the second place as follows: A property does not constitute in being that of which it is a property, as the risibility does not constitute a man in the being of a man. Paternity, filiation, and the like constitute the persons in the being of persons; therefore, they are not properties of them. But

---

1   See *SQO* art. 34, qu. 2; ed. R. Macken, p. 170.
2   See *SQO* art. 56, qu. 3; ed. Badius 2, fol. 114rL–115vA.

in God none are not said to be properties more truly than these, as will be seen below.[3] Therefore, and so on.

3. <It is argued> in the third place as follows: In simple beings there is no difference between what is abstract and what is concrete save in the mode of signifying, as <there is> between whiteness and white, because [365] *"white,"* according to the Philosopher, *"signifies* only a *quality,"*[4] just as whiteness does. But in God a person is equally as simple as the essence, as will now be seen below.[5] Therefore, there is no difference between the Father and paternity or between the Son and filiation save only in the mode of signifying. But between a property and that to which a property belongs there is necessarily another difference than only in the mode of signifying. Therefore, paternity and filiation are not properties of the Father and of the Son. But besides these and similar ones there are no other properties of the persons in God. Therefore, and so on, as before.

4. To the contrary there is the statement of Damascene in book one, chapter ten: *"The Son and the Holy Spirit have all the things they have on account of the Father. The reason is that <the Father> has them apart from non-generation, generation, and procession. For they differ from one another only in these hypostatic properties."*[6] And in chapter eleven he says: *"The Father and the Son and the Holy Spirit are one in all things apart from non-generation, generation, and procession. For we recognize the one God in the properties of paternity, filiation, and procession alone, and we understand their difference according to their manner of existence."*[7]

<The Resolution of the Question>

5. It must be said that in those things whose nature is hidden, before it is known whether they are, it is necessary to know what it is that is signified by the name, as [366] the Commentator says on the chapter, "On the Void," in book four of the *Physics.*[8] But the properties have being in God in a very hidden way, and a sign of this is the multiplicity of errors about them. Therefore, it is firstly necessary to see here what we ought to understand is signified by the name "property," and then from this whether and how we ought to understand something of the sort in God. It must therefore be known according to what Ambrose determines in the book, *On the Incarnation*, that both in creatures and in God there are certain words that express a nature, as "man," "lion," and "God." But some express some manner or a quality of a nature, if quality is

---

3   See below qu. 3, par. 8.

4   See Aristotle, *Categories* 5.3b19–20; trans. Boethius, ed. L. Minio-Palluello, p. 11.

5   See *SQO* art. 56, qu. 1; ed. Badius 2, fol. 113vD.

6   John Damascene, *On the Orthodox Faith* 8, 13; PG 94: 823; ed. E. Buytaert, p. 40.

7   Ibid., 8, 17; PG 94: 830; ed. E. Buytaert, p. 44.

8   Averroes, *Commentary on the Physics* 4, comm. 5; ed. Juntas 4, fol. 147rV.

taken in a broad sense. For, as he says, "*In God the signification of one generating and of one begotten expresses a quality of a substance.*"⁹ But it must be known that some of such qualities belong to a substance as it is a substance, such as goodness, truth, and the like, which in God are called attributes. But some belong to a supposite, and they are the ones that are called properties. And according to this it must be said that in God it is necessary to hold properties, as it is also necessary to hold attributes.

<Replies to the Arguments>

6. To the first argument to the contrary that "*a property is something outside the concept of that to which a property belongs,*"¹⁰ it must be said that it is true when a property is the same thing as the <proper> fifth universal,¹¹ but it is not taken in that way here, as was said.

[367] 7. To the second argument that "*a property does not constitute in being that of which it is a property,*"¹² it must be replied in the same way.

8. To the third argument that "*in simple beings there is no difference between what is abstract and what is concrete save in the manner of signifying,*"¹³ and so on, the Master Praepositinus, paying attention to the divine simplicity, said for this reason that no property should be held to exist in God. And he spoke in this way: "*It is known that there are diverse opinions on the properties. For some hold almost infinite properties, as Master Gilbert; some hold six, as Master Radulphus; others hold three, as Master Robert; some none, and Master Ivo of Chartres is said to have long been of this opinion, and we agree with this opinion.*"¹⁴ And he explains all the authorities and propositions that teach that there are properties in God, by holding that in them something abstract is used to indicate a property, either by the common name "property," or by a proper name, that is, "paternity" or "filiation," instead of something concrete that indicates a person. He speaks in this way: "*When we say that paternity is in the Father or that the Father is distinguished from the Son by paternity, these are manners of speaking, and the sense is: 'Paternity is in the Father,' that is, 'the Father is the Father,' just as when I say: 'I ask, your love,' that is, 'you who are loved.' When we say 'the Father begets the Son,' the same thing is predicated of itself, because the sense is: 'The Father is the Father of the Son,' or 'The Son is from the Father.'*"¹⁵

---

9   Ambrose, *On the Incarnation of the Word* 9; PL 16: 878B; ed. O. Faller, p. 272.

10   See above par. 1.

11   See Porphyry, *Introduction*; trans. Boethius, ed. L. Minio-Palluello and B. Dod, pp. 19–20.

12   See above par. 2.

13   See above par. 3.

14   Praepositinus, *Summa against the Heretics* 12, 2; ed. J. Garwin, p. 277.

15   Ibid., 12, 5; ed. J. Garwin, p. 279.

9. "*But,*" as he says, "*all the authorities seem to cry out against this. For Augustine says: 'It is proper to the Father to generate; it is proper to the Son to be generated, and it is proper to the Holy Spirit to proceed.*" Similarly, "*There is one property by which the Father generates, another by which the Son is generated,*" and so on. *The authority is to be understood in this way: it is proper to the Father to generate, that is, only the Father generates, and so on* also *in the others.*"[16]

[368] 10. "*Hilary says: 'It is proper to the Father that he is the Father; it is proper to the Son that he is the Son; it is proper to the Holy Spirit that he is the Holy Spirit. Therefore, the property is different, and so on.' This authority is explained as the one before: 'Only the Father is the Father, and so on.*"[17]

11. "*Likewise,*" Ambrose says, '*In the persons property, in the essence unity,'* and so on. *We say that this authority must be explained in this way: in the persons property, that is, the persons are distinct, and they are one in essence and adored as equal in majesty.*"[18]

12. "*Jerome says: 'We confess not only the names, but also the properties of the names.'* But if it is considered carefully, it is seen that he did not say: '*We confess the properties of the persons,'* but '*those of the names,*' and a property is usually said to be its signification. Therefore, the sense is: '*We confess not only the names, but the properties of the names,'* that is, the significations. But he explains what are the significations of the names when he adds, that is, the persons.*"[19]

13. But "*John Damascene rather seems to be opposed, when he says: 'Idiomata are characteristics of the hypostases, not of the nature; that is, properties* [369] *are determinative of the persons, not of the nature.'*[20] John likewise says: '*Each of the hypostases possesses a proper manner of existing.'* In that way we reply: '*The idiomata, etc., that is, the persons are distinguished in relation to one another, but the nature is not distinguished from one of them.*"[21] "*Each person has a proper manner of existing,*"[22] that is, each person is the one substance in such a way that < it is > not another.

----

16   Ibid., 12, 2; ed. J. Garwin, p. 277. See Augustine of Hippo, *Answer to an Arian Sermon*, PL 42: 696; ed. P.M. Hombert, p. 219; also *On the Trinity* 5, 6; PL 42: 915; ed. W. Mountain and F. Glorie, p. 211, as well as Fulgentius, *On the Faith for Peter* 2, 7; PL 49: 755. See below qu. 5, par. 4.

17   Ibid. See Hilary of Poitiers, *On the Trinity* 12, 23; PL 10: 447; ed. P. Smulders, p. 597.

18   Ibid., ed. J. Garwin, p. 278. See also Pelagius, *Confession of Faith for Pope Innocent*; PL 48: 489C.

19   Ibid.

20   Praepositinus, *Summa against the Heretics* 12, 2, ed. J. Garwin, p. 278, quoting John Damascene, *On the Orthodox Faith* 50; PG 94: 1002D; ed. E. Buytaert, p. 187.

21   John Damascene, *On the Orthodox Faith* 49; PG 94: 999C; ed. E. Buytaert, p. 184.

22   Ibid.

14. He also replies to the argument that is raised as an objection against him, speaking as follows: "*But it is objected to us in this way: By no property is the Father distinguished from the Son, nor the Son from the Father, and the Father is the same in essence with the Son; therefore, the Father is the Son. It is argued with insistence: By no accident is the Father distinguished from the Son, nor the Son from the Father, and the Father is the same with the Son in essence; therefore, the Father is the Son.*"[23] And he means that they are distinguished by themselves, as simple beings are. "*For otherwise the process would run on to infinity.*"[24] Hence, he adds: "*It is asked of us: If the persons are not distinguished by the properties, by what are they distinguished? To this we say that they are distinguished by themselves. For Jerome says: The persons are distinguished by themselves and their names; therefore, the Father is distinguished by himself from the Son and from the Holy Spirit, and so it is with the others.*"[25] And he introduces in his own favor one argument, saying: "*But they ask whether that property by which the Father is distinguished from the Son is substantial, and if it is, then the Father is substantially distinguished from the Son; therefore, he is not of the same substance with the Son.*"[26]

15. Praepositinus really saw quite well that the properties that are properties in God in the most proper sense have to be maintained only on account of distinguishing the persons from one another. Hence, those who imagine only one person in God, as the Jews and pagans do, do not need to maintain some properties in that person. For this reason, since he denied that there are properties in God, he needed to hold that the persons are distinguished by themselves. For otherwise in holding that they are distinguished, it was necessary to hold [370] that they are distinguished by some things that belong to them, and they have to be called only properties, as was said. Hence, Ambrose says in the beginning of *On the Trinity*: "*The Father is not who the Son is, but between the Father and the Son there is expressed the distinction of generation,*"[27] that is, so that they are distinguished by the property of active and passive generation.

16. But it is most efficaciously shown by a fourfold argument against Praepositinus that we can only maintain that the divine persons are distinguished by themselves insofar as they are distinguished by something belonging to them. And by these arguments it is clear that there is an error in his statement and that one necessarily has to maintain that there are properties in God. The first of these is as follows: Whatever simple beings differ by themselves differ by everything that which belongs to them. For otherwise they would differ by something that belongs to them and would not differ by something <else that

---

23   Praepositinus, *Summa against the Heretics* 12, 2; ed. J. Garwin, p. 279.

24   Ibid.

25   Ibid., 12, 4; ed. J. Garwin, p. 279.

26   Ibid., 12, 3; ed. J. Garwin, p. 279.

27   Ambrose of Milan, *On the Faith* 1, 2; PL 16: 555A; ed. O. Faller, p. 10.

belongs to them>. But whatever things differ in that way are entirely different and agree in nothing, as the genera of the categories of substance and accident differ. Therefore, if the divine persons differed in that way, they would be entirely different and agree in nothing. The consequent is false; therefore, the antecedent is also.

17. The second is as follows: Anything simple that differs by itself in terms of the whole, not by some part of itself, from other simple beings completely differs from one by that by which it differs from another. If therefore the three divine persons differ among themselves in this way, then by that by which the Father entirely differs or is distinguished from the Son, he also differs and is distinguished from the Holy Spirit. But the divine persons are not distinguished by something absolute, for then they would differ in substance and nature. Rather they only differ by something relative, therefore, the Father would differ from the Son and the Holy Spirit by one and the same relation. And if that is so, then, conversely the Son and the Holy Spirit would also differ from the Father by one and the same relation and would be one [371] and the same person, since in God only a relation makes the persons many.[28] But it is clear that the Son and the Holy Spirit would differ from the Father by one relation, if the Father differed from them both by one relation, because by the relation by which some would differ from another, they are also related to it, and all relatives are related to one another by the same relations by which they would be opposed to one another. But if there is one relation by which the Father is related to the Son and to the Holy Spirit, there is similarly also one relation at least according to species by which both are related to the Father. For the character of a relation consists in its being toward something else, but in terms of many specifically different relations many cannot be related according to a relation one in species, just as many cannot be related in terms of many specifically different relations, such as filiation and servitude, to the one Father who is the Father by a relation one in terms of species, which is paternity.

18. The third argument is as follows: If the divine persons differ among themselves in terms of their whole, therefore, that is either absolute or relative. It is not absolute because in that case, as before, they would differ in absolute characteristics. It is not relative because in that case the divine persons would be only certain respects, and that is opposed to the statement of Augustine in *On the Trinity*: "Everything that is said to be relatively is something besides its being said to be relatively."[29] And since the Father and the Son are related to the Holy Spirit by the same respect, the Father and the Son would be entirely the same person, as they are also one principle of the Holy Spirit.

---

28   See Anselm of Canterbury, *On the Procession of the Holy Spirit* 1; PL 158: 288–290; ed. F. S. Schmitt, 2, p. 181–183.

29   Augustine of Hippo, *On the Trinity* 7, 1; PL 42: 934; ed. W. Mountain and F. Glorie, p. 247.

[372] 19. And from this there is taken the fourth argument that Praepositinus introduces against himself for the same point as follows: If the Father and the Son are one principle of the Holy Spirit, but are not one in person, they are therefore one in the property by which they are related to the Holy Spirit, and for this reason it is necessary to maintain a property in God, and if <it is necessary to maintain> one, <it is> also <necessary> for the same reason <to maintain> more.[30] And Praepositinus replies, saying that for this reason "they are *one principle* of the Holy Spirit, *because they spirate in the same way.*"[31] And this is not valid for his purpose because they would not spirate in the same way unless there were something the same in them by which they would differ from the Holy Spirit, which can only be a property, because by reason of the common substance they are not one spirative principle. For otherwise the Holy Spirit himself would spirate.

20. Therefore, to the third principal argument introduced above that "*in simple beings something abstract and something concrete only differ in the manner of signifying,*"[32] it must be said that there is something simple in which there is signified only pure unity and in no way a plurality of some things, such as is signified by this name "God" or this name "wisdom." But there is something else simple in which there is in some way signified a plurality, still not one opposed to simplicity, as in this name "person" or "Father" or "Son" or "Holy Spirit." The objection proceeds correctly concerning something simple in the first way, but a person is God is not simple in that way, but is simple in the second way. And concerning it it is not true that something abstract and something concrete differ only in the manner of signifying. Rather, they differ in what is signified because what is abstract signifies something of that which the concrete signifies, such as that from which the name is imposed quasi formally, which is the property itself. But what is concrete [373] signifies along with this the common substance, as will be seen below.[33] And according to this, because a property falls as if formally in what a person signifies, it is substantial to the person insofar as "substantial" is distinguished from "accidental." Still, it does not follow from this that it is the substance nor that one person is distinguished from another substantially, that is, according to substance. It can nonetheless correctly be said that it is distinguished substantially in opposition to that which is to be distinguished accidentally. And in that way the argument that Praepositinus introduces for himself does not hold.[34]

---

30   See Praepositinus, *Summa against the Heretics* 12, 6; ed. J. Garwin, p. 280.

31   Ibid..

32   See above par. 3 and 8.

33   See below par. 22.

34   See above par. 19.

21. Praepositinus' claim that all predications that seem to imply that there are properties in God should be explained as emphatic language in putting the abstract for the concrete is not true.[35] For if, according to what he says, "it is the same to say that *paternity is in the Father* or the Father generates as *that the Father is the Father*,"[36] then it would similarly be the same to say that the Father generates and similarly that the Father spirates as that he is the Father. Hence, since that the Father is the Father is always the same, and "*whatever things are the same as one and the same thing are the same with one another*,"[37] it would therefore be the same to say: "The Father generates" and "The Father spirates," and as a consequence, the same one would be the person generated and spirated, which is false. The Master disproves this in another way in book one of the *Sentences*, distinction twenty-six, the chapter "This can be asked."[38]

22. Similarly his statement that "it is the same to say: '*It is proper to the Father to generate and* that *only the Father generates*,"[39] is not true, although one accompanies [374] the other. For he alone generates only if he alone has the property that is for generating. He perhaps explains the authority of Ambrose correctly because nothing in God is to be adored except by reason of the deity.[40] And on account of this the Trinity is to be adored by one adoration. But this has nothing to do with the present question, nor does it prevent there being properties in God, although they are to be adored because they are rooted in the essence of the deity and constitute the divine persons. And as for his statement that one should note in the authority of Jerome that "*he does not say the properties of persons but of names*,"[41] one need not. For Jerome clearly explains this in the beginning of the authority, when he speaks as follows: "*Apart from the words that indicate a property of the persons, whatever is said of one person can be understood of the three*,"[42] and in that way, "*avoiding the impiety of Sabellius, we distinguish the three persons expressed under a property*."[43] And in that way the properties belong to the persons as constituting and distinguishing them, and they belong to the names as those things from which the names are imposed as if formally, and they still do not signify the names alone, but <signify them> along with the

35   See Praepositinus, *Summa against the Heretics* 12, 2; ed. J. Garwin, p. 277. See above par. 8.

36   Ibid.

37   Aristotle, *Physics* 1.2.185b15–16.

38   See Peter Lombard, *Sentences* 1, d. 26, 7; PL 192: 594; ed. I. Brady, 1, p. 201.

39   See above par. 9.

40   See above par. 11.

41   See above par. 12.

42   Pseudo-Jerome, rather Pelagius, *Confession of Faith for Pope Innocent* 3; PL 192: 591

43   Ibid.

common substance, and they are both included in what is signified by a person. On this account he adds: "*that is, the persons,*" not because a person is signified by the name [375] and not the property of a person, as Praepositinus wants.[44] Hence, the Master of the *Sentences*, in book one, distinction twenty-five, the last chapter, proves by that authority that "person" stands there for a property, and also in distinction twenty-six, the chapter, "Hence."

23. But he clearly explains the statement of Damascene in book three, chapter six, contrary to the intention of the text that reads this way: "*Nor do the hypostases differ from one another according to substance, but according to accidents that are characteristic, that is, that designate, but <are> characteristic idiomata of an hypostasis, not of a nature. For they determine an hypostasis, a substance*[45] *along with accidents. Hence, an hypostasis, that is, a person, has what is common along with the properties.*"[46] But he calls the properties accidents by a very broad use of the name. See how he clearly does not intend that by these words alone that "*persons* are distinct among themselves, and *not the nature from the persons,*"[47] as Praepositinus says, but that the persons are distinct among themselves according to the properties, not according to the substance, and that the properties are determinative of the substance, not of the nature, as will be explained below,[48] so that in what it signifies a person contains both the substance and a property.

24. And what he says in the explanation of the second authority from book three, chapter five, that "*each person possesses a proper manner of existing, that is, each person is one substance so that it is not another,*"[49] is clearly against [376] that statement of Damascene in book one, chapter eleven: "*According to all things the Father and the Son and the Holy Spirit are one apart from non-generation, generation, and procession. For we recognize one God, but in the properties alone of paternity and filiation and procession and according to cause and effect,*"[50] because the Father is the cause, and the Son and the Holy Spirit are from this cause, "*And we understand their difference according to the perfection of an hypostasis, that is, of an existence.*" See that by his words: "*each person possesses his proper manner of*

---

44   See Praepositinus, *Summa against the Heretics* 12, 2; ed. J. Garwin, p. 278; see above par. 12.

45   I have conjectured "substance, *substantiam*" instead of "subjects, *subjecta.*"

46   John Damascene, *On the Orthodox Faith* 50, 1; PG 94: 1002C–1003A; ed. E. Buytaert, p. 186. See also Peter Lombard, *Sentences* 1, d. 27, c. 3; ed. I. Brady, p. 205.

47   See above par. 13.

48   See *SQO* art. 56, qu. 2; ed. Badius, 2, fol. 113vG–114rL.

49   Praepositinus, *Summa against the Heretics* 12, 2; ed. J. Garwin, p. 279; see above par. 13.

50   John Damascene, *On the Orthodox Faith* 1, 8; PG 94: 827D–830A; ed. E. Buytaert, p. 44. Also see Praepositinus, *Summa against the Heretics* 12, 2; ed. J. Garwin, p. 279.

existing,"[51] he does not understand that each person is the substance of the deity and no other, but that each person has a proper manner of existing, that is, of subsisting, according to his property, that is, as that from which another is, or that which is from another, or that which is from the others.

25. And in accord with this there is used in God a threefold manner of asking or predicating, and they are: by "what," which is with regard to the substance, by "who," which is with regard to a person, by 'how," which is with regard to a property. But "who" and "how" are reduced to one manner, namely, that of relation, because "who" corresponds to that which is related, "how" corresponds to that by which one is related, whether it is signified by a noun or by a participle.

26. And to Praepositinus's argument that it does not follow that "persons are not distinguished by the properties; therefore, they are not distinguished, just as it does not follow that they are not distinguished by accidents, therefore, they are not distinguished,"[52] it must be said that there is no similarity because in those things that are distinguished according to accidents, there remains another distinction that is according to substance. On this account [377] it does not follow that "if some things are not distinguished according to substance, they are not distinguished." But in God, besides the distinction according to properties there does not remain another distinction, as has been seen.[53] And for this reason it correctly follows that "they are not distinguished according to properties, therefore, they are not distinguished."

---

51   Ibid. 49; PG 94: 999C; ed. E. Buytaet, p. 184.

52   See above par. 14.

53   See above par. 16.

QUESTION TWO

Whether in the Divine Persons It Is Necessary to Hold Many Properties of the Persons

1. With regard to the second question it is argued that one should not hold that there are many properties in God, in the first place as follows: A proper characteristic follows upon the form and species of the reality or upon character of the species and of the form, as an accident follows upon the character of an individual. But in God there is only the one form of the deity; therefore, there is only one proper characteristic or one property.

2. <It is argued> in the second place as follows: Many properties can only exist according to the same character or according to diverse characters of a species. But in neither way can diverse properties held to be in God because neither the former nor the latter are able to be with regard to the numerically same thing, just as two whitenesses cannot, nor blackness and whiteness. But whatever is in God has being with regard to the numerically same thing, as with regard to the divine essence. Therefore, and so on.

3. <It is argued> to the contrary that there is a property in God only on account of the plurality of persons, as was already established above.[54] But it is necessary that a plurality of persons have many properties. Therefore, and so on.

[378]   <The Resolution of the Question>

4. It must be said to this that we necessarily have to maintain many properties in God with regard to the persons because many qualities are found to denominate them according to the manner already stated, as will now be explained in the following question.[55]

<Replies to the Arguments>

5. To the first argument to the contrary that *"properties follow upon the form and species of the reality,"*[56] and so on, it must be said that there is a certain absolute property, and it is only one in one form and species, and this is the case if one is speaking in a strict sense about a proper characteristic or about a property, as we maintain that "risible" is proper only to a human being. Hence, such a proper characteristic is often placed in the description of a reality when

---

54 See above qu. 1, par. 15.

55 See below qu. 3, par. 5–8.

56 See above par. 1.

its specific form is not known. But there is another relative property, and it can quite well be multiple in the same form and species because it does not follow so much upon the essence of the form as upon the manner of having it and of subsisting in it, as will now be seen.[57] But such is a property of a person in God, about which we are speaking, as will be seen below.[58]

6. To the second argument to the contrary that many properties whether of the same species or of a diverse species cannot exist with regard to the numerically same thing,[59] and so on, it must be said that it is true of absolute properties, as with regard to the subject in which they inhere. And in that way there is in God no property at all with regard to the divine essence, as Richard says in book four of *On the Trinity*, chapter sixteen: "*It is proper to every substance that truly has from itself the name to have composite being and to be subject to accidents. But the divine substance alone has simple being and is subject to nothing that inheres.*"[60] But with regard to the [379] numerically same thing, as with regard to the foundation in which they are founded, there can very well be diverse relative properties on account of the diverse manner of having that same thing, as not from another, as from which another is, and the suchlike, as will now be seen.[61]

---

57   See below qu. 3, par. 5–8 and *SQO* 56, 2; ed. Badius 2, fol.113vG–114rL.

58   Ibid.

59   See above par. 2.

60   Richard of Saint Victor, *On the Trinity* 4, 16; PL 196: 940C; ed. J. Ribaillier, p. 179.

61   See below q. 3, par. 5–8.

QUESTION THREE

Whether in the Divine Persons It Is Necessary to Hold Only Five Properties

1. With regard to the third question it is argued that in God there are not more than two properties because there is a property in God only from the manner of one person's being in relation to another, since there is no absolute property, as will be said below.[62] But in God there are only two ways of a person's being in relation to another, namely, "as that from which <another is>" and "as that which is from another," as is seen from what was determined above.[63] Therefore, there are only two properties in God.

2. Richard says that they are only three in book five of *On the Trinity*, chapter twenty-five: "*The number of the persons will be according to the number of the properties, and as we will not be able in any way to find a fourth property, so we will not be able to find a fourth person.*"[64]

3. It is argued that there are only four because there is only a relative property in God, as will be seen below.[65] And similarly there is not a relation in God unless it is a property. For whatever is in something besides its substance is a property in it. But in God there are only four relations according to the two emanations, as is clear from what has been already determined.[66] Therefore, and so on.

[380] 4. But it is argued that there are more than five and quasi infinite properties from what Ambrose says in book two of *On the Trinity*: "*The properties are generation, God, Son, Word, likeness, imprint, splendor, power, truth, life,*"[67] and others of this sort, which are only with regard to the Son, and there are many others with regard to the Father, such as unbegotten, first principle, and suchlike, and very many with regard to the Holy Spirit, such as love, gift, and suchlike. Likewise, there are many with regard to the three in common, such as equality, likeness, and suchlike, which are quasi infinite. Hence, and so on.

---

62 See below art. 55, qu. 5, par. 7.

63 See above art. 55, qu. 2, par. 6

64 Richard of Saint Victor, *On the Trinity* 5, 20; PL 196: 963D–964A; ed. J. Ribaillier, p. 218..

65 See *SQO* art. 58, qu. 3; ed. Badius 2, fol. 134rR–134vI.

66 See above art. 53, qu. 9, par. 5 and art. 54, qu. 9, par. 9–11.

67 Ambrose of Milan, *On the Faith* 2, prol.; PL 16: 584A–B; ed. O. Faller, p. 58,

<The Resolution of the Question>

5. It must be said to this that "property" is spoken of in four ways in God: in a very broad sense, in a broad sense, in a strict sense, and in a very strict sense. In a very broad sense whatever things have to be considered with regard to the persons are called properties in God, just as whatever ones have to be considered with regard to the divine essence are called attributes, and Ambrose speaks in that way in *On the Trinity* in the authority cited.[68] And in speaking in this way, Praepositinus says that *"certain men hold almost infinite properties in God. For they say that certain properties follow upon the essence, as equality, coeternity, likeness,* but *certain ones follow upon an hypostasis, as paternity, filiation,"*[69] and suchlike. In this way all the essential divine attributes can also be said to be properties, according to the statement of the Philosopher who says on [381] the number three in the beginning of *On the Heaven and the World: "According to this number we apply ourselves to magnify the one God eminent with the properties of those things that exist."*[70]

6. But if one is speaking in a broad sense, as the same Praepositinus says: *"Our masters say there are only five properties: two in the Father alone, which are innascibility and paternity, one in the Son alone, namely, filiation, one in the Holy Spirit, namely,* passive production, *and one in two in common, namely, in the Father and in the Son, which is said to be active spiration."*[71]

7. But if one is speaking in a strict sense, there are only four properties because active spiration is not said to be a property in the proper sense because it is common to two and proper to none.

8. But in a very strict sense there are only three properties, which are paternity, filiation, and passive spiration because they alone constitute and distinguish the persons from one another. Hence, they are also only according to the number of the persons, as Richard says in book three of *On the Trinity,* chapter sixteen: *"The plurality of persons shows that a difference of properties cannot be lacking in that Trinity."*[72] And in chapter seventeen he says: *"It is without a doubt necessary that in that Trinity there are as many personal properties as there are persons."*[73] And in book five, chapter fifteen he says: *"But the distinction of properties turns about two things. For* [382] *it consists in giving and in receiving. For the property of one consists only in giving, that of another only in receiving, but*

---

68   See above par. 4.

69   Praepositinus, *Summa against the Heretics* 10, 1; ed. J. Garwin, p. 258.

70   See Aristotle, *On the Heavens* 1.1.268a9–24; ed. Juntas 5, fol 2rb, as in Albert the Great's *Commentary*; ed. P. Hossfeld, p. 3.

71   Praepositinus, *Summa against the Heretics* 10, 2; ed. J. Garwin, p. 259.

72   Richard of Saint Victor, *On the Trinity* 4, 15; PL 196: 939C; ed. J. Ribaillier, p. 177

73   Ibid., 4, 17; PL 196: 941A; ed. J. Ribaillier, p. 180.

between *these one consists in both giving and in receiving.*"[74] And because these three properties alone constitute and distinguish the persons, for this reason *"they are said to be personal properties,"*[75] as Praepositinus says, but <they are> not the only properties of a person, since all the others are nonetheless[76] said to be properties of the persons.

<Replies to the Arguments>

9. To the first argument that *"in God there are only two ways of being,"*[77] and so on, it must be said that it is true. Still <there are> common and general ones under which other special ones are contained because the way of being as *"that from which there is another"* necessarily entails the way of being *"as <that which is> from none."* For otherwise it would go on to infinity from the quasi anterior side so that the one from whom there is another would be from some other. And thus the way of not being from another would also be included in the way *"from which there is another."* And that way contains two, of which one is by generation, but the other by active spiration. Similarly the way *"that is from another"* contains two, one by generation, the other by passive spiration. And in that way the five others are reduced to those two ways.

10. To the second argument that *"there are only three,"*[78] it must be said that it is true that the personal ones or those constitutive of the persons <are only three> and by that the other two are still not excluded, as was touched upon and will be seen more below.[79]

11. To the third argument that *"in God there are only *four* relations; hence, there are only four *properties,"*[80] it must be said according to what has already been said that it is true that <there are only four> stated positively and that are understood in accord with the hypostases; still besides these [383] there is one negative property signified by the name *"innascible"* and similarly many that are understood in terms of the essence, of which there will be a discussion below.

12. To the last argument that *"there are many *and quasi infinite ones,"*[81] it must be said according to what has already been said[82] that it is true if one is speaking of a property in a very broad sense.

---

74   Ibid., 5, 15; PL 196: 960D–961A; ed. J. Ribaillier, p. 213.

75   Praepositinus, *Summa against the Heretics* 10, 2; ed. J. Garwin, p. 259.

76   I have conjectured *"nonetheless, tamen"* instead of *"only, tantum."*

77   See above par. 1.

78   See above par. 2.

79   See above par. 5 and 8, as well as qu. 1, par. 15–20 and below qu. 4, par. 11.

80   See above par. 3.

81   See above par. 4.

82   See above par. 5.

QUESTION FOUR

Whether in God All the Properties Are Notional

1. With regard to the fourth question it is argued that all properties are notional in the first place as follows: That by which something becomes known
is a notion. But a divine person becomes known to us by any property because, according to Ambrose,[83] there are certain quasi qualities and, according
to Damascene,[84] certain quasi accidents, as is seen from what has already been
said. And, according to the Philosopher in book one [384] of *On the Soul*, such
"*<accidents> contribute the greatest part to knowing the quiddity.*"[85] Therefore, and
so on.

2. <It is argued> in the second place as follows: The properties by which the
persons are mutually with respect to one another belong more essentially to
God than those by which God is with respect to creatures because the former
are also more truly said to be notions of the persons than the latter are of the
deity. But the latter are notions by which the essential attributes of the deity
become known to us, of which sort are being creator, being ruler, and such like.
Therefore, and so on.

3. It is argued to the contrary in the first place that no property is a notion.
For since only the reason and principle for knowing a thing ought to be said to
be a notion. But in God with respect to the persons such is only the common
essence from which they have being because, according to the Philosopher:
"*The reason for being and for knowing is the same.*"[86] Therefore, and so on.

4. <It is argued> as follows in the second place that the common action,
spiration, ought not to be said to be a notion: Only that ought to be called a
notion that reveals the proper knowledge of a thing, and on this account the
Philosopher says of a definition that it is for the sake of making known.[87] For it
conveys a proper knowledge of a thing, and for this reason it is properly said to
be a notion of a thing, but a genus that conveys common knowledge of a thing
<is> not <said to be a notion of a thing>. But because active spiration is com-

83   Ambrose of Milan, *On the Incarnation of the Word* 9, 98; PL 16: 878B; ed. O.
      Faller, p. 272.

84   John Damascene, *On the Orthodox Faith* 50, 1; ed. E. Buytaert, pp. 186–187.

85   Aristotle, *On the Soul* 1.1.402b21–22; ed. F. Crawford, p. 14.

86   Aristotle, *On the Soul* 3.7.431a1–2; ed. F. S. Crawford, p. 464.

87   See Aristotle, *Metaphysics* 7.4.1039a7–17; anon. trans.; ed. G. Vuillemin-Diem,
      p. 128.

mon to the Father and to the Son, it conveys no proper knowledge. Therefore, and so on.

5. Besides, according to the Philosopher, the principles of being and of know-ing are the same.[88] But common active spiration is the principle of being for no person because it is not constitutive of a person. Therefore, and so on.

6. It is argued in the third place that innascibility is not a notion because it implies nothing besides the other personal properties except a negation. But a negation [385] is not by itself a principle of knowing of the sort that a notion in God ought to be. For otherwise many other negations in God ought to be said to be notions, as will be seen further below.[89] Therefore, and so on.

---

88   See above par. 3.

89   See *SQO* art. 57, qu. 1; ed. Badius 2, fol 117vM–118rQ.

7. It is argued in the fourth place that passive generation and passive spiration cannot be said to be notions because a notion ought to be a principle of making known something of dignity in that of which it is a notion, and passive generation and passive spiration do not do that because they say that a person exists, but exists from another. Thus, although that he exists is something of dignity, it is still of no dignity that <the Holy Spirit> has being from another. Rather, it seems to be more a defect because someone does not have from himself what he has only from another, and that is mark of a great lack of dignity. Hence, and so on.

<The Resolution of the Question>

8. It must be said to this that "notion" is said in many ways. For in one way something is said to be a notion formally because it is the very knowledge of a reality absolutely impressed upon the mind. In that way it is nothing other than a simple concept of the mind in which a thing is known. But in another way something is said to be a notion effectively because it produces and causes knowledge of a thing in the mind, and this in two ways. For it is either something outside the thing, but having an order to the thing, and in that way every effect can be said to be a notion with respect to its cause, or it is something in the thing. And this is said either as something of the essence of the thing by which it is constituted in being, and in this way the definition and universally that which is the essential form in a thing is said to be the notion of the thing. And thus only the three personal properties constitutive of the persons are to be said to be notions of the persons. Or <it is said> as something virtually existing in that by which the thing is constituted in being, as [386] the moving power of all things universally exists in the moving power of the first moveable being, and it is a notion with respect to the mover of the first moveable being. And in this way "innascible" or "unbegotten" is a notion of the Father, in accord with what will be explained below in speaking about "innascible."[90] Or <it is said> as something accompanying a thing essentially constituted in being, as accidents follow upon a substance and are notions. And according to this way, with every sort of accidentality nonetheless removed, there are two notions in the divine persons because they either follow upon the person by reason of the person or by reason of the divine essence in him. In the first way, the common "action-spiration" is a notion of the Father and of the Son. For the fecundity of spiration follows upon generation in a certain order, as was established above.[91] In the second way, all the other properties that are in the person in accord with the essence or those of the persons compared among themselves, such as are equality, likeness, and suchlike, or of individual persons in terms of themselves, such as are the essential attributes, are said to be notions.

---

90   See *SQO* art. 57, qu. 1; ed. Badius 2, fol. 118rP.

91   See *SQO* art. 52, qu. 2; ed. M. Führer, p. 250 and above art. 54, qu. 6, par. 34.

9. Hence, if one looks at what has been said, it is clear that in the present question only those properties that are constitutive of the persons or are in the persons by a character by which they belong to a person, not by a character by which they belong to the essence, are said to be notions. And such are only five, whose number is understood as follows. For since in accord with what has been determined above,[92] a person in God is only relative, and this according to the character of origin. But a relation according to the character of origin can be either of one to one, of which one [387] is the person from whom the other is and the other the person who is from the other, and one is from one. In that way there are two notions: one of the Father, as paternity or active generation by which the other is from him, but the other <that> of the Son, as filiation or nascibility by which he is from another. Or <a relation> can be of many to one who is from those many, and in that way there is the notion of common active spiration of the Father and of the Son. Or <a relation> can be of one to many, and this either of one from whom there are many, and in that way innascibility is a notion of the Father, as will be seen below,[93] or of one who is from many. In that way passive spiration is a notion of the Holy Spirit.

<Replies to the Arguments>

10. For the resolution of certain arguments one must distinguish here concerning a notion, as we distinguished above concerning a property[94] because something can be said to be a notion in a very broad sense, in a broad sense, in a strict sense, and in a very strict sense. In the first way, if "property" is taken in a very broad sense, every divine property can be said to be a notion, and in accord with this the first two objections proceed. But if one is speaking in a broad sense concerning the notions of the persons, only the five properties[95] that are in the persons in terms of the persons are said to be notions, not those <that are in the persons> in terms of the common essence, as was said.[96] But if one is speaking in a strict sense, only four of them are. For common active spiration produces no proper knowledge of a person. But if one is speaking in a strict sense that cannot be said to be a notion in accord with which the fourth argument proceeds,[97] and similarly the fifth.[98] But if one is speaking in a very strict sense, only the three personal properties are notions [388] For innasci-

---

92 See above art. 53, qu. 6, art. 53, qu. 9, par. 7 and qu. 9, par. 5

93 See *SQO* art. 57, qu. 1; ed. Badius 2, fol. 118rP.

94 See above qu. 3, par. 5–8.

95 See Praepositinus, *Summa against the Heretics* 10, 2; ed. J. Garwin, p. 259; see above qu. 3, par. 6.

96 See above qu. 3, par. 6.

97 See above par. 4.

98 See above par. 5.

bility cannot be a notion by reason of the negation it implies, as the second last argument proceeds.[99] But whatever of dignity the character of an understood affirmation implies is contained in generation and spiration and in this regard is reduced to them, as will be seen below in speaking of innascibility.[100]

11. To that which is assumed in the third argument, namely, that "*no property is a notion because it is not the principle of being in the persons, but only the essence is,*"[101] it must be said that in the persons there is being and there is being toward something else. The first is from the essence and is common to the three. But the second is from a property and is distinguished in accord with the distinction of the properties, as Augustine says in book seven of *On the Trinity*: "*The substance of the Father is the Father himself, not that by which he is the Father, but that by which he is.*"[102] And thus in one way the essence is the principle and reason for knowing the persons, and in another way a property is. But this is proper to the persons insofar as they are persons, and for this reason they are said to be notions of the persons and the essence itself is not.

12. To the last argument that "*generation and spiration, <if they are taken>, passively cannot be said to be notions,*"[103] it must be said that in what has being from another through generation or spiration, it is necessary to consider three things, namely, having being that is of dignity, but common to all, and for this reason it does not provide the character of a notion. And having it without qualification from another, which entails neither a character of dignity nor also one of a lack of dignity, and for this reason it too does not provide the character of a notion. And it is necessary to consider a third thing in it,[104] namely, having being from another in this way, that is, through natural generation or spiration that, because they are noble ways of having, for this reason entail the character of a notion. [389] But how they are noble ways of having is sufficiently explained in book one of the *Sentences*, distinction twenty-five, on the Son, the chapter, "Here it is asked," and concerning the Holy Spirit in the chapter, "So also."[105]

---

99   See above par. 6.

100   See *SQO* art. 57, qu. 1; ed. Badius 2, fol. 118rP

101   See above par. 3.

102   Augustine of Hippo, *On the Trinity* 7, 6; PL 42: 943; ed. W. Mountain and F. Glorie, p. 262.

103   See above par. 7.

104   See *SQO* art. 57, qu. 1; ed. Badius 2, fol. 118P–R and fol. 120rD–E.

105   See Peter Lombard, *Sentences* 1, d. 26, c. 4; PL 192: 952–953; ed. I. Brady, 1, pp. 199–200 and c.6; PL 192: 593–594; ed. I. Brady, 1, pp.. 201–202.

QUESTION FIVE

Whether the Notions or Properties in God Are Relations

1. With regard to the fifth question it is argued in the first place that no property in God is a relation as follows: A property in God is the essence or substance. For paternity is the deity. But that which in God is the substance is not a relation because they are distinguished as opposed, as the two categories in God, as is clear from what has been determined above.[106] Therefore, and so on.

2. <It is argued> in the second place as follows: The weakest way of being does not belong to the truest being because the way <of being> ought to correspond to the reality. Whatever is in God is the most noble being, and the manner of a relation is the weakest manner of being, as the Commentator says on book eleven of the *Metaphysics*, chapter eleven: *"Relation has the weakest being among all the categories."*[107] Therefore, and so on.

[390] 3. It is argued in the third place that not every property in God is a relation as follows: According to Damascene, in book one, chapter eleven: *"The Father and the Son and the Holy Spirit are one in terms of all things apart from generation, non-generation, and procession."*[108] But there are other properties apart from these; therefore, they are one in them. But they are not one in the relations; rather, <they are one> in substance alone. Therefore, all the other properties in God are substances and not relations.

4. In the fourth place it is shown that a property in God, such as "unbegotten" at least, is not a relation, as follows: There is not a relation unless there are two extremes, one of which it is said and the other that with respect to which it is. But "unbegotten" has only one extreme, namely, that of which it is said, and does not have the other with respect to which it is said. Therefore, and so on.

5. But if it is said according to Augustine in book five of *On the Trinity* that he is said to be related "to the non-begetter"[109] this cannot stand because that "non-begetter" cannot be a divine person like the Son and the Holy Spirit because the Father is related to them by other relations. But the same person is

---

106   See SQO 32, 5; ed. R. Macken, p. 79 and pp. 81–84 and pp. 89–90, as well as 32, 4; ed. R. Macken, p. 57.

107   Averroes, *Commentary on the Metaphysics* 12. comm. 19; ed. Juntas 8, fol. 306raB:

108   John Damascene, *On the Orthodox Faith* 1, 8; PL 94: 827D; ed. E. Buytaert, p. 44; see above q. 1, para. 4 et 24.

109   See Augustine of Hippo, *On the Trinity* 5, 6; PL 42: 915; ed. W. Mountain and F. Glorie, p. 211; see above qu. 1, par. 9.

not related to the same person by many relations, as will be explained below.[110] And besides in that case "non-begetter" would be a property of the Son or of the Holy Spirit, as "unbegotten" <is> of the Father, and that is not true, as will be seen below.[111] Nor can it be a creature because God does not have an essential respect to it, nor is a notion in God understood with respect to it because it asserts nothing of nobility in God, and a notion ought to be a property that pertains to [391] nobility. Nor can it be without a respect to something else because there is not something else. And a notion in God is no more to be understood with respect to that which is nothing at all than with respect to a creature.

6. It is argued to the contrary that whatever is in God besides the substance is a relation. For there are not many categories in God, according to what has been established above.[112] All the properties in God apart from the substance are relations, as Augustine says in book nine of *On the City of God*: "For this reason a person is said to be simple because he is what he has, except what each person is said to be relatively to another."[113] Therefore, and so on.

<The Resolution of the Question>

7. It must be said to this in accord with what has already been determined[114] that the properties in God are nothing other than certain qualities of the substance, and in that way, although they are really the substance or the essence—for paternity is the deity, and the rest of them are so in the same way—still insofar as they are properties, the character of them is other than that of the substance. And it cannot be some absolute character because it would necessarily assert besides the substance some absolute reality on which it would be founded, and there would be composition in God. It is necessary therefore that it be a relative character that requires some absolute reality only as its foundation. But a respect or a relation is implied in different ways through the properties of the substance that are the attributes and through the properties of the persons that are more truly said to be properties because the former like goodness, truth, and suchlike signify the essence under the character of a respect, as was determined above.[115] But the properties of the persons do not <signify the essence> in that way, but signify by their name only respects, as paternity does not signify the essence along [392] with a respect to another. For

110   See *SQO* art. 56, qu. 3; ed. Badius 2, fol. 115rR.

111   See SQO art. 59, qu. 4; ed. Badius 2, fol.146rN.

112   See *SQO* art. 32, qu. 2; ed. R. Macken, pp. 36–50.

113   Augustine of Hippo, *On the City of God* 10; PL 41: 326; ed. W. Dombart and A. Kalb, p. 330.

114   See above qu. 2, par. 4.

115   See *SQO* art. 33, qu. 2; ed. R. Macken, pp. 130–141 and art. 35, qu. 8; ed. G. Wilson, pp. 76–78.

the person that is the Father signifies this, as will be said below,[116] but <paternity> signifies the pure respect by which the Father is the Father, and it is that way with the rest. Hence, the Master says in book one of the *Sentences*, distinction twenty-seven, the chapter "Nor nonetheless": *"The name "Father" does not denote only a relation, but also an hypostasis, that is, it signifies the substance; and in that way "Son" and "Holy Spirit" do also. But the words for the relations, namely, 'paternity,' 'filiation,' 'procession,' 'to beget' or 'to be begotten,' 'to proceed,' signify only relations."*[117]

<Replies to the Arguments>

8. To the first argument to the contrary that *"a property is the essence, as paternity is the deity,"*[118] it must be said with regard to what is signified by the expression that, although the reality of the property or respect and of the foundation on which it is founded is the same, it will be explained in the following question what is signified both by the name of the foundation and by the name of the property both in God and in creatures. Hence, as in God a property is predicated of the essence, and the other way around, as will be explained below when explaining the manner of speaking and predicating in God,[119] still the manner of the one and of the other is always different, and although they are distinguished from each other as opposed, they are not <opposed> with respect to their foundation; rather, they agree in it. For the category of relation is not distinguished in reality from the realities of the categories on which it is founded, but only [393] in the manner and character of the predicament, as was explained above.[120] And in that way by reason of the reality the substance in God is a relation, although not by reason of its manner. And from this it comes about that, although the properties are the very divine essence, still the divine persons are distinguished by the properties and the essence is not, according to what the Master determines in book one of the *Sentences*, distinction thirty-three through the whole.[121] And in that way it truly turns out that it is held that in God the properties are relations despite the fact that they are the divine essence.

---

116 See below, qu. 6, par. 23 and 29, and also SQO art. 58, qu. 3; ed. Badius 2, fol. 134rF–vH and art. 75, qu. 1; ed. Badius 2, fol. 289vA-291vO and art. 75, qu. 2; ed. Badius 2, fol. 292rP–295rL.

117 Peter Lombard, *Sentences* 1, d. 27, c. 2; PL 192: 595; ed. I. Brady, 1, pp. 204–205.

118 See above par. 1.

119 See below qu. 6, par. 26.

120 See SQO art. 32, qu. 5; ed. R. Macken, pp. 79–107.

121 Peter Lombard, *Sentences* 1, d. 33, c. 1–2; PL 192: 610–613; ed. I. Brady, 1, pp. 240–246.

9. To the second argument that *"the weakest way of being belongs to relation.* which ought not *belong to* the most noble *being,"*[122] it must be said that in creatures a relation's way of being, even one that is a relation according to being, is most weak, because it is in them through a certain dependence, not only on the reality of its foundation and of its subject, but also on its object. For relative beings are founded upon diverse subjects according to being, as paternity is upon the substance of a father and filiation on the substance of a son, and likeness in two whitenesses, so that if the reality is destroyed in the object, the reality is also lacking in each extreme. Hence, certain men thought that relation is among the second intentions and is a thing of reason existing only in the mind.[123] But it is not so with regard to real relations in God because in God a relation is not in one [394] extreme through some dependence, but only through some order to the other extreme because the relation is founded upon the essence in both extremes. In this way the essence is naturally under such respects, and it cannot be without them any more than it can be without its own way of being, which is proper to it insofar as it is the substance or essence. On this account in God the manner of a relation is not weaker than that of the substance, and the reality of a relation is not weaker than that of the substance because it is one and the same.

10. To the third argument it must be said that Damascene is speaking of properties in the most strict sense,[124] and under one of them he includes active and passive procession and under non-generation he includes active generation, as will be seen below.[125] But in the other properties the <persons> agree because they are substantial, such as likeness, equality, and suchlike. And for this reason by the fact that they are one in them, it is not excluded that they are one only in substance, because their unity in the persons is through the unity of substance, as will be explained below.[126]

11. To the fourth argument "concerning 'unbegotten' that *is not a relation,"*[127] it must be said that this is not true. For the understanding of this it must be known that "unbegotten" is said with respect to something else, not with respect to itself. And Augustine shows this in book five of *On the Trinity*, chapter seven, when he says: "But this negative particle 'un-' does not bring it about that what without it is said relatively is said substantially when it is added, but there

122   See above par. 2.

123   See Averroes, *Commentary on the Metaphysics* 12, comm. 19; ed. Juntas 8, fol. 306rB, and Thomas Aquinas, *Commentary on the Sentences* 1, d. 26, q. 2, a. 1; ed. P. Mandonnet, pp. 629–630. Also see below qu. 6, par. 13.

124   See above par. 3.

125   See *SQO* art. 57, qu. 4; ed. Badius 2, fol. 122vB–C.

126   See *SQO* art. 56, qu. 4; ed. Badius 2, fol. 116rB–117rH.

127   See above par. 4.

is only denied what without it is done, just as in the other categories. For when we say: 'He is a man,' we point out the substance. Therefore, someone who says 'non-man' *does not indicate another sort of category,* [395] *but only denies that one,* and so on. *Therefore, one does not depart from a relative category when one says 'unbegotten.' For as 'begotten' is not said with respect to itself, but because he is from the begetter, so when one say 'unbegotten,' it is not said with respect to itself, but it is shown in that way that he is not from a begetter, because as the Son is related to the Father and the non-son is related to that non-father, so it is necessary that the begotten be to the begetter, and the non-begotten to non-begetter."*[128] But because this relation is negative, for this reason some have denied that "unbegotten" is a relation, and they hold that of the number of the five notions only four are relations.[129] And it is true that there are only four positive relations, but a negative one is still no less a relation than the others, according to the words of Augustine,[130] and it is real because as those affirmative ones have from the nature of the reality to be founded without consideration of the intellect, this negative one also similarly <has to be>, and this makes the relation real, as will be explained below.[131]

12. To the argument that "'non-begotten' is not said in relation to 'non-be-getter' as to another divine person or to a creature,"[132] it must be said that it is quite true; it is rather related to something else that does not exist and cannot exist in the nature of things, as to a non-begetter. And to the argument that "with respect to something of the sort there cannot be a notion,"[133] it must be said that it is true by reason of a pure negation or of a negative relation. It is nonetheless a notion by reason of the relation understood along with it, as will be seen below.[134]

[396] 13. But Praepositinus replies in another way, speaking as follows: *"To the objection that if innascibility is a relation, it is necessary that its correlative be another, we reply in this way that not every relation has a correlative. For a certain relation exists in or is present to a creature with respect to the creator, still no relation exists or is present <in him> with respect to a creature."*[135] And that is true in terms of

128   Augustine of Hippo, *On the Trinity* 5, 7; PL 42: 915–916; ed. W. Mountain and F. Glorie, pp. 213–215.

129   See Thomas Aquinas, *Commentary on the Sentences* 1, d. 26, q. 2, art. 3; ed. Mandonnet, p. 638

130   See Augustine of Hippo, *On the Trinity* 5, 7; PL 42: 916; ed. W. Mountain and F. Glorie, p. 214.

131   See qu. 6, par. 6.

132   See above par. 5.

133   See above par. 5.

134   See *SQO* art. 57, qu. 1; ed. Badius 1, fol. 117vN–118rO.

135   Praepositinus, *Summa against the Heretics,* 11, 5; ed. J. Garwin, p. 268.

reality; it nonetheless exists in or is present to him according to reason and the consideration of the intellect. And in that way in the present question the relation is present negatively to the other extreme according to the consideration of the intellect, and in that way it is not and cannot be something in reality. But Praepositinus says that "unbegotten" is said relatively to the Son and the Holy Spirit, when he speaks as follows: *"Besides, by that property he is said to be related to the Son and to the Holy Spirit because by it the property of the Son and the property of the Holy Spirit are shown to be removed from the Father,"*[136] which is not entirely absurd, as will be seen below.[137]

136　Ibid.

137　See *SQO* art. 57, qu. 1; ed. Badius 2, fol. 117vM–118rR.

QUESTION SIX

Whether the Properties in God Are Real Relations

1. With regard to the sixth question it is argued that all the properties in God are real relations as follows: Something is said to be "real" from "reality."[138] But no absolute reality is or can be in God except the essence itself, from which everything [397] relative, which of itself is not a reality, takes its origin, according to Boethius who says in chapter twelve of *On the Trinity* that three categories, namely, substance, quantity, and quality *"reveal a reality, but the other categories reveal circumstances of a reality."*[139] Nothing therefore in God has any real being except from the divine essence. But any properties equally have reality from the divine essence because they have reality from it only because they are founded on it, and all are equally founded on it because <they are founded on it> immediately. Therefore, and so on.

2. Besides, if a relation is real from the substance on which it is founded although it is not said to be real except because it is also some reality—for otherwise it would not constitute a person that is a reality—but it can only be a reality on account of the reality of the substance because it is the substance, therefore, for the same reason that a relation can be called a reality, it can be called a substance. The consequent is false; therefore, and so on.

3. But it is argued that some of them are real. Boethius says in the book, *On the Trinity*, that only *"relation makes the Trinity many."*[140] But what makes something really many can only be real. But the multiplicity of the Trinity of persons in God is real, not merely according to reason, for Augustine says that *"the Father, the Son, and the Holy Spirit are three realities."*[141] Therefore, and so on.

4. But it is argued that these are not real; therefore, for much better reason one of them is not, as follows: John Damascene says in book one, chapter eleven: [398] *"It is one thing to consider <something> in reality and another to consider <it> in reason and knowledge. In all creatures the division of hypostases is considered in reality, but their community is considered in reason and knowledge.*

---

138 The Latin says literally: "Real ... from thing; *reale ... a re.*" I have generally translated "*res*" as "reality," which seems to be preferable in most cases.

139 Boethius, *On the Trinity* 4; PL 64: 1253C; ed. C. Moreschini, p. 177. See *SQO* art. 32, qu. 5; ed. R. Macken, pp. 81 and 87 as well as below par. 13.

140 Ibid. 6; PL 64: 1255A; ed. C. Moreschini, p. 180.

141 Augustine of Hippo, *On the Trinity* 5, 8–9; PL 42: 916–918; ed. W. Mountain and F. Glorie, p. 217. See also his *Answer to Maximinus* 2, 22; PL 42: 793; ed. P.-M. Hombert, pp. 631–639.

But in the supersubstantial substance *it is just the other way around. For there what is common and one is considered in reality, but it is considered by knowledge as divided.*"[142] But this division is only in terms of the personal properties, as the same author says: *"For we know one God, but we understand a difference only in the properties of paternity, filiation, and procession according to the manner of existence."*[143] Therefore, in terms of such properties the persons differ only by knowledge or reason. But this would not be so if they were real relations. Therefore, and so on.

5. Likewise, Boethius says in *On the Trinity* that *"the relation of the Father to the Son in the Trinity and of both to the Holy Spirit is similar to the relation* of the same thing to itself."[144] But that is only <a relation> of reason. Therefore, and so on.

<The Resolution of the Question>

6. It must be said to this in accord with what was determined above[145] that the properties that are attributes are not real respects or relations, and the reason for this will now be seen.[146] But concerning the others it must be known that, since every relation consists in a certain order and certain comparison of things related among themselves, this order has to vary in accord with the variety of things that are ordered. And this occurs in three ways because it either consists in the order of things ordered from the nature of reality so that from both sides the character of the order is from the nature of the reality, or <it consists> in the order of things ordered from the character of the intellect so that from both sides the character of the order is from the character of the concepts, or <it consists> partly from the order of the things ordered from the nature of the reality and partly from the character of the intellect. In that way, for example, on the one side the character of the order is from the nature of the reality and on the other from the character of the intellect. If it consists in the order of the things ordered [399] from the nature of the reality, in that case the relation is real. If it consist in the order of the things ordered from the character of the intellect, in that case it is a relation of reason. If it is partly in one way and partly in another, in that case it is partly from the one side a relation of reason, but partly and from the other side a relation of reality.

---

142   John Damascene, *On the Orthodox Faith* 1, 8; PG 94: 827A and C; ed. E. Buytaert, pp. 42, 43, and 44.

143·   Ibid.; PG 94: 830D; ed. E. Buytaert, p. 44.

144   Boethius, *On the Trinity* 6; PL 64: 1255A–1256A; ed. C. Moreschini, p. 180.

145   See above qu. 5, par. 7.

146   See below par. 25.

7. An example of this third way is found if a man is compared to a column at his right side,[147] this relation that the man has to the column as to his right and the column to the man as to its left, because it is to his right—this relation of the man to the column is, I say, real because the right side on which it is founded in the man is in the man in terms of reality, but the relation of the column to the man is only one of reason[148] because the left side on which it is founded in the column is not in column except according to a concept of the intellect, that is, from a respect to the right hand of the man.

8. An example of the second is found when the intellect takes one thing as two[149] and in this way understands it under a certain order and respect to itself, as when something is said to be the same as itself. For in that case the relation is according to reason from both sides because this duplication of the same thing is only in a concept of the intellect. Or when it is said "in God the Father is equal to the Son," the relation is according to reason on both sides, and this is the case because the equality of some things is only according to the commensurate magnitudes among themselves or insofar as they have commensurate magnitudes among themselves. And for this reason the equality of two or more of them is not a real relation except according to two or more commensurate magnitudes really diverse from one another in terms of which they are really commensurate with one another, on which are founded the diverse real respects. But the spiritual magnitude of the Father and the Son is the divine essence itself that is one [400] in the two of them in terms of reality and is in no way made many. When therefore the equality of the persons is said to be in terms of it, it is necessary that it be taken twice in terms of the intellect, once as it has being in one person and once as <it has being> in the other, or <it has to be taken> three times, if the equality of the three persons is to be taken in accord with it so that in accord with this the diverse respects can be founded on it. And for this reason the equality of the persons in God is a relation of reason from both sides.

9. And there is no difference in these two examples except that in the former they are both doubled by the intellect, namely, that upon which the order and relation is founded as it is the substance of the reality and that to which it belongs. For there is identity only by taking the same thing twice by the intellect and similarly the same substance. But in the latter example there is doubled by the intellect only one, namely, that on which is founded the order of the relation. For the divine persons are many of themselves, not as a result of a work of the intellect, but the essence of the deity that is only one in them, insofar as equality is founded on it, is taken within the intellect as made many, insofar as

---

147　See Aristotle, *Physics* 4.1.208b14–19; ed. Bossier and J. Brams, pp. 136–137.

148　See *SQO* art. 51, qu. 1; ed. M. Führer, pp. 217–219.

149　See above par. 6.

it belongs to this one and insofar as it belongs to that one, and in this respect there is more reality in the relation of this equality than of identity.

10. An example of the first[150] is found in all things ordered according to a relation following upon quantity, quality, action and being acted upon, at least when the corresponding character of order and respect is found on both sides. For in that way equal and similar things are related to each other in creatures because in both there is quantity or quality in terms of reality by which they have an order and respect between each other, and similarly things that are naturally active and passive because there really is something in both on which action and being acted upon are founded, and that real element in creatures is always two things in absolute reality, as one quantity and another, or one quality and another, or one motion and another, or [401] something else according to which the related extremes are necessarily two things in absolute reality. For if that real element is not really one thing in one extreme and really another in the other, there is not a real relation in creatures from both sides. In fact, if it is really one thing in both differing only by reason from both sides, it is a relation and order according to reason alone, as was said concerning the relation of identity.[151] Similarly, if there is something real in one to which something real does not correspond in the other, the relation and order is real from the one side, but one of reason only from the other side, as was said of the man and the column.[152]

11. This then is what troubles us most in God where we necessarily have to hold according to the faith and the statements of the saints that there is a real relation between the divine persons lest we hold that the persons are distinguished by reason alone. For because there is no absolute reality in God except the essence of the deity and for this reason it is necessary that the individual respects in the individual persons be founded upon it, it is very obscure how a relation is more real between the divine persons according to their active and passive characters, which are to generate and to be generated, than according to the characters of quantity and quality, which are equal and similar, since all these respects are nonetheless founded on the identity of the divine essence. And although reason cannot grasp it fully, one must still try to attain it somewhat.

12. For the understanding of this it must be known that in accord with what has been already said, "*relation has weaker being* among all *the categories*,"[153] and this is especially so because the category of substance signifies in the manner of being. For the character of substance is to exist in terms of itself. But the abso-

---

150 See above par. 6.

151 See above par. 9.

152 See above par. 7.

153 Averroes, *Commentary on the Metaphysics* 12, comm. 19; ed. Juntas 8, f. 306raB.

lute categories of accident, such as quantity and quality, signify in the manner of something inhering. For the character of an accident is to be in. But relation signifies in the manner of something [402] that is toward something else. For the character of a relation is being toward something else, as if it is nothing of that which is related by it, as Boethius says in chapter twelve of *On the Trinity*: "*All this predication is attributed to external things*."[154] And the Philosopher says in book five of the *Metaphysics* that knowledge insofar as it is a relation belongs not to the knower, but to the known.[155]

13. "Hence, some *have thought* relation *is* from among the *second* intentions,"[156] which are only realities of reason that do not exist outside the intellect, such as are the intention of genus and species. And Boethius seems to hold this when he said in the book *On the Trinity*, when speaking of the difference of the predication of substance, quantity, quality, and relation. "*Is it therefore clear*," he says in chapter twelve, "*what is the difference of the categories? For some disclose a reality as it were, but others the circumstances as it were of a reality. But the latter do not disclose being, but signify something in some way extrinsic*."[157] And as he says in chapter twelve, "*One therefore cannot by a relative predication alone add or subtract or change anything of the reality of which it is said. And the whole of it consists* [403] *not in that which is being, but in that which is to be in some way in comparison*."[158] And at the end of the chapter he says: "*Hence, if the Father and the Son are said to be relatively, they differ in no other way than by relation. But relation is not predicated of that of which it is predicated as if it were itself a reality, and it does not in terms of reality produce an otherness of the reality of which it is said*."[159] And on this account Gilbert of Poitiers also says in the commentary on this passage that relations are not in or subsisting in the persons, but attached to them, when he says: "*Because the theological persons cannot be other than one another by the opposition of essences, they are proven and are other than one another by the opposition of those things that are said to be extrinsically attached*."[160]

14. And this is not entirely false. For a relation is a reality and is a mode, but of itself it is only a circumstance or a certain mode, unless someone wants to extend "reality" to the point that he also calls a mode of a reality a reality, especially one that follows a reality from the nature of the reality and not from the

154 Boethius, *On the Trinity* 4; PL 64: 1253C–D; ed. C. Moreschini, p. 176.

155 See Aristotle, *Metaphysics* 5.15.1021a30–34; ed. G. Vuillemin-Diem, pp. 104–105.

156 Averroes, *Commentary on the Metaphysics* 12, comm. 19; ed. Juntas 8, f. 306rB.

157 Boethius, *On the Trinity* 4; PL 64: 1253C; ed. C. Moreschini, p.177.

158 Ibid., 5; PL 64: 1254A; ed. C. Moreschini, p. 178.

159 Ibid., 5: PL 64: 1254B; ed. C. Moreschini, p. 178.

160 Gilbert of Poitiers, *Commentary on Boethius's On the Trinity*; PL 64: 1295D–1296A; ed. N. Häring, p. 147.

nature of the intellect, which is also called a reality of reason since it has being only from the intellect. And yet it is not called a reality without qualification because although a respect that follows from the nature of the reality can be called a true reality in some way, this does not belong to it by that character and comparison by which it is toward something else or from the fact that it is a respect or a relation. For otherwise that respect that would be toward many terminuses would not be one thing, but many, nor one reality but many. And in that way there would not be one relation in terms of reality by which one is equal to two, nor one paternity by which one [404] is the father of two sons in creatures, when there are two terminuses toward which, and that is false.

15. Besides, if because it is a respect and is toward something else, a relation of itself were a reality, then if compared to substance, it would not be just only a mode, and thus in one way it would be a reality and in another way only a mode, which is impossible, just as it is impossible that something is an accident in one way and a substance in another. And on this account a relation takes that it is a true reality or real from something else as from its foundation because it cannot have this from anything else. For it has comparison to something else only as to a foundation or to a terminus.

16. Specifically, however, with regard to the relations of the notions in God it is clear from what has already been said that they take their reality from their foundation so that they are called real. For this is necessary on account of the fact that they consist in a comparison of things ordered from the nature of a reality existing in them without any consideration of the intellect. In accord with what has been determined above,[161] the deity by itself formally has being; rather, it is being itself, and in terms of itself it has being from nothing as from a principle, and on this account, as a pure form, it is the first reason for being a principle of all things, and there is founded on it the respect or order to those things of which it is a principle and by a certain order of nature firstly to that which is firstly derived from the principle. And this respect to what is firstly derived from the principle along with the form of the deity constitutes the first person, which by reason of his primacy is necessarily innascible, and he does not have being from another, but every other person and every other thing has being from him, but the first one derived from a principle <has being> firstly by a certain order of nature. For because the deity in this first person is a certain act of understanding in act, the deity is fecund and the reason for being a principle actively in the manner of nature and intellectual operation as that by which one has producing and similarly <the other has it> passively as that from which one has its being produced. And because it is the reason from

---

161   See *SQO* art. 21, qu. 3, 4, and 5; ed. Badius 1, fol. 125vA–129vK; ibid. art. 30, qu. 1; ed. Badius 1, fol. 178rQ–vR; ibid, art. 30, qu. 3; ed. Badius 1, fol. 179vI–180rN; ibid. 33, 2; ed. R. Macken, pp. 130–141; and ibid. art. 39, qu. 2; ed. G. Wilson, pp. 198–199.

which there is founded on it a respect that is being produced by another, it also constitutes along with the essence the second person. And as existing in both persons, it is at the same time fecund so that it is the reason for producing actively by which the two produce in the manner of the will [405] its and similarly passively as that from which it is produced, and through this the respect, which is being produced by another in the manner of the will, is founded on it and constitutes with it the third person. And in that way because the notional relations in God are founded on the divine essence itself, they are real from its nature alone without any consideration and comparison of the intellect, as in creatures relations also are called real that are founded on a reality from the nature of the reality without any consideration of the intellect.

<A Doubt>

17. But it is doubtful whether the relations can be called realities along with the fact that they are real. And it is undoubtedly true that, insofar as they include in themselves their foundation, just as they are said to be real because they are founded on a reality, so they are also realities because they include in themselves the reality of their foundation. But in accord with this they are only one reality, although they are three or four relations.

18. Some[162] think that, just as a respect founded on a reality from the consideration of the intellect is said to be at least a reality of reason both in terms of the order that it has to the foundation and in terms of the order it has to an object, because it has both orders from the consideration of the intellect, so that a respect that is founded on a reality from the nature of an absolute reality ought to be said to be a reality in terms of both orders. For both belong to it from the nature of the reality, that is, that it is founded on an absolute reality and that it is in respect to an object.

[406] 19. But if one holds this with regard to real relations in God, <one should hold this> also in creatures for the same reason, that is, so that paternity in creatures is not only said to be a reality and real from the foundation that is the natural potency for generating, but also from the fact that it is toward an object, which many[163] hold, and that that reality from an order to the object is proper to the category of relation.

<A Question>

20. But then I ask when the category of relation is transferred in terms of something that remains in God, does the reality remain in God when the category of relation is transferred or it does not <remain>, but passes into sub-

---

162   Giles of Rome, *Commentary of the Sentences* 1, d. 33, qu. 3, resp.; ed. Venice, f. 171vM–172vL.

163   Ibid.

stance. And whether this way or that, either this reality is absolutely the same as the mode of the category, which is to be toward something else, or it is not. If it is not, then if when a relation is transferred to God, such a respect does not remain because, according to some,[164] it is an accident in creatures, but passes into substance, then what remains of relation in God is only the mode alone and not a reality any more than in creatures. But if it remains in God as something other than that mode, then some reality of a creature would be in God besides the reality of the deity and besides the mode of being toward something else, and that is false. But if that reality in creatures is the mode itself and it is transferred to God, it is necessary that it remain because otherwise nothing of the category of relation would remain in God.

21. In God therefore the reality of a relation from the order to an object is only the mode itself. And in that way insofar as there are diverse modes of being toward something else insofar as there are diverse objects, so there are also diverse realities. But in that case there is only a dispute about a name in calling a reality [407] what others call a mode of a reality. Nonetheless, if respects can in that way be said to be realities, this is only because they are from the nature of reality founded on a true reality. For because really and from the nature of the reality they are founded on the reality in accord with the manner stated so that they are said to be realities from their order to the foundation, for this reason they also have a respect toward an object and are said to be realities in an order to the object, but not because of an order to an object. For to have a respect to an object does not give them that they are also realities in comparison to the object, but it is rather the other way around. For because they are realities from their order to the foundation, they are also realities in relation to the object and also really have a respect to an object.

22. It is nonetheless quite true if a respect is said to be a reality that, "just as respects are diverse from comparison to diverse objects, so the realities are also diverse,"[165] but this never comes about as from the cause on account of which it exists, but only as that without which it does not exist. For at times there are diverse respects toward the same object, as those of two sons to the same father, as was already said. Hence, given that two sons have two filiations to the same father, the cause or reason that they are diverse respects or diverse realities is not one object, but rather the foundations that are the diverse passive potencies of being generated in the diverse matters from which the two sons are generated, and the diverse filiations are founded on the diverse passive potencies, although a single paternity in terms of reality still corresponds to them in

---

164 See M. Henninger, *Relations: Medieval Theories, 1250–1325* (Oxford: Oxford Universtiy Press, 1987), pp. 4–6.

165 See above par. 21.

the object, because it is founded upon the unique active potency of generating, which is in the substantial form of the one who generates.

23. In that way in God, the objects are not the cause or reason that the respects toward the diverse objects are diverse, although they are not without their diversity, because according to the Philosopher, "*relative terms are by nature simultaneous.*"[166] But neither is the cause of the other's being; rather, the cause and reason is the divine essence by itself, insofar as it is the foundation of all the divine properties according to the way that has been [408] already touched upon.[167] For although it is unique in absolute reality, it is by itself on account of its infinity and unlimitedness the reason that there flow as it were from it the diverse respects corresponding to one another in the mode of action and being acted upon and further the diverse products, as by the mode of action <there flow> to generate and to spirate for actively producing the Son and the Holy Spirit and in the mode of being acted upon <there flow> to be generated and to be spirated for producing passively as it were the Son and the Holy Spirit so that the simple and unique divine essence is the complete reason of their being diverse respects, not only because the respects are without qualification to generate, to spirate, to be generated, and to be spirated. And because the products are diverse or distinct, and not the other way around, the diversity of the products is the reason for the diversity of "to generate," "to be generated," "to spirate," and "to be spirated."

24. And from this it is seen something presupposed above,[168] namely, that the quiddity and reality in accord with which one relation is different from another is not taken from the order to its opposite, but rather from its foundation. Hence, that the properties of the emanations are distinguished among one another is not due to the fact that one is toward another or one is from another nor from the fact that they are toward diverse persons that are produced or from diverse persons that produce, but from that fact that they flow in diverse ways, or rather that they are as if diverse outpourings from the same substance. Hence, the persons are also diverse among themselves not so much because one proceeds from another as because they proceed in diverse ways from the same person, as was said above.[169] Hence, although one person proceeds from another, they are not nonetheless diverse because one is from another, but because they are constituted by diverse properties of the emanations. For the Father is other than the Son, not so much because the Son is from him as because he is constituted by [409] the property by which the Son is from him actively and the Son <is constituted> by the property by which he is as if passively from

---

166   Aristotle, *Categories* 7b15; tr. Boethius; ed. L. Minio-Pauluello, p. 21.
167   See above par. 15–16.
168   See above art. 54, qu. 6, par. 31
169   Ibid.

the Father so that constitution in being through such a property in the Father is previous according to reason to the character of the emanation of the one produced.

25. But the usage of the Church does not seem to admit this way of speaking by which the respects are called realities. For since there are four real relations in God, there would then be a quaternity of realities in God besides the reality of the essence, which the <Church's> usage in speaking does not seem to admit, although the concept is not contrary to the truth. On this account, if it must absolutely be said that the relations are diverse and many realities in the way already stated, it seems to me that it is better to say with a qualification that there are many and diverse realities of relation than that there are many and diverse realities, with reality understood without qualification. For if it were said to be a reality without qualification, although it is not a reality existing in itself, since it is not a substance nor subsisting in itself, because it is not a person nor something subsisting in another in God, because there is no accident in God, and similarly it is not in creatures, then something that remains would not be transferred in God. It would therefore necessarily be in accord with the opinion of the man from Poitiers *"a reality externally* [410] *attached,"* as that mode seems to be something attached to substance insofar as it is a reality in accord with the opinion mentioned that does not hold that it has this reality from the subject, but rather from the object, although it has another reality from the foundation, that is, because many respects have it from the foundation that they are realities and one reality, but have from diverse objects that they are diverse realities. But as has already been said,[170] they have both modes of reality from the foundation, one so that they are one in it, the other so that they as if flow from it in diverse ways, for much better reason than that diverse creatures flow from it. For the interior emanations are the reasons for the exterior emanations.

26. Besides, if someone wants to say that in creatures the foundation of a relation is one thing, but the relation itself another, and that it is an accident inhering in a subject, as the other categories of accident and that this is the proper mode of this category, which is a pure mode and not a reality, and similarly in God, he is confronted in this way: Since in God there are two categories transferred from creatures, namely, substance and relation,[171] so that when they are taken up in predication about God, whatever is of reality in them as they are with regard to creatures does not remain, but passes as a whole into the divine substance and there remain only the two modes and characters of those categories, which are also the same in creatures. If therefore there were in God diverse realities, that is, of substance and relation, they would both be there by the nature of the deity, and to one there would correspond one mode transferred

---

170   See above par. 16 and 23–24.

171   See *SQO* art. 32, qu. 5; ed. R. Macken, pp 79–107.

by creatures and the other to the other. Hence, since a proper mode is alone founded immediately in the proper reality and not in another except through the proper reality, that is, because one of them has being in the other, just as therefore in God the mode of substance, which is to exist in terms of itself, has of itself and immediately being with regard to the reality of the substance and being founded on it, so [411] the mode of relation, which is being toward another, also has of itself and immediately being with regard to the reality of a relation and being founded on it. Thus because in God the mode of relation, which is a certain respect and being toward another, does not have being with regard to the reality of the substance or being founded on it except through the reality of a relation existing in the substance or with regard to it, just as in creatures the respect, which is being toward form, is not said to be in the essence of matter except through another reality of the relation existing in it.

27. And from this it necessarily follows that that reality of the relation other than the reality of the substance would be something absolute because that respect that is nothing but a mode of being toward another is founded only on an absolute reality. For whatever is apart from absolute being is only a mode of that which is either being in terms of itself or being toward another. But a mode does not have its being founded on a mode because for the same reason that one is founded on another, that other is founded on a third, and it would be necessary to go on to infinity. One must therefore stop in something that is an absolute reality on which every mode is immediately founded. And thus in God it is not to be said without qualification that it is a reality apart from the reality of the substance so that the reality of a relation is said to be in God with a determination besides the reality of the substance, that is, according to the already stated way of calling the mode of a reality stated without qualification a reality, and we do not want to oppose this because there would only be a dispute about a name that is fruitless when there is certainty about the reality.

<Replies to the Arguments>

28. To the first argument to the contrary that "a relation cannot be real from the subject substance because in that case all the divine relations would be realities and real respects, because they are all founded on the divine substance,"[172] it must be said that a property can be founded on the substance in two ways. In one way so that it perfectly has its being founded on the substance from the nature of the substance without [412] any consideration of the intellect and any comparison of it to anything real of another character. Every property founded on the divine substance in the first way is real, and such are only the personal properties. But in the second way <they are> not <real>. For similar and equal are not real relations in God because they are not founded in God on

---

172 See above par. 1.

the divine essence without consideration of the intellect, as was said above.[173] Similarly, the respects of the attributes also are not because they are not founded on the divine essence without all consideration of the intellect and comparison to something real. For according to what was determined above,[174] they do not have being in God except from the consideration of the divine intellect in terms of itself or also from comparison to the real distinction of the persons or from consideration of the divine intellect under comparison to things distinct in creatures, as others say.[175] Some also hold that they have being in God only from the consideration of the our intellect and comparison to corresponding things in creatures.[176]

29. To the second argument that "*if a relation is real, it is some reality; therefore, it is substance*,"[177] it must be said to this that it is true insofar as it is real and otherwise not. Because this name "relation" in one way signifies a respect as it is a mere intention and the character of the category, and in that way relation is not a reality, neither a substance, nor an accident, nor something real, but a mere mode of being toward something else, unless in accord with the manner already touched on in calling a mode of a reality a reality or in calling a mode real because it follows upon a reality. In another way it signifies [413] a respect as it is the reality of the absolute category on which it is founded, as all the names of the species of relation also signify, such as paternity, filiation, and suchlike. And in that way in God it signifies the reality that is the substance, and it is the substance but signified under the character of a respect. For there is with regard to this point a difference between the respects signified in the names of the attributes that are wisdom, goodness, and in the names of the properties that are paternity, filiation, and in the names of the persons that are Father and Son. For the names of the attributes signify the substance under the character of a respect of reason and are not imposed to signify the respect, but the substance under the character of the respect. But the names of the properties are imposed to signify the respect founded on the substance and not <to signify> the substance under the character of the substance, but they only include it in their signification. But the names of the persons are imposed to signify the substance under the character of a respect so that <the substance> also signifies that real respect and is principally imposed from it.

---

173   See above par. 16 and 23–24.

174   See *SQO* art. 51, qu. 1; ed. M. Führer, p. 216–223.

175   See Thomas Aquinas, *Commentary on the Sentences* 1, d. 2, q. 1, art. 3; ed. P. Mandonnet, pp. 63–72 and also *SQO* art. 32, qu. 4; ed. R. Macken, pp. 63–65 and art. 51, qu. 1; ed. M. Führer, pp. 2221–226.

176   See Moses Maimonides, *Guide for the Perplexed* 1, 52; ed. 1520, fol. 19v–20r. See also *SQO* art. 32, qu. 4; ed. R. Macken, pp. 60, 68, 70, and 72.

177   See above par. 2.

30. To the other argument that "what is divided in God is considered *by reason and knowledge*,"[178] it must be said that in God what is divided has a twofold comparison, one to that which is common, the other to what is divided along with it. In the first way it is certainly considered by reason and knowledge because the substance and a property differ only by reason, but they <do> not in the second way. But this reply is contrary to the statement of the Damascene because it compares in the opposite way what is common and divided in creatures. For he expressly states that "*what is divided is considered in reality*,"[179] so that things divided under something common really differ among themselves. Therefore, according to his mind, in God what is divided is considered by reason, that is, that things distinct under something common differ from one another only by reason.

[414] 31. Therefore, one must speak in another way because, although in God, as was said,[180] a property signifies the substance, it still is not distinctive of a person as it is the substance, but only as it is a respect so that in that way there is one mode of substance as it is a substance, but only as it is a respect so that there is one mode of substance as it is substance and another as it is under the character of a respect. In that way the difference of two persons is in the modes of reason with respect to the differences of two persons in creatures in terms of absolute substances. And thus with respect to this, according to the intention of the Damascene, "it is divided by consideration or reason."[181] And in this way in looking at the mode of a respect, Boethius says, in accord with what has already been established, that relation does not express a reality, but only a mode.[182]

32. To the last argument that "*the relation of the persons among themselves is similar to the relation of the same thing to itself*, which *is only according to reason*,"[183] it must be said that it is true with regard to the fact that from each side the relation is founded on the same thing in reality, but it differs with regard to the fact that <in the relation of identity> the duplication of the relation is founded on the same thing on both sides and the distinction of the related extremes comes only from reason and the consideration of the intellect, <and it is> not so in the present case, as has been seen.[184]

---

178 See above par. 4.

179 John Damascene, *On the Orthodox Faith* 1, 8; PG 94: 827A; ed. E. Buytaert, p. 42.

180 See above par. 26–27.

181 See John Damascene, *On the Orthodox Faith* 1, 8; PG 94: 827A; ed. E. Buytaert, pp. 42, 43, and 44.

182 Boethius, *On the Trinity* c. 4; PL 64: 1253C; ed. C. Moreschini, p. 177. See above par. 1 and 13.

183 See above par. 5.

184 See above par. 16–27.

INDEX OF SCRIPTURE CITATIONS

INDEX OF SOURCES CITED BY HENRY

SELECT BIBLIOGRAPHY

LATIN TEXTS

RENAISSANCE EDITIONS

Henry of Ghent, *Quodlibeta*. 2 vols. Paris: Badius, 1518; photographically reprinted Bibliothèque S.J., Leuven, 1961.
_____. *Summa quaestionum ordinarium*. 2 vols. Paris: Badius, 1520; photographically reprinted St. Bonaventure, NY: The Franciscan Institute, 1953,

MODERN EDITIONS

Henrici de Gandavo, *Quodlibet VI*, ed. Gordon A. Wilson. Leuven: Leuven University Press, 1987.
_____. *Quodlibet VII*, ed. Gordon A. Wilson. Leuven: Leuven University Press, 1991.
_____. *Summa (Qaestiones ordinariae)*. Art. I–V, ed. Gordon Wilson. Leuvern: Leuven Univerity Press, 2005.
_____. *Summa (Quaestiones ordinariae)*. Art. XXX–XXXIV, ed. Raymond Macken; intro., L. Hödl. Leuven: Leuven University Press, 1991.
_____. *Summa (Quaestiones ordinariae)*. Art. XXXV–XL, ed. Gordon Wilson. Leuven: Leuven University Prsss, 1994.
_____. *Summa (Quaestiones ordinariae)*, Art. XLI–XLVI, ed. Ludwig Hödl. Leuven: Leuven University Press, 1998.
_____. *Summa (Quaestiones ordinariae)*. Art. XLV–XLII, ed. Markus Führer. Leuven: Leuven University Press, 1998.

OLDER, BUT STILL VALUABLE GENERAL STUDIES

Jean Paulus, *Henri de Gand: Essai sur les tendances de sa métaphysique*. Paris: J. Vrin, 1938.
José Gómez Caffarena, *Ser Participado y Ser Subsistente en la Metafisica de Enrique de Gante*. Rome: Gregorian University Press, 1958.

OTHER GENERAL SOURCES FOR HENRICIAN STUDIES

Henry of Ghent: Proceedings of the International Colloquium on the Occasion of the 700th Anniversary of his Death (1293), ed. W. Vanhamel. Leuven: Leuven University Press, 1996.
Henry of Ghent and the Transformation of Scholastic Thought: Studies in Memory of Jos Decorte. Ed. Guy Guldentops and Carlos Steel. Leuven: Leuven University Press, 2003.
A Companion to Henry of Ghent. Ed. Gordon Wilson. Brills: Leiden, 2010.

BIBLIOGRAPHIES ON HENRY

Pasquale Porro, "Bibliography," in *Henry of Ghent*, pp. 405–34 and "Bibliography on Henry of Ghent (1994–2002), in *Henry of Ghent and the Transformation*, pp. 409–26. Gordon Wilson, "Bibliography," in *A Companion to Henry of Ghent*, pp. 399–422.

HENRY'S BIOGRAPHY

Pasquale Porro, "An Historiographical Image of Henry of Ghent," in *Henry of Ghent*, pp. 373–403.

ENGLISH TRANSLATIONS

Henry of Ghent's Summa of Ordinary Questions: Article One: On the Possibility of Knowledge. South Bend, IN: St. Augustine's Press, 2008.
Henry of Ghent's Summa: Questions on God's Existence and Essence. Articles 21–24. Translated by Jos Decorte and Roland J. Teske, S.J.; Latin Text, Introduction, and Notes by Roland Teske, S.J., Dallas Medieval Texts and Translations 5. Leuven: Peeters, 2005.
Henry of Ghent's Summa: Questions on God's Unity and Simplicity. Articles 25–30. Latin Text, Translation, and Notes by Roland J. Teske, S.J. Dallas Medieval Texts and Translations 6. Leuven: Peeters, 2006.
Henry of Ghent's Summa of Ordinary Questions: Articles Six to Ten on Theology. Translated and annotated by Roland J. Teske, S.J. Mediaeval Philosophical Texts in Translation 48. Milwaukee: Marquette University Press, 2011.0
Henry of Ghent's Summa of Ordinary Questions. Articles 35–36, 42 & 45. Translated with an Introduction and Notes by Roland J. Teske, S.J. Mediaeval Philosophical Texts in Translation. 50. Milwaukee: Marquette University Press, 2013.

STUDIES RELEVANT TO THE ARTICLES TRANSLATED

BOOKS

Hissette, Roland. *Enquête sur les 219 articles condamnés à Paris le 7 Mars 1277.* Louvain: Publications universitaires, 1977.
Marrone, Steven P. *The Light of Thy Countenance: Science and the Knowledge of God in the Thirteenth Century.* Volume 2: God at the Core of Cognition. Leiden: Brill, 2001.
Marrone, Steven P. *Truth and Scientific Knowledge in the Thought of Henry of Ghent.* Speculum Anniversary Monographs 11. Cambridge, Mass.: The Medieval Academy of America, 1985.
Pickavé, Martin. *Heinrich von Gent über Metaphysik als erste Wissenschaft: Studien zu einem metaphysikentwurf aus dem lestzten viertel des 13. Jahrhunderts.* Leiden: Brill, 2007.
Teske, Roland. *Essays on the Philosophy of Henry of Ghent.* Milwaukee: Marquette University Press, 2011.

ARTICLES

Decorte, Jos. "Relation and Substance in Henry of Ghent's Metaphysics." In *Henry of Ghent and the Transformation*, pp. 3–14.

Flores, Juan Carlos. "Intellect and Will as Natural Principles. Connecting Theology, Metaphysics and Psychology." In *Henry of Ghent and the Transformation*, pp. 277–305.

_____. "Henry of Ghent's Metaphysics and the Trinity, with a critical edition of question six of article fifty-five of the *Summa Quaestionum Ordinarium*. Ancient and Medieval Philosophy Series 1, XXXVI. Leuven, 2006.

Friedman, Russell L. "Relations, Emanations, and Henry of Ghent's Use of the 'Verbum Mentis' in Trinitarian Theology: the Background in Thomas Aquinas and Bonaventure." *Documenti e Studi sulla Tradizione Medievale* 2 (1996), pp. 37–42.

Hödl, Ludwig. "The Theologian Henry of Ghent." In *A Companion to Henry of Ghent*, pp. 103–134.

Laarman, Matthias. "God as *Primum Cognitum*: Some Remarks on the Theory of Initial Knowledge of *Esse* and God According to Thomas Aquinas and Henry of Ghent," In *Henry of Ghent: Proceeding of the International Colloquium*, pp. 171–191

Marrone, Steven P. "Speculative Theology in the Late Thirteenth Century and the Way to Beatitude." In *Les philosophies morales et politique au Moyen Âge*. Ed. B. Carlos Bazán, Eduardo Andújar, Léonardo G. Sbrocci. New York: Legas, 1995. II, pp. 1067–1080.

Porro, Pasquale. "Filosofia e scienza teologica in Enrico di Gand." In *Verum et certum. Studi di storiografia filosofica in onore di Ada Lamacchio*. Ed. Constantino Esposito, Pauolo Ponzio, Pasquale Porro, and Veneranda Castellano. Bari: Levante Editori, 1998.

Porro, Pasquale. "Metaphysics and Theology in the Last Quarter of the Thirteenth Century: Henry of Ghent Reconsidered." In *Geistesleben im 13. Jahrhundert. Miscellana Mediaevalia 27*. Eds Jan A. Aaertsen and Andreas Speer. Berlin: Walter de Gruyter, 2000. Pp. 265–282.

Teske, Roland J. "Henry of Ghent's Apophatic Theology. In *Essays on the Philosophy of Henry of Ghent*. Pp. 220–246.

_____. "Henry of Ghent on the Analogy of Being." In *Essays on the Philosophy of Henry of Ghent*. Pp. 247–263.

Wilson, Gordon. "Supposite in the Philosophy of Henry of Ghent," in *Henry of Ghent: Proceedings of the International Colloquium*, pp. 343–372.